Afghanistan and the Soviet Union

Afghanistan and the Soviet Union

Henry S. Bradsher

Duke Press Policy Studies

Durham, N.C.   1983

Printed in the United States of America on
acid-free paper.

Library of Congress Cataloging in Publication Data

Bradsher, Henry S. (Henry St. Amant), 1931–
    Afghanistan and the Soviet Union.

    (Duke Press policy studies)
    Bibliography: p.
    Includes index.
    1. Afghanistan—Foreign relations—Soviet Union.
2. Soviet Union—Foreign relations—Afghanistan.
3. Afghanistan—History—Soviet occupation, 1979–
I. Title. II. Series.
DS357.6.S65B7   1983   327.58′1′047   82–21015
ISBN 0–8223–0496–1
ISBN 0–8223 0563–1 (pbk.)

Second printing 1984

Contents

Acknowledgments

Both Afghanistan and the Soviet Union pose problems for a writer of recent history. Many of the developments in Afghanistan during the last few decades lack adequate documentation. Some of the key participants have disappeared without giving testimony on what happened. Statements made by Afghan leaders both in public and, with apparent sincerity, in private to visitors have to be taken with great caution. So do Soviet statements. The need for an analytical approach to the Soviet side of the equation is more obvious because of long-standing difficulty understanding Soviet actions that emerge from secrecy and dissembling. Further problems result from inadequate sources of information and inadequate analysis of Afghan developments; consequently, the events that led to the Soviet army's December 1979 move into Afghanistan have become wrapped in rumors and half-truths. Some writers have approached the overall problem with a background in studies of Afghanistan, some with a knowledge of Soviet affairs. This book is an attempt to pull together both sides of developments affecting the two countries and to show the interrelationship.

Most of the people who helped me sort through the murkier corners of the subject in an attempt to understand and clarify it have not wanted to be identified by name. They have included present and former members of several governments in Asia and Europe, some of whom have been my friends for a quarter-century and had risen by the late 1970s to positions in which they were personally involved in some of the events related here, officials of the United States government, scholars, and others. Most especially, they have included some of the many Afghans whom I have known over the years (some others have been killed in successive waves of political murder in Kabul) and other Afghans whom I met in the course of research. The interviews referred to in the footnotes were all conducted by me in the latter part of 1980 and during 1981 in Washington, London, and the United Nations headquarters. An old friend who is a senior journalist in India, R. Ramanujam, conducted several interviews and did research in New Delhi that shed new light on an important point. Some of these people might not agree with my conclusions and are not to blame for them.

My friendships with Afghans, and an appreciation of their country from travelling in it, go back to the period from 1959 to 1964 when I was an Associated Press correspondent in South Asia and visited Afghanistan a number of times. I am grateful to The Associated Press for starting me on my Afghan interests and then, when I was AP bureau chief in Moscow from 1964 to 1968, furthering my long-time interest in Soviet affairs. Later, *The Washington Star* enabled me to revisit Afghanistan while I was its specialist on Chinese affairs based in Hong Kong from 1969 to 1975. A paid leave from the post of the *Star*'s diplomatic correspondent in Washington, D. C., enabled me to accept the hospitality of the Woodrow Wilson International Center for Scholars and its Kennan Institute for Advanced Russian Studies in the winter of 1980–81. The Center provided me with a magnificent office sixty-seven steps up a tower in the Smithsonian "castle" building overlooking the Mall in Washington and provided other support that made it possible to write this book. A research assistant at the Center, Mark Wasserman, helped locate materials outside the immediate Afghan and Soviet fields. The closing of the *Star* a few months after I returned to work there provided me with paid time between jobs to revise the manuscript.

My thanks to all these people and organizations. They gave me the opportunity to write this, but they have no responsibility for the results.

A note on style: Rather than impose some personal system of rendering into English names and words from a diversity of languages and scripts, I have followed the styles of the sources used—even though this results in some inconsistencies in, for instance, some names being "Mohammad" and some "Mohammed."

Afghanistan and the Soviet Union

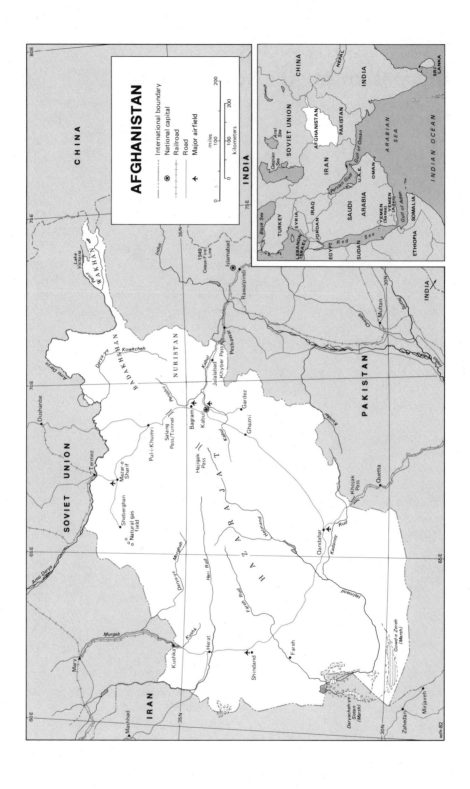

AFGHANISTAN

- – – – – International boundary
- ⊛ National capital
- ——— Railroad
- ——— Road
- ✈ Major airfield

miles
0   100   200
0 100 200
kilometers

CHINA

SOVIET UNION

IRAN

PAKISTAN

INDIA

WAKHAN

Lake
Victoria

Amu Darya

Darya-ye Kowkcheh

BADAKHSHAN

NURISTAN

1949
Cease-Fire
Line

Islamabad

Rawalpindi

Kabul

Jalalabad

Khyber Pass

Peshawar

Gardez

Bagram

Kabul

Ghazni

Salang
Pass/Tunnel

Pul-i-Khumri

Dushanbe

Termez

Mazar-e
Sharif

Sheberghan

Natural gas
field

Hajigak
Pass

H A Z A R A J A T

Helmand

Kunar

Qandahar

Khojak
Pass

Quetta

Kadanay
Rud

Multan

INDIA

Amu Darya

Murghab

Darya-ye

Hari Rud

Farah Rud

Fareh

Shindand

Herat

Kushka

Marv

Murgab

Kushk

Helmand

Gowd-e Zereh
(Marsh)

Daryacheh-ye
Sistan (Marsh)

Mirjaveh

Zahedan

Mashhad

weh-82

CHINA

SOVIET UNION

NEPAL

INDIA

AFGHANISTAN

PAKISTAN

IRAN

Caspian
Sea

Aral
Sea

ARABIAN
SEA

Persian Gulf

U.A.E.

OMAN

Gulf of Oman

SRI
LANKA

INDIAN OCEAN

TURKEY

LEBANON
ISRAEL

SYRIA

IRAQ

JORDAN

SAUDI
ARABIA

YEMEN
(Sana)

YEMEN
(Aden)

Gulf of Aden

SOMALIA

ETHIOPIA

SUDAN

EGYPT

Red Sea

Black Sea

Introduction

During 1978 and 1979 the people of Afghanistan were forced into a bloody struggle to defend themselves against incorporation into a new form of colonial empire ruled from Moscow. This book is a study of the Afghan and Russian developments that produced these people's difficult situation of the early 1980s. For those who knew Afghanistan before it fell under Communist control in April 1978, it is a sad account. But it is an important one for all those seriously interested in this remote Asian land—important and tragic for everyone who respects the right of the proud, diverse, and formerly free Afghan people to determine their own fate.

The fate willed by the leaders of the Soviet Union was the conversion of Afghanistan into a quietly obedient member of "the socialist community of nations." That is, aside from the forms of national identity that will always make it a distinctive country, Afghanistan must follow both internal and external policies whose basic outlines conform to Soviet patterns and desires. Although the *mujahideen*, or resistance fighters, of Afghanistan were, in the early 1980s, able to prevent the Soviet Union and its local supporters from gaining more than limited control inside the country, there was little reason to expect the guerrilla war to end Soviet determination to enforce that conformity. Neither was there any willingness on the part of foreign countries to provide more than a few weapons to the *mujahideen*; nor was there a balance of power in the region that could neutralize Soviet pressure on the Afghan people. There was little prospect of the country's being spared a painful conversion into Soviet Afghanistan, little chance of avoiding what is essentially an extension into Central Asia, of Great Russian control of other ethnic groups.

The presence of Soviet troops in Afghanistan after December 1979 was both a new development in world power relationships and part of an old pattern. It was a new reach for Soviet Army control, the first territorial expansion by direct use of Soviet military power in the thirty-four years since World War II ended. That was what made the world take so much notice of the Christmastime invasion: this intervention in Afghan affairs was easier to interpret as aggression than indirect Soviet military involvement from Indochina to Angola. But it also fit into the historic pattern of a dynamic, thrusting Great Russian people who were building an empire; they subdued weak, economically undeveloped Central Asian descendants of peoples who had both terrorized and enlightened the world during centuries of Slavic silence. The 1979 military move was only another, long-delayed, step forward in a lurching Russian advance, a step into the only sector on the Soviet periphery (a sector perhaps later to include Iran) where the lack of cross-border cohesion and strength, and the absence of a regional balance of power, made such movement possible.

The Russian advance in the nineteenth century had destroyed the separate identities of other political entities as weak and unconsolidated as Afghanistan then was, but imperial Britain checked that advance in order to protect its domain in India. That bought time during which Afghanistan was able to develop into its modern form and become accepted as a sovereign member of the community of nations. But in the twentieth century the rules of imperialism changed. It was no longer necessary to extinguish the separate identity of a people or nation and absorb them into the metropolitan power's own national structure in order effectively to destroy their sovereignty. So when the advance of Russian power resumed, the political form was new but the political goal was not.

The advance was not a revival of the old imperialistic march toward warm water ports. The Soviet Union does have motives for wanting to expand its power toward the Persian Gulf and elsewhere, but Afghanistan in 1979 was not immediately pertinent to any strategic plan. A more likely motive was the age-old tendency for any powerful nation to seek the territorial limits of its power, to seek to fix a secure and stable frontier.

Modern Afghan leaders were aware that their weakness could tempt the Soviet Union to resume the tsarist Russian search for a boundary defined by the interests of a strong, stable power. When Britain removed itself from that role by giving independence to India in 1947, Afghanistan sought help from the United States to reestablish some counterweight and also to help modernize the country. The American government saw little reason, however, to become involved in such a remote, unfamiliar, primitive and, in its official view of the world, strategically unimportant land. The United States was also wary of becoming committed to Afghanistan at a time when Kabul was pursuing the Pushtunistan issue.

One of those troublesome legacies of unthinking colonial convenience still found on several continents, the Pushtunistan problem arose from the British drawing their Indian empire's northwest frontier deep into the Pushtun tribal area that was the traditional home of the dominant Afghan ethnic group. A strongly felt emotional need of that group to redeem the separated brethren was seen by outsiders more as an irredentist claim that could destabilize the region by opening the way to redrawing borders. Afghan frustration over the United States' wariness of showing support for its Pushtunistan position affected thinking in Kabul about the Soviets. Afghanistan turned to Moscow for help in building a modern army and air force for two reasons: to maintain internal order during the social and political strains of modernization; and to confront Pakistan, the successor to British India as holder of Pushtunistan.

As in so many undeveloped countries, most of them newly independent, Afghanistan's efforts to modernize and achieve economic progress disturbed the traditional political system. The political lectures given to military personnel as part of their training in the Soviet Union were only a contributory factor. More important was the Communist claim of a way to overcome poverty and social inequality. The Communist message reached Afghanistan in many ways, but the Communist parties of India, Pakistan, and Iran played particularly significant roles because of their ethnic and cultural similarities. The key to the development of a Communist movement in Afghanistan, however, was the creation of a new stratum of society through education. Afghan aspirations had been rigidly defined by the old outlooks of the governing elite, the small merchant community, the peasantry, and the village religious leaders who were often also the main land owners. Although drawn from these groups, a newly educated element developed that was unwilling to accept the elite's slow, limited version of progress. The Soviet embassy in Kabul encouraged and in various ways supported this element. By the early 1960s it had evolved into an identifiable Communist movement.

In more than a decade of semi-clandestine existence, the divided, squabbling People's Democratic Party of Afghanistan (PDPA) never achieved more than a gadfly role in Afghan affairs. But neither the royal governments before 1973 nor Mohammed Daoud Khan, who seized power that year, recognized the importance of political pressures created by the PDPA and an offshoot Maoist group. Not appreciating what was happening, they did little to counter it. Daoud used old-fashioned strongman methods to neutralize one PDPA faction that gained a toehold in his republican government. That success led to overconfidence in Daoud and contributed to leftist strength by frustrating hopes that he would carry out social and economic reforms.

The overthrow of Daoud in 1978 that ended with the PDPA in power was a more confusing event than is indicated by the new regime's official account, which has been accepted uncritically in most foreign versions of it. It is questionable whether what became known as the Saur Revolution (from the Afghan name for the month in which it occurred) was actually a Communist coup at the beginning or only developed into a PDPA regime by default of the soldiers who led it. But the 1973 and 1978 coups both pulled Afghanistan back from pragmatic or rightist policies disliked by local Communists and the Soviet Union. That fact, combined with obvious Soviet involvement in the September and December 1979 changes of government, raised the broader question of a pattern of Soviet involvement going back to the two coups. Soviet military advisers were well integrated into the Afghan military structure; they had to know that the tanks were rolling in both 1973 and 1978. They may even have known slightly before, whether or not they had been involved in planning or directing the military takeovers.

Does the limited available record indicate that the Soviet Union masterminded successive coups in Afghanistan from 1973 onward? This question cannot be answered definitely without access to Soviet secrets. Any attempt at an answer without such information risks becoming an exercise in ideological preconceptions rather than analysis. The pattern is, however, clearly suggestive: on all four occasions the Soviets had reason to want changes in Afghanistan's leadership. The 1973 and 1978 coups involved Marxists who made no secret of their connections with the Soviet embassy in Kabul—indeed, in Babrak Karmal's case, flaunted it—as well as more secretive leftists both in and outside the armed forces. Both coups depended upon military units whose leaders had been exposed to Soviet political indoctrination during military training courses and therefore had, if not become Communists, at least been inspired to revolutionary dissatisfaction with their homeland's status quo. More broadly, the coups involved a political movement that had been fostered, aided and even, when differences between feuding factions were papered over in 1977, steered by direct or indirect Soviet tactics. The Soviet Union had provided encouragement for the ideological impatience with successive Afghan regimes that exploded into the coups. This is the background.

The foreground is less certain. A knowledge of what was going on is the minimum assumption that should be made about Soviet responsibility. If Soviet officials had really wanted Afghanistan to maintain the nonaligned position to which they paid public tribute, rather than having it turn to a Soviet bloc embrace, they might have warned endangered governments of danger and also tamped down or discouraged the leftist sources of danger. Such warnings or preventative actions are not unknown in the murky world of espionage. But the Soviet Union had no motive in 1973 or 1978 for helping governments that were drifting away from policies it preferred; it had motives for wanting their replacement. In September and December 1979, the motivation was much stronger, the advance Soviet involvement more obvious. The Soviets' failure in September to get rid of Hafizullah Amin made their determination greater to use whatever force was necessary in December to seize control of Afghan political developments.

Once leftists had come to power in a neighboring country and been embraced by Moscow as being Socialists in the Leninist tradition, Afghanistan's fate became a matter of ideological commitment to the Soviet leadership as well as practical concern based on the country's location. Soviet leaders could not ignore or fail to help the cause of Communist success without betraying the Soviet regime's own rationale. But the Soviet Union did not simply rush in to take over Afghanistan. In the seventeen months between the 1978 coup and the abortive attempt to oust Amin, Soviet involvement in Afghanistan increased by stages in response to developments within the country.

Within weeks of the formation of the new regime on 30 April 1978 by Nur Mohammed Taraki, Soviet Communist Party officials were trying to keep the PDPA unified and were helping it develop a structure capable of controlling a country. At the same time, Soviet advisers were filling gaps in the government created by purges of non-Communist officials. Increasing armed opposition to PDPA rule brought greater Soviet military involvement in advisers, weapons, and combat support roles such as flying helicopter gunships. Evidence is scanty that the Soviet Union was doing anything other than meeting needs as they arose, rather than carrying out some master plan for taking direct control of Afghanistan. When, finally, the Amin regime was on the verge of losing its grip on the country, Soviet military transport planes appeared over the Hindu Kush late on the night of 24 December 1979 and began landing fully armed troops at Kabul airport. On 27 December they seized control of the Afghan capital.

Soviet leaders chose direct intervention rather than allow Afghanistan to turn from its professedly Marxist course toward a more neutral and independent— and under the circumstances, more chaotic—course.

That choice was a product of several factors. Geography was a major one; Afghanistan was inescapably exposed to the security concerns of its powerful neighbor. The dynamism that Communism gave to Soviet foreign policy, in economic aid and military training programs, was another factor. So was the growing military power of Moscow, with its greater ability in the 1970s to project that power beyond the marching distance of its soldiers. Soviet leaders had shown an increased assertiveness in world affairs, a readiness to seize opportunities to extend Soviet influence in tumultous situations, and a changed attitude toward the role of Soviet soldiers, shifting the emphasis of their responsibilities from defense to Kremlin-defined international duties.

The strength of the December 1979 action, the culmination of progressively more direct involvement in Afghan affairs, was intended to guarantee that there would be no more problems of Afghanistan's turning away from Soviet interests. This, and Soviet attitudes toward (if not direct initiatives of) the earlier coups, form a pattern that should discourage speculations about any future Soviet willingness to withdraw from a neutralized Afghanistan.

Two lines of thought emerged in the West about how to create such a willingness. One method was to arm the Afghan resistance in order to make the Soviet Army occupation too expensive for some future Soviet leadership that would be overly burdened with more urgent economic and political problems and might decide to cut its losses in Afghanistan. Well into the third year of the occupation, however, those losses were low; besides, Russian history and Soviet politics argued against this line. The other method was diplomatic rather than military. It proposed negotiating a neutral status for Afghanistan insuring that the country would not oppose Soviet interests if direct Soviet military control were withdrawn—somewhat like the situation that had normally existed before 1978. Western and Third World diplomats plus others talked of Austrian and Finnish neutralization models without taking into account the balance of power within those European countries' regions that checked Soviet military power. No such balance existed in Afghanistan's region.

Such ideas also failed to take into account the major difference between preserving a status quo in Europe and rolling back Soviet power by neutralizing a country once under Kremlin control. A rollback in Afghanistan would be a precedent unacceptable to the leaders of the extended Soviet empire, with its vulnerabilities already repeatedly exposed in Eastern Europe. Beyond these burdens for any diplomatic scheme lay the ideological refusal of the Soviet Union to allow the collapse of a ruling Communist Party that it had supported. The official pretense of Karmal and the Soviets that only outsiders opposed the regime, and that Soviet troops could not leave without guarantees against outside interference, hid an unwillingness to test Karmal's popularity. It was impossible to negotiate a withdrawal of his Soviet sponsors and leave him securely in power, or to leave any secure government led by Communists trying to implement Soviet policies. The alienation of the Afghan people by the PDPA's policies before December 1979 created that impossibility; the attempt after that to impose foreign rule on a defiantly independent people blighted future prospects of Afghan leaders who were in any way tainted with Soviet-style politics or Russian support.

If there were fewer people inside Afghanistan opposing the Karmal regime after its first few years in power, it was not because the regime had won support. It was because so many people had fled or been driven abroad. In the early 1980s some one-fifth to one-quarter of Afghanistan's population was in refugee camps in Pakistan or Iran or further abroad, judging from the few, vague statistics available on either refugee numbers or the country's original population. Estimates of the part of the countryside beyond control of the Soviet Army and the depleted Afghan army were as high as 80 to 90 percent. Important cities like Qandahar were periodically lost to guerrilla uprisings and their old marketplaces devastated by Soviet firepower in retaliation. While some regional cooperation among *mujahideen* had developed, there was no overall unity among the resistance groups. Instead, there was fierce competition among some. This left no clear alternative to Karmal's regime.

But no alternative was likely. The Soviet Union intended to remain in Afghanistan, shaping the country to its will. The prospect was endless guerrilla warfare, endless refugee suffering, endless pain and bloodshed that developed out of the events recounted here.

Chapter 1. Country of Conflict

The tough character of the Afghan people was bred out of the land's ruggedness. The terrain is harsh and demanding, mostly bleak mountains and deserts broken only by small verdant patches. Equally challenging has been its location. At a crossroads of ethnic migrations, marauding armies, and modern empires, this area has a more continuous history of fighting invasions than any other part of the world. In wars and guerrilla clashes, fighting each other when not resisting outsiders, Afghanistan's varied peoples have sharpened their combative instincts over the centuries for the resistance to Soviet control.

Political and Cultural Boundaries

The modern nation of Afghanistan was not created by internal coalescence. Like many countries of the Afro-Asian world, it is a product of external forces. Its boundaries were formed in the nineteenth century by the interaction of the British empire on the Indian subcontinent and the Russian empire in Central Asia. The result is that Afghanistan lacks either ethnic or geographic cohesiveness. Its very name is an expansion of the Afghan label first put on only one of its peoples, the Pushtuns, whose distinctively craggy character still is stamped upon world perceptions of the whole country. National unity was forged by a combination of Pushtun and Tajik political and cultural dominance, but the Communists who came to power in 1978 emphasized ethnic differences in a way that weakened unity.

British success from 1600 onward in developing a valuable trade with India inspired Peter the Great of Russia in 1717 to seek an overland route to the subcontinent. By the 1830s the tsarist empire had taken over the degenerate remains of some Central Asian Moslem emirates that before the Age of Discovery had prosperously dominated trade between Europe and China and preserved and added to world knowledge during Europe's Dark Ages.[1] The Russian thrust southeastward from Moscow and the British thrust northwestward from Calcutta met in the "Great Game" of competition for control over the lands between.[2] Like many international affairs before and since, it was played over the course of sixty years on the basis of apprehension more than actual developments, emotional reactions more than cold analysis, and inadequate information more than hard facts.

Twice the British invaded Afghanistan out of fear that Russia would establish control there. Both times they retreated in the face of Afghan hostility. The first time was in 1839 after Dost Mohammed Khan, the ruler of little more than the Kabul and Qandahar areas, had appealed to the Russians for help in recapturing Peshawar, the Afghan winter capital, from Sikh control. St. Petersburg was not prepared to help, but the Army of the Indus marched across the Khojak Pass to ward off possible Russian entry into Afghanistan. Resistance to British occupation of Kabul forced a retreat beginning 6 January 1842. Only a handful of the 4,500 fighting men and 12,000 others survived guerrilla attacks in the mountain defiles east of Kabul.[3]

The continued press of Russian armies southward revived British fears four decades later after diplomacy had failed to establish a limit to tsarist power. To protesting British diplomats, Russian officials repeatedly professed surprise at their armies' capture of new territory, saying it was unauthorized—but never relinquishing anything. The armies thus played in the nineteenth century the role that foreign Communist parties sometimes played in Soviet foreign policy of the twentieth century when they were manipulated to Soviet advantage despite official insistence that Moscow had no control over them.

The clash of Russian and British interests was a result of their similarity. In what could just as well have been an expression of the British compulsion in India, the tsar's foreign minister, Prince Alexander Gorchakov, propounded in 1864 a rationale for expansion:

> The interests of security on the frontier, and of commercial relations, compel the more civilized state to exercise a certain ascendancy over neighbors whose turbulence and nomadic instincts render them difficult to live with. . . . The state . . . must abandon the incessant struggle and deliver its frontier over to disorder, which renders property, security and civilization impossible; or it must plunge into the depths of savage countries, where the difficulties and sacrifices to which it is exposed increase with each step in advance. . . . The greatest difficulty is in knowing where to stop.[4]

British efforts to impart that knowledge led to another invasion of Afghanistan in 1878. Russia had established diplomatic relations with Kabul, which British India lacked, and had promised military support. When the British marched, support was not forthcoming. Dost Mohammad's successor, Sher Ali Khan, appealed for Russian help, but the Russian commander in Central Asia replied that it was impossible in winter to send troops across Afghanistan's mountain backbone, the Hindu Kush, to Kabul. The reply came 101 years almost to the day before Soviet troops, claiming to be responding to another Afghan plea for help, flew over the wintry Hindu Kush and drove through a Soviet-built tunnel in it to seize control of Kabul.

British tutelage of Afghanistan then lasted for forty years. During that period Britain completed a process already begun with the Russians of giving legal definition to the country. Correspondence between London and St. Petersburg in 1873 fixed a boundary from Lake Victoria (Ozero Zorkul to the Russians), 13,400 feet up in the Pamirs, down the river system that begins with the lake's snow-fed waters and eventually takes the name Amu Darya (*darya* means "river"), the Oxus of antiquity, until the river turns northwestward toward the

Aral Sea.[5] With colonial carelessness, neither British nor Russians cared that this divided Uzbek and Tajik peoples in what had been one ethnic, economic, cultural, and historic region. Nor did they clarify the precise river boundary, leaving islands in dispute until a 1946 Afghan-Soviet frontier agreement.[6] The remaining northern border was fixed in 1885 from the Amu westward overland to the Hari Rud, the river marking the Iranian border, and in 1895 from Lake Victoria eastward to the Chinese border.[7] The result was a border 1,481 miles long between modern Afghanistan and the Soviet Union.[8]

That length depended upon settlement of a Chinese-Soviet border dispute in the Pamirs, however. In 1963 Afghanistan and China defined a forty-seven-mile border at a watershed more than 16,000 feet high, but its juncture points with the Soviet Union and Pakistan were in doubt.[9]

The approximately 550-mile-long Afghan-Iranian border was defined under British supervision after 1857, when the shah in Tehran renounced Persian claims to what were then identified separately as Herat and Afghanistan.[10] At the southern end of that border the Helmand River's Hindu Kush waters disappear into lakes and marshy areas. Sharing the waters was a cause for disputes between the two countries as late as the 1970s. Although the problem was dormant in the first few years of Communist rule in Kabul, it retained the potential for causing future trouble between Afghanistan and Iran.

The remaining Afghan border marches with Pakistan for 1,510 miles.[11] This is the Durand Line agreed in 1893 between Sir Henry Mortimer Durand, foreign secretary to the government of India, and Amir Abdur Rahman Khan, who unified Afghanistan after 1880. It zigzags southwesterly from the Chinese border at 20,000 feet altitude through mountains and desert to a rock 5,400 feet high on the Iranian border.[12] On the way, it divides Pushtun (or Pathan) tribes—the fabled Afridis and Waziris, Yuzufzais and Mohmands, and others who sniped at the British Indian Army for decades—as well as Baluch and Brahui peoples. It was drawn across traditional routes of nomads who grazed their sheep and goats in the Afghan highlands in the summer and wintered in what is now Pakistan. These *powindahs* or *kuchis* ignored the line until the 1960s, when an estimated 200,000 were still crossing annually with their flocks and with small trade goods that supplied remote Afghan villages.[13]

The population of Afghanistan within these boundaries has never been accurately known. There has not been a complete census.[14] In 1980 the Afghan government used a figure of "more than 15 million" persons living in some 15,000 villages and a handful of towns. Other estimates run from fewer than 13 to more than 20 million,[15] including the millions who by 1982 were refugees in Pakistan or Iran.

Pushtuns were estimated to number only 6 to 6½ million in Afghanistan.[16] Some 3½ to 4 million other Pushtuns lived in Pakistan, but the figures were unclear and politically sensitive on both sides of the line. Some 70,000 to 100,000 Baluch were in Afghanistan before refugees began to leave, perhaps ten times as many in Pakistan,[17] and others in Iran. The Brahui, a culturally and

Borders —

economically similar ethnic group, also divided among the three nations, numbered perhaps 200,000 in Afghanistan.

The most important of the three ethnic groups divided across the Soviet border is Tajiks. Between 3 and 3½ million in Afghanistan outnumbered the 2,898,000 shown in the 1979 Soviet census.[18] An estimated 1 to 1½ million Uzbeks live south of the Amu, 12,456,000 in the Soviet Union. Turkmen were variously estimated from 125,000 to 400,000 in Afghanistan, while Soviet Turkmen numbered 2,028,000.[19]

The Afghan-Iranian border divides not only Baluch, Brahui, and Turkmen but also Farsiwan, who numbered approximately 600,000 in Afghanistan; Aimaq estimated at 800,000 in Afghanistan; and Qizilbash, variously estimated from 60,000 to 200,000. The only sizeable ethnic group unique to Afghanistan is the estimated 875,000 Hazara people of vaguely Mongolian appearance in the mountainous central part of the country.[20] Numerous other smaller ethnic groups also exist, the remains of invasions as varied as Alexander the Great's blue-eyed Greeks and pure Mongols of Genghis Khan's devastating armies.

At least twenty languages are spoken in Afghanistan.[21] The two dominant ones, with some 80 percent of the people speaking one of them, are the provincial form of Persian known as Dari and the Pushtun language, Pashto. Dari, the language of Afghan Tajiks, is the lingua franca of modern Afghanistan despite Pushtun political domination. Whatever the language, the religion is Islam. Some 80 percent adhere to the Sunni form that lacks any religious hierarchy or authority. The independence of local holy men joins ethnic, language, and geographical differences in buttressing village resistance to centralized governmental control. This resistance is compounded by the lack of a tradition of respect for the abstract authority of political institutions in a tribal system held together by personal, family, and clan ties.[22]

According to available statistics and best estimates, living standards in Afghanistan at the time it came under Communist control were appallingly low. The infant mortality rate was one of the highest in the world. Between a third and a half of all babies died in childhood. Life expectancy was around thirty-five at birth; for those who survived childhood, it was about fifty years. Malnutrition was so chronic as not to be considered a major problem; perhaps half the population was debilitated by tuberculosis and a quarter by malaria; afflictions such as measles were common.[23] Literacy was estimated to be between 10 and 12 percent.[24] Communist efforts after 1978 to expand education and medical care were coupled with political indoctrination. Village schools and health care centers therefore became targets for burning by resistance forces.[25]

The poverty of Afghanistan's people was a result of a limited amount of fertile, well-watered land and of isolation from modernizing influences. But the country had natural riches. Commercially, the most important development by the early 1980s was the discovery of natural gas around Sheberghan on the north slope of the Hindu Kush. Only small oil resources were reported in the north,[26] but better prospects were believed to exist in the southeast.[27] An unusually large and rich deposit of iron ore existed some 12,000 feet high near the Hajigak Pass,[28] but its inaccessibility made it uneconomic to exploit. This problem also limited interest in "one of the 10 most important copper deposits in the world,"[29] located near Kabul. Excellent coal seams, [30] high-grade chrome near the Pakistani border,[31] uranium in the southwestern desert,[32] gold, emeralds, and other resources were also known.

Political Activity to WWII

The first ruler of Afghanistan to seek to take advantage of the country's potential by modern development was Amanullah Khan.[33] This grandson of Abdur Rahman seized the throne on the mysterious murder of his father, Habibullah Khan, on 20 February 1919. In the turmoil that followed, he found it expedient to divert national attention by fighting the British for release from their control over Afghan foreign relations. It was a short war. Airplanes and radios gave the British advantages they had lacked in 1842—a foretaste of the difference that helicopter gunships would make to the Soviets in fighting the Afghan resistance. But in writing the 8 August 1919 peace treaty, Britain was wearied by World War I, involved in the Russian civil war, and keenly aware of previous costs of trying to control Afghanistan. It gave the surprised and skeptical Afghans "complete liberty . . . in internal and external matters."[34]

Even before this, Amanullah wrote on 7 April 1919, to the "High-Born President of the Great Russian Republic," Vladimir I. Lenin, proposing diplomatic relations.[35] Lenin's reply on 27 May was later taken as recognition of Afghan "independence and autonomy," with the Bolsheviks as the first to accept that status.[36] "In turn, Afghanistan became the first state to officially recognize the Republic of Soviets," *Pravda* said in 1981.[37] This statement is unsupported by standard Western histories of the Soviet Union. Any legal ability of Afghanistan to recognize anybody was questionable: 27 May was the day before Amanullah sued for peace in his battlefield attempt to win from Britain the right to such direct foreign ties. Lenin's reply rang with revolutionary rhetoric, and he later urged Afghanistan to take "the great historic task of uniting around itself all enslaved Moslem peoples and leading them on the road to freedom and independence."[38]

Lenin's intentions were clouded, and Afghanistan's situation complicated, by events in the former tsarist Central Asian empire. These events north of the Amu Darya in many ways paralleled developments sixty years later south of the river. Bolsheviks, who before coming to power had recognized "the right of all the nations forming part of Russia freely to secede and form independent states,"[39] were engaged from 1918 into the early 1920s in suppressing Uzbek and Tajik efforts to exercise that right.

At the time of the Bolshevik Revolution in 1917, tsarist Central Asia was in turmoil. Its Moslem peoples had revolted twice during 1916. The second time they exploded with hatred of Russian settlers, massacring many of them. The Russian reply used overwhelming firepower in savage and uncontrolled retaliation.[40] The revolution left the only effective power in the region to a group of Russian railway workers, skilled laborers, and soldiers who formed the Tashkent Soviet. Local Moslem leaders withdrew to Kokand in the Ferghana Valley. There on 10 December 1917, a group of 203 persons, drawn from the region's upper classes, proclaimed what became known as the Kokand Autonomous Government. It sought self-rule for the region within a Russian-led nation. The Tashkent Soviet responded to this challenge to colonial authority with an attack in February 1918 that laid waste Kokand, looted the valley, and killed between 5,000 and 14,000 persons.[41] In March the Soviet's army tried to recapture Bukhara, a former tsarist protectorate that technically had become independent.[42]

Basmachi Resistance

These events inspired the largest, most popular, and most persistent resistance movement to Communist rule in Soviet history.[43] It also became for a time the most threatening because of the weakness of Soviet power during the Civil War. Moslem partisans who fought Russian control became known as *basmachi*, a term that Soviet media made pejorative by defining it as "bandits" or "robbers."[44] But the *basmachi* had popular backing. It was "almost a mass movement of the peasant population," a Soviet encyclopedia conceded, led by "the local national intelligentsia," and religious and temporal leaders as well as partisan commanders.[45]

Well-armed, mounted on horseback for mobility, able to vanish into the supporting population when pursued by the Red Army, *basmachi* bands reached a peak of power between 1920 and 1922. Soviet sources estimated that they numbered 20,000 men.[46] But old clan, tribal and ethnic divisions prevented a concerted drive against Russian control. A description of the *basmachi* could well apply to the Afghan resistance in the early 1980s:

> The principal weakness of the *basmachi* movement was its lack of unity. The various detachments operated independently of each other under the leadership of ambitious and jealous chieftains, who refused to coordinate their activities. . . . [It] represented essentially a number of unconnected tribal revolts and exhibited all the shortcomings of such forms of resistance. It never attained its ultimate purpose—the overthrow of Russian rule in Turkestan— because the Russians were infinitely better organized, controlled the cities and the lines of communications, and had at their disposal a more numerous and more experienced armed forces.[47]

The Russians also used for the first time airborne forces, and airpower,[48] a hint of the advantage that Soviet helicopter gunships and other modern weaponry would have over Afghan guerrillas.

Despite some help from Amanullah and, according to the Soviets, British help,[49] the *basmachi* were ultimately defeated by a combination of military pressure, economic measures, and political steps. Some of the economic and political moves were similar to changes that the Soviet-directed Afghan government made in 1980 to try to win popular support. These will be discussed in chapter 12 as an apparent model for Afghanistan. By the mid-1920s the *basmachi* problem had been brought under Soviet control, self-determination denied. A revival of guerrilla operations as a response to collectivization was quelled in the early 1930s. Many Tajiks and Uzbeks fled across the Amu Darya to join their kin in northern Afghanistan, and some Turkmen also. Estimates run from 50,000 to ten times as many.[50]

Although relations were troubled by the *basmachi* situation, Amanullah's government signed a friendship treaty with Soviet Russia on 13 September 1920.[51] Independent Afghanistan's first treaty, it specified a Russian gift of a million gold rubles, 5,000 rifles with ammunition, several aircraft and the establishment of an aviation school, a gunpowder plant, and sundry technical aid.[52] The gold suggested that Moscow was trying to pick up where the British had left off—subsidizing the Afghan government as part of controlling it. The whole package, promised when the Bolsheviks were struggling to survive in the Civil War and were cut off from Afghanistan by White armies and the *basmachi*, developed into the first Soviet foreign aid program.

The alarmed British imposed on Moscow, in a 1921 agreement to supply the Soviets with badly needed industrial goods, a pledge not to use Afghanistan as a base for Bolshevik agitation in India.[53] But the "Great Game" died hard. The new Russian ideological zeal gave a sharper edge to activity in the area. The British Indian government became increasingly fearful of Bolshevik influences through Afghanistan as Amanullah became more friendly with Moscow.[54] The friendship intensified when the Soviets capitalized on a regional rebellion in Khost, southeast of Kabul, in March 1924. Accusing the British of instigating opposition to Amanullah's tentative efforts at social reform,[55] Moscow outbid them with aid and quickly built up its advisory personnel to 120, the largest group of foreigners in Afghanistan. Soon, "The so-called Afghan air force [was] to all intents and purposes a Russian service and [was] indeed [to] be regarded as a Russian advanced base," a British intelligence report said.[56]

Soviet preeminence in presence and influence in Kabul did not last long, however. After a tour of Europe, including Moscow,[57] and of Egypt, Turkey, Persia, and India, Amanullah returned home in July 1928 inspired to modernize Afghanistan in the way that Mustafa Kemal Ataturk was then forcibly changing Turkey. But he lacked Ataturk's power. A new, wider rebellion erupted. Amanullah fled Kabul to Qandahar in January 1929, and the throne was claimed by an Afghan Tajik highwayman named Habibullah but known as Bacha-i-Saqao ("Son of the Water Carrier").[58] The Russians, who eight years earlier had sent a military column into another backward neighboring state, Mongolia, to install a friendly government, decided to intervene to help Amanullah. The Afghan ambassador to Moscow, Ghulam Nabi Charkhi, crossed the Amu Darya accompanied by 800 to 1,000 armed men of Central Asian origin under command of the Russian military attaché from Kabul. Afghans were different from Buddhist Mongols, however. They remembered Soviet repression of their *basmachi* cousins and resisted. Ghulam Nabi's force gave up the fight in June and withdrew to Soviet territory after receiving word that Amanullah had fled to Italy.[59]

British influence was then reestablished. The highwayman's chaotic rule ended on 13 October 1929 when he was driven from Kabul by an army led by five brothers from a branch of the Afghan royal family. The army was raised among tribes on the Indian as well as the Afghan side of the Durand Line, creating suspicion of British connivance.[60] When the eldest brother, Mohammad Nadir Khan, took the throne, Russian influence was eclipsed and the Russian presence virtually disappeared. Nadir Shah, as he became known, summarily executed Ghulam Nabi in 1932 on suspicion of conspiring to restore Amanullah. A year later the king was murdered by a youth associated with Ghulam Nabi's family.[61] The king's brothers crowned his nineteen-year-old son, Mohammad Zahir Shah, who under their guidance continued a pro-British policy.

Afghanistan remained neutral during World War II, acquiescing to an Anglo-Soviet demand to expel nondiplomatic Germans and Italians. The 13 June 1946 agreement between Kabul and Moscow to define the Amu river border, thus settling the ownership of some 1,192 islands,[62] showed a relatively benign post-war Soviet attitude toward its weak neighbor. During or immediately after the war, Afghanistan was the only country bordering the Soviet Union not to be subjected to Soviet efforts to chisel off territory—except for northern Korea, where a Soviet puppet had been installed across an unchanged 10.4-mile river border.[63] Why this exception? There is no clear answer. Perhaps Afghanistan seemed too quiet, too unimportant, too unthreatening to be worth the trouble and outcry of a territorial grab. From 1945 to 1949, however, Soviet provocateurs were sent across the Amu to proselytize among Uzbeks, Tajiks, and Turkmens. They had no success because of bitter memories of the way their brethren had been treated under Soviet control.[64]

Chapter 2. The Cold War in Afghanistan

Two goals of Afghanistan's ruling royal family set up conditions in the three decades before 1978 that allowed local Communists and the Soviet Union to establish the foundations for their eventual control. One goal was a desire to modernize the country, to bring the benefits of economic development to still medieval villages and early nineteenth-century towns. The other was winning independence for the Pushtun peoples across the Durand Line in what became the Moslem nation of Pakistan, with the unstated hope of later absorbing their "Pushtunistan" brethren into Afghanistan.

Modern Economic Development

The basis for modern economic development was laid in the 1930's. Commercial agriculture, industrialization and investment banking were started with local resources and drew on trade with the Soviet Union and India. Earnings accumulated during World War II (from sale of fruit, food, and karakul skins) made the government feel prosperous enough by 1946 to undertake projects intended to improve living standards. It turned to the United States. During the war, Americans had proven able to build roads and airfields in remote parts of the world, and they were a distant, relatively neutral source of help compared with either Soviet or British involvement. But the first approach to the United States legation in Kabul, on 25 April 1946, was dismissed as too vague in economic concepts.[1]

The government therefore went ahead without official United States help. It signed a $17-million contract with the Morrison-Knudsen Company of Boise, Idaho. Gravel roads were to be substituted for the rough tracks linking Kabul and Qandahar with each other and with Durand Line crossing points. They also contracted to repair old irrigation dams and build some new canals in the Helmand Valley.[2]

With these and other improvements, the Helmand, Afghanistan's most important internal river, was to water a new breadbasket. Warnings of salinity and waterlogging problems, and of the soil's thinness, were ignored. Difficulties mounted from working in little-known terrain remote from logistical support. Although Morrison-Knudsen's technical work was good, and it trained a generation of Afghans in modern construction, the company inevitably was blamed for the project's inability to fulfill dreams of large new fertile areas farmed by former nomads—who did not want to settle down. American prestige suffered as the Helmand project became known as a vast white elephant. In two decades it absorbed some $55 million of Afghan money plus another $60 million of

United States loans and grants. The World Bank said in 1977, however, that, "Whatever the past failings, the Helmand Valley now makes an important contribution to the national economy, notably in supporting a rapidly growing cotton-textile complex and providing a substantial surplus of wheat."[3]

The Helmand project epitomized a number of continuing problems. They included the unwillingness of an illiterate, isolated peasantry to play its assigned role in modernization. This attitude led in 1978 to resistance to Communist changes and in the early 1980s to a division in the Afghan resistance movement between those who did not want any strong central government, Communist or otherwise, fighting instead to return to traditional ways, and those who wanted to modernize but not by a Communist model. The project also showed the tendency of developing countries to overreach their resources, human as well as economic, in schemes that were poorly planned, badly implemented, inefficiently run, and unable to repay their costs.

The appeal for an American development loan was made more specific in 1947. "The Afghan government tends to think of the loan," the United States legation reported later, "as of political as well as economic importance, possibly increasingly so in the light of manifestations of Soviet interest and offers to be of assistance to Afghanistan."[4] The United States Export-Import Bank was asked for $118 million. But the bank was unmoved by a Soviet scare. It took a dim view of the economic rationality of Afghan plans. To the bitter disappointment of the Afghan government, which saw economic development as a way of enhancing its domestic support, the bank finally approved on 23 November 1949 only $21 million in credits to continue Morrison-Knudsen's work in the Helmand Valley.[5]

By 1949 the aid atmosphere was beginning to change. The massive program of American foreign aid to developing countries in the 1950s and 1960s was starting. Up to 1979, when aid was halted, the United States had provided $532.87 million in aid to Afghanistan. Of this, $378.17 million was in outright grants, or gifts, and the remaining $154.7 million was in loans on concessionary terms.[6]

Immediately after World War II, Afghanistan hoped to divert to economic development some of the money it had been spending on an antiquated 90,000-man army. Shah Mahmud Khan, who became prime minister of nephew Zahir Shah's government in May 1946, said he was

convinced that America's championship of the small nations guarantees my country's security against aggression. America's attitude is our salvation. For the first time in our history we are free of the threat of great powers' using our mountain passes as pathways to empire. Now we can concentrate our talents and resources on bettering the living conditions of our people.

He envisaged "a small but well-trained internal security force." By 1955 the army had been cut in half, while the central police force was expanded to 20,000 men.[7].

Attempts to Gain Arms

But the developing chill of the Cold War, and the Soviet encouragement of revolutionary seizure of power by Communists across Asia, soon caused a change of Afghan tone. A well-trained force required foreign arms. As the British, who had supplied some weapons, began withdrawing from India, the Afghan war minister told the British military attaché in Kabul on 10 June 1947 that he was concerned. The only potential enemy was the Soviet Union, he said, and he feared more pressure from Moscow than its already insisting on a veto over foreigners' movements in northern Afghanistan near the Soviet border.[8]

For weapons, as for economic aid, Afghanistan turned to the United States. Washington had ignored an arms request during World War II,[9] but in late 1948 a new request was made. While in Washington in late 1948 seeking the $118-million loan, the minister of national economy, Abdul Majid Khan Zabuli, also asked for American weapons to maintain internal security in case of revolts by well-armed tribesmen. Fear of tribal revolts was an aspect of development plans founded in Amanullah's experience. It was justified by the burning of the army base at Jalalabad in 1949 by tribesmen protesting reforms. But it was not a theme well understood in Washington. The Soviet danger was. A second reason for seeking United States weapons, Zabuli said, was

> to make a positive contribution in the event there is war with the Soviets. Properly armed, and convinced of U.S. backing, Afghanistan could manage a delaying action in the passes of the Hindu Kush which would be a contribution to the success of the armed forces of the West and might enable them to utilize bases which Pakistan and India might provide. . . . When war came Afghanistan would of course be overrun and occupied. But the Russians would be unable to pacify the country. Afghanistan could and would pursue guerrilla tactics for an indefinite period.[10]

When the Soviets tried to pacify the country three decades later, most of the weapons used to resist them had been supplied by the Soviet Union.

The Truman administration was not impressed then. It paid little attention to Afghanistan. Its South Asian specialists were more concerned with India and Pakistan, with Afghanistan merely an exotic land beyond the Northwest Frontier; its Middle East experts were busy with the Arab-Israeli problem and Iranian alarms; its Soviet affairs specialists dismissed Afghanistan as small and unimportant. The country was not seen as occupying a central position where influences from three diverse areas came together and influences might be directed outward into those areas. The perceptions of the "Great Game" were forgotten.[11]

Repeated requests for weapons were put off, even though in 1949 Afghan officials suggested that "unless US gave Afghan more assist Afghans might turn to USSR," as a cable from the American mission in Kabul—now raised to an embassy—put it in 1949.[12] A study for the United States Defense Department's joint chiefs of staff said: "Afghanistan is of little or no strategic importance to the United States. . . . Its geographic location coupled with the realization by Afghan leaders of Soviet capabilities presages Soviet control of the country whenever the international situation so dictates." The study recommended neutrality for Afghanistan in case of a Soviet-American war and warned that any "overt Western-sponsored opposition to Communism" there "might precipitate Soviet moves to take control of the country."[13]

The United States embassy in Kabul endorsed arms sales on 4 January 1950 "to exclude Soviet influence, cement Afghan-American friendship, maintain internal security, and promote settlement of differences with Pakistan."[14] But in early 1951 the National Security Council in Washington said:

> The Kremlin apparently does not consider Afghanistan's relatively meager assets to be worthy of serious attention and probably believes that it can take Afghanistan easily whenever its broader objectives would be served. There is little doubt that Afghanistan could be conquered regardless of its will to resist. In the event of an invasion, it is possible that certain elements—particularly the Afghan (Pathan) tribesmen—would continue to resist.[15]

When Shah Mahmud visited Washington in April 1951, the State Department told President Harry S. Truman that Afghan arms requests were being ignored rather than refused. It advised him to tell the prime minister of "the limitations of the ability of the US to furnish military assistance," to stress reliance on collective security within the United Nations, and to hold out hope for more financial and technical aid.[16]

Afghanistan persisted. It presented a formal request and arms list on 13 August 1951. The United States reply on 27 November was that the $25-million cost would have to be paid in cash, Kabul would have to arrange transit through Pakistan, and the sale would be made public. These terms were unacceptable; Shah Mahmud called it "a political refusal." The war minister who had drawn up that arms list, Mohammad Daoud Khan, renewed the request after becoming prime minister in 1953. On 28 December 1954 it was in effect rejected again. A United States diplomat then in Kabul, Leon B. Poullada, said that "a month later, in early 1955, Daoud opened negotiations with the USSR on their long-standing offer of military aid which the Afghans had previously ignored."[17]

Pushtunistan

In both the 1951 and 1954 arms rejections, the United States urged Afghanistan to settle its Pushtunistan dispute with Pakistan as an implied condition for reconsideration. This dispute was the expression in a new international situation of the ruling Pushtun elite's emotional inability to renounce part of traditional Pushtun territory on the other side of the Durand Line. The desire for ethnic unity was too deeply ingrained in the psychological and political makeup of the Afghan governing system and the tribal structure on which it rested to be renounced.

Although the British had reinforced Durand's 1893 agreement by 1919 and 1921 treaties with Afghanistan, there was an administrative distinction between parts of India governed by British officials and the northwest frontier tribal agencies that were governed by local khans. This difference had left some doubt about the status of most Pushtun areas. As Britain began moving toward freeing India, the Afghan government asked about recovering Pushtun areas. Britain rebuffed it as having no legal interest beyond the line. Afghanistan then demanded that Pushtun territories be given independence, instead of only being offered a choice between becoming part of Hindu India or Moslem Pakistan. Britain ignored this, and the choice naturally followed religious ties. The Pushtunistan (or Pakhtunistan) issue was born.[18]

Afghanistan then began a long, costly struggle to try to shake the areas loose from Pakistan, which became independent 14 August 1947. First Kabul voted against Pakistan's joining the United Nations. Then a *loya jirgah* [meeting of tribal leaders] in Kabul on 26 July 1949 repudiated the old frontier agreements with Britain. On 12 August a tribal meeting just inside Pakistani territory announced the establishment of a new nation of Pushtunistan. Its definition was vague. One official Afghan version said its territory ran from the Durand Line to the Indus River and from near the Chinese border to the Arabian Sea. It "covers an area of more than 190,000 square miles and has a population of over seven millions."[19] This was more than just Pushtun areas. Afghan media later talked separately of Pushtunistan and Baluchistan, advocating independence for each.[20] But there was no vagueness on one point: Pushtuns on the Afghan side of the Durand Line would not be included in an independent state. The inevitable conclusion of the outside world was that Afghanistan was simply trying to detach territory from Pakistan as the first step toward taking it over.

Pakistan, struggling against great odds for national cohesion and survival, reacted with pressure to try to halt the Afghan campaign. Almost all Afghan imports passed through Karachi harbor and across the Khyber or Khojak passes. Slowdowns occured from late 1947 onward. The Pakistani government virtually halted the movement of Afghan goods through Karachi in December 1949 and stopped Afghan tank trucks from picking up petroleum products.[21]

Beginning of Soviet Opportunities

This was the beginning of postwar Soviet opportunities in Afghanistan. There was no economically feasible transit route across Iran, but a Soviet railroad reached the north bank of the Amu Darya. In July 1950 the Soviet

Union signed a four-year trade agreement with Afghanistan to barter Soviet petroleum products, cotton cloth, sugar, and other commodities for Afghan wool, furs, raw cotton, fruit, and nuts. It also provided duty-free transit for Afghan goods and gave Kabul a politically high currency exchange rate.[22] Soviet diplomats in Kabul began to express cautious sympathy for the Pushtunistan campaign, emphasizing racial affinity. A Soviet journal hinted in 1951 that Moscow envisaged Afghanistan's taking over Pushtun areas of Pakistan while the Soviets took over the Tajik, Uzbek, and Turkmen areas of Afghanistan, thus tidying up the ethnically messy nineteenth-century boundaries,[23] but this was never explicitly advocated.

The United States government was "displeased by [Afghan] efforts to gain our support in their campaign against Pak[istan] through threats to place themselves under Sov[iet] auspices."[24] Both Washington and London tried diplomatically to halt the campaign. They failed. Aghanistan was therefore considered a potential aggressor against Pakistan in a more real and immediate danger than any Soviet threat to Afghanistan which might have justified providing United States weapons to Kabul.[25] But the Soviet threat in its broader dimensions was sufficient to make the United States arm Pakistan, thus alienating Afghanistan.

The idea of America's arming Pakistan arose in 1951, during the Korean War. By mid-1952, agreement in principle had apparently been reached, but the decision was not formally approved until 8 February 1954. The decision was made over the objections of United States specialists on South Asia. They argued that it would worsen relations with India—which quickly proved true—but they paid little attention to its effects on Afghanistan.[26] Pakistan joined in September 1954 what became the Southeast Asian Treaty Organization, and a year later the Baghdad Pact that became the Central Treaty Organization. While the United States had global issues in mind, plus encouraging the Pakistani army as an element of stability in a fragile nation,[27] the army's commander had other ideas. Mohammad Ayub Khan, who later became president, wrote that Pakistan was seeking local security, particularly against India, in joining ostensibly anti-Communist alliances.[28] In 1956 SEATO endorsed Pakistan's position that the Durand Line was a fixed border where the question of self-determination for Pushtuns did not arise.[29]

The American attitude on Pushtunistan was a key factor in difficult United States relations with Daoud while Soviet influence in Ahghanistan began to grow. Daoud was a first cousin of King Zahir Shah, who was two years younger. Daoud became prime minister in 1953, at the age of forty-one, because his generation of the royal family had become impatient with his uncle, Shah Mahmud. The younger generation was unhappy on three grounds: Helmand Valley problems and related slowness of economic progress and social reforms; concern that growing dependence on the West, especially on the United States, might compromise Afghan neutrality and complicate relations with the Soviet Union; and displeasure with what Daoud in particular considered inadequate official support for the Pushtunistan issue.[30] Daoud's attitude clashed with that of the United States ambassador, Angus Ward, who soon drifted into hostile relations with him. "Misunderstandings of innocent actions were common on both sides" as Daoud turned to Moscow for first economic and then military aid.[31]

The first major Soviet-Afghan agreement was announced on 27 January 1954, after the United States plan to arm Pakistan was known. The Soviets lent $3.5 million for the construction of grain elevators at Kabul and Pul-i-Khumri, and a flour mill and bakery at Kabul.[32] This was the first such loan outside the Soviet bloc since the death ten months earlier of Joseph V. Stalin, who had not believed in helping neutral nations. Its low rate of interest, 3 percent, and a delay in repayment until the projects were completed in 1957, qualified it as foreign aid, even though not a gift. It was therefore the beginning of a major change in Soviet policy and the beginning of competitive aid-giving in the Soviet-American struggle for influence in nonaligned countries.

After World War II, Soviet policy toward these Third World countries emphasized support for local Communist insurgencies in colonial territories or newly independent nations. Those national leaders who had assumed power from the European masters were in general regarded by Stalinist ideologists as lackeys of imperialism. All those not with Stalin were considered against him. Neutralism was if anything more immoral to him than it was to some Americans in the depths of the Cold War. But failures of Communist insurgencies to win power began to cause doubts in Moscow before Stalin's death. Circumstances were changing; the old anticolonial line was becoming outdated. New tactics were needed to appeal to independent leaders in the majority of cases where economic backwardness meant there was no proletariat to be mobilized. At the same time, post-war recovery was beginning to turn the Soviet economy outward for foreign trade and new sources of supplies. This offered chances to detach former colonies from economic dependence on Europe or America.[33]

After Stalin's death on 5 March 1953, the official Kremlin attitude toward the Third World quickly began to change. National leaders like India's Jawaharlal Nehru and Egypt's Gamal Abdul Nasser were no longer criticized but instead praised as leaders of free peoples. Attacks on the Moslem religion were muted in external propaganda, although repression continued at home. A trade pact with India—not aid, not yet—was announced in December 1953. The following month came the first loan to Afghanistan, and within two years many other aid agreements. Moscow began to represent itself abroad as the champion of developing nations, helping them to establish economic as well as political independence, to raise living standards, and to prosper in a condition of world peace for which it had long tried to claim credit. This was a pragmatic policy, not a revolutionary one.[34]

The first secretary of the Soviet Communist Party, Nikita S. Khrushchev, told visiting United States congressmen that "We value trade least for economic reasons and most for political reasons."[35] It was, however, unclear how large an element economic considerations initially played in the new policy. There were cases of the Soviet Union's selling surplus and antiquated industrial plants to unsophisticated countries in return for primary products of use to the Soviet economy, and even for products that the Soviets sold at a profit in Western markets so as to undercut the original supplier's own sales and rob it of badly needed foreign exchange. But there were also cases of Moscow's supplying equipment and technical services at obvious cost to its domestic needs, perhaps on a long-term calculation of later benefit.

Economic Justification of Soviet Aid

After Khrushchev was ousted from power in October 1964, however, a reaction set in against foreign aid, which had never been popular inside the Soviet Union. Officials began to emphasize the returns, such as cotton from Egypt to make clothing for Soviet consumers. Some Soviet economists began to develop an economic, rather than political, rationale for trade and aid, although the Kremlin continued to preach to the Third World that it offered escape from Western exploitation. Soviet internal literature came more clearly to reflect the benefits of an international division of labor, which meant attaching aid recipients to the Soviet economy for its own gain. Assured supplies of raw materials and fuel, including natural gas from Afghanistan, were claimed. A regular flow of repaid credits also became important, with countries like India repaying more on old loans in the 1970s than they were getting in new ones. Regardless of whether aid had led to Communist triumphs abroad (and it will be argued later that it was a major factor in Afghanistan's case), it was of benefit in building up the overall economic strength of the Soviet Union.[36]

Deriving such benefit was what Marxists accused colonial powers of doing with trade to the detriment of their colonies, and post-colonial Western powers of doing with their form of aid. Moscow covered its gains with assertions that it was selflessly helping poor countries, many of which suspected otherwise. This help—from 1954 to the Soviet invasion of Afghanistan in 1979—amounted to $18,190 million worth of aid commitments to non-Communist developing nations, of which only $8,170 million had been drawn by the end of 1979.[37] The proportion drawn was low because of bureaucratic, planning, or technical problems, or because some countries began to find that the terms and quality of equipment offered were inferior to free-market offerings. Military aid was valued at $47,340 million offered, $35,340 delivered.[38] Very little Soviet aid was in the form of gifts; most was in the form of loans.

Of these totals, about $1,265 million in economic aid had been extended to Afghanistan up to the time of the coup in 1978. These were almost entirely loans. While 71 percent of the $532.87 million of American aid to Afghanistan was in outright gifts, the Soviets expected a return on what they sent across the Amu Darya. But interest and repayment terms on loans to Kabul were more generous than those that Moscow allowed to any other poor non-Communist country. East European countries, which were cajoled if not required by Moscow to provide loans as part of a coordinated Soviet bloc program of Third World penetration, had extended about $110 million to Afghanistan. Some 5,000 Afghan students had been trained in Soviet academic institutions and 1,600 in technical institutions by 1979. Soviet military aid for Afghanistan was valued at roughly $1,250 million, and some 3,725 Afghan military personnel had received military training in the Soviet Union through 1979.[39]

After the first Soviet aid agreement, others soon followed. In July 1954 an agreement worth $1.2 million was signed for construction of a gasoline pipeline across the Amu Darya and three gasoline storage centers, and in August an agreement for $2 million for road-building equipment. Also in August, Czechoslovakia, which was the first East European country to assist the Third World, provided a credit of $5 million to build three cement plants; these ran into problems—cost overruns, and raw material supplies proved inadequate. In October a $2.1-million Soviet loan agreement was signed providing for an asphalt factory and equipment to pave the dusty streets of Kabul. The United States Export-Import Bank had twice refused to let the Kabul paving project be added to loans for Helmand development. But, while it did not contribute directly to agricultural development, the project contributed greatly to the image of Soviet friendship.[40] These were early examples of a Soviet talent for getting maximum propaganda value from aid projects while United States aid provided essential but often inconspicuous things.

Pushtunistan Support

Another flareup of the Pushtunistan problem in 1955 led to a five-month closing of the Pakistani border, giving the Soviet Union an opportunity to intensify its developing relationship with Afghanistan. Moscow promptly provided such essential imports as gasoline and cement to continue construction projects, even American aid projects. In June the Soviets made a new duty-free transit agreement with the Afghans as another step toward reorienting the country economically from the Indian subcontinent to the north.[41]

An effort to convert this into a political reorientation was made during the visit to Kabul in December 1955 by Khrushchev and Soviet Premier Nikolai A. Bulganin. Up to that point, major powers had tried to maintain a cautious attitude toward the Pushtunistan problem, avoiding commitment to either side beyond formally recognizing Pakistan's border and hoping to exercise restraint. But the Soviet leaders chose to support a friendly neighbor against a recipient of United States military aid and member of Western alliances. "We sympathize with Afghanistan's policy on the question of Pushtunistan," Bulganin said. "The Soviet Union stands for an equitable solution of this problem, which cannot be settled correctly without taking into account the vital interests of the people inhabiting Pushtunistan."[42] In later years, however, Moscow tried to avoid any direct restatement of its position.

Khrushchev explained in his memoirs what Soviet thinking was at the time by emphasizing security, thus foreshadowing Kremlin attitudes in the late 1970s. "America was courting Afghanisan," he wrote,

> appearing to give that country economic aid but actually being much more interested in currying political favor. . . . At the time of our visit there, it was clear to us that the Americans were penetrating Afghanistan with the obvious purpose of setting up a military base. . . . The capital which we've invested in Afghanistan hasn't been wasted. We have earned the Afghans' trust and friendship, and it hasn't fallen into the Americans' trap. . . . The amount of money we spent in gratuitous assistance to Afghanistan is a drop in the ocean compared to the price we would have had to pay in order to counter the threat of an American military base on Afghan territory. Think of the capital we would have had to lay out to finance the deployment of our own military might along our side of the Afghan border.[43]

More Loans

Khrushchev and Bulganin announced the gift of a 100-bed hospital to be built in Kabul and fifteen buses to run on its newly paved streets. They promised a thirty-year credit of $100 million at 2 percent interest. This was a major increase in Soviet bidding for Afghan favor. After some disagreement on how to use the credit, projects included construction of a military air base at Bagram, 20 miles north of Kabul, and new roads in northern Afghanistan, with a tunnel 1.7 miles long at an altitude of 11,100 feet through the Hindu Kush at the Salang Pass.[44] While unquestionably desired by Afghanistan at the time, the air base, roads, and tunnel would prove to be key facilities for the Soviet invasion.

Other Soviet loans followed. When Zahir Shah visited Moscow in August 1957, he was promised $15 million for the development of natural gas exports to the Soviet Union, to replace primary products like wool and cotton in repaying loans.[45]

After the invasion, Soviet media repeatedly emphasized how helpful the Soviet Union had been to Afghanistan over the years. By then seventy-one aid projects had been completed, with fifty-two of them still being operated with Soviet technical help, and another sixty projects had been agreed upon. "As regards the volume of cooperation, Afghanistan is in the front rank of the developing countries which receive our assistance," *Pravda* reported.[46] An American who assessed Soviet foreign aid all over the world wrote in 1967: "Soviet aid to Afghanistan has been immensely successful. The Russians have avoided most forms of political interference. . . . Russian aid projects on the whole have been well-suited to Afghanistan's needs. . . . The record indicates that flexibility and determination to show that the Soviet Union can co-exist with a smaller nation have been of equal importance" to the advantages of geographic proximity.[47]

But Daoud was cautiously skeptical. He reportedly turned down a Soviet offer to finance the entire second five-year development plan, for 1960–65, on condition that Soviet advisers be placed at the highest level in all Afghan ministries[48]—a placement that occurred after Daoud was killed in a coup d'etat led by Soviet-trained military officers. When questioned about Soviet subversion in 1956, Daoud snapped, "Does anyone think we have not heard of Czecho-slovakia?," referring to the 1948 Communist takeover there. Daoud similarly dismissed a 1956 warning from an American ambassador, on instructions from Washington, that Soviet economic aid was laying a logistical infrastructure for invasion and that Soviet training of Afghan military officers could create a fifth column in the armed forces.[49] By the early 1960s, Afghans

> were quite sure that Soviet actions were always motivated by their own interests and by those alone. But, [the Afghans] reasoned, assuming Soviet planners to be reasonable men, those interests could only be injured by an attack on Afghanistan. The country would be an economic liability to the USSR; to control it would be difficult and costly; and, most important, any such aggression would have disastrous repercussions among the neutralist nations in Asia and Africa.[50]

Growth of Soviet Military Influence

The greater danger, however, than overt attack was the development of Communist influence in the Afghan armed forces. Daoud, who personally supervised all middle-level and senior military assignments, was almost arro-gantly confident about the loyalty of *his* men. His failure to develop in the late 1950s some system to meet the possible dangers of a Soviet military relationship was continued by the leaders who succeeded him in the 1960s. American diplomats noted in 1971 that: "There is . . . no effective organization within the military to counter or even catalog the long-term, possibly subversive effects of Soviet training of the many military officers who go to the USSR for stints as long as six years."[51]

In economic aid, Afghanistan was first; it was second in the Third World to receive Soviet military aid. Moscow had offered to barter arms to Egypt as early as the autumn of 1951, when Egypt demanded that Britain withdraw its military forces from the Suez Canal Zone. After the 1952 coup that led to Nasser's presidency, Soviet arms began reaching his country clandestinely. In February 1955, Czechoslovakia secretly concluded the first commercial arms deal with Egypt as the Soviet bloc sought to offset the developing Western alliance system in the Middle East that became the Baghdad Pact.[52]

A cash purchase by Afghanistan of $3 million worth of Czechoslovak weap-ons was negotiated in August 1955,[53] before Egypt's deal with Prague was publicly known. The summer 1955 confrontation with Pakistan seemed to complete a shift in Afghan thinking—or at least Daoud's thinking—away from Shah Mahmud's feeling that money might better be used for national improve-ment than a large army. Daoud was dedicated to improvement, and he needed a strong army to maintain internal order during the social upheaval of modernization. But his personal commitment to the Pushtunistan issue was a powerful added incentive for turning to Soviet bloc armaments. Daoud manipulated the trouble with Pakistan to win approval from a *loya jirgah* in November 1955 for a military aid relationship with Communists[54] whom tribal elders regarded with religious hatred and secular apprehension. The eventual effect was to reduce those elders' power as the central government acquired a stronger military force to back its policies.

Czechoslovak arms began arriving on the Soviet border in October 1955—the first substantial quantity of new weapons received since British shipments early in World War II. But Daoud wanted more. Military aid did not figure publicly in Khrushchev and Bulganin's visit, although United States diplomat Poullada says it was secretly agreed. In July 1956 a loan of $32.4 million was agreed with Moscow for military aid.[55] That began a Soviet orientation of the army and air force. Their technical language became Russian, and they became dependent upon Soviet expertise and spare parts. From armed forces of 44,000 men, plus 20,000 central police, with almost antique weapons and fewer than twenty-five old piston-engine warplanes in 1956,[56] the Afghan armed forces had grown by the time of the 1978 coup to an army of 100,000 men and an air force of 10,000, both moderately well equipped with modern, but not the very latest, Soviet weaponry, plus 30,000 paramilitary central police.[57]

United States Aid—Too Little, Too Late

Five months after the Soviet arms deal was made, the United States National Security Council found that "the capability of the United States to shape events in South Asia is severely limited," among other reasons because it could not supply all the desired aid. The NSC recommended United States efforts to resolve the Afghan dispute with Pakistan and to "encourage Afghanistan to minimize its reliance upon the Communist bloc for military training and equipment, and to look to the United States and other Free World sources for military training and assistance."[58] There was no detectable sense of irony in the secret NSC study, no reference to the repeated American spurning of Afghan military aid requests before the Soviet deal, no recognition of the effects of America's arming Pakistan, apparently no institutional memory of what had gone before.

The United States began to offer places in United States military schools to Afghans. This was part of a low-budget program run for a large number of allied and neutral countries. In cases such as Indonesia, the program had had significant impact in orienting some foreign armed forces toward the West at times of domestic or foreign Communist pressures. One Afghan went to the United States in 1958, and by 1962 enrollment had risen to 68 in the Command and General Staff School, tank maintenance school, and other specialties. The numbers dropped after that. By the last year, 1978, when twenty Afghans were enrolled, a total of 487 courses (some Afghans took more than one course) had been provided free to the Afghan armed forces[59]—compared to the 3,725 trained in the Soviet Union.

The advent of large-scale Soviet economic aid to Afghanistan caused a change in the American attitude on development projects, too. Until 1956 United States loans were made on economic calculations, if not strictly banking ones, as rejection of the Kabul street paving showed. But in that year the United States International Cooperation Administration (ICA), that later became known as the Agency for International Development (AID), began helping Afghanistan on a more consciously political basis. While the United States should "not undertake an economic aid program aimed at matching in size and scope the credit and aid activities of the Soviet Union," a secret study said, the National Security Council concluded that Soviet bloc military aid posed "problems for the United States government which are primarily of a political-economic nature and should be included among the factors affecting our political relations with Afghanistan and the size and nature of our economic assistance."[60] The State Department designated Afghanistan as an "emergency action area," and it began in 1959 studying ways to compete with the Soviets there, although some deliberate competition had started earlier in fields like commercial aviation. "Vital United States objectives are best served if Afghanistan remains neutral, independent and not over-committed to the Soviet bloc," it concluded.[61]

While the Soviet Union was training future military leaders, the United States decided to make a major effort to train civilian leaders. Increased educational aid was provided in Kabul. Grants were made for Afghan students to attend American universities. The United States aid program also began building hard-surface roads in the eastern and southern part of the country that connected with Soviet road-building in the north and west. President Ayub Khan of Pakistan began to worry aloud in the late 1950s that the new roads would enable the Soviet army to drive to his border, eliminating the historic buffer of difficult terrain.[62]

American aid for transportation and communications also included the curious case of the Qandahar International Airport. It was supposed to make Afghanistan a modern air center comparable to its historic Central Asian role in caravan days. Qandahar would become a major refueling point for flights across southern Asia. ICA provided $10 million in grants and $5 million in loans for Morrison-Knudsen to build the airport. But before it was opened in December 1962, modern jets had come into use and were speeding across the area without need to refuel.[63] The airport was then labeled by the State Department "a monument to poor planning. Kandahar will never be an international jet center," with the town not even a significant tourist attraction, and, "since all [fuel] must be imported by truck across the mountains, the airport is not economic even as a refueling point."[64] Two decades after the project was launched, in the year 1976, the airport handled only 6,600 international passengers, compared with 106,000 at Kabul.[65] In 1980 it became the Soviet military regional headquarters.

Qandahar was not simply a matter of poor planning, however. According to United States diplomats who negotiated with the Afghans, the Kabul government insisted on the airport as part of a package of American support for Afghan civil aviation. The United States feared that rejecting the project would mean losing the chance to organize the local airline, Aryana, and running the risk of having the Soviets organize it and use it to penetrate nearby Asian countries. So Washington knowingly agreed to fund a white elephant at Qandahar, the diplomats thought, and Pan American World Airways took Aryana in hand.[66]

But that does not seem to have been the whole story, perhaps not even the main reason, for building the airport. A number of sources, both military and civilian Americans who declined to be identified, said Qandahar was a potential United States Air Force base for wartime use. It became, in American military planning, a "recovery base" where bombers could land after attacking Soviet targets in Siberia or Central Asia that were too distant from their takeoff points in Western Europe or North Africa for them to have fuel to get home. A consistent pattern of deletions from secret United States government documents about Afghanistan in the later-declassified versions seems to support the oral reports of this military purpose in an ostensibly wholly civilian aid program,[67] but no documentary evidence passed unclassified into the public domain.

Washington's decision to compete with Moscow in trying through aid to influence Afghanistan faced major problems. Remoteness from the United States was a primary one. Poullada evaluated the aid program as having been good "from a political and strategic viewpoint" but "ineffective as a barrier to Soviet penetration" because of "fundamental internal weaknesses":

1. It was inefficiently executed, cumbersome, burdened with red tape and plagued by long and unjustified delays. Many of the aid administrators and technicians willing to work in Afghanistan were of poor quality.

2. It lacked steadfastness. As the global Soviet threat shaded off into détente, the program lost momentum and received declining appropriations.

3. It could not compensate for bumbling American diplomacy, which mishandled the military aid and Pushtunistan issues. Soviet diplomacy, on the other hand, exploited these issues brilliantly.[68]

Whether the Soviets were always brilliant is questionable, but they were in a position to benefit in a more ruthless way from their growing involvement in Afghanistan.

Daoud's economic and social changes combined with other factors to stir up riotous opposition to the government in Qandahar in late 1959 and in other parts of the country. Daoud blamed Pakistan for fomenting trouble inside Afghanistan. Border trouble led to a break of diplomatic relations on 6 September 1961 and another closing of the border to Afghan goods.[69] Once again the Soviet Union provided help.[70]

Daoud's brother, Foreign Minister Mohammad Naim Khan, appealed to President John F. Kennedy for help in quickly developing an overland route through Iran so Afghanistan could avoid complete logistical dependence upon the Soviet Union. Kennedy replied that such a route was too expensive to replace access through Pakistan. Afghanistan needed to make adjustments in its policy to resolve its problem with Pakistan, because no country could readily maintain its independence by complete dependence on one country like the Soviet Union, Kennedy added.[71]

But Daoud was too proud, too rigid, too committed to the Pushtunistan issue, to adjust. So a consensus developed in the royal family in Kabul that he had to go. In a decade of unchallenged command, Daoud had shaped the future of Afghanistan, but he went quietly.

Chapter 3. Royalists and Communists

During the decade from Daoud's forced retirement in 1963 until he returned to power in 1973, King Zahir Shah tried to turn a traditional Asian royal dictatorship into a modern constitutional monarchy. He failed for a number of reasons. They included the lack of preparedness of his primitive country for self-rule, his own hesitancy about permitting the development of institutions essential for a functioning popular government, and administrative incompetence that compounded economic difficulties.

By his hesitancy, the king hindered the evolution of political parties composed of people loyal to himself and dedicated to the kind of westernized, guardedly democratic system that he professed to seek. But he did not hinder the development of political groups that were prepared to work in a semi-legal twilight. The result was that the decade saw the maturing of tendencies toward radicalization of Afghan politics. Several types of Marxist movements developed as well as Moslem groups dedicated to strictly traditionalist Islamic practices. The 1950s had laid the foundation for a Soviet military role in Afghanistan; the 1960s established trends that developed during the 1970s into the conflict of the 1980s in which the Soviet military role took an expanded form.

A foreign-educated Afghan technocrat took charge of the government in 1963. Kabul Radio announced on 9 March that Daoud had submitted his resignation to King Zahir on 3 March, that it had been accepted, and that the minister of mines and industries, Dr. Mohammed Yousuf, had been asked to become prime minister. The announcement added that when he resigned, Daoud "presented His Majesty with several proposals for stabilizing the social conditions in the country and improving the administrative structure. After further study the new government is expected to incorporate these suggestions into future policies."[1]

The changes that Daoud had initiated during his decade as prime minister had created the very problems that he proposed to solve in his final proposals. By moving from cautious, low-budget economic development efforts to extensive foreign-financed aid projects; by extending schooling into long-neglected provinces and bringing the brightest boys to Kabul for further education or sending them to the Soviet Union for military training; by a number of other steps, Daoud had shaken traditionalist, localized Afghan society and tried to drive it into the modern world. The inevitable result, which he foresaw and wanted to control with a strong and loyal army, was a destabilization of social conditions as a wider circle of Afghans was educated to ask questions.

If an economists' catch-phrase of the period, "the revolution of rising expectations," did not really apply to most of the villages of the less-developed world because they lacked any perception of potential change, it did at least begin to apply to a growing number of Afghans as the Kabul elite was broadened and made more representative of the country as a whole. At the same time, the administrative structure needed to be improved because it was still essentially a control system for the ruler. Like bureaucracies in most traditional Asian countries, and in many colonial situations, it was well-adapted to preventing the wrong things from happening by an elaborate system of checks and balances. But it was psychologically incapable of initiating actions or guiding economic development with any efficiency.

Problems of Self-rule

While Daoud recognized these problems, there were three reasons why he was the wrong man to make the changes himself. One was his personal identification with strong, centralized control; a new face was needed to revitalize the system. A second reason went much deeper. Other traditional monarchies in the Moslem world had been overturned by violent revolution during the 1950s, and in 1962 the one most nearly comparable to the Afghan one had been ousted in the North Yemen. The extended family descended from the victors of 1929 recognized the desirability of disengaging from direct responsibility for the government, of turning it over to a trusted commoner member of the government establishment like the German-educated Yousuf and giving him a chance to seek a broader mandate under a constitutional monarchy. Daoud therefore retired and left his cousin the king as the only member of the family with a visible role in running the country. The third reason was immediate—the need to back out of the Pushtunistan dead-end.

Economic Difficulties

About 40 percent of the government budget came from customs duties. The closure of the Pakistani border had cut receipts so deeply (even after some traffic had been rerouted by mid-1962 over the long, uneconomic rail and truck route to Khorramshahr on the Persian Gulf as a supplement to trade through the Soviet Union) that ministries' budgets had to be slashed 20 percent and development projects postponed. With Daoud gone, the shah of Iran brought Afghanistan and Pakistan together in an agreement, 28 May 1963, to reopen diplomatic and trade relations.[2]

In general, Daoud's tough and hard-driving style, his royal status, and his emotional approach had done much for the country but by 1963 had been exploited to their limit or just beyond. He recognized this and went willingly when the family consensus had developed in favor of a change, although the king was concerned about the reaction of the new men trained by Daoud. While Daoud supporters spread stories that American influence had ousted him and that the king was an American puppet, the king "made discreet arrangements with key military officers to deal with any active opposition which Daoud or his supporters may seek to generate," according to a United States Central Intelligence Agency report from Kabul.[3] None developed.

Apparent Calm

The quietness of the change seemed to confirm the belief of Afghan officials that they had no real political problem. The only subject for open political activity up to then was agitating over Pushtunistan, an issue that Daoud might have cultivated at least partially as a foreign distraction, sort of a safety valve. Foreign missions in Kabul were closely watched in an attempt to prevent political infection from them. When the Soviets established an Afghan friend-ship society in Moscow as part of their pattern for cultivating foreign countries, Daoud's government responded with a Soviet friendship society headed by a non-political member of the establishment, and officials controlled attendance at its few meetings. The combination of government vigilance, the traditional dislike for Russians in Central Asia and for what they had done to the Moslem religion north of the Amu Darya, and the upward mobility within the Afghan system were assumed to reduce or even eliminate any Marxist pressures.[4]

There was confidence in Kabul that Afghanistan was avoiding problems created in other rapidly modernizing countries that produced frustrated intellectuals who would turn to Communism. The low subsistence level of most Afghans' lives was egalitarian if not elegant, and the displacements caused by such development projects as the Soviet irrigation and fruit-growing scheme around Jalalabad were not seen as significantly disruptive. The tribal organization of society, combined with an extensive system of political police, was assumed to keep malcontents in line.

Some effort was made to avoid contamination from the training of military personnel in the Soviet Union. Trainees there were all required to study the Marxist view of history and to learn about the international Communist movement. Since many of them came to see the monarchy as the expression of social injustice, when they returned home they were viewed with suspicion. For a time they were denied responsible positions, kept below less well-trained Afghans in a system that emphasized personal ties to Daoud, who had been the military commander before becoming prime minister. This created frustrations, as did a wide pay gap between senior and junior ranks. But the monarchy, while somewhat apprehensive, felt that the lack of a political tradition in the armed forces would protect it from a military coup of the Nasser type.[5]

Political Reality

There was, however, a political tradition in Afghanistan in 1963, alive if submerged. Modern, as distinct from Asian court, politics had had its first flowering during the period after World War II when Shah Mahmud started moving toward economic developments, enabling some of Amanullah's young reformers such as Ghulam Mohammed Ghubar to return to public life. Within the small educated elite of government officials, merchants and landowners, a liberal political movement developed in 1947 named *Wikh-i-Zalmaiyan* ("Awakened Youth"). In 1949 Shah Mahmud eased up on controls used on previous parliamentary elections, which under the 1931 constitution had insured tame and virtually powerless assemblies, and permitted some 40 to 50 reform-minded liberals to enter the 120-member body.[6]

This "liberal parliament" began subjecting ministers to unprecedented cross-examinations, asking about traditional and widely prevalent governmental corruption, about failure of Helmand Valley development to produce the promised results, and other awkward questions. It also passed a law permitting limited freedom of the press. A number of crude newspapers with small circulations immediately appeared, attacking government officials and conservative religious leaders and calling for completely free elections in a more rapid movement toward real democracy. At Kabul University, twenty or thirty students formed a society to discuss religion, Communism and other sensitive subjects.

The government reacted by trying unsuccessfully to form its own political party. Twice it closed student societies. Before the 1952 parliamentary elections, it jailed about twenty-five liberal leaders, including Ghubar, and closed the non-government newspapers. Despite having talked of going underground when a crackdown came, *Wikh-i-Zalmaiyan* disappeared.[7]

An American specialist on Afghanistan, Louis Dupree, wrote that Shah Mahmud's attempt to loosen the reins a little and bring liberals into the system had failed because

(1) The Opposition was directed against an established independent regime, not against a colonial oppressor; (2) to many, in and out of government, a freer society would have meant less graft; (3) the central government maintained tight control over the civil service, which did not participate widely in the "Liberal" movement for fear of retaliation; (4) the almost 100 percent illiteracy prevented the "liberal" press from having an impact outside its own inbred circle; (5) personal attacks on the royal family and religious leaders antagonized many fence-sitters; (6) the government looked on all opposition as preparation for its overthrow, and refused to believe that the "liberals" merely wanted to liberalize the existing government.[8]

Some of the jailed liberals agreed to work within the system and attained ministerial rank under Daoud. Those still in prison in 1963 were released at the beginning of Yousuf's government. One of the 1949–52 liberals, Mohammed Siddiq Farhang, was then named by the king to the seven-member committee to write a new constitution. The committee, which started with a draft left by Daoud, finished its work in 1964, and a *loya jirgah* met to give the nation's assent.

Zahir Shah signed the new constitution into law on 1 October 1964. It provided for a bicameral parliament, with the lower house fully elective and the upper one partly elected and partly appointed by the king. Members of the royal family were barred from politics, a provision that was understood to have been aimed particularly at Daoud. While the constitution did in theory permit political parties to function, the king never agreed to implementing legislation that would make them legal. Unofficial parties began to fill the resulting void.[9] Some of the parties' leaders had first gotten a taste of politics during the "liberal parliament" period, a formative time in Afghanistan's development. Among them were Nur Mohammed Taraki and Babrak Karmal.

Taraki

Taraki was a self-made man from plebeian origins, the kind of background that a true Communist is supposed to have but that sometimes is fabricated to hide the sort of bourgeois family that produced Karmal. Taraki had a genuine concern with social justice that came out strongly in his novels and short stories. But he was a writer and dreamer, a teahouse talker rather than a schemer or organizer, a man with lofty goals but little realistic sense of how to achieve them. Although shy and somewhat retiring, he could fire others with his mission of reform, but they had to find a way to carry out his dreams because he was incapable of following through effectively. That was his undoing. When hoisted to power by men whom he had inspired but was unwilling or unable to control, he overreached himself with unrealistic and unwise policies. He then watched almost helplessly as their results deprived him of power and eventually of life.

While Taraki was introverted, Karmal was a gregarious politician who relished public attention. Karmal was the fiery, dramatic leader of the leftists in the parliament elected in 1965, a man who wanted to be at the center of the political action, even if that meant splitting the Marxist movement. Chastised by time in prison, and tempered by working within the bureaucracy, he had a realistic sense of what was possible within Afghan society, if a warped sense of what ends might be acceptable to achieve it.

In different degrees, ideology meant something for both men. As for most leftist leaders in poor countries, however, it was for them not the kind of ideology that Moscow had redefined as Marxism-Leninism so much as it was initially a desire to achieve change, to attain both progress and social justice. In a way that was pragmatic rather than dialectic, they and many others throughout the developing world gravitated toward Moscow's offering primarily because it was the most obviously available alternative to the system in which they lived, with its backwardness and its cautiously slow approach to change under the control of a governing elite.

Perhaps Karmal's motivating drive was more to achieve power than Taraki's, less to benefit the poor masses of whom he had no personal knowledge the way Taraki did. But the clearer contrast is with the third leader of Afghanistan's first few Communist years, Hafizullah Amin. Amin, who emerged as a leftist a decade after the other two, never showed much sign of having an ideological commitment to progress or social justice. It was, therefore, easy for him to twist others' commitments into tools of raw power, in the way all Communist systems have allowed. Amin was a man who sought power for its own sake, seeking to have his friends and acquaintances serve his purposes. Highly efficient and hard-working, he was the organizational tool for Taraki's inspirational leadership, the man to put some structure and backbone in a fuzzy message of opposing the royal system. A primitive brutality that has been notable throughout the history of Central Asia was comfortable for Amin—he lived and died by it.

Taraki was born 14 July 1917 into a Pushtun family[10] that sometimes farmed at Soor Kelaye in the Naweh district of Ghazni province of southeast Afghanistan, sometimes followed flocks in the seasonal migration of nomads in the region. At the age of five he began working for a widow, but his father wanted him to have an education, and he finished the Naweh Primary School. In 1932 he went to Qandahar to seek a job. The Pushtun Trading Company hired him as an office boy and, impressed by his brightness, sent him to its Bombay office as a clerk for its fruit export business.

His years in the British Indian port city seem to have been critical for Taraki's intellectual development. He attended night school, learning English and finishing tenth grade. Some reports say he met Communists then, although his official biography when he was president did not claim that he became a Marxist at that time.[11]

In 1937 Taraki returned to Afghanistan and got a job in the government's press department, which posted him to Badakhshan in the northeast. With time on his hands, Taraki began the writing that eventually gave him prominence within the narrow Afghan intellectual circles—and attracted Soviet notice. One piece written between 1948 and 1953, when his works were later said to have been "compiled on the basis of class struggle," was about Maxim Gorky, a hero of Stalinist literature. This suggests that he was by then already in touch with the Soviet Embassy in Kabul and receiving material from it. In 1957 a Soviet specialist on Afghanistan praised some of his stories as "interesting for their social direction . . . [and] show[ing] his sympathy for the Afghan peasantry."[12] After he became president, the Soviet press reported that Taraki "wrote many stories on acute social issues which have been translated into various languages, including Russian. . . . These stories relate the formation of the proletariat in Afghanistan and the transformation of rural peasants into city inhabitants and workers."[13]

Efforts by Westerners to find Russian translations of Taraki's works were unsuccessful.[14] If they appeared at all, they were probably in very small editions, the demand being limited to Central Asia or to Russian specialists on Afghanistan. The significance of publishing Russian editions, or saying they were published, however, is that it provided a seemingly legal and legitimate reason for Soviet money to be given to Taraki in the guise of royalties. This technique has been used by Moscow in a number of Third World countries to flatter and subsidize promising politicians, not all of them necessarily Communists when first singled out for such attention.

Transferred back to Kabul, Taraki became active in *Wikh-i-Zalmaiyan*. His apparently was a minor role, although his official biography as president claimed that he founded the organization.[15] It also claimed falsely that during the "liberal parliament" period he started the newspaper *Angar* ("Flame," or "Burning Embers"), an opposition weekly published by Faiz Mohammad Angar, a Pushtunistan advocate. Soviet writers later attributed to Taraki[16] *Angar*'s political statement, entitled "What do we want?" It called for food, clothing, enlightenment, "equality for all in the service of society . . . legal parties for our political education . . . the annihilation of national and social traitors . . . the elimination of tribal and kinship privileges." These demands were to be realized "by unifying and awakening the people, by asserting a people's government . . . to insure that all strata of society have a voice in social affairs." Shah Mahmud closed the paper.[17]

Then, according to a colleague in the Afghan leftist movement[18] and implicitly confirmed by Taraki himself, he sold out. After returning to Kabul from Badakhshan, he had become director-general of publications in the ministry of press and information in 1950 and 1951, then editor-in-chief of the official Bakhtar news agency.[19] During this time he was also, in semi-secrecy, helping the opposition. When the crackdown came and others were jailed, however, Shah Mahmud reportedly personally offered Taraki the alternative of going abroad as an embassy press attaché if he would stop his opposition activities. This indicated that Taraki was regarded as a minor figure, neither important nor threatening enough to justify imprisonment. Taraki agreed to go abroad, saying later he had been given a good job to silence him,[20] and went in early 1953 to Washington.

When Daoud became prime minister in September 1953, Taraki publicly denounced him in Washington.[21] Taraki's official biography says Daoud then recalled him,[22] but at a news conference in New York City on 11 November Taraki said he had quit to protest the dictatorial government in Kabul and planned to go into exile in England because he would be shot if he returned home. "They will confiscate my house and property in Kabul, and may persecute my brothers and wife living there," Taraki declared.[23]

But a month later, reportedly after intercession with Daoud by another exiled former liberal,[24] Taraki issued a statement through the Afghan embassy in Karachi accusing American newspapers of misreporting his remarks. "The story not only embarrassed my government, which I have served faithfully for 16 years, but also caused me great anxiety," Taraki said, and he was going home.[25] The official biography says imperialist lackeys tried to keep him from returning to "spare himself from Daoud's wrath" but that as a true patriot he went anyway, phoned Daoud from the Kabul Cinema to ask if he should proceed to prison or home, and was told to go home but was put under police surveillance[26] —a normal step in Afghanistan. Taraki came out of the episode looking fairly unimportant, somewhat weak, and nursing a continuing hatred for the government. His integrity had been compromised.

Unable to work for the government, Taraki took a job in 1955 as a translator for the United States aid mission in Kabul,[27] a fact omitted from his official biography. All jobs for foreigners in Afghanistan were monitored by the political police, and some Afghans were questioned regularly about their work. In 1958 Taraki quit to start a commercial translation service that supplied the American embassy and other missions with material from the local press and other things.[28] From May 1962 to September 1963 he worked for the United States embassy[29]—and as an Afghan government informer on the Americans, Dupree suggests.[30]

During these years, Taraki continued his writing. He later said he had written about a dozen books, "largely novels about the life of peasants."[31] Some of his works embraced "scientific socialism," advocated a Soviet economic development model for Afghanistan, supported Soviet positions against the West, and even seemed to incorporate material from Soviet works on materialist philosophy.[32] This was when his works were reportedly translated into Russian.

By 1964 Taraki had become a contact man for the Soviet embassy, using the tea shops where he liked to sit and talk as a place to introduce young Afghans to embassy staffers who were presumed to be members of the Soviet police responsible for foreign espionage, the KGB.[33] Taraki was later credited with "transmitting his progressive ideas on the struggle against despotism and exploitation" to a younger generation during this period.[34] After the new constitution was promulgated and elections were planned, but political parties had not been legalized, he gathered together about 30 young men and formed the People's Democratic Party of Afghanistan (PDPA).[35]

Karmal

One of the young men was Babrak Karmal. His name can be translated as meaning "working tiger," but after he became president, Kabul whispers said his last name was an acronym of Karl Marx Lenin.[36] He was born in 1929 at Kamary, near Kabul, into a prominent Pushtun family, possibly related to Daoud, that had become divorced from the culture of its tribe, the Kakars. A pillar of the royal establishment, his father, Lt. Gen. Mohammed Hussein Khan, served in various responsible posts, including governor general of Paktia province.[37] The Kabul elite sent its sons to foreign schools in the capital; Karmal attended German-language schools for thirteen years, graduating from Nejat High School in 1948.[38] He entered the faculty of law at Kabul University in 1949, just as the "liberal parliament" began to agitate intellectual life with politics.

Caught up in the excitement, Karmal became a leader in student politics and played a prominent role in demonstrations protesting the closing of student debating societies.[39] It was at this time that Karmal began to emerge as an effective orator—in Dari, the main language of the Kabul elite and of government, not his tribal Pashto, showing his urban alienation from his roots. He was a natural politician who cultivated a wide range of contacts. While Taraki was connected with *Angar*, Karmal contributed to Ghubar's newspaper *Watan* ("Homeland"). When Shah Mahmud cracked down, Karmal as well as Ghubar was imprisoned.[40]

Up to then, politics seems to have been excitement for Karmal more than an ideological commitment, a way to achieve personal importance and possibly power rather than a matter of any strongly held beliefs. There was little sign that this youth born with the Afghan equivalent of a silver spoon in his mouth had the understanding of the common people's plight that sprang from the personal experience of a Taraki, or that as a result he had the burning sense of social injustice that motivated some other leftists. His very flexible career suggests that this never completely changed for Karmal, but he later said that during the years 1952 to 1955 which he spent in prison he was converted to Communism. Karmal attributed this to Mir Akbar Khyber,[41] a fellow prisoner who taught himself Russian while in prison. Khyber's own Communist history is obscure, but a foreign adviser who knew him as a minor police official in the late 1950s and early 1960s found him to be a very bright, efficient, and inquisitive man who somewhat surprisingly and dangerously advocated leftist views over lunch at the police academy.[42]

Karmal returned to law school after his release, graduated in 1957, and then did a year of compulsory military service. In 1958 he became a minor official in the planning ministry.[43] The ministry soon was headed by another person who had been imprisoned in the 1952 crackdown; Daoud was trying to harness the energies of bright Afghans to economic development within the royal system.

Some time during his government service, which lasted until 1965, Karmal became involved with Naheed Anahita Ratebzad, a medical doctor who was the wife of the king's personal physician. After Daoud dropped the veil in 1959, Ratebzad had organized the Democratic Movement of Women to demonstrate for severe punishment for Moslem fundamentalists who attacked unveiled women in the streets.[44]

Amin

The third man who was to become president of a Communist Afghanistan, Hafizullah Amin, not only lacked the lengthy history of leftist activities that Taraki and Karmal brought to the new PDPA but also was abroad when the party was founded and only rose slowly to his later prominence.

Amin was born in 1921 in the Paghman mountain area just west of Kabul where his father was a low-level civil servant. An elder brother, Abdullah Amin, taught in the Paghman primary school and saw Amin through it after their father died. A bright student, Amin began moving up through the egalitarian system of choosing future leaders on the basis of merit and training them at government expense. Amin became a boarder at the high school in Kabul for training teachers, then received a degree from Kabul University's science faculty, returned to the high school to teach, became its vice principal, and then became principal of another Kabul high school.[45]

In 1957 the American aid program sent him to Teachers' College at Columbia University in New York City, where he earned a master's degree in educational administration. Before school opened, he lived for six weeks with a family in Hamden, Connecticut, that later remembered him as "a very decent sort of guy" who liked to discuss everything from democracy to Communism, education to agriculture, and was taught to swim by the family's seven-year-old daughter.[46] His faculty adviser at Columbia found Amin "smooth and personable . . . a bright guy with lots of ability."[47]

Just when and how Amin was attracted to Communism is unclear. Some Afghans who were students in the United States at the time say they were approached by leftists, others say they were not, and one reports that a military attaché at the Soviet embassy in Washington offered some students money and weapons to stage a revolution at home.[48] Just as the United States aid program was intended to inculcate American principles in the future leaders of foreign countries trained in the United States, so was it Soviet practice to try to use Western Communists to indoctrinate or even recruit, whenever possible, students from Third World countries studying in the West. An Afghan who knew Amin back in Kabul in the mid-1960s says that he had in his living room Communist literature printed in New York City.[49] Amin's official biography says that on his return home in 1958 "he established close contact with Nur Mohammed Taraki and made use of his political, revolutionary and scholarly views."[50] If true—Amin's official biography is suspected of being dressed up later—this indicates that he had developed Marxist views in the United States and possibly was even put in touch with Taraki as a result of Soviet influence on both. But in an interview while he was president, by which time the ties to Taraki had been expunged from his biography, Amin said that "my stay in the United States is not the reason for my political beliefs. My beliefs and thoughts emanate from the reality of the ideology of the working class."[51]

Whatever his beliefs, Amin cultivated government connections to get ahead. He worked in a new teachers' training institute in the education ministry in Kabul, which was virtually run by American aid advisers. Afghan sources say that he was influential in the selection of students to study in the United States, working with Daoud's political police on deciding who was trustworthy.[52] If he was already a Communist by then, he presumably was favoring leftists or those whom he thought might be influenced, thus double-crossing the police. A powerful personality, Amin developed his own network of followers with a manner that was said to polarize people, making them either devoted to him or dislike him, and this network was later taken into the PDPA with him.

In 1962 he was selected by competitive examination to return to Columbia University on another United States aid scholarship for a doctorate in education.[53] On his second stay he became active in the Associated Students of Afghanistan in the United States, one of many foreign student organizations receiving money and guidance from United States groups that were later accused of being CIA fronts. A struggle within the ASA over whether to affiliate with the Moscow-run International Union of Students or the Western-oriented International Students' Conference indicated that both Communists and non-Communists were seeking to influence Afghan students. Another student, Abdul Latif Hotaki, who in 1967 exposed CIA links,[54] was the revolutionary firebrand of the ASA, but he did not want its formal leadership, and in 1963 his friend Amin became president. In this position Amin represented Afghan students in welcoming Zahir Shah on a visit to the United States. An American who worked with ASA remembers Amin as an efficient, reliable, and serious person who ran the organization with a stern hand. He seemed a dedicated educator, although inadequately prepared to earn a doctorate.[55]

Amin's biography says he used his growing influence with Afghan students to launch in 1963 "a progressive organization" separate from ASA, and he sent word to Taraki that his group considered itself part of the Afghan leftist movement.[56] This might well have been a later exaggeration to enhance Amin's importance, but he showed political views in his message in the 1964 ASA yearbook. Amin wrote that the Afghan youth movement "must go forward with all possible speed toward social justice, individual freedom and a democratic political system. . . . We faithfully conceive of a strong united youth movement which will work to speed up any progressive change and act as a counterforce against any oppressive or suppressive force in Afghanistan."[57] The Afghan government, which tried to keep close watch on students abroad, became angered. It asked the United States government not to renew Amin's visa, forcing him to return home in 1965 without completing his doctorate. His Columbia advisor said Amin went with "some bitterness [because] we did not fight to have him stay on. . . . We could not justify our taking a position against his government."[58]

Amin returned to Kabul a few months after the thirty young men had, according to the PDPA's official history, gathered at Taraki's house in the Sher Shah Maini section of Kabul on 1 January 1965 and founded the party.[59] The fact that Amin was able to join as a junior member and work his way into the party leadership showed that his role in America was accepted as a leftist one. But after Soviet soldiers had killed him in 1979, Amin was accused of having been recruited by the CIA during his United States student days and from then on been an American "mole" assigned to destroy the true Marxist leadership in the PDPA. No evidence was ever offered for this extraordinary charge, but as part of its propaganda campaign the Karmal government made a public demand that the United States government—with which it had only cold, formal relations—hand over "all the documents pertaining to the cooperation of the treacherous and criminal Amin with the CIA."[60]

Taraki claimed that the party's founding meeting "was the result of piecemeal activities during the past 25 years. The nucleus of this party was formed 20 years before it was established,"[61] that is, even before *Wikh-i-Zalmaiyan* was organized but at a time when World War II had sparked a desire for change among educated Afghans. The biographies of some officials in the regime that Taraki formed after the 1978 Communist takeover said they had become members of the PDPA in 1963. This early date presumably refers to Taraki's gathering of a group of leftists. One biography that gives the 1963 membership date then inconsistently says the member "participated . . . in founding congress of" the PDPA.[62]

During the period before the 1965 congress, Pushtun members of the small, underground Communist Party of Pakistan reportedly maintained contact with the leftists. One source says Taraki had kept in touch with the Communist Party of India ever since his Bombay days almost three decades earlier.[63] Either or both of these parties might have played a more formative role in the PDPA than Taraki's KGB connections. The Soviets have long used a foreign Communist party to supervise and aid another less-developed one. There is, however, no evidence of how substantive the Pakistani and Indian party ties were.

Foundation of the PDPA

The timing of the formal organization of the PDPA obviously was a result of the promulgation of the new Afghan constitution and the prospect of parliamentary elections. According to a version of the party's history that was circulated secretly in July 1976 by Taraki's faction in an already-split PDPA,[64] the 1 January 1965 meeting chose a central committee. Its members were identified as "comrade," thus following Soviet organization and style. The seven full members were Taraki, Karmal, Ghulam Dastagir Panjshiri, Dr. Saleh Mohammed Ziray, Shahrollah Shahpar, Sultanali Keshtmand, and Taher Badakhshi. Alternate members were Dr. Shah Wali, Karim Misaq, Dr. Mohammed Taher, and Abdal Wahab Safi. The central committee "unanimously selected the long-standing Communist and revolutionary and prominent writer Comrade Nur Mohammed Taraki as general secretary of the PDPA's central committee," the secret history said, thus clearly labeling Taraki a Communist. His title at the time might have been first secretary, as Leonid I. Brezhnev was then called in Moscow, where he had just taken the title from Khrushchev and later changed it back to Stalin's preferred form of general secretary. Karmal was named deputy general secretary, or second secretary.

The party constitution—it is uncertain whether this was adopted at the founding meeting or was written later—proclaimed that "The PDPA is the highest political organ and the vanguard of the working class and all laborers in Afghanistan. The PDPA, whose ideology is the practical experience of Marxism-Leninism, is founded on the voluntary union of the progressive and informed people of Afghanistan: the workers, peasants, artisans, and intellectuals of the country."[65] Copying the dictatorial system of the Soviet Communist Party, the constitution went on that "The main principle and guideline of the structure of the PDPA is democratic centralism." This was defined as "adherence of lower officials to the decisions of higher officials; [and] enforcement of collective basic leadership and individual responsibility." Party members were held responsible by the constitution for "learning the political theories of Marxism-Leninism" and "expanding and strengthening Afghan-Soviet friendly relations and such relations between Afghanistan and the socialist fraternity, international workers' movements, [and] people's liberation movements of Asia, Africa, and Latin America." The organizational structure was a strict imitation of the Soviet party's.

The secret history said that the founding meeting set the party's goals "as building a socialist society in Afghanistan based on adapting the morals of general truths and the Marxist-Leninist revolutionary principles to conditions in Afghanistan." The history summarized the first meeting as having "established our Marxist-Leninist party . . . the Communist Party of Afghanistan." Public identification with Marxism or its Soviet version was avoided, however, and the relatively neutral name of People's Democratic Party chosen instead of Communist.

But attitudes were not neutral. The history not only expressed "joy and happiness" over the 1975 Communist victories in Indochina and the Soviet and Cuban interventions in Angola but also accused "American imperialism" of trying "to prevent the establishment of the PDPA prior to its formation."[66] After the PDPA was formed, the history said, efforts were made to destroy the party by attacks on its members by the "Moslem Youth," described as a reactionary religious band that "was clandestinely led by the royal court and American imperialism." The party continued, the 1976 document said, its "struggles against imperialism, and particularly aggressive American imperialism and its open ally, Maoism, and is fighting alongside our brother parties, foremost among them the Leninist party of the Soviet Union, for the unity of the world Communist movement and the union of the revolutionary forces of the world."[67]

The worker class that the PDPA claimed to lead was almost invisible in Afghanistan. In the 1960s the government civil service numbered some 60,000, few of whom would qualify as Marx's proletariat. Just before the PDPA came to power in 1978, 38,000 persons worked in 174 industrial units, most of them government-owned aid projects; in the mid-1960s the number of industrial workers was probably nearer 20,000—or about one-seventh of 1 percent of

Afghanistan's population. In 1978 another 50,000 or so worked in construction.[68] This meant there was a problem in building what was supposed to be a worker's party—a problem common to the less-developed Third World of illiterate farmers and petty bourgeois merchants. But Lenin had never doubted that his middle-class clique knew best for the workers, and neither did Taraki. "It is not necessary that the workers should be leading," a PDPA official explained in 1979. "A working-class party does not mean that the majority is constituted by workers, but rather that the members are equipped with the ideology of the working class."[69] The original PDPA leadership contained government doctors and administrators, students and writers, but no workers in the Marxist sense.

The task of expanding the original membership was therefore difficult. The lack of a meaningful working class to recruit was only one problem. The parlor leftist inclinations of the leaders seem to have kept them from even trying to enlist the downtrodden of Afghan society whom they never seemed to understand anyway. Another problem was that, outside a narrow elite somewhat alienated from the bulk of the people, the operation of Western-style or Communist political parties was alien. Afghanistan's tradition was for strong men to establish their authority by winning acceptance at a *jirgah*, where everyone was free to speak and a consensus was reached without formal voting. This is a system generally found in primitive societies, and it has carried over into some advanced ones like the Japanese, but it did not fit the modern concept of large numbers of people pooling their individually meager strength in a political party. It certainly did not fit the Leninist concept of "democratic centralism," which means dictatorship that can go beyond the limits of social custom and acquiescence that limited the *jirgah* system.

Another reason was that the royal government seemed to offer ample rewards for most of the bright youngsters whom it brought to Kabul at a time when government operations were expanding with the inflow of foreign aid. The impression, perhaps unfair, of some Afghans was that those just bright enough to get government scholarships but not capable enough to expect to win their way to the top of the bureaucracy were the ones attracted to Communism, while in the military it was men faced with the prospect of retiring as majors rather than the most promising officers. The same could be said for Communist parties in many poor countries, however, and if true it explains a brutal vindictiveness shown by second-raters who attain as Communists the power they could not hope to win competitively in other ways.

Recruiting

The first obvious target for Communist recruitment was Kabul University and the high schools in the capital that fed it. In 1965 the university had some 3,200 students, with a third to a half living in dormitories, and the high schools another 17,000, many of them also boarders.[70] The poor boys from the provinces in the dorms lacked any organized activities such as social clubs, athletic organizations, or professional societies, and the resulting boredom left them open to outside penetration by political activists.

The Communists moved in. Two leftist poets who in 1966 joined the PDPA central committee, Mohammed Hassan Bareq Shafi'i and Gholam Mojadad Sulaiman Laiq, were particularly effective in attracting students with their social messages. Indoctrination was in gradual stages. It began with discussions analyzing the importance of Amanullah's reforms; then discussions emphasized the present royal family's ties to British imperialism since 1929. Further discussions analyzed the *Wikh-i-Zalmaiyan* movement and the "liberal parliament." Finally, leftist literature was circulated, including some in Persian—in written form, virtually the same as Dari—that seemed to originate with the Tudeh party, the underground Iranian Communist party that operated under Soviet control from a base in East Europe.[71]

In the spring of 1965 students at a technical high school in Kabul went on strike to protest food and other conditions. A pamphlet appeared mysteriously that urged students to seize their rights because no one would readily give them any. The government arrested several students and expelled others, but the source of the pamphlet never became public, although the Soviet embassy was generally suspected.[72] With student unrest an obvious problem, the government obtained advisers on student activities from the United States Peace Corps and from the Asia Foundation, an American organization later identified as receiving CIA funds. But as fast as the advisers could develop non-political diversions, such as sports clubs, leftists would try to take control of them.[73] With Western-style political parties not technically legal, and with Moslem fundamentalist organizations at a disadvantage among students trying to escape the control of *mullahs* in their villages, the clandestine activities of the new PDPA found fertile ground.

The United States embassy in Kabul observed in 1971 that in the previous four years leftists "have made important gains among students and the urban-oriented, lower-level professionals," especially high school teachers. It added:

> Unfortunately, moderate political leaders are ineffectual, divided, by and large members of the establishment, and of an older generation. They are not, in effect, offering the younger generation alternatives to leftist programs. . . . In sum, we are confronted with a real and present danger that the left will preempt control over the politically conscious youth and the disenchanted.[74]

The suspicion of a Soviet embassy involvement in student agitation and the reports that Taraki had long had a KGB connection came together in the way Moscow honored him after the official founding of the PDPA. He was invited to visit the Soviet Union, officially for the medical treatment that had long been offered to foreign Communist leaders. But, while Taraki might have received some treatment, his extensive travel during forty-two days in the Soviet Union in 1965[75] suggests something other than medical purposes. Taraki was quoted after he became president of Afghanistan as saying that as a Communist party leader in 1965 he had been treated by the Soviets like a head of state.[76]

PDPA Activities

The first parliamentary elections under the 1964 constitution were held in August and September of 1965. Few Afghans outside the towns bothered to vote. With each candidate supposedly running independently, in the absence of political parties, the government controlled the results. The PDPA later blamed this for the defeat of Taraki in Naweh and of Amin in Paghman,[77] while two central committee members were imprisoned during the campaign. Only three PDPA members were elected: Karmal, Nur Ahmad Nur Panjwa'i, and Feizan Alhaq Fezan. Anahita Ratebzad also won a seat and, working closely with Karmal, was later counted as a PDPA member.

When parliament opened in October, Karmal and Ratebzad led angry attacks on Prime Minister Yousuf and his interim cabinet in which some liberals and opponents of the monarchy joined the attack. They accused the government of corruption and nepotism. Students were brought in to block parliamentary action, and finally demonstrations on 25 October ended with the police opening fire, at least three persons killed, Yousuf resigning, and Karmal tasting power. It was his personal power, more than the PDPA's. In following years, 25 October became a day for leftist demonstrations, but observers in Kabul at the time were left perplexed about who had wanted the trouble, and why. Suspicion fell on Chinese Communists studying at the university, as well as on Russians using the Tudeh party, as inspiring the agitators. But there were also indications that Zahir Shah was behind student opposition to Yousuf, whom the king had begun to consider too independent.[78]

Yousuf's interim government promulgated a press law that led between January and July 1966 to the appearance of six newspapers, some published by "liberal parliament" leaders who after time in prison wanted to pick up again efforts at reform.[79] On 11 April 1966 the first two issues appeared simultaneously of *Khalq* ("The People," or "The Masses"), which the PDPA later described as "its propaganda organ."[80] Taraki was the publisher, Bareq Shafi'i the editor. Using both Dari and Pashto, the two issues contained the "democratic aim of *Khalq*." This was in fact the policy statement of the PDPA in somewhat disguised form to avoid too obvious an identification as a pro-Soviet Communist party. To anyone familiar with Soviet jargon about the Third World, however, it was obvious enough.

The lengthy statement, as rendered into English by Taraki's translation service for sale to foreigners in Kabul, began by analyzing Afghanistan as "a country with a feudal economic and social system. The oppressed people of this nation have suffered from the most difficult and tyrannical kind of oppression

and exploitation and illiteracy and poverty under the authority of feudal lords."
It blamed "the pathetic condition" of the Afghan people on feudalists, some big
businessmen, foreign traders, "corrupted bureaucrats and the agents of mono-
polists and international imperialism." A national democratic government was
prescribed to improve their condition, with its "political pillar . . . [a] united
national front representing all the progressive, democratic and nationalist forces,
that is, workers, farmers, and enlightened progressives." A new, noncapitalist
economic system was advocated, with emphasis on industrialization and the
nationalization of foreign trade, although how the plan was to be financed was
left unexplained.[81]

A number of social and economic changes were proposed in a foreshadowing
of the major reforms introduced after Taraki came to power—which stirred up
the nationwide opposition that became a civil war and led to the Soviet invasion.
Land reform was outlined only sketchily, but the most innovative of the 1978
reforms for farmers was clearly promised: "Laws must be changed so that they
can be released from mortgages, creditors, unemployment and other difficulties
created by the feudal landlords and the city usurers." Breaking with Pashto and
Dari domination, the statement called for "the establishment of compulsory
and free primary education in the mother language of the children in all parts of
the country" and efforts "to develop the languages and the cultures of the
various people and tribes of the country." Only Taraki's 1978 decree on women's
rights is absent from the 1966 statement, suggesting that the all-male PDPA
leaders had not yet focused on the subject. Their lack of economic realism was
apparent in their idealistic pronouncements on minimum-wage laws, guaranteed
vacations with pay, no work for children under the age of fifteen—the ones who
tended the flocks and wove the rugs, both jobs basic to the economy—and
other ideas befitting a mature industrial nation.[82]

On international relations, the statement said that "The most outstanding
subject of contemporary history is . . . class struggle and war between international socialism and world imperialism which began with the Great Socialist
Revolution of October," meaning the Bolshevik Revolution. Without being
named, the Soviet Union was praised for its contribution to world peace and the
weakening of imperialism.[83] Summarizing this statement later, the PDPA history
more candidly said it included "non-capitalist growth and turning toward socialism . . . and friendly relations with the socialist countries, primarily with the
Soviet Union and other peace-loving countries."[84]

Some 20,000 copies of each of the two issues of *Khalq* were circulated,
although later circulation was about 10,000. Some readers who studied the first
two papers found the statement's phraseology untypical of usual Kabul writings
and more like Tudeh documents or materials from Soviet Tajikistan, but it is
unclear whether this meant that the PDPA was simply transmitting foreign
doctrine or was trying to adapt the only Marxist literature available in a
familiar language. In any event, the government closed *Khalq* after six issues,
on 16 May 1966, under a provision of the press law for protecting public

security and dignity and "safeguarding the fundamentals of Islam, constitutional monarchy, and other values enshrined in the constitution."[85]

PDPA Split

By the following year the PDPA had split into two factions—further splits followed—led by Taraki and Karmal and named for their newspapers, *Khalq* and *Parcham* ("The Banner," or "The Flag") which Karmal started in 1968. In its 1976 history of the party, the Khalqis claimed that the brief publication of their newspaper in 1966 had so alarmed reactionaries and the royal regime that they set out to split the PDPA, and Karmal became their tool. Karmal was quoted as arguing in the central committee that *Khalq* had been too leftist, and instead the party should proclaim its loyalty to the king while working within the system for change. In a speech to parliament on 7 August 1966 Karmal said he respected "such a progressive king" and called for steps "so that the authority and prestige of our king will be established and preserved."[86]

This attitude later earned the Parchamis a scoffing title of "the royal Communist party," but there was a serious point behind it. Karmal believed that it was necessary for Marxists to build their strength gradually by co-opting others from within the government. This suited his extroverted politician's desire to stay on the public stage as well as his sense of reality for a tiny, weak movement. It was not Taraki's way, despite the initial *Khalq* endorsement of a national front. Shy, introverted, he preferred to follow a lonelier course of what he considered Marxist purity by fighting the system from outside.

The split was a personality conflict and a fight for power within the leftist movement, but it had a basis in tactical differences that grew into ideological bitterness. Both factions paid tribute to Moscow, which was publicly supporting the king's regime while giving private support to the Marxists. While Karmal frequented Soviet embassy parties, flaunting his connection, Taraki was by one account invited to Moscow to receive a literary prize shortly after the split.[87] It is conceivable, because it has happened in other countries, that KGB agents encouraged or even inspired the split so that local Communists would have one foot in both the royal and opposition camps and be able to benefit whichever came out ahead in the long run.

As the split was developing, Taraki saw himself in danger of being supported by only a minority of PDPA leaders as the more politically adept Karmal won supporters. Taraki therefore resorted to a tactic that had worked in other Communist parties. He expanded the leadership, bringing in people whose personal loyalty he could count on. In mid-1966 the central committee was enlarged "in order to check unprincipled and divisive activities," the Khalqis later said.[88] Amin was added to this leadership group, along with Bareq Shafi'i, Sulaiman Laiq and five others. Karmal tried to get Khyber, who was still a police officer, into the central committee on his side but failed. He then submitted his resignation from the PDPA leadership on 24 September 1966, but apparently not from the party itself. It was accepted.[89]

In July 1967 Karmal broke with Taraki's organization completely, taking with him a majority of the full members of the founding central committee—Panjshiri, Shahpar and Keshtmand plus himself—and some other members, including Sulaiman Laiq. With Badakhshi from the original committee dropping out to form a Maoist group, only Ziray remained with Taraki. Each side then claimed that it was the true party, the other a splinter group. Taraki, who had begun to depend upon the organizational efficiency of Amin, charged Karmal with being a royal stooge, citing official permission to start *Parcham* while Khalqis were repeatedly denied permission to open another newspaper.[90] Karmal's supporters said Taraki "adopted a bureaucratic attitude and imposed divisive policies . . . [while] he tried to keep his ulterior motives hidden." This Karmal version, published 23 June 1976 by an Iraqi Communist newspaper,[91] added that Karmal "was practically the founder of the party," and Taraki was the first leader only because of his greater age. That version, and similar ones circulating in foreign Communist circles, provoked the Khalqis into writing their secret history in July 1976 to give their side. Curiously, while the Iraqi paper backed Karmal, the Tudeh Iranian journal *Dunia* published Taraki's materials,[92] a further sign that Moscow—which subsidized and indirectly controlled both publications—wanted to keep a line open to both sides.

The split left the Parcham faction with an orientation toward urbanized and westernized intellectuals from a number of ethnic groups, especially Tajiks, while Khalq was predominately Pushtun and embraced a wider economic cross-section of the population with a more diverse background.[93] While Parcham took a pragmatic line of seeking temporary alliances on the long road to Communism, Khalq favored class struggle and a hard line. Two other factions appeared. One, named for its newspaper *Shu'la-yi-Jawed* ("Eternal Flame"), was openly inspired by the Cultural Revolution then under way in China. The other was *Setem-i-Melli* ("Against National Oppression"). It was led by Badakhshi from the original PDPA central committee, who came to represent regional resentment to Pushtun domination, especially Tajiki opposition to it.[94]

By 1972 a United States State Department report estimated that there were between 300 and 500 Communists in Afghanistan, "divided among five separate factions [the fifth, Kargaran, lasted only briefly], all illegal as political parties and some with only a tenuous connection with international Communism." The report said that "The main emphasis in recruitment . . . seems to be among students and teachers." Despite the small number of members, however, the report noted, the Communists could marshal students and others for noisy demonstrations.[95]

The late 1960s and early 1970s were riotous by normal Kabul standards, and a few demonstrations and strikes occurred in other towns, although politics remained an essentially capital phenomenon—again, typical of less-developed countries. One angry demonstration, against visiting United States Vice-President Spiro Agnew in 1970 because of the United States role in Vietnam, did not include the Parchamis, however. In their moderate role of going along with

Agnew's host government, and aware of Soviet attempts to improve United States relations despite the Vietnam war, they let the United States embassy know they would abstain.[96]

Worsening Conditions

Aside from Communist agitation, the demonstrations and strikes were signs of growing malaise in Afghanistan. The government tried to get tough, closing both *Parcham* and *Shu'la-yi-Jawed* plus other opposition papers before the 1969 parliamentary elections, in which Taraki again lost but Amin and Karmal were elected as the only Communist members.[97] Amin, who had returned to teaching and then a government bureaucracy job after losing in 1965, was no match for Karmal's oratorical brilliance, and the personal animosity grew.

Though still technically illegal, other political parties were being formed. Mohammed Hashim Maiwandwal, who succeeded Yousuf as prime minister and remained in office two years, formed the Progressive Democratic Party. Another group of Westernized liberals formed the Afghan Social Democratic Party.[98] The Islamic fundamentalist right was also growing in strength, partly because Communist activity polarized some elements in the population and intensified awareness of a choice among Moslem traditionalist, Western liberal, and Soviet Leninist models for Afghanistan's future. The sharpening of choices then led to some of the conflict after the Soviet invasion in 1979, when all three elements were in a contention that weakened resistance to foreign domination.

Agnew's visit was part of an American effort to preserve an Afghan opening toward the West that would keep the country from foreign domination. Shortly after he came into office with President Richard M. Nixon, the National Security Council under Henry A. Kissinger's direction convened interdepartmental groups from various parts of the administration to define United States interests abroad in a series of country policy statements. The one on Afghanistan, approved on 6 August 1969, defined American objectives in the country as:

1. The preservation of Afghanistan's independence and territorial integrity;
2. The creation of a viable political and economic system, responsive through evolutionary change to the needs and desires of the people;
3. The prevention of Soviet influence in the country from becoming so strong that Afghanistan would lose its freedom of action; and
4. The improvement of Afghanistan's ties with Pakistan and Iran.[99]

In a policy review in 1971 citing these objectives, the United States embassy in Kabul observed:

For the United States, Afghanistan has at the present limited direct interest; it is not an important *trading partner*; it is not an access *route for U.S. trade* with others; it is not presently as far as is known a *source of oil or scarce strategic metals* nor does it appear likely that it will become so; there are *no treaty ties or defense commitments*; and Afghanistan *does not provide us with significant defense, intelligence, or scientific facilities.*[100]

Both the 1969 objectives and the 1971 statement of interests were repeated in the embassy's policy reviews prepared annually until the eve of the 1978 Communist takeover and were considered valid up to then. The 1972 review added the comment that Afghanistan was "a minor element in our policy toward central-south Asia," but "Soviet military or greatly increased political presence in Afghanistan would clearly be against American interests. It is difficult, however, to perceive any combination of circumstances which would make such crude, overt, highly visible action essential or desirable to Moscow."[101]

Although Afghanistan maintained its international position as a nonaligned country aided by both East and West, the parliamentary experiment was by the early 1970s being generally adjudged inside the country as being a failure. The government seemed unable to accomplish much. Parliament, dominated by provincial landlords despite the excitement provided by Karmal and other radicals, dithered. The World Bank found the economy ineffectively run, development projects muddled, good management missing. "Disillusionment about the past and pessimism regarding the future" prevailed in Kabul, it said.[102] And then the weather, too, was unkind. Between 1969 and the winter of 1971–72, little rain fell in some parts of the country. By late 1971 famine had developed. Official relief efforts were slow, inefficient, and plagued with corruption. Estimates of hunger-related deaths start at more than 80,000 and go much higher, with nomads and people in remote villages suffering the most.[103]

The delayed political impact led in December 1972 to the installation of the fifth prime minister since Daoud, Mohammad Moosa Shafiq Kamawi. Moosa Shafiq, educated in Moslem theology at al-Azhar University in Cairo and in international law at Columbia University in New York, and an author of the 1964 constitution, was seen at the time as Zahir Shah's last best chance to make the constitutional monarchy system work.[104] Attacking problems with vigor, he resolved the long-deadlocked dispute with Iran over Helmand River waters,[105] launched anti-corruption and literacy drives, sought to reinvigorate economic development activities, and generally improved administration with personal dynamism. Whether he could have turned around and salvaged the old system, or he was by mid-1973 already beginning to flag, became a moot point when Daoud reappeared on the public stage to overthrow his first cousin and brother-in-law, King Zahir Shah.

Chapter 4. Daoud's Republic

Daoud's comeback meant a return to traditional strongman rule, but circumstances had changed in a way that he fatally failed to appreciate. The five years of his second period in power frustrated the economic and social hopes of political factions that had emerged after his retirement in 1963. Not only had domestic pressures become stronger than he remembered, but also stronger were the pressures of living on the border of an increasingly assertive superpower. Halting, hobbled constitutional government had been inadequate to Afghanistan's problems; government by traditionalist cronies and tough-minded but unimaginative followers of Daoud's branch of the royal family proved to be equally inadequate. There was, then, a certain logic that Daoud's new government was replaced with a third alternative—dictatorship by very untraditionalist and unrealistic Communists.

After 1963, Daoud had quietly watched the difficulties of the rapidly changing cabinets, though he was barred by the 1964 constitution from politics. When the 1969 elections failed to produce a more decisive second parliament—in fact, made worse the incompetent dithering of that body, which was unwilling to accept cabinet proposals to move the country ahead—Daoud widened the circle of persons with whom he regularly discussed events. As the man who had opened Afghanistan to Soviet aid and military influence, his circle included leftists. His political seminars developed into a conspiracy for a coup d'etat, accelerated at first by the government's weak response to the drought and then by the vigorous new leadership of Moosa Shafiq.[1]

In early 1973 Moosa Shafiq was beginning to make constitutional monarchy look viable again by overcoming decade-old deadlocks with new approaches on domestic problems. He was also improving relations with Pakistan and Iran.[2] In Afghanistan's awkward situation, and particularly when done by an American-educated leader, such an improvement had an automatic but unfortunate connotation of moving away from Soviet influence.

After his coup, Daoud said that, "For more than a year, the subject was being considered by some friends, and various plans discussed. Only when anarchy and the anti-national attitude of the regime reached its peak was the decision for taking action made."[3] Although obviously self-serving, this statement is a significant indication of Daoud's thinking. There was no anarchy beyond the usual administrative incompetence, which Moosa Shafiq was moving to reduce after the drought. Perhaps the ambitious Daoud feared not the government's collapse but its success, which could have reduced his chances of ever making a comeback. What was anti-national? The Helmand waters agreement with Iran was under heavy political attack, sapping Moosa Shafiq's authority for accomplishing more immediate domestic goals, but its service to Afghan national interests was shown by Daoud's later ratifying it. Moosa Shafiq was tamping down the

Pushtunistan issue, to Daoud a prime national concern. And he was doing nothing to improve relations with Moscow, which Daoud had always kept at the top of his priority list. But that did not mean Moosa Shafiq was destabilizing Soviet relations in any normal sense of international affairs. Only a nation whose independence has already been compromised is suspected of weakening its relations with one neighbor because it improves relations with another.

Daoud's own realignment of foreign policy after returning to power indicated that Moosa Shafiq's foreign policy was not so much a factor in the plot as his improvement in the workings of the government. The surge of optimism in Kabul after he became prime minister in December 1972 that Afghanistan could be hauled out of its lethargy and mismanagement threatened to eliminate the justification for a return to power that had started Daoud's conspiracy sometime before July 1972.

Some of Daoud's friends were military officers who had been his protégés when he was prime minister or were the sons of his colleagues then; some were officers who had been drawn to him after 1963 because of his reputation for having run a decisive government; some were officers who had developed a loathing for the monarchy under the impact of political lectures while attending military courses in the Soviet Union or were unhappy about slow promotions because of royal suspicions about their exposure to Communism; and many were civilians. The latter included Karmal.

Karmal was suspected by some Afghans of having been in touch with Daoud for many years, even of being used by Daoud as his agent in, and source of information on, the leftist movement, and of adopting a position in favor of leftist cooperation with other political elements under Daoud's influence.[4] The fact that Karmal's father was a trusted general in Daoud's service[5] was suggestive. Certainly, the trouble that Karmal caused in parliament for the monarchical government would have drawn the outcast Daoud to him even if the suspicions that Daoud put him up to it were wrong.

Whether their similarity of interests extended into the armed forces is less certain. The Parcham faction had begun by around 1970 to seek converts to Communism among military officers, but it is unclear whether this was done in some sort of connection with Daoud. Khalq, meanwhile, maintained the position that ideological purity forbade recruiting military personnel to a supposedly workers' party. From all indications, Parcham had not built up much strength in the armed forces before Daoud decided to move, although some accounts of the period suggest unconvincingly that Parcham took the lead and then brought Daoud into its plot.[6] This is unlikely. Daoud had his own network of informers in the government and supporters outside it. The question was later confused by some of the coup leaders joining Parcham or Khalq after 1973.

If Parcham, whose leader was regularly seen to be in close touch with Soviet diplomats in Kabul, was to some degree involved in Daoud's coup, what then was the Soviet role? This has been a subject of rumors and speculation without any definite proof being produced. Among pertinent factors, however, was the fact that the Soviet Union was cooperating with the Afghan government by providing aid, while encouraging discontent with it by the indoctrination of its officers in Soviet training courses and by the sympathetic attitude toward both Karmal and Taraki. It was pressing Kabul to take an implicitly anti-Chinese stand of adhering to Brezhnev's 1969 concept of an Asian collective security agreement, thus trying to draw Afghanistan closer to it.

But instead, it found the Moosa Shafiq government improving relations with Pakistan, which by then had become a recipient of Chinese economic and military aid while still retaining loosened ties to the United States, and with Iran, whose shah had in 1972 taken on the role of the United States ally responsible for defending his region against Soviet threats. If this worried Daoud simply because he believed in a carefully balanced neutrality for Afghanistan, it must have bothered the Kremlin much more. Iran and Turkey were strong enough bordering countries to take positions that the Soviet Union did not like, but Afghanistan never had been, and the Soviets had in the past shown themselves reluctant to give up positions of foreign influence without a struggle. With Moosa Shafiq trying to salvage a bankrupt system, it would from Moscow have seemed simply a matter of protecting Soviet interests to finish off that system and return to the known and tolerated—if not completely trusted—figure of Daoud. He could not last forever. If Parchamis could establish themselves in his shadow, perhaps they could eventually replace him.

Such reasoning does not, of course, prove that the Soviets gave a wink and a nod to Karmal or to non-Parchami military officers known to Soviet military advisers in the Afghan armed forces. But it suggested as much to a number of observers, including one high official of a nearby country who kept a close eye on Afghanistan.[7] This official contended that the movement of Afghanistan toward Soviet control began in 1973, not 1978, and Western nations like the United States simply did not want to recognize the fact because they were in that late Vietnam era pulling back from foreign involvements. Admitting a Soviet gain in Kabul would have made the pullback less justifiable, more difficult, so the Americans ignored it instead, the official thought.

On the other hand, there was evidence that, for all their ties inside the Afghan armed forces and their key role in warplane and armored vehicle operations, Soviet military advisers who might have gotten wind of a coup did not adequately inform their government. Or, if they did, the information was held very tightly, because some Soviet diplomats in Kabul professed to be surprised when it happened, and there were some corroborating signs of this. A certain confusion within the Soviet establishment in Afghanistan would not disprove some Soviet involvement, however. Moscow later felt compelled to deny any involvement,[8] and Daoud also denied outside influences.[9]

Daoud was not the only person who had concluded by 1972 that the constitutional system was a failure and should be replaced. There were discussions within the ruling elite of calling off the parliamentary elections scheduled for the autumn of 1973 and having Moosa Shafiq rule by decree with royal support.[10] A key participant in the discussions was the king's first cousin and son-in-law, Major General Abdul Wali Khan. Throughout the constitutional period, only one man had held the same post in every cabinet, the defense minister, General Khan Mohammed Khan, who was supposed to be the king's guarantor of the loyalty of the armed forces. But toward the end of the period, real military power and a large measure of political influence as well had gravitated toward Abdul Wali, who commanded the Kabul region and the palace guard. Abdul Wali was becoming increasingly disliked as the power behind the throne, and leftists particularly hated him for having ordered troops to fire on the demonstrators on 25 October 1965. With his own intelligence network, Abdul Wali reportedly knew shortly before Daoud's coup occurred who was plotting it, but he failed to realize the need for quick preventive action. Maiwandwal was also reported to have been starting a coup plan with the support of military officers who had been ousted by Abdul Wali,[11] but Daoud preempted him.

The 1973 Coup   ZAHIR SHAH

The king left Afghanistan 25 June 1973 for eye treatment and the medicinal mud baths at Ischia, Italy.[12] Before dawn on 17 July, a small group of officers leading several hundred troops seized the palace in downtown Kabul, the radio station, airport, and other key positions. There was little resistance; only four soldiers and four policemen died. Abdul Wali, who was Daoud's first cousin as well as the king's, was arrested along with other key royalists.[13] At 7:20 A.M. Kabul Radio announced that Afghanistan had become a republic, and, after some martial music, Daoud spoke in Pashto. He had left the nation on the right path a decade earlier, Daoud claimed, but "my weak colleagues did not follow" it. Instead, there developed "bankruptcy of the country's economic, administrative, social and political stature. . . . Democracy was changed into anarchy and the constitutional monarchy into a despotic regime." Daoud promised "real democracy" and friendship with all nations, although he noted "differences over the Pakhtunistan issue" with Pakistan.[14]

The next day it was announced that a "central committee" of supporters had named Daoud founder, president, and prime minister of the Republic of Afghanistan, with personal control of the defense and foreign ministries.[15] Zahir Shah later abdicated and settled down in Rome,[16] where he was joined— upon his release from house arrest almost two years later—by Abdul Wali. Membership of the central committee, reported at between fifteen and thirty-five men, was never made public.[17] After that first meeting it was not known to have met again, presumably because Daoud found it safer to deal with members separately in order to avoid united pressure.

The king's army chief of staff, General Abdul Mustaghni, was reported to have played a key role in the coup, but younger military officers became more prominent. They included a Tajiki major, Abdul Qadir, and engineer Pacha Gul Wafadar, both of the air force, and Mohammed Aslam Watanjar and Faiz Mohammed from the army, plus other senior officers who did not figure in later political maneuvering.[18] Their political allegiances at the time of the 1973 coup were the subject of conflicting reports, and the subject was further confused by conversions of Parchamis to the Khalqi faction by the time of the 1978 coup.

Other officers later claimed that they had taken part in the coup and had been PDPA members at the time,[19] but essentially it was not a Communist military coup and Daoud was no front man. At his first news conference after the coup, Daoud said there would be few military men in his cabinet.[20] At least two leftists became ministers, Faiz Mohammed in the key position of minister of interior responsible for police, and Pacha Gul as minister of frontier affairs dealing with Pushtunistan areas. Karmal was not mentioned in the new regime, and Daoud rebuffed efforts by Taraki to see him.

Daoud moved steadily and fairly rapidly, behind a cloak of secrecy that left Kabul uncertain just who was really in charge,[21] to reduce the influence of both the military and the leftists. One action was the shifting of military assignments to insure that people loyal to him personally, without leftist taint, were in key positions. Another was the sending of eager, young Parchamis out to provincial administrative positions to try to put their reformist ideas into practice. Not then having the full power of the state behind them, as they did in 1978, the approximately 160 urbanized leftists were unable to make the kind of changes that so alienated rural people later. But neither were they able to convert the masses to their ideas—any more than the 2,500 educated young Russians who exactly a century earlier went to the Russian countryside as *narodniki* with the same idealistic notions of working great social changes. Instead, the Parchamis soon sank into the same lethargic inefficiency and corruption that had always marked Afghan provincial administration, or trickled back to Kabul disillusioned with the harsh reality of a countryside about which they had only theorized.

Parcham under Daoud

Parcham, which immediately after the coup had been reported to be recruiting new members on an unprecedented scale, lost its dynamism.[22] Daoud made it clear that he was not adopting a leftist attitude or accepting the claims of any ideological faction. "We have no connection with any group, and linking us to any group or movement is a sin," he said on 28 February 1974 to graduates of the Polytechnic Institute, a Soviet aid counter to United States predominance in educational aid. The official report of that speech was significantly headlined, "National Interests Above Every Thought, Ideology."[23] Soon after, Daoud began easing leftists out of his cabinet. Pacha Gul was made ambassador to Bulgaria, for instance.

Daoud carefully avoided any mention of ideological or political factional connections in dismissing leftists, instead putting out the word that corruption or inefficiency were the reasons. While the latter reasons were certainly likely, this approach showed his political caution, possibly for the sake of relations with the Soviet Union as well as domestic reasons. By 1975, Parcham was a beaten force, its ideology uncertain, its claim to point the way to the future discredited.[24]

Khalq under Daoud

Khalq "supported Daoud, hopeful and confident that he would allow us to participate in the government," Taraki recalled later. "We thought that Daoud would indeed carry out actions in the interests of the subjugated class. Daoud deceived not only himself," Taraki said, "but also the whole nation" with his original program[25]—which, others noted, echoed points from the PDPA program. While calling for a national front, so that it could get a share of power under Daoud, Khalq accused Karmal's faction of occupying profitable government positions and calling for the PDPA to be disbanded on the grounds that it was no longer needed because Daoud was carrying out its program. This, Khalq proclaimed, was treason.[26] It was also short-term politics. But Khalq was not above trying to make its own factional gains at Parchami expense. It was reported to have sent a letter to Daoud in late 1974 offering to provide honest officials to replace corrupt Parchamis. Daoud ignored the offer.[27] He did not want ideologues.

Instead, as he eliminated leftists from his regime, he brought into the government old hard-line supporters, especially General Abdul Qadir Nuristani as interior minister, in charge of police. He put some proven old pro-Western bureaucrats into key jobs, such as former finance minister Mohammad Khan Jalallar as minister of commerce. And he rehabilitated Moosa Shafiq as an adviser.[28]

Daoud also crushed the group of plotters that Maiwandwal had been organizing, and the former diplomat and prime minister died in October 1973 under torture in Daoud's palace dungeon. A mistake, the regime said; he was just being questioned, and his questioners were being punished.[29] At least one other plot was reported crushed in the first six months of the republic—others were reportedly foiled in 1974, 1975, and 1976—and hundreds of persons arrested.[30] Gruesome details of torture soon began to circulate in Kabul. Five persons died in the first publicly acknowledged political executions in Afghanistan in more than forty years.[31]

In 1975, Daoud set up his own political party, the National Revolutionary Party, and required all political elements to come under its umbrella.[32] This was the final blow to Parcham's hopes of having separate influence on his regime since the move was clearly intended to neutralize independent influences. At the same time the armed forces' leadership was purged. A new constitution was approved by a *loya jirgah* on 30 January 1977 that established a presidential one-party system.[33] Daoud's constitution was a bitter disappointment to leftists.

It was contrary to the clandestine advocacy by some Afghan Communists of a *jirgah*, or parliamentary, form of government. These Communists, claiming to speak for the PDPA, said, "Our party believes that accepting the presidential system instead of democracy in the shape of *jirgah* will not be in our national interests."[34]

Under this system, Daoud named a new cabinet that was supposed to tackle long-unresolved problems, to give new vigor to government. But he packed it with his old friends and their sons, with royal hangers-on, people incapable of providing fresh dynamism for a still cumbersome, inefficient administration, people with vested interests that prohibited a meaningful implementation of a promised land reform program.[35]

As he aged and tired, Daoud seemed to become more suspicious, choking effective government by insisting upon personally approving too wide a range of matters. He saw plots everywhere, probably rightly. He asked—virtually ordered—the American embassy to quit keeping contacts with leftists, just as the shah of Iran had halted United States intelligence contacts with the religious opposition that was to overthrow him. The Americans generally complied, but there was no restriction on Soviet contacts with Afghan Communists.[36]

Results of Daoud's Rule

By the latter part of Daoud's second period in power, that is, just before the Communist takeover, Afghanistan was in poor shape. Ample rainfall and good harvests after 1972 had enabled the economy to recover from the drought, but its growth was just keeping pace with the population increase, and therefore low living standards were not improving. Infant mortality remained among the world's highest, life expectancy among the lowest, average incomes among the poorest.

Although by the mid-1960s state enterprises were not considered to be successful, and there was a swing back to private enterprise to develop the country, Daoud brought back into office his statist policies of the 1950s that emphasized the government's role in the economy.[37] A seven-year economic development plan, 1976–83, was drawn up following Soviet models. But Afghanistan was unequipped for such grandiose schemes. It could only compound earlier mistakes of pouring money into large projects without relating them directly to human needs or providing either money or managers to run them properly. The World Bank found that the situation had improved somewhat since 1971, but the "obstacles to development remain daunting." It said the new plan "seems to draw its inspiration too much from the dreams of the future, and too little from the harsh realities of the present.[38] In short, Afghanistan under Daoud had a politically repressive, economically drifting regime.

Foreign Policy Changes

The seven-year plan was based primarily on expectations of massive amounts of financial aid from the shah's Iran—up to $2 billion at first and the hope of more later. This was part of a major reorientation of Afghanistan's foreign policy that began to develop after Daoud had been back in power a year or two. Taraki later charged that Daoud pretended to be non-aligned but "In reality he capitulated to the reactionaries within and without. He collaborated with royalists and imperialists . . . accept[ing] foreign loans with political and economic strings and conditions attached and thus acced[ing] to the wishes of neocolonialism."[39] This was a Communist judgment on a move that was reducing Afghan dependence upon the Soviet Union.

Daoud, the man who had started sending soldiers across the Amu Darya for training, diversified this by arranging military programs for Afghans in India, Egypt, and even, just before he fell, in Pakistan. India had close Soviet ties, but military cooperation with the other two was certain to antagonize Moscow. Egypt had expelled Soviet military missions in 1972 and was openly feuding with Moscow, and Pakistan had moved from a close military relationship with the United States to one with China, the Soviets' most-hated antagonist.

Relations with Pakistan and Afghanistan's most anti-Communist neighbor, Iran, were improved, and friendlier relations developed with traditionalist and therefore also anti-Communist Moslem countries like Saudi Arabia.[40] These included countries that—after the sharp rise of oil prices in 1973—were able to provide some of the aid that Daoud wanted. American aid had been declining in the late 1960s, and the era of détente in the early 1970s had reduced United States interest in aid competition with the Soviets in remote countries like Afghanistan.[41]

At the same time, there was growing disillusionment in the Third World about the benefits of Soviet aid, growing recognition that it tended in the long run to reduce flexibility of the recipients' economies, tie them to the Soviet economy, and ultimately benefit Moscow—such as Afghan natural gas traded for unprofitable infrastructure projects. With advice from Moosa Shafiq and another American-educated official, Ali Ahmad Khuram, the minister of economic planning, Daoud might have been acting simply out of economic rationality, although the statist nature of the new seven-year plan weakens that argument. All three men were soon killed, and Daoud's thinking on the move to reduce Soviet economic dependence remains unclear, although a desire for more aid than Moscow would offer might be an adequate explanation.

Nor is it clear why Daoud moved away from primary reliance on Soviet military training. A purge of leftist military officers in 1975 indicated that he feared political influences in the armed forces in a way that he had not in the late 1950s and early 1960s, presumably as a result of having seen the political connections of some officers who helped him seize power. Even before he felt sufficiently in control of the new regime to conduct that purge, he had started in early 1974 to arrange the military training program with India[42]—where Afghan soldiers could use Soviet-made equipment without being subjected to Marxist indoctrination. If Moosa Shafiq's supposed compromise of carefully pro-Soviet Afghan neutrality in early 1973 was in fact one reason for Daoud's coup, then Daoud had come by the mid-1970s to see his country's problems in a different light. This might have been a fatal mistake, but it was a major change that could be explained as the result of a new realism in Kabul about how best its national interests would be served—if not a sufficient caution in revising policies.

Relations with Iran

After the April 1978 coup had killed Daoud, a theory developed abroad that Iran's Shah Mohammed Reza Pahlavi had lured the Afghan leader to his doom by offering to replace the Soviet Union as Afghanistan's main benefactor and chief foreign influence; and the Soviets in reply organized Daoud's downfall.[43] The extension of that theory by Western leftists is that the United States was ultimately responsible because the 1969 Nixon Doctrine, which encouraged nations to reduce their security dependence on the United States by assuming more responsibility for their own regional problems, had led the shah to try to seduce Afghanistan away from its Soviet-influenced neutrality and into his own anti-Communist orbit.[44]

The theory of a lure or seduction is doubtful, however, and the shah given more importance than he deserved. Daoud wanted money; for a few heady years the shah thought he had enough to give it away; and Iran tried to use it to influence both Afghanistan and Pakistan, its only two oil-poor neighbors. Pakistan was an Iranian ally in CENTO, but from the time the Soviet Union began arming Afghanistan, the shah had been apprehensive about it.[45] Already uncertain about Daoud, because of his earlier Soviet opening and his exacerbation of Pakistani relations, the shah was disturbed by the precedent of abolishing a next-door monarchy. He extended a hand of friendship to Daoud after the coup, however, rather than trying to isolate him and thus force him into greater dependence upon the Soviet Union—an alternative that United States diplomats in Tehran warned him against, as they warned other Moslem countries. Some of those diplomats say that neither the United States nor Iran ever expected to draw Afghanistan away from its geographically imposed close relationship with the Soviet Union, instead only trying to provide enough alternative support for it to maintain true neutrality,[46] but that could be a later excuse for having destabilized the Afghan situation.

By mid-1974 intensive talks were underway between Kabul and Tehran on economic development plans. Afghanistan was also talking to the Saudis, Iraqis, Kuwaitis and other oil-rich Moslem nations; Iran was not the only non-Soviet alternative. Daoud had held up approval of Moosa Shafiq's Helmand waters settlement with Iran, which Parcham, Khalq and Maiwandwal's party all criticized, not finally ratifying it until 1977.[47] Despite this, Afghan-Iranian relations blossomed. On 22 October 1974 Iran gave Afghanistan $10 million for feasibility studies on a number of projects, including construction of the country's first railroad. The understanding then was that up to $2 billion of aid might eventually be forthcoming for these projects over a ten-year period[48]—almost as much as total East-West economic aid to Afghanistan up to then. Saudi Arabia made a $10-million grant and promised an interest-free loan of $55 million, Iraq put up a $10-million loan and a grant of $2 million, and Kuwait promised help.[49]

But it was Iran that made the most noise. When Daoud visited Tehran in April 1975, the shah agreed to lend $400 million on easy terms for a variety of small industry, transportation, and Helmand Valley projects, and it was expected at the time to cost some $1.1 billion to link the Iranian, Pakistani, and Soviet rail systems through Afghanistan.[50] The railroad estimate later rose to $1.7 billion, but by then the illusion was beginning to dissipate.

Iran was over-extended, unable even to finance the shah's ambitions of regional military dominance combined with domestic economic growth, while Afghanistan lacked the talents to spend wisely all the money originally discussed. The shah had to announce a cutback of foreign aid after magnificently promising up to $10 billion in all directions. Numerous consultations on specific projects had by 1977 exposed the tiny reality behind talk of Iran's becoming the dominant benefactor in Afghanistan. While Afghan migrant laborers who used to go to Pakistan for jobs were drawn in increasing numbers to Iran by the shah's development programs, and their remittances home became an important source of foreign exchange for Kabul, economic relations cooled.

Irritated Afghan officials offered to release Iran from all its promises, but the proud shah insisted he would go ahead with some aid.[51] His political standing in Kabul was clearly diminished, however, well before what could later be seen as the possible preliminaries to the April 1978 overthrow of Daoud. Although the question of Iranian political police—SAVAK—operations in Afghanistan would arise later, the fact was that by 1977 any Soviet fears of Iran's cutting Afghanistan away from Soviet influence should have been waning. The Soviet bloc ended up putting far more aid into Afghanistan during the Daoud presidency than the combined total of Iran, other Moslem countries, and the West. The United States continued a small-scale aid program. It included the introduction of some space-age technology to the primitive country, including satellite communications for resource surveys and seismological equipment.[52] These led the Soviets to charge that "sinister espionage nests were built" by the Americans in Afghan territory before 1978.[53]

Relations with Pakistan

While in his generous phase, the shah used his influence in Kabul to tamp down the Pushtunistan dispute between Afghanistan and Pakistan.[54] Soviet support reportedly was behind Afghan backing for a Baluchi autonomous movement in 1974.[55] The situation had become agitated enough by that autumn for Pakistani Prime Minister Zulfikar Ali Bhutto to talk of possible war with a trouble-making Afghanistan. Daoud's government was diverted by a tribal revolt north of Kabul—stirred up by Pakistan as a counter-irritant, some said.[56] Gradually, the situation cooled off with Iranian diplomatic efforts as well as United States and other advice to both sides. Pakistan made a gesture of sending relief supplies after an Afghan provincial disaster.

Relations began to improve. Daoud visited Pakistan twice, and both Bhutto and his successor, General Mohammed Zia ul-Haq, paid visits to Kabul. On the last of these visits, when Daoud went to Islamabad on 5 March 1978, agreement was reached that both Afghanistan and Pakistan's own Pushtun (Pathan) and Baluch leaders would tone down the Pushtunistan issue, Zia would release from prison those Pakistani leaders who had been agitating against his military rule, and Daoud would send home Pakistani political exiles. After Daoud was overthrown the following month, the exiles were allowed to remain, and the Pushtunistan issue was briefly stoked up again,[57] but the new Communist government soon had too many other more pressing problems to agitate it.

One reason Daoud backed away from his quarter-century support for the Pushtunistan cause, in addition to Iranian and other foreign urging, was a noticeable cooling of the Soviet attitude. The cooling had begun in the mid-1960s when Moscow decided to compete with new Chinese influence in Pakistan by softening its attitude toward the old United States ally. A more neutral tone was adopted on the Pushtunistan issue.[58] Then in 1969 Brezhnev launched his Asian collective security plan as a gambit in competition with China. One element in it was a reaffirmation of Asian borders. The Kremlin wanted this because of its dispute with China over land taken in tsarist times by what Peking insisted were "unequal treaties" that should be revised, and over some areas even beyond those treaty lines. Daoud noted in 1974 that "we do not like [the plan's] emphasis on inviolability of frontiers. That will mean accepting Pakistan's present frontiers, which are the doing of the British."

Relations with the USSR

But on his first visit to Moscow as president, from 4–7 June 1974, Daoud accepted Soviet-drafted language in a joint communiqué endorsing the plan.[59] The Soviets did not repay the favor. They omitted from Tass or Moscow Radio his Kremlin banquet denunciation of "the unlawful and stern attitude and course adopted by the rulers of Pakistan toward the Pushtun and Baluch patriots and people."[60] While censoring Daoud, the Soviets also lectured him. His official host, President Nikolai S. Podgorny, who joined Brezhnev and Premier Alexei N. Kosygin in private talks with Daoud, said publicly that Afghanistan's "great and complex tasks [of] renovating political, economic and cultural life . . . . can be solved successfully when the course charted is pursued firmly, when broad popular masses are drawn into the work of building a new life, and when the forces which are sincerely interested in strengthening the new system act vigorously and in close unity."[61] Decoded from the veiled language of diplomacy and the jargon of Soviet ideology, that meant Daoud should carry out his initial promises of reform by working closely with the PDPA, which by Communist definition represented the "broad popular masses."

This was said at a time when Parcham's role was already being diminished, but it had not yet lost out completely and the leftist military officers had not yet been purged. The Soviet impression that Daoud was still on a favorable, leftist-influenced course was suggested by the presence at some of his official Kremlin functions of Boris N. Ponomarev, the Soviet Communist Party secretary in charge of the party's international section that maintains relations with Communist and leftist parties outside the Soviet bloc; he does not show up on visits of Western, capitalist leaders. Kremlin leaders obviously were concerned about prospects in Afghanistan. Still, they said the proper things about "cordiality, friendship and mutual understanding," while the Soviet press favorably noted "a number of social reforms" in Afghanistan. Protecting its already huge investment in the country, the Soviet Union granted an interest-free ten-year moratorium on a $100-million debt and promised another $428 million in development aid.[62]

Podgorny returned Daoud's visit in December 1975. Again proper things were said. But by then Daoud had embraced the shah, he had banned all political parties except his own organization, Parcham was ignored and dispirited, and government policies generally were shifting away from what the Soviet Union favored. Official statements lacked the warmth of the previous year. Official Soviet reports of Podgorny's visit spoke coolly of Soviet-Afghan relations "as a model of the peaceful coexistence of countries with different social systems," rather than suggesting a similarity of support by "broad popular masses."[63] The 1975 communiqué referred obliquely to the Asian security plan in a way that avoided having to spell out Afghan endorsement, probably deliberately. But, most significantly, the communiqué spoke of "mutual trust, mutual understanding, frankness and good will."[64] No cordiality this time, and no more official friendship.

The Soviet system uses finely tuned language to convey precise shades of ideological and diplomatic meaning—almost a special vocabularly for insiders. The arcane art of Kremlinology, when applied to small differences in language and to omissions as well as to what is said, has over the years proven a reliable indicator of attitudes and hidden policies in the Soviet Union. The word "frankness," for instance, is carefully used only when some disagreement has been openly discussed and left unresolved. Its use in Kabul in December 1975 meant trouble in the relationship. The trouble was papered over with polite official expressions, however, and *Izvestiya*'s report tried to put a good face on the situation by saying the official talks "were frank and friendly, as is the custom with real friends."[65]

Strains were increasing, with worse yet to come. Daoud visited Moscow again 12–15 April 1977, the month after he had under his new constitution appointed a cabinet of personal supporters and some known anti-Communists. Parcham had been left out, along with other leftists who might claim to represent "the broad popular masses." Daoud had clearly reverted to rule in the old royalist, tribal manner. He had removed Soviet military advisers from the lower levels of the Afghan armed forces, cutting their numbers sharply, as he sent men to train on Soviet-made military equipment in India and Egypt. Some sources say that by then Soviet aid had begun to slow down, Soviet technicians in Afghanistan to work less enthusiastically.

But in the official record of the 1977 visit there is nothing direct to show the deterioration of relations. The descriptive language was chosen carefully, even leaving out any communiqué reference to "frankness."[66] Podgorny, who soon after was ousted by Brezhnev in a grab for the Soviet presidency to add to his party leadership, lectured Daoud again about the need for a "concerted effort of all the people,"[67] but it was less direct than in 1974. In reply, Daoud lectured the Soviets. Good relations, he said, "stand on the firm foundations of good-neighborliness, frankness, sincerity, and disinterested and worthwhile cooperation."[68]

The message was clear: Moscow should accept the fact that Kabul would disagree with it but should continue to provide aid anyway, without attaching strings. Reiterating the disinterested theme, Daoud claimed that his country was "creating premises for rapid socio-economic and political development . . . [that] demand all-round efforts from the people and government of Afghanistan. Cooperation and disinterested aid from friendly states will play a valuable part in this undertaking."[69] The communiqué later said that talks "took place in an atmosphere of friendship, trust and understanding, and there was a circumstantial exchange of opinions on urgent world problems."[70] When he got home, Daoud said he was confident that the visit would strengthen relations, "which are based on good-neighborliness, mutual respect and noninterference in domestic affairs."[71]

Daoud's proclaimed confidence was more diplomatic than real. Reports soon reached Asian diplomats from Afghan officials of an angry confrontation between Daoud and Brezhnev. In their formal secret talks, the Soviet leader reportedly complained to Daoud about the composition of his new cabinet, accusing some of its members of working for foreigners—implicitly, for the United States—and saying new men should be brought into the government who better represented the masses—again implicitly, PDPA members. Brezhnev also asked for the expulsion of some American experts working in Afghanistan, including the satellite and seismological specialists, according to some accounts. And he was unhappy about Daoud's criticism of Cuba for trying to steer the nonaligned movement—of which Daoud had been an original founder, in

Belgrade in 1961—in a pro-Soviet direction.[72] There might have been other complaints.

The basic point is that Brezhnev was trying to bully Daoud, the powerful Russian benefactor trying to influence or even control the policy of a weak Afghan nation. It might work with East Europeans or Mongolians, but Brezhnev had misjudged Daoud. The Afghan president was reported to have slammed his fist on the conference table, said that Afghans were masters in their own house, and no foreign country could tell them how to run their own affairs. Then, some versions say, Daoud stalked out, other versions that the meeting continued sourly. A senior Afghan official with long experience of dealing with the Russians is said to have whispered to a colleague, after seeing the anger on Brezhnev's face, that Daoud had just written his death warrant.[73]

Relations with Other Countries

After that, Daoud's desire to diversify his foreign support became more obvious, perhaps more desperate. The new Carter administration was interested in having Daoud visit Washington, and Daoud wanted to, but when scheduling efforts began in the summer of 1977 obstacles arose for technical rather than political reasons, United States officials later said. Finally, by the spring of 1978 the visit was tentatively planned for September. The United States was expected to voice support for Afghan nonalignment and to make at least a gesture of increasing the long-dwindling level of aid. Behind this lay confidence in Washington that Afghanistan would remain the quiet political backwater that it had traditionally been.[74] A senior State Department specialist on Soviet affairs, Adolph Dubs, who was then overseeing South Asian affairs in the department, told a House of Representatives subcommittee on 16 March 1978, just six weeks before the coup in Kabul, that, "Internally, the political situation is stable" in Afghanistan. "President Daoud remains very much in control and faces no significant opposition."[75] Daoud apparently thought so, too, and devoted much of his time to foreign affairs.

In addition to improving relations with Pakistan and inviting the shah of Iran to visit Kabul in June 1978, he went to India, Yugoslavia, and Egypt, the original pillars of the nonaligned movement. He joined in Yugoslav President Josef Broz Tito's effort to block Soviet-dominated Cuba from assuming leadership of the movement at the nonaligned summit scheduled for Havana in September 1979. Daoud's role was important because foreign ministers of nonaligned nations were scheduled to hold a preparatory meeting for the summit under his auspices in Kabul 6–10 May 1978.[76] Then Daoud went to Saudi Arabia, a country that had long been using its oil riches to try to fight Soviet influence in the Moslem world. Daoud and King Khalid issued on 4 April 1978 a communiqué calling for a peaceful solution of the Horn of Africa conflict between Ethiopia and Somalia "on the basis of self-determination for the people of Ogaden."[77] While consistent with Daoud's Pushtunistan stand—and with the one-time Soviet position on both Pushtunistan and the Ogaden—this was clearly opposed to the Soviet stand with weapons, advisers, and Cuban troops in support of Ethiopia's refusal to yield the disputed Ogaden to Somalia. Then Daoud went home and was overthrown, and the PDPA came to power.

PDPA Politics

The 1967 split in the party had produced continual squabbling as well as competitive activities by Khalq and Parcham. Each organized strikes and other agitations, and each published underground newspapers and books. A list of Khalqi publications, containing translations of Lenin and other Soviet writers plus original material by Taraki and his comrades,[78] indicates that Taraki's faction was receiving material and probably also publishing subsidies from the Soviet embassy in Kabul, despite Karmal's better publicized connection there. When Parcham seemed to be on the winning side of Daoud's coup, Khalq reassessed its policies. From its semiclandestine position it campaigned "for the establishment of a basic united front against imperialism and feudalism composed of all parties, groups and individuals who . . . support . . . a National Democratic Program."[79] Clearly, it wanted a share of the official action.

At the same time Khalq began trying to recruit military men. Until 1973, Taraki had taken the position that Marxism required a country to reach socialism through the efforts of its worker class, a term loosely interpreted to include worker-oriented intellectuals. However, the bitter experience of seeing some Parchami military officers help Karmal's faction to gain an initial foothold in government, and the realization of how easily a small band of soldiers could seize the government, made Khalqi leaders decide that they needed military supporters, and perhaps the revolution did not need to await the development of a strong, politically conscious proletariat.

Amin, a key PDPA member but not yet on the party politburo, was assigned the job of recruiting Khalq members in the armed forces.[80] Some Parchami soldiers switched their allegiance to Khalq when Karmal went into a slump in 1975, but mostly Amin found new members on the basis of grievances against Daoud's favoritism, poor pay and conditions, general poverty, and the host of other problems plaguing Afghanistan. Khalq's appeal was essentially nationalistic, and its lesser public identification with the Soviets than Parcham helped it win adherents. By 1976, Khalq later claimed, Amin reported to Taraki at one of their regular early Sunday morning meetings sitting on rope beds in Taraki's courtyard that the party "could, with a certain amount of casualties on the part of the armed forces, topple the Daoud government and wrest the political power." But Taraki, "with his profound far-sightedness," said to wait until conditions were ripe and the party stronger.[81]

Efforts to reunify the PDPA had been going on sporadically ever since the split, punctuated by angry personal attacks when they broke down. Khalq accused Parcham of plotting with Daoud to have its leaders murdered; Parcham accused Taraki of being a CIA agent because he once worked for the American embassy. Each faction claimed to be the true PDPA.

In 1975, having lost its gamble on Daoud, Parcham began to revive itself after the rustification of the 160 members and other setbacks. This led to a Khalqi accusation that Parcham was running a parallel party which was "treason against the working class and the matter of democratic unity of patriotic forces."[82] But, Khalq said in late July 1975, it was ready to discuss in secrecy "unity and the union of forces." A Soviet authority on the PDPA wrote later that unification efforts were accelerated because Daoud had begun "preparations for the complete elimination of the PDPA."[83] But the talks quickly broke down, leading in July 1976 to Khalq's circulating clandestinely its account of party history up to then.[84]

Three months earlier, on 4 April, the Communist advocacy of a parliamentary rather than presidential form of government had been linked to an appeal for the creation of an Afghan Democratic National United Front of "all the national progressive parties and organizations belonging to left-democratic sides (in and out of the regime)." The appeal prefaced the spurned advice on what sort of a constitution Daoud should have. This document,[85] which reached Western hands during the brief period in May 1978 when Khalq and Parcham were united in the new Afghan regime, avoids the polemics that were raging between the two factions when it was written in 1976. Internal evidence suggests that it was of Parchami origin. Parcham was at the time more desperate for a united front because of its setback.

Newspaper Battles

Khalq was more inclined toward bitter polemics. Its secret history was written at least partly to counter curious and confused comments on the Afghan political situation and on the PDPA itself by foreign Communist publications with ties to the Soviet Union. One of the earliest known comments in this period was by *Tariqust al-Shaab*, an Iraqi Communist newspaper. On 22 February 1976, it used the transparent technique of replying to a reader's request for information in order to publicize the PDPA. Aside from some factual errors, the reply made it sound as if Taraki headed the one true party.[86]

Then a statement by the "Committee of the Afghan Communists Abroad," dated 18 March 1976, turned up in the West accusing Taraki of having "exploited the progressive magazines of India and Iraq to publish material . . . incorrectly showing him to be a great Communist leader of Afghanistan. . . . Mr. Taraki is not recognized as a leader of the Khalq Party of Afghanistan, nor is his party recognized as a Communist Party of Afghanistan on an international level." Accusing him of harming the interests of the Afghan working class, it concluded that, "If Nur Mohammed Taraki does not mend his ways, he will have to face grave consequences."[87] What these consequences might be was not explained.

In May came an appeal for PDPA unity in a Communist Party of India

(CPI) journal. On 23 June *Tariqust al-Shaab* apologized for misinforming its readers, corrected its errors, and proceeded to attack Taraki. It called Parcham "the real proletarian party" in Afghanistan and Taraki's a "splinter group [that had] caused the interference of the American CIA."[88] The Iranian Tudeh journal *Dunia* also got involved, seemingly supporting Taraki.[89] Then on 24 November *The Socialist*, the newspaper of Australia's pro-Soviet Communist party, reported on a letter that Karmal apparently wrote to Communist parties all over the world that were aligned with Moscow. Karmal claimed that he and his party were playing a central role in Afghanistan's "democratic movement" but were under right-wing and Maoist attack. Asking other parties' support, he wrote: "Let us express categorically that the success of the national liberation movement of the peoples in general and of the people in Afghanistan would not have been possible in the past, nor shall it be possible in the future, without the support of the Soviet Union."[90]

PDPA Unity

And yet, despite this heated history of an internal feud that spilled over into foreign publications, Khalq and Parcham formally agreed in March 1977 to restore PDPA unity.[91] Four months later, in July, they held a conference that "adopted a decision on the organization reunification of the factions and on the development of a program of joint action. . . . [and] considered the question of the removal of the dictatorial regime of M. Daoud."[92]

Why did men with bitter personal antagonisms unexpectedly overcome their differences and make what later proved to be only a temporary, insincere alliance? The answer seems to have been Soviet pressure. After coming to power, Karmal wrote in *World Marxist Review* that unity was achieved "with the help of our international friends and brothers," but he did not elaborate. The help was apparently channeled primarily through the Communist Party of India. The article in the CPI journal *Party Life* on 22 May 1976[93] is the earliest clear sign that the Soviet Communist Party's secretariat had lost patience with Afghan infighting.

The article appeared under the byline of a CPI secretary and politburo member, N. K. Krishnan. Beginning with praise of Daoud's proclaimed policies, it said that "unity of the democratic, progressive and patriotic forces of Afghanistan [is important] in order to get the new policies of the republic implemented and to defeat the forces of foreign and internal reaction which are chafing under the new regime and are planning to weaken and sabotage its policies." Krishnan called the PDPA "a focal point of the progressive democratic movement in Afghanistan" and lamented the 1967 split. "It appears that basic political-ideological differences were not the main factors leading up to this split," and, whatever the original reason—Krishnan delicately avoided referring to personal factors—"there seems to be even less reason for the continuation of the split in the circumstances of today."

Both factions believe in scientific socialism and cooperation with the Soviet

Union, he said, both have welcomed the policies announced by Daoud, and both desire unity for implementing these policies. "It is undeniable that the unity of these two groups can become the lever for building up a broad united front of all popular patriotic forces in Afghanistan in support of the republic and for effective implementation of the new policies enunciated by President Daoud Khan." The article also praised Soviet economic aid for Afghanistan in details that indicated at the least a Soviet input into its writing.[94]

Soviet Pressure

The overall implication was that the CPI, which Moscow had in the 1920s and 1930s controlled indirectly through an official of the Communist Party of Great Britain, had similarly been delegated the task of supervising the Afghan party. For economic, cultural, and political reasons, Afghans were in close touch with Indians. Members of the CPI already knew Taraki, Karmal, Anahita Ratebzad, and Khyber, and Amin was friendly with Romesh Chandra, the president of the Soviet-sponsored World Peace Council who was also a member of the CPI's central executive.[95]

The continuing polemics both in the PDPA secret history and in publications abroad indicate that the *Party Life* appeal did not have immediate effect, and the dating of Indian efforts to follow up the article is uncertain. Krishnan said in an interview in March 1981 that he sent copies of the article to Taraki and Karmal, and they sent representatives to see him in New Delhi in June or July 1976.[96] Another senior CPI official, who declined to be identified, replied in writing to a January 1981 query on this point that the CPI invited Khalq and Parcham representatives to India in 1977 "for a detailed discussion of their internal dissensions."[97] These two dates are not necessarily contradictory. Krishnan could have been referring to an abortive early reconciliation effort and the other official to a subsequent effort that succeeded.

From this information, it can be deduced, but not confirmed, that the agreement in March 1977 to restore unity was made in the discussions in India by representatives of Khalq and Parcham, whose names have not been disclosed. The CPI representatives in the talks were Krishnan and M. Farooqi, another member of the CPI's central executive. Krishnan and Farooqi felt that Parcham was more responsive to their advice, which probably meant that it was aware of being in a weaker position inside Afghanistan.[98] The PDPA representatives then went home to arrange the unification conference in July 1977.

Soviet pressure for unification therefore existed even before Daoud's confrontation with Brezhnev in mid-April 1977. The senior CPI official who declined to be identified said the invitation to the 1977 discussions was issued "with the knowledge and consent of [the] Communist Party of [the] Soviet Union; otherwise, [the] CPI would not have undertaken it. Possibly, the suggestion for such an initiative on the part of [the] CPI also came from Moscow."[99] The May 1976 article by Krishnan seems to indicate that the initiative began in early 1976.

Perhaps it did not at first have enough Soviet pressure behind it. The Soviet embassy in Kabul had leverage at its disposal—in the form of subsidies to the PDPA, favors, and ideological arrogance—that until early 1977 it apparently did not start to use effectively in order to weld the factions together.[100]

The Soviet attitude at the time was reported not to be one of expecting the reunified PDPA to replace the Daoud regime immediately. If Khalq's contacts at the Soviet embassy knew of Amin's claim to be able to stage an armed coup by 1976, they presumably discounted it as unrealistic boasting. After all, the Soviets had their own advisers and agents in the Afghan armed forces to keep informed on military politics. The small group of Soviet specialists who watched Afghanistan wanted the PDPA to get ready for an eventual succession, by fair means or foul depending upon events, to Daoud.

In typical dictator suspiciousness, Daoud had not allowed any acknowledged political heir to emerge. Taraki, as the senior figure of Afghan Communism, presumably was to be groomed and positioned by Soviet specialists as the eventual successor, a status that was beginning to be discussed in wider Kabul circles than just PDPA adherents. Karmal, twelve years younger, would be prepared as *his* successor. But in 1977 Afghan Communists were believed by Moscow to be too few, too weak to be able to assume responsibility for the country. Indeed, some Soviet officials told Westerners after the April 1978 coup that they had not wanted the PDPA to come to power so soon because both the party and the country were too underdeveloped, and unwanted burdens would inevitably be thrown on the Soviet Union. Perhaps in five years or so, some Russians suggested.[101] This might only have been a later excuse to avoid any blame for the coup, or hindsight as the burdens mounted.

But while Daoud ruled, what Moscow apparently wanted—so far as its sparse public references to Afghanistan can be interpreted—was the gradual development of a political force inside the country that would have to be taken into account in the making of policy, a source of leverage on Daoud. This was the kind of political influence that Soviet leaders sought for Communist parties in other developing nations under strongman rule. That the long-term Soviet goal was a Communist Afghanistan cannot be doubted. The question was timing. But Moscow was encouraging forces that soon got out of hand, and so the overthrow of Daoud was its responsibility to a degree that is still debatable.

Further Factionalism

The feuding between Khalq and Parcham did not end with the July 1977 unification agreement. Both factions were small at the time. After further intensive recruiting in careful secrecy, especially by Khalq in the armed forces during 1977, by the time of the coup Khalq had perhaps 2,500 members at the maximum, Parcham maybe 1,000 to 1,500.[102] The figures are uncertain, lost in the secrecy and deliberate organizational looseness needed to escape detection by Daoud's political police and in the claims made after the coup of much larger memberships. As head of the larger faction and the original PDPA leader, Taraki became general secretary. Karmal became his deputy. Some observers thought Karmal uncharacteristically accepted second place because he had decided the Daoud regime was failing fast and feared he would be left out if the better-prepared Khalq faction alone managed to snatch power from the collapse.

All civilian operations of the factions were supposed to be unified immediately under a thirty-member central committee, with members of each faction treated equally. Naturally, there were later charges of cheating and keeping secret cells separate from the unified party. The more sensitive and dangerous work in the armed forces was treated differently. Khalq had perhaps four times as many military adherents as Parcham, according to a later estimate,[103] and the divergence might have been as great in 1977. The Khalqis were unwilling to merge their military networks with people whom they suspected of a continued willingness to work with Daoud, thereby creating a danger of betrayal. Each faction continued to try to recruit its own military supporters. The resulting overlap and competition caused confusion and hostility. The official account published while Khalq was in power—which must be treated more as party mythology than history—says Amin prepared Khalqi military officers to be ready "in case someone else toppled Daoud or in case Daoud attacked the party or arrested Comrade Taraki."[104]

The PDPA was aware of Moslem traditionalists' unhappiness with Daoud's modernization and centralization of authority, which threatened villagers' virtual autonomy. It is doubtful that the religious right was developing any real potential to overthrow the regime, although Daoud himself was more apprehensive of the power of the *mullahs* than of the leftists, but that was another element in the smoldering power struggle. Yet another was resistance within the government to the increasingly harsh, repressive steps being taken as Daoud became more paranoid about his problems. His younger brother, Naim, and six cabinet ministers broke with him temporarily in November 1977 over his policies; but he managed to lure them back and began to realize that his domestic policies were leading to a dead end. On 17 April 1978, according to Dupree, Daoud told close associates that he would broaden his regime by bringing in technocrats and liberals.[105]

Murder of Khyber

On the same day, Mir Akbar Khyber was murdered. That set in train events which led ten days later to Daoud's own death. The murder was the third of a prominent person in eight months. In August 1977, the chief pilot for Ariana Afghan Airlines, Captain Inam Gran, who had recently led a strike, was shot outside his apartment house. There were several possible explanations, but the most interesting was that he might have been confused with Karmal, whom he physically resembled and who lived nearby.[106] This theory leads to a further question of whether Daoud's tough new interior minister, Abdul Qadir Nuristani, a non-Communist participant in the 1973 coup, wanted (with or without Daoud's approval) to kill Karmal as the first step toward wiping out the Communist leadership. Or did Khalq kill Gran while gunning for Karmal, as some Afghans believe? The question cannot be answered. Neither can questions about the murder in November 1977 of Khuram, the planning minister.[107] As the Westernized leader of economic modernization, he might have been a target of Moslem reaction, or he could have been killed simply as a matter of honor in the kind of family feuds that continue to ripple though Afghan society.

Khyber's murder was not only the most significant but also the most mysterious. Generally known as the ideologue of the Parcham group, he was also its organizational brains, thus playing for Karmal the role that Amin did for Taraki. His death was initially blamed by most observers on Daoud's police. Some unsubstantiated versions attribute a role to advisers from Iran's anti-Communist SAVAK, but the best available evidence discounts this.[108] Shortly after coming to power, Taraki publicly charged Daoud's "fascist and terrorist regime" with the killing.[109]

But, after Soviet troops had murdered Amin, Anahita Ratebzad said there was evidence that Amin was responsible.[110] Although it had then become policy to blacken Amin however possible, some independent Afghan sources agree that it was he. They say Khyber was trying to recruit Khalqi military officers for Parcham or the two factions were competing for the same recruits, and the murder resulted from this conflict. Karmal said in 1980 the PDPA decided shortly after reunification "to investigate Amin's divisive factional activities," apparently meaning his resistance to combining Khalqi and Parchami military cells. "Exactly one month before the Saur Revolution, the central committee of the united PDPA passed a decision . . . to punish Amin and to remove him from the central committee. But implementation of this decision was delayed by some invisible hand and slackness in the central committee."[111] Karmal did not elaborate. He probably meant the hand of Taraki, who needed Amin too much to drop him, but whom Karmal did not want to criticize openly. The failure of the PDPA in power to investigate the murder, either under Taraki who would have had some complicity if Amin arranged the murder, or under Karmal after he tried to assume Taraki's mantle, suggests that there were dark secrets which various Communists wanted to remain hidden. Anahita Ratebzad's statement apparently was quickly seen to be fraught with dangerous implications, and there was no further public mention of the subject.

Whoever killed Khyber, in death he became a convenient martyr for the Communist cause. A crowd of unusual size for Kabul (estimates go up to 30,000, but the United States State Department later cited "some 15,000" and Dupree said 10,000 to 15,000[112]) turned out for the funeral on 19 April. Taraki and Karmal both made strong graveside orations. Although leftist wrath was primarily directed at the American embassy, Daoud was alarmed at the show of strength. He ordered the arrest of PDPA leaders.

Chapter 5. The Saur Revolution

The murder of Khyber triggered a confused sequence of events. The net effect was to put Afghanistan under the control of a small Communist movement. The movement was totally unprepared for the power that unexpectedly, even accidentally, fell into its hands. Its misuse of that power with a combination of idealistic reformism and brutal authoritarianism started the country on a downward spiral into civil war and foreign occupation.

In the years just before Khyber was killed, Daoud's police had watched the PDPA with the same inefficiency shown by the rest of his administration. He knew the party had continued to operate underground despite his order that all political parties be abolished except his own. During 1977 he had indirectly received a warning that the reunified party would resist any attempt to suppress it. But until Khyber's funeral on 19 April 1978, he tolerated it on the assumption that it was as small and ineffectual as Parcham had proven to be in 1973–75. The funeral told him otherwise. Had Khyber been murdered by the government, then it logically would have been ready to follow up with arrests of other PDPA leaders, but it was only when Daoud took fright at the crowd that plans were hastily made to crack down. It took six days to decide upon and organize the arrest of the party's leaders. They were, during that time, just as blind as Daoud had been, not realizing that the funeral would cause a strong government reaction. Although Amin later claimed to have been working on a military coup plan for some time, the fall of Daoud came in a hasty, ill-organized manner.

Shortly after midnight on the morning of 26 April, police arrested Taraki and took him to prison. In the PDPA mythology that was later embroidered around this and subsequent events,[1] Taraki and his wife defied them, to no avail. At the same time, police went to the homes of other PDPA central committee members. Most apparently were taken directly to prison, but Amin was only put under house arrest. There followed one of the stranger episodes of a peculiar period.[2]

Amin sent his teenage son Abdur Rahman to find out what had happened to Taraki. At 6:00 A.M. the youth reported Taraki's imprisonment. So at 6:30 Amin sent his son to an air force officer and 1973 coup participant named Sayed Mohammed Gulabzoy with instructions to tell other PDPA members at the air force headquarters at Kabul to attack the government at 9:00 A.M. the following day, 27 April. Amin also used a brother and a cousin to summon party leaders who had not been arrested.

When the first comrade arrived at 7:30 A.M., Amin wrote out for him a plan for the coup, including the assignments of Watanjar to command ground forces, Abdul Qadir to command air force units, and orders for twenty other individuals, according to the PDPA history. At 8:00 A.M. another leader, Ziray, arrived but was blocked by police from going into the house to talk with Amin, so Amin wrote out another set of instructions and sent them out to him. By 10:30 Amin's work was finished; at 10:45 more police came to take him to prison. So the coup was organized while Amin was under house arrest!

Such is the official history. It would be easy to dismiss this apparently amazing development as official Afghan incompetence. Two other explanations are possible, however. One is simply that Amin did not in fact organize and send out orders for the coup as later claimed by media under his control—that instead the coup's military leaders acted pretty much on their own. Their reason for an essentially spontaneous uprising would have been fear.

The government announced on the evening of 26 April the discovery of an "anti-Islamic" plot and its leaders' arrests.[3] Daoud's defense minister, Lt. Gen. Ghulam Haider Rasuli, put the armed forces on alert in apparent apprehension of wider plot ramifications—although he also, contradictorily, decreed singing and dancing in military units the next morning to celebrate the plot's defeat. Even if Gulabzoy, Ziray, and others were not spreading plans from Amin, therefore, PDPA members and sympathizers in the armed forces would have learned of the crackdown. They had reason to fear that the arrested leaders might disclose their own connections with the illegal PDPA.

Even persons having known differences with Daoud but no PDPA connection had reason to worry that the crackdown might be broadened into a general roundup of those whose loyalty was suspected by the increasingly paranoid president. For both categories, with and without PDPA connections, a preemptive move against the government might be safer than awaiting unpredictable official actions. Men like Watanjar and Qadir knew that the combination of their roles in overthrowing the royal regime in 1973, their falling out with Daoud over his failure to implement the reforms that they had expected then, and their connections—however tenuous—with the illegal PDPA created considerable risk of severe action against them in Daoud's widening cleanup of potentially troublesome elements on the excuse of a plot. The nature of initial coup announcements tends to support this explanation: that it was not actually Amin's party-directed plan; that the coup's hasty initial purpose was not to permit Taraki's group of Communists to reorder the nation in accordance with the 1966 PDPA statement of principles. But that must remain only an unproven possibility.

The second explanation was offered by some Afghans. They say that even after becoming a Communist, Amin kept his connections with the political police. A senior police officer from his home area, Paghman, maintained close contact with his boyhood friend.[4] The police apparently believed that Amin was a source of information on the PDPA, a line into the underground movement. Whether Amin was playing both sides—maintaining ties with the police against the possibility of the Marxist movement's being crushed, or was outsmarting the police from the beginning, as he later claimed, can never be determined. Those who seize power and manage to hold on to it usually destroy any incriminating records—as did the Bolsheviks with records that might have shown Stalin to have been a double agent working for the tsarist police as well as for Lenin.

After Amin had been killed by the Soviets and his reputation blackened by Karmal, no public attempt was made to reexamine his role in the coup. That might have been as politically dangerous as investigating Khyber's murder. If Amin's claims were true, they would have detracted from the glory of the newly beatified Taraki; if false, the PDPA's claims to have overthrown Daoud as a consciously Communist action would have been weakened. And any investigation into PDPA members' ties to Daoud and his police probably would have gotten uncomfortably close to Karmal. Despite the uncertainties, however, there is a strong possibility that the delay while Amin was under loose house arrest was part of a police attempt to use him for the police's own purposes, presumably to expose more of the PDPA network. If so, the police moved too slowly. The coup that overwhelmed them might have been partially attributable to what was slipped out of Amin's house that morning without anything more than arrest warnings being sent.

Coup—Military or PDPA?

Whatever the genesis of the downfall of Daoud, it was accomplished by a small number of military men.[5] Thursday, 27 April 1978, dawned dull and gray. The coup began to develop about 9:00 A.M., the time supposedly ordered by Amin, with the first reported movement at the military air base side of Kabul International Airport. Only some 600 men, 60 tanks and 20 warplanes were involved in approximately nineteen hours of rebel action against the more numerous loyalist forces.

Watanjar, the deputy commander of the Fourth Armored Brigade at Kabul, led the tanks to attack the Arg, the old walled royal palace in the center of Kabul that contained Daoud's residence and office complex and the barracks of the presidential guard. The palace came under attack about noon. About 4:00 P.M. Qadir, a deputy commander of the air force, brought MiG-21 and SU-7 jet fighters into the attack, strafing and rocketing the palace in an attempt to break its determined defense by the 1,800 guards there. Taraki said later that only seventy-two persons died in the coup,[6] but his opponents' estimates went into the thousands. The exact figure is unknown, but Taraki's count is probably too low. It almost certainly does not include senior officials who were executed during or immediately after the takeover.

Successful coups are later described by the victors to sound inevitable. In fact, chance played a large part in the outcome. Both sides blundered. If Amin did write the plan, it was an incompetent one. It failed to target Daoud's communications as the first objective. Amin's lack of military experience could account for that. An alternative explanation is the absence of a plan, and hasty independent movements by various ill-coordinated soldiers happened to succeed.

When the soldiers began to move, Daoud was holding a cabinet meeting in the Arg to decide the fate of the seven arrested Communist leaders[7] and, presumably, what other steps were required to insure security. Word came of rebellious movements by tank units east of Kabul. Rasuli left the meeting to rally loyal divisions around the capital, keeping in contact with Daoud through the untouched telephone exchange. Troops were hard to round up, however. One reason was that the singing and dancing order had temporarily dissolved some units. Usual Afghan army inefficiency could have caused difficulties, too, and there is the possibility that PDPA infiltration blocked orders.

By late afternoon rebels had freed the PDPA leaders from prison, the official history said, and tanks and infantry had captured Kabul Radio, next to the compound of the modern United States embassy building. The delay of six or seven hours from the first rebellious action to the freeing of the PDPA leaders strongly suggests that they were a low priority for soldiers who were not looking to them for orders. There are contradictions about what happened after they were freed. The official history says that Taraki was taken to the radio building, which had become the military command post, along with Amin and other PDPA leaders. The soldiers reported to Taraki on the continuing fight with Daoud's loyal troops. At the insistence of Karmal, who was described as arguing that the coup would fail and PDPA leaders should flee into hiding in villages, Taraki was moved to the greater safety of the air base, the history says. Amin was left in command at Kabul Radio.[8] Taraki claimed later that he had "issued all orders" during the fighting.[9] But Amin said that, when he arrived at the station, "the officers automatically gave me the command of the revolution. So from 5 o'clock at the evening [although the history said the station was captured at 5:30] until 9 o'clock in the morning of 28 April, I was commanding the revolution."[10]

There is no independent evidence that either Taraki or Amin was in command. The available evidence suggests otherwise. The first known announcement that Daoud had been overthrown—premature, because the palace was not completely captured and he and his family killed until around 4:00 A.M. on 28 April—was broadcast on Kabul Radio at 7:00 P.M. 27 April by Qadir.[11] "The power of the state fully rests with the revolutionary council of the armed forces," Qadir declared. He made no reference to the PDPA or a civilian leadership.

Listeners to the Dari broadcast were told that Qadir headed the council, and Watanjar's name was also mentioned. One version of the official history says Amin suggested that Taraki read the initial announcement, but Karmal opposed this. Taraki broke the deadlock between Amin and Karmal by asking Amin "to allow the Khalqi officers to read the communique." This version does not mention that Amin spoke on the radio. But another version, also official, says Amin introduced Qadir on the radio, and Qadir read a communiqué in Dari, and Amin then introduced Watanjar, who read it in Pashto.[12]

Aside from that version of the history, there is no record that Amin played this role, which seems likely to have been a later invention. The United States embassy in Kabul, listening to the radio for clues to what was happening, reported hearing only Qadir's and Watanjar's names, not Amin's.[13] The confusion in the official versions makes them highly suspect. The soldiers seemed to be acting on their own, not under direct PDPA orders and possibly not even under much Communist influence. Amin wanted the history to show his dominant role. The version that says only that Taraki asked Amin to let the officers speak, without saying Amin spoke, could have been concocted to obscure an inability of the PDPA political leaders to control what the officers did.

Such an inability is strongly suggested by the issuance at 10:00 P.M. of a policy statement by "the revolutionary council of the national armed forces." It was short and simple enough to have been just written on the spot. The council's domestic policy "rests on the preservation of the principles of the sacred teachings of Islam, establishment of democracy, freedom and security of the individual, and the promotion of advancement and progress of our beloved people of Afghanistan." Its foreign policy "consists of the pursuance of the policy of positive active neutrality, supporting peace in the region and world, cooperation and friendship with all countries on the basis of amicable coexistence and respect of the United Nations' charter."[14]

This sounded like the generalities of many non-Communist Third World coup leaders. There was no mention of the PDPA's own program or of a civilian leadership, a significant omission. If the soldiers had considered themselves as only a transitional team clearing the way for the PDPA, then there logically would have been no reason for them to issue their own policy statement. The clear implication is that for the first few days the Communists as an organized party were not in control, despite later assertions to the contrary.

But some Communist influence was distinguishable in the soldiers' broadcasts. Marxist rhetoric was used. The initial announcement warned against any "anti-revolutionary element" that might defy the revolutionary council, who represented power "of the people of Afghanistan."[15] The next day, 28 April, when Qadir read most radio announcements, he said that those who failed to return to work on 29 April—a Saturday, the beginning of the Moslem work week—would be considered "enemies of the people."[16] Soldiers with Soviet military training might easily have picked up such Soviet terminology without having been simply PDPA agents. On 29 April, Kabul Radio announced that, "On the order of the Revolutionary Military Council," four of Daoud's senior officials had been killed after rejecting the council's repeated calls to surrender.[17]

The Soviets seemed to think this was another military coup. For the first three days, reports by the Soviet government news agency, Tass, called it a coup d'etat and said the armed forces' council had seized power.[18] An authoritative Soviet journal later avoided claiming that it was a PDPA coup, even after that had become the conventional claim with coup redefined as revolution. The journal only cautiously said instead that PDPA work in increasing "its influence among the popular masses and in the army . . . played the decisive role in ensuring the success of the national-democratic revolution." This could be read as meaning that the party had only influenced rather than led events. The journal said that "a Military Revolutionary Council was formed during the 1978 April Revolution. . . . On April 29 [it] handed over all power to the Revolutionary Council, which was set up as the supreme body of state power and merged with it." A later Soviet book said the military council "headed by Colonel Abdul Kadir, . . . which directed the revolutionary coup, adopted a decision at 9 P.M. on April 29, 1978, transferring all power to the Revolutionary Council of the Democratic Republic of Afghanistan."[19]

The PDPA official history does not mention that Qadir's council ever existed or that any domestic and foreign policy statement had been issued independent of the PDPA program. Deliberately obscuring what happened in the first few days, it says that "On the 27th and 28th, the Khalqis made preparations for the meeting of the Revolutionary Council of the Democratic Republic of Afghanistan and on the 30th the real revolutionary commander, general secretary of the central committee of the PDPA, Comrade Nur Mohammed Taraki, was unanimously elected" president and prime minister.[20] This later version is not, however, what foreign embassies in Kabul were told on 30 April in a foreign ministry circular note requesting their governments' diplomatic recognition of the new regime. The note said: "The Revolutionary Council of the Democratic Republic of Afghanistan in its first meeting, *dated* 7 Saur 1357 [27 April 1978], elected Mr. Nur Mohammed Taraki, who is a great nationalist and revolutionary person, as the president of the Revolutionary Council . . . as well as prime minister."[21]

Aside from the difference in identification of Taraki, the key point is the dating. There was an apparent effort to claim direct continuity from the Daoud regime, ignoring the armed forces' council period, by dating the meeting that elected Taraki on 27 April even though it was not held until three days later.[22] There were many such tamperings with the record. On 3 May Taraki said the "revolutionary armed movement" had occurred "under the leadership of patriotic officers and the brave army,"[23] but on 9 May he said it occurred "under the guidance of the [PDPA] and by the patriotic officers and valiant soldiers."[24] Two years later Karmal said that "it was the uprising of the progressive forces of the Afghan army that caused . . . the regime of Daoud to be overthrown in 1978."[25]

By 30 April, then, the soldiers were being shouldered aside by men who had devoted their lives to semi-clandestine political organization while maintaining contacts with the Soviet embassy in Kabul. What happened in those few days has not become known. If the soldiers had not seized power on direct orders of the PDPA, if they had not acted with the intention of turning power over to the party, they at least remained silent when later downgraded. Whether this was a matter of loyalty or of having been so out-maneuvered that they had lost any chance to protest effectively is unclear. There was no attempt to explain the situation to the public, just bald announcements.

"Decree No. 1 of the Revolutionary Council of the Democratic Republic of Afghanistan," read on Kabul Radio 30 April, said the military council had been disbanded.[26] All the military council's members were included in the new revolutionary council, however, making plausible the Soviet version that the soldiers had merged with the civilian Communist leaders. In addition to reporting Taraki's election, the decree said the new council "shall elect, as soon as possible, the vice president" of the council and members of Taraki's cabinet. It also "will adopt and announce its policy." Why a delay? Presumably there was a struggle for position underway. The jockeying for power obviously was a three-way contest, among the military leaders and the Khalq and Parcham factions. The decree also declared the next day, 1 May, to be a holiday for all workers. May Day is a traditional Marxist holiday, and the language used to describe it in Kabul was the first clearly Marxist rhetoric heard from the new, little-known Afghan leaders.

At 9:00 A.M. on May Day, Decree No. 2 said that Karmal had been named the new council's vice president, followed in order by Amin, Watanjar, Qadir, and then a number of old PDPA civilian leaders. The decree also named the new cabinet with approximately the same lineup of names as the council's. Karmal was senior deputy prime minister.[27]

Not until 9 May was a policy statement made by Taraki.[28] It was very different from the military council's. Domestically, Taraki promised "democratic land reforms." He said the new regime would "promote and consolidate the state sector of the national economy . . . eliminate imperialist influences in various economic, political, cultural and ideological fields . . . [and] clear the state organizations of anti-revolutionary, anti-democratic and anti-people elements." A purge was thus underway. Taraki promised a foreign policy of nonalignment and good relations with all neighbors, but he singled out such goals as "to further strengthen and consolidate friendly relations and all-round cooperation with the USSR" and to campaign "against the old and the new imperialism and support the national liberation movements in Asia, Africa and Latin America."

The contrast between the two policy statements suggests that the main link between the soldiers and the PDPA leaders was a common hostility toward Daoud—whom Qadir in particular hated for failing to carry out the reforms for which Qadir and Watanjar too had helped lead the 1973 coup. It was the armed forces' victory, and they initially sounded as if they intended to keep control of the result with their own program. Just how the disciplined PDPA stalwarts managed to wrest the command away from them, as appears to have happened, remains a mystery. The one-day delay in agreeing on the full lineup of the new leadership is significant. That the 1 May result of the jockeying for power was an uneasy compromise was soon shown by events. The key point, which Lenin had proven sixty-one years earlier, was that a determined leader, backed by a small but dedicated band of supporters, can dominate a larger number of less well organized, less ideologically inspired persons.

The change of government that started with the arrests early on 26 April and ended with the secret meetings on 30 April, came to be known in Afghanistan as The Great Saur Revolution, from the local name for the month. It was not a revolution, however. It was a palace coup d'etat. No mass uprising occurred, no widespread public support was evidenced. In fact, people in Kabul tried to ignore the fighting around the palace, traffic dodging among the tanks, life continuing pretty much as usual until the realization spread that Daoud was under attack.[29] Then, most people and many military units waited to see who would win before committing themselves. Outside of the capital, the country remained quiet.

Similarity to Bolshevik Revolution

Of all the times that Communists have come to power in the world since Lenin arrived in Petrograd in 1917, only a few cases, such as China and North Vietnam, can be accurately categorized as revolutions in the strictest sense of the population's being mobilized to seize control of the government. In the majority of the cases, like most East European countries and North Korea, outside military power and police control were used to impose Communist rule. But the Afghan case is the one that most clearly resembles Lenin's own Bolshevik Revolution, which was really a coup . In both cases, a small group without any popular mandate, primarily drawn from or later claiming to have represented just one part of a divided and feuding Marxist movement, used armed force to seize the center of the governmental structure and then spread its control over a populace in whose name it claimed to act. Though Lenin actually organized the military move, and Amin may not have, at least the small scale of the seizures was similar.

And just as the 1917 German decision to inject Lenin into the tumultuous Russian situation, by returning him from Swiss exile in the famous "sealed train," was an important foreign factor in the downfall of the troubled post-monarchical Kerensky government to a handful of Bolsheviks, so was Soviet encouragement of the PDPA over a long period a factor in the downfall of Daoud's faltering post-monarchical regime. Civil war followed in both cases, and in both cases some of the original coup supporters ended up fighting what they considered a perverted or even betrayed outcome of the change that they had helped create: Kronstadt sailors in Russia, Khalqi officers who joined the resistance in Afghanistan.

Just as a legend had to be created in Russia, so did Afghans and Soviets go to work to deny that it was just another military coup. "It is not necessary that [the working class] should be in the majority so that the working class revolution takes place," Amin said. "But it ought to be noted that the working class revolutionary ideology is the torch of our revolution and its leadership, that is, the People's Democratic Party of Afghanistan. It is on this basis that the same dictatorship of the proletariat has been established in this country and is in the service of the peasants."[30]

A Soviet commentator was more explicit in describing the position of the tiny PDPA, which represented a radical elite group of government employees, military officers, and students. What, he asked, could this "political vanguard do? Was it supposed to sit impassively on the shore of a vast sea of human privation and suffering? Was it supposed to wait until the political conscience of millions would awake completely? No, they chose another course, namely, leaning on the army to take political power, and, in the process of social transformation, to involve the millions in the revolution."[31] In other words, it was not a case of a revolution but of a small group's arrogating to itself the right to decide what the millions must want. It soon turned out that the decision was wrong, that most Afghans rejected the PDPA version of revolution, that the country was not ready for the excesses of a new ideology.

The ideological inspiration was kept half-hidden at first. Other than the May Day celebrations, the language of Taraki's policy statement, and a brief use of the title "comrade" in Kabul newspapers before it was dropped, the new regime was cautious. An admission of Communism would automatically antagonize many Afghans as well as neighboring Moslem countries because of the belief— based on observation of what the Soviets had done in Central Asia—that Communism was deadly to Islam. So on 3 May Taraki denied any foreign involvement in "a democratic and nationalist revolution of the Afghan people" and insisted that "Afghanistan never had a party called the Communist Party and there is not a Communist Party now."[32] A Yugoslav journalist in Kabul, who presumably would be able to recognize a Communist, was not put off. He reported the next day that the new council included "representatives of the reunited Communist Party" as well as soldiers.[33]

Taraki soon gave a classic definition of a Leninist organization: "The Afghan People's Democratic Party, led by the central committee, guides, leads and controls the country's affairs. The revolutionary council and the . . . government execute government affairs."[34] On another occasion, he said that "We consider ourselves to be radical reformers and progressive democrats. Marxism-Leninism is not a formula which we apply or claim."[35] Amin told interviewers who asked if the PDPA was Communist, "Call us whatever you want . . . We will never give you a clear-cut answer."[36]

But over the next few months speeches became more obviously Marxist. On 7 November 1978, the anniversary of the Bolshevik Revolution, Amin said the Saur Revolution was a continuation of the Russian event. "Though we are not the first socialist country of the world, we have the honor of being the neighbor" of it, Amin said. Afghanistan's duty is to defend "its evolution on the basis of scientific socialism."[37] This was pure terminology from the Soviet Union, which says it is using "scientific socialism" to reach the eventual goal of true Communism.

Soviet Role in the Coup

If this was a continuation of the Bolshevik Revolution, what were the Soviet role and attitude? A direct role had not been identified by outsiders, but the buildup to the coup was an indirect role as old as the inculcation of dissatisfaction with the Afghan regime in the minds of military personnel sent to the Soviet Union for training. The Soviet-urged unification of Khalq and Parcham just nine months earlier, when Daoud's turn to the Moslem world and the West had antagonized Moscow, was an important element in the background to the coup.

When the coup suddenly erupted, however, the Soviet embassy in Kabul acted as surprised as other embassies—and as Daoud. Soviet Ambassador Aleksandr M. Puzanov, an alcoholic seventy-two-year-old castoff from Kremlin political struggles two decades earlier, was off trout fishing in the Hindu Kush, and the embassy was being run by his deputy, Yuriy K. Alekseyev, an experienced Asian hand. What the KGB team in Kabul was doing is uncertain. The CIA—which for years kept in Kabul a man with previous Soviet experience to watch the Russians there—had by 1978 eliminated that position in a budget cut; however, the CIA station chief and the United States ambassador spoke Russian and were under instructions from Washington to regard watching Soviet activities as a higher priority than monitoring Afghan domestic affairs.[38]

Some of the 350 Soviet military advisers then in Afghanistan observed the rush of activity, or perhaps were informed by the leftist-inclined Afghan officers whose friendship they had cultivated. These advisers joined in the coup activities. Soviet officers were observed with the Afghan armored units that seized control of Kabul airport's military section early in the coup.[39] Other Soviet advisers were known to have helped organize and launch the MiG-21s and SU-7s from Bagram air base. The accuracy of some of those warplanes' rocket attacks on the palace inspired rumors among Western observers that Soviet pilots had flown them, but that seems to have been an unjustified vestige of a colonial mentality that denied mere Afghans such competence. Western intelligence reports concluded that Soviet advisers, whose technical expertise played an important continuing role in Afghan armored and air forces, had taken a significant role in the coup.[40] It is not possible to say if it was a decisive role, if it developed only after some initial hesitancy when word of the coup began to go around, or if the advisers took the time or effort to obtain political clearance from the Soviet embassy before participating.

It is possible to speculate, however, that sometime during the approximately thirty-two hours between the arrests of PDPA leaders and the beginning of the coup, reports about a military move against Daoud reached the Soviet embassy and Moscow. Soviet military advisers are always under tight political control. It is completely unbelievable, if not actually impossible, that they would get involved in a coup without high-level authorization. Therefore, the least assumption that foreign governments and others have drawn is that the Soviet Union prepared the way for a Communist coup in Afghanistan over many years, saw it coming, and might have helped block or thwart it had Moscow wished to warn Daoud, but did not plan it in advance or trigger it—not then, not when the PDPA was still so weak, the country so unready for tight Leninist central control, and anyway Daoud was likely to die naturally before too long. A greater assumption that governments and others have seriously considered without taking as definite is that Moscow authorized a Soviet role in helping the coup succeed while not becoming publicly committed in case it failed. A significant delay points toward the greater assumption. Moscow denied "imperialist propaganda" of Soviet involvement in the 1973 coup immediately after it occurred.[41] In 1978 the essentially same Soviet leadership only felt compelled by nine days of mounting Western suspicions of a Kremlin hand to issue a belated denial.[42]

Recognition Granted

While Soviet diplomats rushed around Kabul trying to find biographical information on many of the new leaders, there was something happening behind the scenes that enabled Moscow to preserve its record dating back to Amanullah of being the first capital to recognize a new Afghan government. At 5:00 P.M. on 30 April Kabul Radio reported in Decree Number One that Taraki was in charge. Kabul Radio later said that at 5:30 P.M. Puzanov had met the new president in his office and given him a message of diplomatic recognition. The United States embassy in Kabul did not receive until 6:25 P.M. its copy of the circular note from the foreign ministry requesting recognition.[43] Curiously, Tass mentioned only India in reporting two days later that some countries had recognized the regime. When Moscow Radio finally reported the Soviet recognition, on 3 May, it cited Kabul Radio as the source,[44] although the Afghan broadcast would not have been quoted by Moscow without official guidance there.

Also on 3 May, Brezhnev and Kosygin's "hearty congratulations" were sent on what they called Taraki's election as president, and wishes for great success, while Soviet Foreign Minister Andrei A. Gromyko sent a similar message to Amin, who had become Afghan foreign minister.[45] But aside from saying that "the Soviet people have heard with satisfaction" that May Day was being celebrated,[46] Soviet media were carefully noncommittal about events in Afghanistan for some days. *Pravda* finally pronounced the official Soviet attitude on 6 May: "The interests of social development demanded a fundamental break with obsolete social relations." It added cautiously, "Complex tasks of forming the new power, the intrigues of internal and external reactionary forces, and struggling for a better future for the Afghan people, lie ahead."[47] The Soviet attitude gradually grew warmer after that. By mid-May Soviet media were reporting favorably on planned reforms.[48] This meant that the Kremlin had decided to go a significant step beyond just recognizing the new regime by endorsing it as a healthy new development to be encouraged—and embraced.

The public embrace was given by Gromyko to Amin. The new Afghan foreign minister stopped in Moscow 18 May on the way to a meeting of nonaligned countries in Havana. Soviet media, and the joint communiqué on their talks, identified the two men not only by their government positions but also as members of the political bureaus, or politburos, that controlled their two parties, the Communist Party of the Soviet Union and the PDPA.[49] This was a clear signal that the Kremlin had accepted the PDPA as a Marxist organization. When Gromyko meets foreign ministers from non-Marxist countries, only his and the visitor's governmental titles are used. But on this occasion the rhetoric was Communist. Amin "stressed that as a result of this revolution . . . power went over into the hands of the people under the leadership of the PDPA," the communiqué said, and he praised Soviet friendship. Gromyko conveyed, "on behalf of the CPSU, its central committee, the politburo of the CPSU CC [central committee] and personally Leonid Brezhnev," wishes of success to the Afghan people, PDPA leaders, and republic. Amin cautiously extended best wishes in the name of Taraki, other Afghan leaders, and the Afghan people, but he did not name the PDPA.[50] This was a milestone in the evolving Soviet attitude.

Non-Communist Views

It was not generally noticed in the non-Communist world. There, some mystification existed about the nature of the new Afghan regime. Alarms in 1973 that Daoud's coup had been communistic, with "the Red Prince" planning to take Afghanistan into the Soviet bloc, had proven so unfounded that chastened Western observers were hesitant in reading the small amount of available evidence in 1978. While some British commentators declared that the "Great Game" was over, with the Russians as winners, United States officials carefully avoided pronouncements that might make it difficult to keep open lines for possibly influencing the new regime or that could trigger the terms of the Foreign Assistance Act of 1961, which prohibited aid for "any Communist country."[51]

Some American officials regarded the little-known PDPA leaders as more nationalistic than communistic. This was supported by Dupree, who had drunk tea and talked over many years with Kabul leftists. "The term 'Communist' is, in my opinion, unjustified—as yet," Dupree said in mid-May. "Governments, like persons, should be considered innocent until proven guilty."[52] In a surprising use of a term that a quarter-century earlier had caused United States political controversy because it had been applied to Chinese Communists, a leading American newspaper published the view that "Taraki and his cabinet colleagues are agrarian reformers, intensely nationalistic and likely to be formidably opposed to direct Soviet intervention."[53]

Adolph Dubs was more skeptical. He had been accepted by the Daoud government as the new United States ambassador to Afghanistan shortly before the coup. Taraki's government reaffirmed the acceptance. Before leaving for Kabul, Dubs recommended that the Carter administration do some contingency planning for a Soviet military takeover of Afghanistan, but South Asia specialists in the State Department dismissed this as mad. Within a few months of arriving in Kabul, Dubs repeated the recommendation, and a junior official in Washington half-heartedly drafted some later-unused ideas.[54]

On 13 July the State Department's third-ranking official, David D. Newsom, visited Kabul, and he and Dubs met Taraki and Amin. The two Afghans, who had within two and a half months signed some thirty new aid and cooperation agreements with the Soviet Union, asked more United States aid than the $20.6 million programed for 1978. The United States wanted friendly relations, but "we are not going to make a special effort to compete or do anything dramatic" on aid, an official said later.[55]

Afghanistan's non-Communist neighbors also took a cautious attitude. Pakistan's President Zia was disturbed by the collapse of his agreement with Daoud to improve relations and by the revival of Afghan propaganda on Pushtunistan and Baluchi problems. Zia decided to go talk with the leaders in Kabul. They tried to put him off, but he insisted, and on 9 September he met Taraki and Amin. Zia offered to talk over any problems that Afghanistan perceived, to provide technical assistance, and to insure that transit routes were unencumbered. Taraki replied with oratory about his popular support and vagueness about specific issues. Zia went away perplexed and finally in May 1979 branded Afghanistan a Soviet satellite, saying the buffer state had ceased to exist. He met Taraki again at the nonaligned summit meeting in Havana in September 1979. By then Taraki was besieged with troubles and he seemed more friendly, telling Zia that any Afghan leadership had to make verbal attacks on Pakistan. They embraced for television cameras, a politically important move for Taraki as he sought to broaden the popular appeal of his regime—as the Soviets were then advising. Taraki invited Zia back to Kabul for full-scale discussions, but within two weeks Taraki had been overthrown.[56]

The shah of Iran was also disturbed by the Afghan coup. Two days after it occurred he told an American visitor, George H. W. Bush, that he considered it one more example of the Soviet grand design and further proof of a Communist drive to encircle Iran.[57] Later, he told diplomats that it would not have occurred if the United States had taken a stronger stand in Angola, Ethiopia, and other places where Soviet power had recently been displayed. While blaming Moscow for the coup, the shah did not feel that his own wooing of Daoud might have been a factor, diplomats reported. A limited amount of Iranian aid continued on projects underway.[58] Other Moslem countries also continued existing aid programs, and a few new commitments were made early in the Taraki government.

Internal Tensions

While the outside world wondered about Afghanistan, tensions inside the country rose rapidly. The old conflict between Khalqis and Parchamis erupted anew, and new conflict developed between the regime and virtually the entire rest of the population. The Soviet Communist Party, aware of the PDPA's internal strife, sent an official to Kabul in May 1978 to try to keep the 1977 unification intact. Suspiciousness and outright hostility were too much for him, however.[59] Khalqis led by Amin felt that they had won control and owed nothing to old rivals like Karmal. Amin suspected Parcham of keeping its own secret cells within the armed forces even after the coup, creating a possible future threat. Karmal, worried about his position, reportedly sought support from Qadir, a nationalistic leftist not committed to either PDPA faction, but was rebuffed, and the Soviet embassy was still some months away from directly intervening in Afghan internal affairs.[60] By 15 June, Karmal had disappeared from Kabul media, and he was rumored to be under house arrest.

Parchamis Exiled

On 26 June Amin's foreign ministry asked the United States to agree to the appointment of the Parchami interior minister, Nur Ahmad Nur, as ambassador to Washington.[61] Kabul Radio announced that appointment and Karmal's as ambassador to Czechoslovakia on 5 July.[62] Anahita Ratebzad became ambassador to Yugoslavia; A. Mahmud Barialay, who is both her son-in-law and Karmal's younger brother, ambassador to Pakistan; and two other Parchamis also became ambassadors.[63] This is a traditional Third World way of getting rid of political opponents gently, but both Karmal and Nur reportedly resisted being exiled. They finally left quietly.

The regime then lurched on into measures that alienated the Afghan people. It is debatable whether the Parchamis—who had always advocated a gradual approach to Communism—were banished partly because of policy differences, or whether if left in the leadership they might have been able to soften the Khalqi policies that stirred up armed resistance.

Taraki's Purges

After "lengthy discussions," a reorganization of the PDPA was announced 8 July.[64] Amin, who was in control of the new political police named the Organization for the Protection of the Interests of Afghanistan (AGSA in the initials of its Dari name), increased his power by becoming a party secretary. In the government, Amin became Taraki's sole deputy prime minister and Watanjar replaced Nur as interior minister. Known Parchamis in the government, schools, and the armed forces were fired and in many cases arrested, with some 800 expelled from the military alone. Many of them were tortured in efforts by Amin and his acting police boss, Assadullah Sarwari, to discover the names of secret Parchamis. Nur said later that some "professional party cadres . . . were forced to emigrate or go underground, others were arrested, and some paid with their lives."[65] By 19 July, Taraki could say that "There was no such thing as a Parcham party in Afghanistan, and there is no such thing now."[66] The entire government is run by Khalqis, Taraki claimed on 1 August, and all military officers are either Khalqis, Khalqi sympathizers, "or are bound to become Khalqis. In other words, the PDP is in full control of the army."[67]

However, anywhere in the world it is in the nature of radical civilians boosted into power by soldiers to worry about continuing military support. Taraki soon denied his own statement about full control of the army by presiding over—Amin's growing power makes it impossible to say flatly that Taraki was responsible for—a second wave of purges that struck at the military leadership. Kabul Radio announced 17 August the discovery of an "anti-revolutionary network" led by Defense Minister Qadir, the army chief of staff Maj. Gen. Shapur Ahmedzai, and others, who were arrested.[68] They were not Parchamis but essentially Moslem nationalists who might disapprove of the regime's radical new course, if they had not already done so, and reportedly opposed Amin's efforts to control all military appointments. But they were accused of being part of a Parchami conspiracy. The PDPA politburo, which had become its key ruling group as the central committee expanded from a handful of members, decided that Taraki would take over the defense ministry, and Amin "shall also help in the affairs" of it. Within a few days two real Parchamis, Planning Minister Keshtmand and Public Works Minister Mohammed Rafi, had also been arrested as part of the plot.[69] Widespread arrests followed. Virtually everyone known to be, or suspected of being, a Parchami was imprisoned. Some were tortured to death. The regime took a harsh attitude that those involved in leftist politics who were not for it were against it.[70]

This culminated with a PDPA central committee meeting 27 November that denounced "an anti-Saur Revolution and an anti-Khalqi regime conspiracy plotted under the leadership of Babrak Karmal,"[71] with Qadir, Keshtmand, Rafi, Nur, Anahita, and others named as participants.[72] Confessions were made public, including one by Keshtmand—who had been personally tortured by Sarwari—saying that "Karmal argued that the present Khalqi state was isolated from the people and the latter were dissatisfied."[73] The truth of that was already apparent, but the leaders did not want to hear it. They focused on an alleged plan for an uprising at the end of the Moslem holy month of fasting, which in 1978 fell on 6 September, with Qadir to be made the head of state. The central committee expelled nine plotters from the party and reaffirmed a 6 September order summoning the banished Parchamis home from their embassies, but instead of going home the ambassadors had all disappeared[74]—presumably with Soviet help, because the first reappearance was when Karmal returned behind smoking Soviet guns more than a year later.

The PDPA meeting on 27 November also reaffirmed Amin's key role. Taraki announced that Amin had become a party politburo member at the time of the Saur Revolution, and he said separately that Amin had been elected a party secretary without specifying that it happened in July. Taraki thus made it clear that Amin held the key jobs in any Leninist party. Now, Taraki said, Amin and Shah Wali "are administering the party and Khalqi organizations' affairs through related commissions."[75] This wording suggested that some Khalq nucleus was being kept separate from the PDPA as a whole.

Taraki was by then well on his way to becoming a figurehead. By early November there were persistent rumors in Kabul of resentment in the leadership about Amin's high-handed behavior, and an Asian official noted that Amin no longer treated Taraki with the deference he had shown immediately after the coup.[76] Though Taraki must bear blame for what happened during his presidency, Karmal's later regime tried to preserve his reputation. The official line became that "Amin and his group, taking advantage of Taraki's credulity, wove behind his back a conspiracy inimical to the people and hounded honest patriots and revolutionaries, not stopping even at the killing of the finest cadres of the Afghan revolution."[77]

Brutality of the Regime

Parchamis were only a minority of those to feel the brutal wrath of the new regime. There has throughout history been a savage streak in the characters of most revolutionaries who come to power, perhaps because they realize that the same violent forces that thrust them to the top could be unleashed against them. Communist revolutionaries have been among the most savage. Men who endured imprisonment as Communists, who even in many cases obtained educations in prison and were converted there to Communism, as in East Europe before World War II, in Vietnam under the French, or in Afghanistan itself, came out able to continue their struggle for power. But once attaining it, they insured that those who went into the same prisons now under their control did not get a later chance as they had gotten. Royalists, capitalists, non-Leninist socialists, liberals, and neutrals—all political types have felt the brutality of Communist regimes as present resistance and future questioning is smashed. Perhaps the reason is the ideological dictate that Marxism is the wave of the future, which is interpreted to mean that no alternative future can be left possible and any means of preventing it is permissible. To keep the wheel of history from turning back, those who had, before the Communists came to power, shown them some civilized tolerance have to be crushed under it. So it was in Afghanistan, where a primitive savagery had always kept in practice forms of man's inhumanity to man more typical of the Middle Ages than the modern world.

Many foreign observers felt that the Communist coup was greeted by most Afghans with relief. The Daoud regime had failed to satisfy popular demands. The PDPA therefore started with hopes that it would carry out reforms that Daoud had promised in vain.[78] Those hopes were quickly shattered. Members of the extended royal family and those who had served them over the years, many of them nonpolitical technocrats, were arrested without pretense of judicial process. Ministers of Daoud's and previous governments were picked up, and most Western-educated officials. Entire families were imprisoned. Many former officials, certainly in the hundreds, perhaps in the thousands, were killed. One of the first to die was Moosa Shafiq, beheaded according to some reports. At the large prison at Pul-i-Charki, on the eastern outskirts of Kabul, executions averaged about fifty a night.[79] In addition to the armed forces, where few above the rank of major kept their jobs, the first round of purges hit hardest at the interior ministry which controlled police and intelligence, at the technical communications network as well as the media, at the foreign ministry, at educators, and at provincial governors who were all replaced by military men.

A decree issued 14 May, abrogating Daoud's 1977 constitution, established "revolutionary military courts" to dispense summary justice for "any behavior running contrary to the interests of the people and the state,"[80]whatever the PDPA decided that to be. The decree also established AGSA, the new political police that Tass explained would "protect the young state from encroachments upon its independence and internal security." West Germans had trained and advised Afghan police; East Germans and Soviets soon replaced them. AGSA became very busy. Taraki explained that "The criterion of our judgment regarding the removal of unhealthy elements from the administration is sabotage, anti-revolutionary action, corruption, bad reputation, bribery, cruelty, oppression and administrative inefficiency of the officials."[81]

Results of the Revolution

There were three quick results: greater administrative inefficiency because large numbers of trained people were purged, a resulting greater dependence on Soviet advisers, and alienation of the educated class. Karmal complained later that "there was not the necessary number of managers and specialists at all levels who could combine devotion to the revolution with sufficient vocational and theoretical training."[82] As a result, some parts of the government almost ceased to function.

Dependence on Soviet Advisers

The PDPA turned to the Soviet Union for help. The number of Soviet military advisers doubled to 700 within three months, some of them helping to run the defense ministry.[83] Many of the estimated 650 Soviet civilians who had been working on aid projects around the country before the coup were summoned to Kabul to show Khalqis how to run various other ministries, or to run the ministries for them. Because of language similarity, Soviet Tajiks and other Central Asians were rushed south to fill gaps, but many of them were phased out when trained Russians became available because the Kremlin did not want to expose its own people with a Moslem heritage to the growing religious intensity of Afghan resistance.[84] The number of Soviet advisers in Afghanistan grew so steadily throughout Taraki's and Amin's regimes that the Soviet embassy had to build new four-story apartment houses for them. Some educated Afghans who tried to work for the regime were antagonized by compulsory lectures on "epoch-making ideology," a euphemism for Marxism-Leninism.[85]

Alienation of the People

The masses of ordinary Afghans were quickly alienated, too. Organized opposition first developed among the Moslem traditionalist groups that had been fighting the leftists on Kabul University campus and in the streets for years. Unlike the outside world, they never had any doubts about the nature of the people who had seized control. By late May, within a month of the coup, a National Rescue Front was founded by nine Islamic and anti-Communist organizations. Under the leadership of a Kabul University law professor, Dr. Syed Burhanuddin Rabbini, it claimed the support of more than 100 members of Daoud's 374-member parliament.[86]

Many of the country's estimated 320,000 mullahs were soon assumed to be supporters, too, as the regime began to implement new policies. Taraki charged that religion was being used as an obstacle to "the progressive movement of our homeland."[87] He later insisted that only "an insignificant minority" opposed his government because the Afghan branch of the Moslem Brotherhood plus "leftist, extremist, conservative and nationalistic elements" had been swept away.[88]

This became a pretense that continued after the Soviet invasion: that basically the Afghan people liked their government, and only outside provocation was responsible for opposition to it; not until late 1980 was a more realistic appraisal admitted. The first reported armed opposition to PDPA rule occurred too soon for any outsiders to have organized, however. The takeover of local administrations by young Khalqis from Kabul in May 1978 was reportedly resisted in the northeast, especially Badakhshan province and adjacent areas of Nuristan.[89] By removing experienced administrators with some understanding of provincial areas, and replacing them with detribalized, urbanized youths, the government unwittingly enhanced the authority of traditional local leaders—who were the most resistant to its attempts at social reforms.[90] The mullahs in particular were treated as enemies, and they reacted as such. Eventually, Karmal's regime would recognize that "the thinking of the predominately illiterate population is still being formed mainly by the mullahs,"[91] but by then the damage had been done.

Land and Language Reforms

Hardly had it finished the first round of post-coup executions when the new regime began working on implementing the reforms outlined in the 1966 Khalq policy statement. Its dedication to them was partly an ideological conviction that such things as land reform were necessary to prove the Marxist credentials of the new leaders, partly a determination not to let PDPA promises prove as empty as Daoud's similar reform statements and thus risk weakening leftist support, partly a lack of reality by teashop radicals without a proper appreciation of conditions or attitudes outside Kabul, and partly a result of having eliminated the experienced officials who might have been able to offer sensible advice about how to achieve change in a demonstrably change-resistant society.

Reforms seemed to build a reckless momentum of their own. At his first news conference as president, Taraki said (6 May) that technical aspects of land reform were being studied, and a month later he declared, "I believe it will be a year or two before we can go through with our plans for land reform. . . . We do not want to over-hasten our reforms; we want to implement them step by step." He also said 6 May, "We believe that social development will only be possible after the economic changes."[92] Yet just half a year later sweeping land reform and radical social changes had been decreed. And the regime had literally waved a red flag in the face of the Moslem peasantry, replacing Afghanistan's flag of black, red, and Islamic green with a new all-red flag strikingly similar in appearance to the flags of Soviet Central Asian republics.[93] Taraki claimed that "We respect the principles of Islam . . . but religion must not be used as a means for those who want to sabotage progress and to continue exploiting and suppressing the people. . . . We want to clean Islam in Afghanistan of the ballast and dirt of bad traditions, superstition and erroneous belief. Thereafter, we will have progressive, modern and pure Islam."[94]

After announcing the "Main Directions of the . . . Government's Revolutionary Tasks" on 9 May 1978, the revolutionary council issued four reform decrees between 15 May and 28 November. Karmal later claimed that he helped write them before being exiled.[95]

The first was intended as a cheap, quick way to win favor among the Uzbek, Turkmen, and other ethnic minorities while at the same time emphasizing the end of the old royal-style Pushtun dominance. The new regime promised "essential conditions for evolution of the literature, education and publication in mother tongues of tribes and nationalities resident in Afghanistan."[96] In the early 1970s there had been some cautious deviation from the traditional use of only Pashto and Dari as national languages, but Daoud curtailed it. Fearful of Persian (Dari) cultural dominance, he insisted on Pashto as the link language for all peoples, while Dari speakers resisted the spread of Turkic tongues because it would reduce the importance of their language.[97] Those Afghans for whom neither Pashto nor Dari were mother tongues were educated—if at all—in one of the two languages and went on to learn English as a compulsory foreign language until the regime changed that to Russian.

While the use of all significant languages was a theoretically desirable policy, especially with the linkage it was given to a literacy campaign, it had several consequences. One was an immediate need for materials in the newly legalized languages. This need was met for Uzbeks and Turkmen by Soviet advisers and the reprinting of Soviet textbooks, with Taraki's name substituted for Lenin's as the founder, thus hastening the Sovietization of northern Afghanistan.[98] Another consequence was the enhancement of provincialism. The language decree accused previous regimes of a language policy that practiced "the administrative approach of colonialists, divide and rule." But the effect of the new policy has been to divide up Afghanistan in such a way that Russian might become the common language of educated people, which would enhance Soviet control. This was the result of a similar policy in Soviet Central Asia, where in the 1920s the Russians had, over regional objections, broken up the cultural unity of the area by imposing deliberately distinct languages on previously only different dialects of related peoples.[99]

The second decree was intended to eliminate land mortgages and rural indebtedness.[100] Mortgages and loans contracted before 21 March 1974 were cancelled on the assumption that interest payments had already more than repaid the original balance. Later debts of tenants and farm laborers were also cancelled, while owners of less than 4.77 acres of "first-grade land" (double-cropped irrigated land, or orchards or vineyards) were assigned an easy scale of payments. It was claimed that some 11 million peasants benefited from the cancellation of $700 million in debts, on which a 50 percent rate of interest had not been unusual.[101]

The decree provided that the existing Agricultural Development Bank would provide credit for productive purposes—much of the indebtedness had been incurred for weddings and funerals—but the bank was incapable of filling the role that bazaar moneylenders and big landowners had played. As a result, many villagers lacked money to buy seeds and other essentials, and agriculture suffered.[102]

But Taraki, the unrealistic theorist, was proud of what he had done; it seemed ideologically right. The decree had "sharpened the class struggle in Afghanistan," he said. "The class struggle which we awaited for many long years is now gaining in intensity."[103] Many debtors who cited the decree in refusing to pay were reported to have been murdered by angry lenders, hardly the kind of class struggle a Communist party would approve. Taraki's hope of rallying the peasantry to the PDPA cause, in opposition to landowners and moneylenders, showed his lack of understanding of rural Afghan society. Villagers were united by bonds of mutual dependence and common hostility to outside interference, and this proved stronger than Marxist theory about class conflict.[104]

Since a decree by Abdur Rahman in 1884, successive Afghan governments had tried to ameliorate the system of a groom's family paying money and goods to a bride's family, regulate the age of marriage, enhance the status of women, and make related social changes. Effects had been minimal. The PDPA government's next decree put a low limit on bride payments and on payments in case of divorce or separation, promised freedom of choice in marriage, said girls must be sixteen years old and boys eighteen to marry, and provided for six months' to three years' imprisonment for violations.[105] In what was considered by villagers to be a related move, the government tried to bring girls into new schools. These changes challenged traditional customs at the heart of Afghan Islamic society. Rural economic relations were partly based on brideprice payments and the related brides' dowries. They were a form of social security for women, who lacked any other guarantees in the male-dominated society. Arranged marriages, often between first cousins, were the glue that held social relations together. And allowing young women to go to school with boys and outsider teachers was considered an insult to honor, made worse by the fact that Khalqi teachers were more concerned with party propaganda than basic education. The reaction to this decree was the opposite of that intended. By stirring up the resentment of rural males, it actually set back the slow development of women's rights, foreign observers felt, and it left women with less security, because of the ceiling on divorce or separation money.[106]

The last of the major reform decrees was potentially the most significant, but it produced more controversy and opposition than effect. Daoud had announced land reform in 1975 but never implemented it.[107] The Communist regime decreed an even more sweeping program, proclaiming that it would eliminate "feudal and pre-feudal relations from the socioeconomic system of the country."[108] A family was limited to 30 *jeribs* (14.3 acres) of first-grade land, or more poorer land according to productivity. Land above that limit was to be confiscated without compensation and distributed free to landless workers on it or other "deserving persons" in shares of five *jeribs* (2.4 acres) of first-grade land or equivalent.

With a foreign-aided cadastral survey and land registration moving slowly in the 1960s and 1970s, the land ownership situation was only vaguely known. Surveys indicated that the poorest 80 percent of the owners held just 29 percent of land, albeit often the more productive tracts, and the number of peasant families owning no land was reported from 400,000 upward.[109] No one knew just how much land would become available under the decree or how many people qualified as deserving. The official press published contradictory statistics. Behind them lay ignorance. This was the most extreme case of economic and social engineering in a vacuum, teashop theories unimproved by being clothed in a newly captured governmental authority.

Failure of Reforms

Tenant farmers had been dependent on landowners for seeds, various forms of credit, and in some cases implements. Where carried out, the reforms cut them off from these necessities. The decree mentioned cooperatives and new credit facilities to deal with such problems, but little was done about them because the skills, experience, and capital to establish them were lacking. Many poor Afghans, fearful of being severed from their long reliance upon their relatively rich and successful landlords, resisted change because it went against the Koran to usurp another's possessions. Some rich Afghans sabotaged efforts of others to work their land. But in general the tradition of villagers' sticking together against outside interference hindered the efforts of young Khalqi administrators to implement a change which the poor—for whom they claimed to speak—had not been enlightened to want or expect. Coming on top of the earlier decrees, land reform's main result was further arousing and disrupting the countryside and turning it against Kabul.[110]

It is, however, human nature as well as a Communist tradition firmly established in the Soviet Union to claim that whatever program is currently in official favor is working splendidly, regardless of the evidence. Afghan land reform was no exception. Implementation began in January 1979. Reports soon said that its success "is indeed beyond dispute. . . . [It] met with the people's ardent support and approval."[111] On 15 July Taraki announced that land reform had been successfully completed ahead of schedule, and despite poor rainfall the reform and other government measures had resulted in abundant crops.[112] On results of the plan to distribute about 1.5 million acres to 676,000 families, claims varied, the biggest saying that more than 1.6 million acres had gone to 285,000 families, and 964 cooperatives of 257,500 acres for 140,000 families had been established. It was, Taraki said, "an immense triumph achieved through the joint efforts of the party, the government and the entire Afghan people."[113]

Only after Taraki and Amin were both dead was it admitted to have been a disaster that caused armed resistance and cut agricultural production, but it never was admitted that the program had under Soviet urging been abandoned prematurely in an effort to contain rural opposition. Farmers had proven unwilling to plant redistributed land, because of uncertainty of ownership, or to market their produce. An estimated one-third of arable land went untilled. "The lack of effective, scientific and practical agricultural plans, the lack of timely provision of improved seed and fertilizer to farmers, the nonexistence of effective publicity and encouragement to farmers on planting" were conceded later by Karmal.[114] Others discussed "the destructive implementation of agrarian reform" that caused large numbers of peasants to abandon the land.[115] This was, naturally, blamed on Amin by Karmal's regime, but Karmal's claim to have helped draft the reforms showed the absence of realism throughout the PDPA leadership that led it into failures. "Ordinary people lost faith in the revolutionary regime," a Soviet writer admitted.[116]

Discussing "deviations from the correct and principled course, [as a result of which] the revolution got off the right track," Karmal blamed "the general backwardness of the country [and] insufficient maturity by the PDPA" as well as blaming Amin.[117] The party "lacked the necessary experience in carrying out government affairs, and how to guide economic and cultural development," he said.[118] *Pravda* said there had been "flagrant errors of the recent past . . . unbridled tyranny . . . [that] led to deep rifts among the people and in the ruling People's Democratic Party . . . Slogans incomprehensible to simple people and far removed from the real situation in the country were advanced. This not only undermined the masses' enthusiasm but also their trust in the leadership."[119]

An unidentified Afghan Marxist told a sympathetic Pakistani journal that

> The principal mistakes were: (1) the strong degree of financial and ideological dependence on the Soviet Union, (2) an obscured vision of the realities of rural Afghanistan, and the rural classes, (3) lack of a clear program of action among the party leadership, (4) lack of discipline, and the degree of corruption within the party, since most of them had personally been underprivileged

before coming to power, and (5) total lack of control over their immediate families, who exploited their kin ties to the leadership exactly as members of the royal family had done.[120]

The new bureaucracy lacked the restraint that previous ones in Kabul had to observe, because it had Soviet military power behind it and thus thought it could ignore domestic opposition, the Marxist said. Therefore, he said, responsibility for the rebellion against Khalqi rule "has to be shared jointly by the PDPA leadership and the Soviet advisers."

Soviet Support

The willingness of the Soviet Union to rush advisers to the help of the new Afghan regime showed a conscious choice to back up the PDPA rather than letting this Communist party founder from its own ineptness. Ziray, who emerged as perhaps the most important single party organization man, said almost three years later that comrades from the Soviet Communist Party "helped us organize party work. In April 1978 our party took power immediately. It emerged from deep underground. When it became the ruling party it did not know what state leadership meant. Now we have ... a well-organized PDPA which is strengthening daily and a party apparatus which is gaining experience."[121] Gromyko's embrace of Amin on 18 May 1978 as a fellow Marxist as well as just a fellow foreign minister was a signal of the decision to move in and build up the PDPA in the Soviet image.

But Moscow tried to keep a low profile. An agreement in July 1978 to provide another $250 million worth of Soviet weapons to the Afghan armed forces[122] was not made public, and Soviet media did not report on the quick buildup of advisers or the increasingly critical roles they were playing in running the modern part of the Afghan government and economy. The Soviet Communist Party's unsuccessful attempt to prevent the Khalq-Parcham split was kept secret. Moscow was reticent about party relations, focusing public comments on the governmental relationship.

It is the nature of the Soviet system to require an ideological categorization for things. The Afghan party's status and general situation required some generalization in Moscow. Sometimes the ideological label put on foreigners is a purely pragmatic result of Soviet national interests that works its way into Marxist-Leninist thinking. At other times, however, that thinking can guide national policy, so that ideology can become a formative influence on policy decisions. Thus, it was significant later, when the decision was taken in late 1979 to invade Afghanistan, that Soviet ideologists had come to accept it as a country that had chosen socialism, which is the stage toward supposedly true Communism that the Soviet Union considers itself now to be in. The most influential ideologist in the Kremlin, and one of the top two or three Soviet leaders, Mikhail A. Suslov, named Afghanistan in a speech 28 February 1979 as one of the "new states of a socialist orientation [that] have emerged" in the last five years.[123] In April 1979, the Soviet journal *World Economics and International Relations* said that "the Afghan people, under the PDPA's leadership, have begun the task of building socialism."[124] *Pravda*'s report from Kabul on the first anniversary of the Saur Revolution hailed Afghanistan's "socialist choice."[125] In late May, Tass listed Afghanistan among "countries of the socialist community" attending a conference in Mongolia.[126] Ideologically, the Soviet Union had become committed to the success of the PDPA regime, whatever the regime's incompetence in everything except antagonizing the Afghan people.

Militarily, it became committed also when Taraki visited Moscow from 4 to 7 December 1978. He and Brezhnev signed on 5 December a treaty of friendship and cooperation[127] that became the justification used by Moscow a year later for the invasion. Although the Soviets were not bound under the treaty to prevent the downfall of the new Communist regime in Afghanistan, they clearly were already preparing the possibility of saving it from its failure and keeping that country under Soviet influence by force if necessary.

The Soviet Union had already shown that it sometimes signed such treaties with specific purposes in mind. Two of the ten friendship treaties it made with Third World countries during the 1970s, with India in 1971 and with Vietnam in 1978, were followed shortly afterward by those countries' invasions of neighbors, East Pakistan (which became Bangladesh) and Cambodia, respectively. In both cases, Moscow had given the backing which helped make the invasions possible. But the other nine treaties were not so specific as the one with Afghanistan, not even the commitment with Vietnam to assist each other in "defending socialist gains." Most of the treaties provided only for the development of defense capabilities and for consultation without any commitment to action.[128] The Soviet-Afghan treaty was more comparable in its provision for taking action to Moscow's ties to Mongolia, a satellite but not part of the automatic military commitment in the Warsaw Pact of Eastern Europe. The 15 January 1966 Soviet-Mongolian treaty, which was aimed at China, said the two "will jointly undertake all the necessary measures, including military ones, aimed at ensuring the security, independence and territorial integrity of both countries."[129]

The treaty that Taraki and Brezhnev signed in the Great Kremlin Hall said:

> The high contracting parties, acting in the spirit of the traditions of friendship and good-neighborliness, as well as the United Nations' Charter, shall consult each other and take by agreement appropriate measures to ensure the security, independence, and territorial integrity of the two countries. In the interests of strengthening the defense capacity of the high contracting parties, they shall continue to develop cooperation in the military field on the basis of appropriate agreements concluded between them.[130]

After formal talks with Taraki—Ponomarev participated in them, showing that the PDPA was regarded as a Third World Communist party—and the treaty signing, Brezhnev said that relations "have assumed, I would say, a qualitatively new character—permeated by a spirit of friendship and revolutionary solidarity." The treaty expressed this, he added.[131] In reply Taraki endorsed the full list of Soviet-backed causes around the world but, perhaps to maintain his membership in the nonaligned group, qualified his position by saying the Afghan and Soviet positions "coincide on most of the major international problems."

The treaty preamble endorsed the 1969 Brezhnev anti-Chinese proposal on Asian collective security that Daoud had considered detrimental to the Pushtunistan case. Taraki mildly said he hoped the Pushtunistan issue would be "settled with due account taken of the historic background of this problem, through friendly talks and by peaceful means."[132] Ponomarev wrote soon after Taraki's visit that the new treaty was an expression of the Soviet duty to "render support to peoples of former colonies taking their first steps along a path which can lead to the building of a socialist society."[133] On 20 April 1979 the Supreme Soviet gave official governmental approval to the treaty at a session of the rubberstamp parliament that criticized China. Approval was given in terms of the friendship aspects of the treaty. There was no mention of the military aspects.[134] The treaty went into effect with the exchange of ratifications on 27 May 1979.

The visit produced two other signs of Afghanistan's being drawn into the Soviet orbit. One sign was a statement in the joint communiqué summarizing the visit that contacts between the PDPA and the Soviet Communist Party would be expanded.[135] This confirmed and extended the CPSU's attempt to restructure the disorganized PDPA in its own image of rigidly disciplined and bureaucratized operations permeating every aspect of national life, a daunting undertaking in Afghanistan. The other was the signing at the same time as the treaty of an agreement to establish a permanent inter-government commission on economic cooperation.[136] Fleshed out later with numerous specific agreements tying various aspects of the Afghan economy to the overpoweringly larger Soviet economy, this was to lead to a virtual takeover of the Afghan economy. It proved costly for Moscow as Kabul's policies ruined the economy. After the Soviet invasion, the Soviet Union had to assume responsibility for keeping Afghanistan functioning economically.

Death of Dubs

The growing Soviet role in Afghanistan was tragically called to United States attention on 14 February 1979 by the death of Ambassador Dubs. "Spike" Dubs had found it impossible to have meaningful conversations with Afghan officials, seeing them only occasionally and then usually on formal business,[137] but his background in both Soviet and South Asian affairs had qualified him to monitor the situation.

On 14 February he was kidnapped by four Afghans and held hostage at the Kabul Hotel in the center of the capital. The four were members of *Setem-i-*

Melli, the predominately Tajiki organization based in Badakhshan opposing Pushtun domination of Afghanistan that had been formed by Taher Badakhshi, one of the PDPA's founding central committee members who broke with the party in the latter 1960s. The four told Afghan authorities who quickly surrounded the hotel room that they wanted to exchange Dubs for *Setem-i-Melli* members who were imprisoned.[138] The names and number of these members were never clear.

Amin, as foreign minister, and other Afghan officials later made contradictory statements about the demand. The United States embassy in Kabul understood that the kidnappers wanted people named Wahez, Majid, and Faizani.[139] The first name might have been a variant of Bahruddin Bahes, whom Afghan authorities came to say had been the only person demanded. But, they insisted, they knew nothing of Bahes, whom others described as "a character with a mystical Che Guevara reputation."[140] Amnesty International said in May 1979 that, contrary to Afghan government denials that "he has been arrested or that it knows of his whereabouts . . . Amnesty International has been reliably informed he was arrested in the summer of 1978. There are unconfirmed reports that he was killed after arrest."[141]

Majid apparently was Abdul Majid Kalakani, a guerrilla fighter against Pushtun authority who had been caught late in Daoud's presidency. On 8 June 1980, Karmal's government announced his execution for "criminal and terrorist activities," indicating that he had been in custody during Dubs' kidnapping.[142] Faizani was never identified, although Amnesty International reported that a Mahmud Farani had been "arrested around July 1978 and reportedly shot immediately after arrest." The Khalqi regime tried to wipe out *Setem-i-Melli*, which it regarded as a Maoist deviation from true Marxism-Leninism, at the same time it purged Parchamis.[143]

Afghan authorities, led by the Kabul police chief at the hotel and backed up by police commandant Seyed Daoud Taroon and Amin, refused to negotiate with the kidnappers. Four Soviet advisers on the scene conferred with Afghan police, and another was with Taroon. The Soviets apparently provided weapons, one helped load them, and another was seen positioning Afghan snipers and signalling when to fire. Overriding objections of United States diplomats, the police with Soviet backing assaulted the hotel room. Dubs and the two kidnappers inside were killed; the other two kidnappers apparently were later killed separately by the police.[144]

The outraged Carter administration accused the Soviet Union of involvement in the bungling that caused Dubs' death, but Moscow denied it. The United States slashed aid programs for Afghanistan that were becoming impossible to carry out anyway because of the spreading guerrilla resistance to the government.[145] On 23 July it announced the withdrawal of most United States diplomats, aid workers, and other official personnel from the country "in light of the security situation."[146] Finally, on 14 August, President Carter signed a law that prohibited any further aid to Afghanistan until the Afghan government had officially apologized and assumed responsibility for Dubs' death and agreed to provide "adequate protection" for all United States government personnel in the country, or "substantially changed circumstances" justified more aid in the American national interest.[147]

Other non-Communist countries halted their aid programs about the same time because of the turmoil and insecurity in Afghanistan. The World Bank and other international aid-giving organizations, which had provided $100.4 million in grants and "soft" low-interest loans to Afghanistan in 1978, began cutting back in 1979. By 1980 only a $2 million grant from the United Nations' Development Program was forthcoming.[148]

The final twist of the bizarre and tragic Dubs case came after Amin had been killed by Soviet troops and denounced by Karmal as a CIA agent. The Afghan interior ministry announced 30 March 1980 that "new discoveries" showed the kidnappers to have opposed "Amin's oppression and suffocating pressure." They recognized Amin as "an imperialist agent" and wanted to force Dubs to "expose the secret link of Amin with the U.S. embassy," the new version said. Fearful of being exposed, Amin instructed Taroon to attack the hotel room and kill everyone in it. Amin had to "destroy all members of this group for his own security," the ministry said.[149] The United States government, which had failed to receive cooperation from Afghan authorities in investigating the case, found this version sadly ludicrous.[150]

Armed Resistance

Armed resistance to the Communist regime mounted during the winter of 1978–79. Winter is a period when farmers have time on their hands to feud and fight. The government's reform efforts, and its purges that broke links between villagers and their friends and patrons in Kabul, provoked increasing numbers of outraged Afghans to use force against official attempts to impose the PDPA's will on them. Spontaneous opposition to governmental interference developed into guerrilla warfare as the government showed more determination to have its way. That determination was sapped, however, by the reluctance of an Afghan army made up of conscripted villagers to fight other villagers. Desertions began, a small start to what developed into a large flight in the winter of 1979–80 as Soviet advisers assumed more control over the army and then the Soviet invasion occurred.

Also beginning that first winter was the development of a network of guerrilla training camps and supply routes across the Durand Line in Pakistan[151] and, to a lesser extent, across the Iranian border. A pamphlet circulated among Afghans in Pakistan said killing one Khalqi was equal to offering 80,000 prayers to Allah. But as the first anniversary of the Saur Revolution approached, resistance was still limited to sporadic attacks in relatively remote areas, while urban areas seemed cowed and under control. Both the government and its Soviet friends acted as if the situation were well in hand.

Then came the Herat uprising. It was a major turning point in the Afghan situation. Moscow's reaction to it led on inexorably, even inevitably, to the Soviet invasion nine months later. With a population of some 150,000, Herat is one of Afghanistan's major towns, the economic and administrative center for the western part of the country. There in mid-March a popular rebellion erupted against PDPA officials, starting with or quickly joined by the army garrison. Mobs surged through the town hunting down and butchering Khalqis. And not just Khalqis: The hatred turned also on Soviet advisers in an explosion of historic enmity for Russians. Those who were found were slaughtered in ancient barbaric ways, some dying slowly, horribly, and their corpses were disfigured in the ultimate primitive expression of contempt. At least twenty Soviet men, women, and children are definitely known to have died, but the toll of Soviet citizens probably was much higher, 100 or more.[152] The government said 3,000 Afghans were killed before loyal troops brought in from Qandahar restored order; other estimates of the four-day battle said 5,000 died.

Unwilling to admit that its own people had rejected it, the government charged that 4,000 Iranian soldiers in disguise had infiltrated across the nearby border and caused the trouble but, it added later, had all been wiped out. No evidence was offered. Iran flatly denied the charge,[153] which might have been inspired by the presence in Herat of thousands of Afghans who had lost their jobs in Iran because of the economic turmoil caused by the shah's ouster two months earlier. Ayatollah Ruhollah Khomeini, the Iranian religious leader, said in June: "The present government in Afghanistan is oppressing people in the name of Communism. We have been informed that 50,000 people have been killed in Afghanistan and that Islamic religious leaders have been arrested there . . . If Taraki continues his ways, he will suffer the same fate as the shah." Khomeini held Moscow to blame for the "killing going on in Afghanistan, thanks to the Soviet interference."[154]

Government Response to Resistance

The Herat uprising produced two important results. One was in the Afghan government, the other in Soviet involvement in Afghanistan. But the logical result, a softening of government policy and a greater effort to win popular support rather than trying to force the people to accept the dictates of a PDPA leadership that was isolated from reality, did not develop. Herat was a warning unheeded. Instead, it served to increase the power of the man most responsible for blindly and doggedly trying to impose a dictatorial will on the nation. That was Amin.

On 27 March he became prime minister, taking over direct responsibility for the government from Taraki. Taraki remained president and became the head of a new High Council for the Defense of the Homeland, but increasingly he became just a figurehead. A new cabinet announced 31 March made Watanjar the defense minister, Sher Jan Mazdooryar minister of interior, and Sarwari head of AGSA, the political police.[155] At his first news conference as prime minister, Amin was asked if Soviet troops would enter Afghanistan. "We have not so far raised this issue with them," he replied.[156] This was one of many such statements that assumed significance later when Moscow claimed that its troops had repeatedly been invited into the country.

Soviet Response

But if not regular Soviet Army units at that time, hundreds or thousands of additional Soviet military personnel did enter Afghanistan shortly after the Herat uprising, while Soviet women and children living there were sent home in April. The Soviet Union's first reaction to the uprising was an alert for its nearest airborne strike force, an elite Russian division at Ferghana in Uzbekistan. If the trouble had not been contained in Herat, and if Soviet citizens working elsewhere in Afghanistan and their families had become similarly endangered, the division presumably would have intervened to protect or evacuate them.[157] The second reaction was to rush military aid to Kabul. On 26 and 27 March Soviet cargo planes delivered to the Afghan capital light tanks, armored personnel carriers, and helicopter gunships. The tanks and APCs were familiar to Soviet-trained Afghans and simply supplemented their weaponry, but the helicopter gunships were new. They were MI-24 Hinds, the Soviet Army's latest, best, and most expensive, firing rockets and heavy machine guns. They had to be flown and serviced by experienced Soviet crews, although ostensibly they were used as part of the Afghan army. Overnight, the traditional guerrilla warfare of ambush and surprise attack by men climbing the rugged Afghan hills had been given a new dimension. The MI-24 "changed the face of the fighting here," an Asian military attaché noted.[158] By late summer thirty of them were reported operating in Afghanistan, along with MI-6 troop-carrying helicopters, hundreds of new tanks and APCs, and some additional MiG-21 fighter-bombers equipped with napalm, which was used on hostile villages.[159]

The first new weapon deliveries were soon followed by a visit of the general in charge of ideology, morale, and discipline in the Soviet armed forces, Alexei A. Yepishev. During the "Prague spring" of 1968, Yepishev had visited Czechoslovakia to assess the situation there and had returned to Moscow favoring Warsaw Pact military intervention to prevent the loss of Soviet-style political control. He arrived in Kabul 5 April at the head of "a delegation of Soviet political workers," including six other generals, and stayed for about a week.[160] They found that "effectiveness was quite low" of ideological work in the army. "The low level of political training, the extreme religiousness and downtrodden nature of the masses of soldiers, and the social heterogeneity of the servicemen" made it possible for opponents of the regime to demoralize the army.[161] One of Yepishev's generals, Lt. Gen. V. Balakirev, said that "Our delegation had many interesting, frank and pithy talks with the organizers of party work and political education" in the Afghan armed forces.[162] The "frank and pithy" part apparently consisted of telling those organizers to do a better job of building military support for the regime and motivating soldiers to fight for it, not against it.

The Soviet Union was plainly worried about the country's holding together. Although *Pravda* much later described the trouble in Herat as a mutiny, on 19 March it showed the worry with unusual front-page coverage of the Afghan accusation of Iranian interference in Herat.[163] It went on to accuse Pakistan, China, Egypt, and "some Western countries" of instigating unrest in Afghanistan. This was the most serious expression of Soviet concern over Afghan stability since the Saur Revolution. *Pravda* thus began a series of worried reports in Moscow media indicating that Soviet concern was growing parallel with the arms buildup and expanding attempt to instruct the Afghan armed forces.

There was no direct mention of the new friendship treaty in the context of possible Soviet intervention, but another authoritative *Pravda* article on 1 June accused the Pakistani government of direct complicity in guerrilla operations across the Durand Line and warned that a crisis "cannot leave the Soviet Union indifferent." With the situation moving toward "a conflict in our immediate vicinity," it is "a case of actual aggression against a state with which the USSR has a common border," *Pravda* declared.[164] Brezhnev spoke even more pointedly, while still avoiding citing the treaty, by saying 11 June that "we shall not leave in need our friends the Afghan people, who have the right to build their lives the way they wish."[165] All this was, of course, predicated on the pretense—which continued, reinforced, after the Soviet invasion—that the guerrilla resistance to the Communist regime in Kabul was essentially a result of outside influences and interference rather than a widespread, genuinely popular rejection of the regime.[166]

Safronchuk

Along with weapons, ideological advice, and a show of international backing, the Soviet Union took another step as a result of the Herat uprising and its review of the subsequent situation. It strengthened its effort to give political guidance to the PDPA and its government. The main agent for this became Vasily S. Safronchuk, who arrived in Kabul a few weeks after the uprising. A trained economist and a career diplomat—his record reads like a genuine diplomat's, not one of many KGB men disguised as diplomats—Safronchuk had been the Soviet ambassador to Ghana after President Kwame Nkrumah had fallen and then the deputy permanent Soviet representative to the United Nations from 1971 to 1976.

It is unclear why the Kremlin chose a man with that background, rather than someone experienced in Afghanistan or at least in Moslem Asian countries, for the job of trying to teach the PDPA how to govern the country better and win more popular support. Perhaps the Soviet experts on Afghanistan were already discredited either in Moscow or with the Kabul regime. While ostensibly part of Puzanov's embassy, but working from the Afghan foreign ministry or from the old royal palace (now known as the House of the People), Safronchuk acquired a status vaguely independent of the embassy.[167] It was also only vaguely influential.

Some changes that might be attributed to him soon appeared, such as Taraki's and Amin's making a show of going to mosques for prayers in an effort to placate aroused Moslem feelings. They began meeting frequently with tribal and provincial representatives, religious leaders, and military officers to explain PDPA aims. The regime made minor admissions of excesses and promised better. The land reform program was halted on the pretense that it had been accomplished.[168]

Safronchuk urged Taraki to broaden the government's base by bringing in non-Communists. Moscow media reported on 13 July a PDPA politburo decision for the establishment of a "united national front" to include all "progressive public and political forces," but significantly this was not publicized inside Afghanistan.[169] But nothing happened on it until, two years later, when, after great difficulty, the Soviets were finally able to have Karmal carry out the idea with the creation of a National Fatherland Front—which failed to rally the desired "progressive public and political forces" to a regime hated for its own policies and for its Soviet sponsorship.

Safronchuk's advice, and other aspects of Soviet pressure, had little or no effect on the Afghan regime. PDPA leaders made it clear that they were not going to welcome Parchamis back into authority—or let survivors of the Parcham faction or other political elements out of Pul-i-Charki prison, where some 12,000 persons were being held by late summer.

Amin reportedly maneuvered to keep Safronchuk or Puzanov from seeing Taraki, as they tried to do almost daily, thus insuring that he became the main contact man with the Soviets.[170] Obdurate, proud of the PDPA's narrow popular base rather than embarrassed by it, determined to do things his own tough and often violent way, Amin became an obstruction to the Soviet effort to save the regime from its own mistakes.

As early as May 1979, intelligence reports reaching the United States government "suggest[ed] that the Soviets are already moving forward with plans to engineer replacement of the present Khalqi leadership of the DRA, perhaps with the exiled Parchamist leaders including former Deputy Prime Minister Babrak Karmal, now believed hiding in Europe."[171] About the same time, however, the United States embassy in Kabul reported, a Soviet embassy official there expressed frustration with the politically inexperienced Afghan government but observed that "at this time" there was no apparent alternative leadership.[172]

Soviet Search for an Alternative

If that were true in May, the Soviet embassy was by July beginning to look for an alternative to Amin. By mid-summer Soviet advisers were running much of the government behind a facade of unqualified Khalqis, but Amin tried to keep control of basic policies. Arrests continued, some widely respected religious leaders who objected to the violation of Islamic traditions were murdered, entire villages were wiped out for individuals' acts of opposition. While the Soviets urged conciliation, the regime conducted new purges. Amin later was assigned the blame, but it was Taraki who said in May 1979 that "whoever stands against our revolution—whoever he may be—we will put him in jail and will really punish him."[173] A reign of terror was conducted against real and suspected opponents of the PDPA, its policies, and its Soviet friends. Urban purges and reports reaching the towns of rural atrocities encouraged opposition, however. An anti-government demonstration occurred in Kabul on 23 June.[174] Something had to be done, despite Amin.

Sometime in July foreign diplomats in Kabul became aware of Soviet efforts to try to make leadership changes.[175] Amin presumably was also aware of them. He tightened his grip. On 27 July Taraki assumed formal control over the armed forces and designated Amin as de facto defense minister to "implement in practice" directives supposedly originating with Taraki. Cabinet changes were "made on the proposal" of Amin. Watanjar was shifted from defense to the interior ministry, Mazdooryar from interior to frontier affairs. At the same time, the PDPA politburo called for deepening intraparty democracy through "enhancing collective leadership of party organs" and other party reforms.[176]

According to a secret source providing information to the United States embassy, "Soviet machinations to alter the Afghan regime . . . moved into a more active phase" in the last week of July. The source, apparently a dissident member of the PDPA hierarchy, said the Soviet efforts were being supported by non-Pushtun cabinet ministers. "An important part of the current political problem is the excessive Pushtunization tendencies of the current Khalqi leadership," the source said.[177] Other charges being whispered around the capital accused Amin of a growing "cult of personality," nepotism, personal profiteering, violent suppression of PDPA dissent, collusion with unidentified foreign enemies, and policy miscalculations.[178]

Reporting the Soviet machinations, the American embassy added: "We frequently hear rumors that the Soviets are still trying to build a new regime around former royalist prime minister [Mohammed] Yousuf," the head of King Zahir Shah's government from 1963 to 1965.[179] Either simultaneously or later—the timing is unclear—the Soviet embassy was also holding late-night talks with Nur Ahmed Etemadi, the king's prime minister from 1967 to 1971. A Westernized career diplomat who had become known to the Soviets as Afghan ambassador in Moscow after 1971, he was ambassador to Pakistan at the time of the Communist takeover. Etemadi had just been called up from Pakistan for consultations with Daoud's government when it was overthrown, and he was imprisoned at Pul-i-Charki shortly after that. Sometime in the summer of 1979 a Soviet embassy car surreptitiously picked him up at prison several times for talks.[180] The ability to take him out of prison not only showed Soviet power in Kabul but also indicated cooperation by some disaffected Afghan officials.

Night Letters

Even stronger signs of opposition to Amin within the ruling group soon appeared. Clandestine leaflets, the traditional Afghan dissidents' *shabnamas* ("night letters"), began to circulate in August. The police made no apparent effort to stop them, and police boss Sarwari was later accused of having encouraged the dissidents who wrote them.[181] One *shabnama*, at least the second to attack Amin from within the Khalq membership, appeared in Kabul on the morning of 29 August. It went far beyond, and made more specific, the earlier whispered accusations. It claimed to speak for "a number of Khalqis . . . [who] decided not to be indifferent to the treachery and rascality of the corrupted band of Amin."[182] Listing fourteen types of mistakes or failures, beginning with "excess of selfishness and personality cult in the leadership," the leaflet charged that "loyal revolutionary personalities" were being dismissed and "thousands of Khalqis . . . who did not come to terms with" Amin were jailed. "Amin's behavior and tyranny are an embarrassment to the [PDPA and have] . . . caused the oppositionist elements to unite to threaten the security and safety of the country," it added. The *shabnama* concluded:

> Although we informed the general secretary of the party [Taraki] of Amin's acts and behavior many times, he told us with much regret that Amin is in charge of everything and he (the general secretary) cannot do anything and every responsibility rests with Amin.
>
> Therefore, it is evident that all Khalqis should join hands against Amin and disarm him of his power. The political bureau of the central committee and the revolutionary council should also take timely action. Otherwise, the loyal members of the party will lose faith in them.[183]

This description of Taraki as helpless to stop the downward spiral of the regime was later contradicted by the version of recent events circulated when Amin had become president. It accused Taraki of having conspired in August to assassinate Amin. The alleged co-conspirators included Sarwari, the AGSA boss, and the last three important military leaders of the 1978 coup left in the national leadership after the purge of Qadir and others. They were Watanjar, who in his new job of interior minister had nominal control of the normal police that were separate from Sarwari's political police; Mazdooryar, now in the frontier ministry dealing with Pushtun tribes that had become hostile to the regime; and Gulabzoy, the communications minister. Amin supposedly learned of the conspiracy and blocked it.[184] Whether in fact opposition to Amin ever got as far as an assassination plot during August—what happened on 14 September could have been something else—is unknown. The military men had proven in 1973 and 1978 that they were capable of it, but Taraki had never shown the decisiveness or ability to organize such an action. The accusation might well have been an exaggeration or even an invention intended to justify Amin's own actions.

While privately working against Amin, and publicly urging national reconciliation, the Soviets were, in the summer of 1979, showing no conciliatory spirit on the military front. Amin attributed to Soviet advice the summer tactic of burning crops to deprive resistance forces of food, saying Moscow had promised to make up any deficits.[185] Food had been a Soviet weapon in fighting the *basmachi*, and first the French and then the Americans had destroyed crops as a tactic against Vietnamese Communists. This was a time-honored way of fighting guerrillas who controlled rural areas, despite the fact that women and children usually suffered more than fighters. It was also a way of insuring that rural alienation increased rather than lessened.

A major army rebellion occurred in Jalalabad in June but was crushed.[186] Daoud had built the modern Afghan army to impose his will on the countryside and tribes more than to defend the nation as a whole, but it was never prepared for the emotional strains that the PDPA put on it. It began to buckle under the pressure, despite a doubling in August of soldiers' meager pay. Rather than be used to oppress those unwilling to accept PDPA policies, whole units deserted. Some soldiers simply went home to their villages. Some units joined the resistance intact, taking with them their Soviet-made weapons.

This process was well underway at the time of the Jalalabad mutiny, but that event seems to have triggered something in the Soviet Union. In late June, Western intelligence agencies picked up indications of unusual military movements, or preparations for movements, in the southern part of the Soviet Union.[187] At first it was unclear whether the Kremlin was preparing for possible military intervention in Iran, then in the early stages of the Khomeini turmoil, or in Afghanistan. Only later, in retrospect, was it possible to date the first signs of Soviet preparations for possibly sending Soviet Army units into Afghanistan as early as June 1979, six months before the invasion. In early July a specially trained 400-man strike unit from the Soviet division at Ferghana, the elite 105th Guards Airborne Division, was stationed at Bagram air base, the key military communications and logistical center for the Kabul region.[188] Moscow wanted to insure that it had an unshakable foothold, an "aerial bridgehead," inside a country that seemed to be coming apart.

A further sign that it was coming apart was an army mutiny on 5 August (well publicized because it occurred within view of Kabul's foreign community). An army regiment at Bala Hissar, the ancient fortress overlooking the old section of Kabul, reportedly rebelled because the political purge of a popular officer caused other officers to feel threatened. Three tanks started from the fortress toward the regime's power center, the House of the People. MI-24 gunships, which received radio orders in Russian, destroyed them with missiles. Then the helicopters and tanks from other units bombarded the fortress. The battle lasted four spectacular hours. The rebellion was crushed.[189] But if Amin, who as defense minister had responsibility for army reliability, was disturbed, he tried to hide it. He continued to reiterate that "We are proud that we have not asked any foreign country to fight for us or to provide our country with security and safety. . . . So far, we have never thought of utilizing foreign forces to defend and protect our revolution," he said 9 September.[190]

The Soviets were less confident of the regime's ability to cope with the widespread opposition, to fight what had become a civil war, without outside help. What further needed to be done about the overall problem was the question assigned to the Soviet deputy defense minister and commander of ground forces who had planned and commanded the invasion of Czechoslovakia in 1968, General Ivan G. Pavlovskiy. He arrived in Kabul in August accompanied by a large team of officers. His team spread out all over Afghanistan to assess the situation.[191] Their secret mission, never publicly acknowledged by the Soviet Union, found that such Soviet-urged steps as setting up "revolutionary defense committees" to broaden support for the government and reduce guerrilla support existed more on paper than in fact. Large areas of the country were out of Kabul's control. In some, such as the Hazara area in the center of the country, resistance forces had begun to try to operate alternative administrations. The army was becoming unreliable.

Under these daunting circumstances, the Soviet Union showed some hesitancy about how much further to get involved. On 16 August a Soviet radio commentary beamed to Afghanistan in Dari pointedly reminded listeners that "the Soviet people were themselves forced to defend the Great October cause [the Bolshevik Revolution] against the conspiracies and sudden hostile attacks of imperialism and foreign reaction which has now attacked the Democratic Republic of Afghanistan." The Soviet people won, and "we are confident" that the Afghan people can, too, the commentary said.[192] Another commentary the next day in English said, "The Afghan people are capable of defending their right to independence. Today they are proving their ability to defend the gains of the revolution."[193] The message was clear: Solve your own problems; don't count on us.

The day after that, 18 August, Afghanistan's national day, Brezhnev and Kosygin sent congratulations that omitted any mention of the friendship treaty.[194] The Kremlin thus seemed to be following a two-track policy. It was preparing to take a larger role in Afghanistan, including a direct military role. At the same time, it was still leaving itself room to back away from the problem.

In these circumstances—Pavlovskiy in Kabul making contingency plans; Safronchuk seeking unsuccessfully to budge Amin on the political necessities for trying to bring the rebellious country under control; Safronchuk also trying to undermine Amin's authority and depose him; Moscow hesitant about having to save the PDPA from its own barbarous and bloody folly; and strong elements within Khalq moving secretly to try to restrict or remove Amin—an opportunity presented itself for the Soviet leadership to talk the situation over directly with Taraki. After Amin's interference in contacts between Soviet officials and "the great leader of the Afghan people," it was a chance for discussions without obstruction from the man whom Moscow had come to be convinced was Taraki's evil influence. Taraki went to Havana for a nonaligned summit meeting. Watanjar was prominent at the Kabul airport departure 1 September, a fact unjustified by his protocol standing—he was not even a PDPA politburo member—and surprising to onlookers,[195] but perhaps explicable in terms of the later accusations by Amin that Taraki and Watanjar had been plotting against him. Taraki stopped on the way home from Havana for talks in Moscow with Brezhnev.

Chapter 6. Amin's Hundred Days

From the Soviet decision in the summer of 1979 that Amin was an obstacle to stability in Afghanistan until the Soviet invasion the following winter to remove him, the country went through a tumultuous and bloody period.

Initially, Soviet leaders hoped to manipulate the situation from a cautiously reserved position, getting the Afghans to correct the policies that had alienated the populace and begun to endanger the Communist regime. But an attempt in September to get rid of Amin failed in such a way that he was left with enhanced power and new bitterness toward his indispensable Soviet suppliers of military and economic aid. Amin took the aid but spurned Soviet advice. He made half-hearted attempts to win popular support that were overwhelmed by measures which guaranteed widening opposition. He made tentative efforts to improve relations with Pakistan, but the only effect was to raise again in Soviet minds the old Daoud spectre of Afghanistan's moving toward a detrimental foreign policy. In short, Amin was a failure, and his tyranny did not last long.

Soviet Talks with Taraki

Taraki was, for all his personal ineffectiveness, a man whom Moscow could appreciate as a loyal friend. His lengthy speech to the nonaligned summit conference in Havana on 5 September 1979 had two main themes, praise for the claimed accomplishments of his government and a survey of world problems that would have sounded no different if written in Moscow.[1] Then, after his talk with Pakistani President Zia about better relations and meetings with other leaders, he flew home via Moscow.

Taraki had stopped overnight in the Soviet capital on the way to Cuba without any meetings with senior officials being reported. On the way home he stayed for two days and "had a friendly meeting in the Kremlin . . . in a heartfelt, comradely atmosphere."[2] The Tass report that so described it named only Brezhnev, Gromyko, and Brezhnev's foreign-affairs adviser, Andrey Aleksandrov, as being present in addition to Taraki. Protocol would normally have required that the Afghan foreign minister, Shah Wali, who had accompanied Taraki in Havana, also participate in the talks, but official accounts left that unclear—a point of some significance because of later reports that Wali was Amin's source of information on what was discussed in secrecy.

The publicly reported discussions included

the continuous strengthening of the close and friendly relations and all-round cooperation between the DRA [Democratic Republic of Afghanistan] and the USSR as well as between the PDPA and the CPSU. . . . Leonid Brezhnev assured Nur Mohammed Taraki that his people and Afghanistan are engaged in a just struggle and, as in the past, he can always count on the Soviet Union's all-round, unselfish assistance. He stressed his belief that the cessation of outside meddling in the internal affairs of the DRA and the establishment of good-neighborly relations between all governments of the Middle East will provide a background for the improvement of conditions in the region and for international security.[3]

With this rhetoric, it was curious that on leaving Moscow for Kabul on 11 September Taraki said that his meeting with Brezhnev had been very useful and had been held "in a frank, fraternal atmosphere."[4] Taraki might not have known the significance of the word "frank," but Tass, which reported his remarks, certainly did. Since Tass does not do such things unadvisedly, there apparently were some disagreements.

Afghan sources and others did not later report on disagreements. Instead, they described an agreement between Taraki and Brezhnev to carry out the kind of domestic changes that Safronchuk had been urging as a way of broadening the regime's popular base and thereby trying to check the growing guerrilla opposition. That would mean, for one thing, bringing Parchamis back into the PDPA and government leadership.[5] Unconfirmed reports said Brezhnev brought Karmal into the Kremlin talks in an attempt to reconcile him with Taraki, but this is doubted by sources who say Karmal was living in exile in Czechoslovakia at the time.[6]

Broadening the regime's popular base would also mean bringing non-Communists into the government, perhaps even at the head of it, if Yousuf or Etemadi would cooperate. Under a Soviet-type system in which the Communist party sets policies for the government to follow and controls who fills important jobs, non-Communist officials would be figureheads, but possibly useful ones in cultivating public opinion. With Amin dumped, someone more attractive as prime minister, and Taraki continuing as the celebrated but ineffectual president, the Soviets would be able to steer Afghanistan. The Kremlin wanted a compliant leadership in Kabul that knew where the financial and military power lay, not a troublemaking and potentially defiant strongman.

The indications, for which there is no hard evidence, were, therefore, that Taraki and Brezhnev agreed on getting rid of the deputy on whom Taraki had come to rely so heavily that his own authority had been stolen away. Amin's later version, however, was that Taraki had already decided to try to assassinate him,[7] with the implication that Taraki only checked out the plot with Brezhnev. After the December invasion, Soviet officials circulated yet another version: that as soon as Taraki left for Havana, Amin began preparing to usurp power.[8] Brezhnev later told a Western visitor he had warned Taraki that Amin was plotting to destroy him.[9]

September Plots

Whatever was happening, Taraki returned to Kabul 11 September to a welcome that exemplified the "cult of personality" that had developed around "the great leader of the revolution." As what Kabul Radio described as "tens of thousands of our noble and patriotic people" shouted slogans like "Good health to Comrade Taraki," the president was greeted with a bearhug by Amin, his "faithful student and great commander of the Great Saur Revolution."[10] They went directly to the palace for a special cabinet meeting. The official account said that Amin reported to Taraki on Afghan affairs during the president's absence, and "This report delighted our great leader."[11] This obscures whether there was an immediate confrontation over the reported plot by Watanjar and the others, or whether that came only a day or two later. Amin's later version said that he demanded the removal of the four from the government and guarantees that Taraki would not plot against him, but Taraki refused both demands.[12]

In this murky affair, there is one shred of evidence that the two leaders' clash did not come immediately upon Taraki's return but a day or two later, and it also points to the plot against Amin being concocted in Moscow on 10 September rather than earlier. It is a report believed by some senior officials of neighboring Asian countries that Amin was tipped off to the made-in-Moscow plot by Shah Wali when he returned home with Taraki.[13] Wali was a close associate of Amin's who helped him run the PDPA organization as well as the government —he was both deputy prime minister and foreign minister—and after Amin became president, Wali was his right-hand man.

Amin's Triumph

On 14 September, Kabul Radio announced that cabinet changes had been made on Amin's recommendation and with Taraki's approval. The three ministers, Watanjar, Mazdooryar and Gulabzoy, and Sarwari also, were out.[14] By the time of the announcement they were already in hiding from Amin's manifestly brutal wrath. Some reports circulating in Kabul said Watanjar and possibly others had escaped to personally loyal army units. Extra tanks were put on guard at the radio station in apparent apprehension of a move by Watanjar's supporters, and several unexplained explosions shook Kabul. But the more probable version is that the four had found shelter in the large Soviet embassy compound.[15]

There was no shelter for Taraki. By the time of the evening announcement, which implied that he was still president, Taraki was being held in the palace as Amin's prisoner. Exactly what had happened is unclear, but Afghan and diplomatic versions agree on the essentials.[16] Taraki summoned Amin to a showdown meeting on 14 September over Amin's desire to fire the four for plotting against him, or his having already fired them without presidential authorization. Amin feared a trap. He was, however, given by telephone the personal assurance of Puzanov that it was safe to go, and the Soviet ambassador urged him to work out his differences with Taraki. Still wary, Amin took an armed escort, including Seyed Daoud Taroon. Taroon, who as police commandant had been involved in the death of Dubs seven months earlier, was then serving as *chef du cabinet* for Taraki. The United States embassy described him as a "brutal, psychopathic killer . . . second only to Amin in the amount of blood on his hands."[17] As Amin was entering the building inside the palace compound where Taraki lived, Amin was fired upon down a staircase. In a brief exchange of gunfire, Taroon died, but Amin escaped uninjured. Amin later said that "Taraki's guard fired at me. . . . Were [Taroon] not there, I would have been shot."[18] Amin hastily rounded up a small military force, went back and fought a sharp, short battle, and captured Taraki.[19]

Effect of Soviet Interference

The Soviet hope of keeping a relatively benign and cooperative Taraki while replacing Amin had blown up. Like a later bungled attempt to remove Amin that led to the overt Soviet invasion instead of a smoother introduction of Soviet troops by internationally acceptable invitation, the September attempt created the worst possible result for the Soviet Union. Amin's power was increased by the elimination of whatever minor moderating influence had resulted from paying lip service to Taraki's leadership, and Amin's suspicion and hatred of the Soviets had been reinforced in a way guaranteed to make more difficult future cooperation between two sides who still needed each other.

Amin needed Soviet military equipment and advisers to run his defensive efforts against spreading guerrilla challenges, and he needed Soviet economic aid to replace collapsing agricultural and industrial production and a sharp curtailment of the foreign trade whose customs duties were the main item in government income. The Soviets needed Amin because, like him or not, he was the center of a system to which Soviet prestige had become committed, along with a large Soviet financial investment and the lives and safety of thousands of Soviet advisers. But, as the Americans found in Vietnam, such a mutual dependence does not produce good relations. The very vulnerability of each side exacerbates the relationship, and the weaker the client becomes, the more destructively self-assertive he can become instead of more gratefully cooperative.

Attack on Taraki's Reputation

At 10:00 the next morning, 15 September, Puzanov called on Amin. Their meeting lasted two hours.[20] It must have been an interesting, even angry, confrontation. One can speculate that Puzanov sought to patch things up and win the release of Taraki. If so, Amin flatly refused. That day the official *Kabul Times* still referred to Taraki as the "great leader . . . genius leader . . . great teacher," and the public did not yet know of the palace shootout. But on the following day, 16 September, the newspaper simply called him Nur Mohammed Taraki, without titles or honorific phrases.[21]

At 8:00 P.M. on 16 September, Kabul Radio announced that an "extraordinary session" of the PDPA central committee had been held, lasting four and a half hours. Shah Wali presided. "At this meeting there was a general discussion at the request of Nur Mohammed Taraki. [He] requested that he be relieved of his party and government positions due to health reasons and physical incapacity which render him unable to continue his work."[22] This was strange. Taraki was known to suffer from various medical problems, including respiratory, stomach, and liver complaints, but none was serious. The "tens of thousands" who had welcomed him at the airport just five days before saw a sixty-two-year-old man in apparently robust health.[23] The announcement went on, "The central committee . . . approved his request by a majority vote. In his place, Comrade Hafizullah Amin . . . was appointed as the secretary general of the PDPA."[24]

The meeting was later reported, in a six-page red-bound pamphlet that circulated secretly among Khalqis, to have adopted a secret resolution on the "unprincipled behavior and terrorist actions of Nur Mohammed Taraki and the gang of four" and decided to expel all five from the party. It said that "Taraki's cult of personality was the main obstacle in the way of accelerated advancement and intensified development. This cult of personality . . . overshadowed all ideological and organizational principles of our party." In order to insure "further individual leadership and satisfy his own selfish motives and intensify the personality cult," the resolution continued, Taraki "finally opted for conspiracies and the anti-party formation of groups against the central committee's politburo and all party organs, and in particular against Comrade Hafizullah Amin, who was a firm pillar against his personality cult in the party." Taroon was martyred during "a terror attempt . . . against our scholarly principled Comrade Hafizullah Amin on September 14, 1979."[25]

Two hours after the central committee meeting, the revolutionary council that was the supreme governmental body met for ninety minutes. Wali was again in the chair. "Discussion was held on the request of Nur Mohammed Taraki for dismissal on health reasons and physical weakness from party and state offices, and the request was evaluated from all sides." It was approved. Amin was named to succeed him as president of Afghanistan. The council also, "in observance of the martyrdom of Engineer Seyed Daoud Taroon . . . stood to their feet and observed a minute of silence."[26] While this meeting was under way, Taroon was being buried with military honors at the Hill of the Martyrs. Flags were ordered to half-staff all over Afghanistan in honor of him, and Jalalabad was renamed Taroon City on instructions of Amin. Lashkar Gah in the Helmand Valley was renamed for Nawab Khan, an AGSA official who was also described as having been "martyred by anti-revolutionary elements" along with two other minor officials.[27] But there were no honors for Taraki. His numerous portraits disappeared from Kabul along with banners hailing him, while security patrols in the capital were strengthened. Amin also took care of another detail. He had Etemadi executed.[28] The Soviets were to be allowed no alternatives.

In an interview 9 September, Amin said that "our decisions are not made by an individual but are made collectively, and the party and leadership assess and analyze them from all sides."[29] But with Taraki out of the way, Amin tried to blame all problems, all causes of public discontent, on Taraki alone. In speeches 17 and 18 September, he said that "from now on . . . Afghanistan will not be ruled by any one person. All government affairs will be handled and moved along collectively . . . No action will be carried out at one person's request or individually." Without naming Taraki, Amin blisteringly criticized "those arrogant ones who were on the seat of power, who engaged in tyrannical acts and swallowed the fruits of other people's hard work . . . who found their own greatness in the humility of others, and who achieved their greatness by crushing other people. . . . This endless greed of the tyrants and arrogant ones" has now ended, Amin said.[30] This attack showed the long-smoldering resentment by the man who claimed to have recruited, organized, and directed the military men who brought the PDPA to power but then had to take third place in the new regime behind Taraki and Karmal, later moving up to second place. Amin seemed contemptuous of Taraki, the impractical intellectual, and jealous of him. Now he was having his revenge.

Taraki's Death

When he held a news conference 23 September, during which he said relations with the Soviet Union were "Excellent, extraordinary," Amin was naturally asked by foreign correspondents what had happened to Taraki. Rumors in Kabul conflicted: he had been killed in the gunbattle, he had only been wounded. In fact, he was unhurt. But Amin replied that Taraki "is definitely sick. . . . He is in Kabul. . . . He is not in hospital, but doctors treat him and give him the necessary medicines. . . . He is so much sick that he could not carry on his responsibilities." Amin claimed that Taraki was satisfied with what had been said about his relinquishing his positions, but then he added enigmatically, "Absolutists who are dominant over the rights of people do not give up power voluntarily unless they are ousted by force."[31] On 10 October the *Kabul Times* published a report that Taraki "died yesterday morning of serious illness, which he had been suffering for some time. The body of the deceased was buried in his family graveyard yesterday."[32]

After Amin had been killed, Karmal's government published a report on Taraki's death.[33] It said that on 8 October Amin told the commander of the palace guards, a man named Djandad, to have Taraki killed. Djandad gave the order to the chief of the palace section of the former AGSA, which was rather peculiarly renamed the Workers' Intelligence Bureau, or KAM by its Pashto initials. The chief, Captain Abdul Haddud, was assigned two senior lieutenants of the guards, Mohammed Eqbal and a man named Ruzi. At about 11:30 P.M. on 8 October the three went to the second-floor room in a palace building where Taraki was being held. Obviously knowing what was coming, Taraki gave them his PDPA membership card, with a request that it be given to Amin, and a bag of money and personal jewelry for his wife—if she were alive; Taraki did not know that Amin had thrown her and other members of his family into Pul-i-Charki prison. Taken to a downstairs room, Taraki was tied up and put on a bed. "Ruzi was strangling Taraki by pressing a cushion against his mouth while Eqbal was holding his feet," Haddud related later, possibly meaning suffocating rather than strangling. "Fifteen minutes later Taraki died." Haddud, Eqbal, and Djandad were among ten former officials whose executions were announced 8 June 1980, along with the execution of Abdul Majid Kalakani, but Ruzi "succeeded in escaping from the investigation."[34]

Soviet Reactions

Soviet media reported the Kabul changes tersely. They had been caught by surprise: *Pravda* was still discussing Taraki's Moscow visit on 16 September, and an hour after Kabul Radio announced Taraki's removal Moscow Radio was praising in Dari broadcasts the "fruitful results" of his meeting with Brezhnev.[35] Amin's criticisms of Taraki were not reported by Soviet media.[36] On 17 September Puzanov called on Amin again,[37] and then Moscow reported that Brezhnev and Kosygin had sent congratulations to Amin on his new jobs. Theirs was a very chilly message. Addressed simply "Comrade Hafizullah Amin," it said, "Accept our greetings in connection with your appointment. . . . We express confidence that fraternal relations between the Soviet Union and revolutionary Afghanistan will be further developed successfully on the basis of the treaty of friendship."[38] Ignoring their curt tone, Amin replied effusively: "Dear comrades, permit me to thank you from the bottom of my heart for your fraternal congratulations on the occasion of my election."[39] Only low-ranking Soviet bureaucrats signed the condolence book placed at the Afghan embassy in Moscow to mark Taroon's death.[40]

There was another Soviet reaction, however. Once more, the airborne strike division at Ferghana went on alert. Pallets of equipment were prepared for loading into transport planes.[41] But the soldiers did not move, not then anyway, and it was unclear what need for them had been apprehended in Moscow. Perhaps the Soviet leadership had expected the planned ouster of Amin by Taraki to evoke some resistance from PDPA military men recruited by and still loyal to Amin personally. If such a situation had occurred, Taraki could have asked for some Soviet military help without provoking the kind of international outrage that was caused by the invasion three months later. After all, Taraki was the acknowledged president, and Amin was known to be the main villain in Afghan atrocities. The Kremlin would have had an excuse of helping Taraki cleanse his regime, an excuse incomparably more acceptable than the one it had to fabricate in December.

There was one suggestive sign that the Soviets were preparing to use such an excuse. It was the reported brief appearance just before the 16 September announcements of a radio station in Termez, the main Soviet transit point on the Amu Darya for traffic to Afghanistan, claiming to be Kabul Radio.[42] It was this false radio that in December first announced Karmal's takeover, but in September it quickly faded away without playing any role. The United States government, which monitored all this, announced that it was "opposed to any intervention in Afghanistan's internal affairs."[43]

Amin's Distrust of the Soviets

Soviet intervention was already a pervasive fact in a less obvious way than sending in army divisions. By that time no significant decision was made, no important order issued in either the civilian ministries in Kabul or the Afghan armed forces without the clearance of Soviet advisers. The advisers had obtained the authority to hold up orders until they countersigned them. What had started in 1978 as the Soviets' helping out by replacing purged officials and officers had developed into a general dependence upon them that must have been as galling to Amin as it was needed by him. He wanted to keep them at arm's length, but he publicly acknowledged the aid. The Soviet Union was providing "whatever we can use" to defend Afghanistan, Amin said in a reference to armaments, but "we will ourselves defend our country . . . [and will] never give this trouble to our international brothers to fight for us."[44]

This hid a burning anger toward the Soviets. It surfaced 6 October when Amin's top deputy, Shah Wali, invited all Communist ambassadors in Kabul except the Chinese one to a meeting. Safronchuk represented Puzanov, who four days earlier had also declined to join other Communist ambassadors at the inauguration of a PDPA training institute. At the meeting Wali accused Puzanov of complicity in the abortive attempt to remove Amin, saying Puzanov was in Taraki's office when he assured Amin on the phone that it was safe to go to the palace. Wali also charged Puzanov with harboring Watanjar in his embassy around 14 September, and possibly the other three fugitives, while denying knowledge of their whereabouts. Safronchuk was embarrassed by the accusation, some of the ambassadors later told diplomatic colleagues, but did not deny it. Wali said that Amin had been invited to Moscow to discuss the Afghan domestic situation but had refused to go.[45]

As a result of the distrust of Puzanov, and as a warning to the Kremlin about meddling in Afghan affairs, Wali as foreign minister formally asked the Soviet Union to replace its ambassador.[46] According to diplomatic protocol, such a request is mandatory, but Moscow deliberately took its time as a sign of unwillingness to yield to the weak client state. Not until 19 November did Puzanov make his required farewell call on Amin.[47] On 1 December the president received his successor, Fikryat A. Tabeyev.[48] While Puzanov's career had peaked in 1952 as a candidate member of Stalin's last Communist party presidium (politburo) and then skidded downward to what was the relatively minor job in Kabul when he arrived there in 1972, Tabeyev was a fifty-one-year-old official still on the rise, being given what was clearly a post of growing importance. A Tatar educated in economic sciences, he had been first secretary of the Tatar region's party committee, a job that rated a seat on the central committee in Moscow from which Puzanov had been dropped in 1971. Safronchuk remained in Kabul with the new ambassador.[49]

During this period, Amin always answered questions of foreign correspondents, whom he seemed to like to meet, by asserting that relations with the Soviet Union were "very cordial and friendly. . . . Whatever we need from the USSR we can get without the smallest obstacle," he said on a typical occasion.[50] On 27 October he told the new American charge d'affaires, Archer K. Blood, that Soviet aid was increasing and necessary because Afghanistan could not maintain itself very long against foreign interference without it. The aid had no strings or preconditions, Amin said. Blood reported that, Amin's usual fluent English faltering as he tried to convey great sincerity, the president said that, "if Brezhnev himself should ask him to take any action against Afghan independence, . . . he would not hesitate 'to sacrifice even one second of his life' in opposition to such a request."[51] In an interview a few weeks later, Amin said:

> We are convinced that if there were no vast economic and military aid from the Soviet Union, we could not resist the aggression and conspiracies of imperialism, its leftist-looking allies and international reaction, and could not move our country toward the construction of a socialist society. . . . There is no limit [to the volume of Soviet aid, and that volume] completely depends on our capacity to absorb and utilize it.[52]

Amin said stories of bad relations between Moscow and Kabul were only "our enemies' propaganda."

But while flying over Afghanistan in late September, Kosygin noticeably failed to send the conventional message of greetings to its leader, in contrast to his message to Taraki on a March 1979 overflight[53] and Brezhnev's to Karmal while passing over a year later.[54] And Amin boycotted Puzanov's embassy reception on the sixty-second anniversary of the Bolshevik Revolution. Amin did, however, send one of his usual flowery messages to Brezhnev and Kosygin on the anniversary.[55]

An unusual sidelight on the Soviet attitude—or, perhaps, on Soviet flexibility—was cast by the clearance on 17 September by the tight and politically sensitive Soviet censorship of a novella for publication in an Uzbek literary journal published in Tashkent.[56] A semifictional account of the Afghan revolution written by a March 1979 visitor to Afghanistan, its hero was Amin. Last-minute editing eliminated the name of Taraki, replacing him with "our Khalq party" or an anonymous revolutionary mentor of Amin's. There was a negative reference to "the errant Babrak Karmal" and allusions to his having maintained a schoolboy acquaintance with a man who became Daoud's chief of political police, with the result that Khalq rather than Parcham had borne the brunt of official repression. If the Kremlin was thinking then of bringing Karmal back to replace Amin, the author and the censors obviously had not been told.

Police Policies

Amin realized the need to seek popular support for his new regime. That meant ameliorating policies for which he was himself primarily responsible but which he could conveniently blame on Taraki. On 18 September he spoke to the old AGSA, now KAM, which he had used for over a year to repress brutally any suspected opposition. He told its members that they were "patriots defending the interests of the masses and are at their service. They [the masses] must realize that you never wish to see any individual arrested without cause, tortured without cause, or in trouble without cause."[57]

Amin did not bother to explain the circumstances under which a person might be tortured with cause. He and the police understood that torture was a routine tool, in fact always had been, in Afghanistan, and the Communist use of it was notable more for quantity than quality. He accepted $6.7 million worth of Soviet equipment for KAM—including, perhaps, the latest KGB torture technology?—that was tied to a strengthened Soviet advisory role in the police organization. But at the same time, he installed his nephew, Assadullah Amin, as head of KAM to protect his interests.[58]

An extraordinary revolutionary court was established by Amin's decree on 23 September to review the cases of those imprisoned since the April 1978 coup.[59] Kabul Radio began announcing the release of what were implicitly political prisoners: 60 the first day, 70 the next, 152 the following, 170 the next, and so on. Karmal's regime later charged that "only a few scores from several thousands of political prisoners were set free while hundreds more were shoved into Pul-i-Charki prison daily."[60]

On 24 September Amin appointed a commission to write a constitution—Afghanistan had had none since the coup—and it began to work two weeks later. Although the PDPA had followed the Soviet Communist Party's example of adopting a resolution denouncing the cult of personality after Stalin had died, as if Taraki were a comparable figure, the opening of the constitutional commission showed that Amin was no more bound by it than Khrushchev or Brezhnev were. The official English-language account of the opening said that "the commander of the Great Saur Revolution" was welcomed with "continued clapping and expression of sentiments [presumably warm] and throwing of petal of flowers,"[61] and at later sessions he was termed "the brave commander" who gave scholarly speeches.[62]

A *loya jirgah* was held in early December to create a National Organization for the Defense of the Revolution. Safronchuk had long been urging this as a way of drawing non-Communists into cooperation with the regime. Moscow Radio had even reported plans for it during the summer, but Kabul had not, and Amin only began mentioning it in late September. "The main aim of the organization," a Soviet newspaper explained, "will be to explain to people in the countryside and the cities the tasks of the April revolution and the principles of the state's foreign and domestic policy."[63] Until then, there had been little or no effort to explain, only to command.

Trying to convey a sense of progress, Amin announced 3 October the success-ful completion of a census taken between 15 June and 5 July. It showed Afghanistan's population to be 15,540,000.[64] Only after Amin had fallen was it admitted that, "with the insurgency going on in most of the provinces, none of his statisticians could venture out of the main towns. . . . He ordered the Central Bureau of Statistics . . . to work on certain estimates based on a few samplings carried out by the United Nations a few years ago . . . and thus give the mass media a round figure."[65] If census takers could not reach the villages, neither could representatives of the new national organization to explain official policies.

Death sentences said to have been given in secret trials of Qadir and Keshtmand were commuted on 8 October to fifteen years' imprisonment, and Rafi's twenty-year sentence was reduced to twelve years.[66] Amin might thus have hoped to win some favor in the military units that resented his treatment of PDPA officers. If so, he was mistaken. The 7th Infantry Division garrisoned at Rishkur on the western outskirts of Kabul mutinied on 14 October. The government blamed "traitorous elements" led by two generals, and it put down the mutiny with jet strikes and other force, but the reported key to the trouble was anger over the treatment of Watanjar. Watanjar's old tank brigade at Pul-i-Charki was not called upon to help quell the trouble, apparently for fears about its loyalty, and Amin instead had to rely on the outdated tanks of his armored militia.[67] Amin later called it a coup attempt rather than a mutiny.[68] Whatever it was, Amin's hold on those remaining in the ranks was weakening.

While a show of leniency was made for Qadir and Keshtmand, few others were so fortunate. The interior ministry began on 16 November posting lists of names of persons who, it said, had died in prison from April 1978 to September 1979 or were no longer in Afghan prisons. The public assumption was that all on the lists had died or been murdered in prison, but the government insisted it had released many and they had secretly fled the country—a story no one believed. The list was said to number 12,000. A public reading of it was confusing, because many Afghans use the same small number of Islamic names. After scenes of strong emotion in front of the ministry building, women weep-ing, men screaming, much angry shouting and wailing, the reading was halted.[69] If Amin's government had hoped to blame Taraki's and thus improve its own standing with the public, the effort was a failure that only reminded people of the brutal nature of the continuing PDPA administration.

How many deaths can be blamed on Amin is lost in inadequate records, deliberately hidden atrocities, and the accusations made later by those Afghans who benefited from the Soviets killing him. Reporting to the State Department on "an amicable, relaxed meeting with President Amin" on 27 September, the then United States charge d'affaires, J. Bruce Amstutz, commented that it was "hard to realize in talking with this friendly fellow that it was he [who] has been directly responsible for the execution of probably 6,000 political opponents."[70] At different times Karmal said publicly that "tens of thousands of Afghan patriots became the victims of Amin's executioners,"[71] and that "Amin . . . mercilessly destroyed more than one million, one and a half million people with mass murders."[72] Official estimates of the number of PDPA members killed by Amin—predominately Parchamis, although this point was not made by Karmal's Parcham-based government—ranged from 1,000 to 4,500,[73] although Soviet media never used a figure higher than 500.

If that were not bad enough, Amin's successors accused him of planning a far worse bloodbath, from which they claimed to have saved the country. "If the change had not come about in December," Karmal said, "they had it worked out so that three to four million people of Afghanistan would have been killed . . . . The regime was a hundred times more cruel than Pol Pot was in Cambodia."[74] This grew wilder in the telling. In December 1980, Karmal said that "if the December 27 [1979] change had not taken place . . . I can tell you that half of the population of Afghanistan would have been sacrificed today."[75]

After discounting such political language, it is still possible to believe that Amin was responsible—both as Taraki's strongman and on his own—for well over 6,000 executions in addition to the innumerable deaths in the civil war that he had such a major role in starting. The United States State Department reported cautiously only that "executions numbered in the thousands,"[76] and Amnesty International cited reports of 9,000 persons still unaccounted for after thousands had been officially listed as dead.[77]

Relations with Other Countries

Amin gave the appearance of trying to create a popular base for his government with a new constitution, the defense organization, claimed leniency toward political prisoners, gestures to appease conservative Islamic elements,[78] and other steps. He also sought to improve relations with neighboring countries. By the time he became president, Kabul had for months been loudly trumpeting accusations against Pakistan and Iran. They were held responsible for the unrest in Afghanistan, which the regime could not admit was virtually a civil war that it had provoked. Foreign training and arming of rebels was the reason for guerrilla warfare, Afghan media charged, and Moscow elaborated the charge. But if angry statements had done nothing to change the situation, then Afghanistan would try a softer approach in hopes of talking its neighbors—particularly Pakistan, where the guerrilla camps were more extensive and better organized—out of permitting insurgent activities across their borders.

Taraki discussed this with the Pakistani president in Havana, asking him to seal the border. General Zia replied that Afghanistan could just as well seal its side of the border. They both knew that the Durand Line was geographically impossible to seal by any ordinary police or military means. Zia added that Pakistan was prepared to have international inspection of the border and of refugee camps inside Pakistan,[79] which then held 194,000 Afghans—a figure that doubled during Amin's three-month reign. Nothing came of that, but Amin picked up the effort to improve relations with Pakistan. In his initial speech as president, his first mention of foreign affairs was a curt and cool expression of seeking continued friendship with the Soviet Union. "Every informed individual in the country can intelligently perceive its importance," he said bleakly. Then Amin turned to Pakistan and said he was interested in eliminating misunderstandings. He hoped Zia and his de facto foreign minister, Agha Shahi, would visit Kabul as soon as possible. "We are also interested in similar contacts with the official and responsible persons in Iran," Amin declared,[80] not trying to fill in the names because of the turmoil in Tehran under Khomeini's religious leadership.

On 29 September Kabul renewed invitations to Zia and Shahi. New outbursts of guerrilla warfare, and the Rishkur mutiny, however, were followed by new Afghan accusations against Pakistan.[81] Zia decided that sending Shahi to Kabul for preliminary discussions under these circumstances would be seen as a sign of Pakistani weakness. Furthermore, it might demoralize the guerrillas, to whose cause Zia was definitely committed emotionally while trying to keep publicly vague any commitment of logistical support. The official Pakistani analysis of Afghan approaches was that Kabul hoped to demoralize the resistance as well as talking Pakistan into restricting guerrilla operations.[82] As Zia's government held back, Amin's became more eager to talk. By early December it was sending word down to Islamabad that Shahi should come soon. Zia said later that the messages from Kabul had become frantic.[83]

The frantic tone could be interpreted as a desperate call for help. But that raises the question of what kind of help Pakistan was capable of giving against the possibility of a Soviet military move. Zia was too realistic to think that his own ill-equipped army, which as always was deployed facing India rather than along the Durand Line, might be able to influence the situation inside Afghanistan. Pakistan might offer more diplomatic support to Afghanistan, but what good would that be? Amin's eagerness to talk suggests that he was following in the footsteps of the Moosa Shafiq government and Daoud, turning to a non-Communist neighbor in an effort to balance and reduce Soviet influence.

Being a Communist, Amin has therefore been labeled by some observers as having been a potential Asian Tito. This overstates the situation. Amin was following some of Safronchuk's advice on domestic policies, such as creating the defense organization. But he lacked the domestic solidarity needed for successfully reorienting his nation. He also lacked much appeal to alternate foreign patrons because of his bloody hands and proven unpopularity. No one was very interested in propping up a tyrant.

So Amin was in too weak a position to hope that he could suddenly shift from Soviet support to some other source of the extensive economic and military aid plus technical and administrative expertise that he desperately needed. Even the Chinese, who were then sustaining the even more bloody-handed Pol Pot clique in its resistance to the Vietnamese takeover of Cambodia, were unavailable to rush to Amin's assistance. They were, from all indications on the Pakistani side of the border, even aside from Afghan and Soviet accusations, deeply involved in helping the guerrilla resistance to the PDPA regime. There was no reason for them suddenly to switch sides, though the Soviets had shown that to be possible by abandoning Somalia to patronize Ethiopia in 1977. Why rush to the aid of a man who obviously is being rejected by his own people?

Nor was there any motivation for the United States to help Amin in the way it had helped Tito sustain his defiance of the Soviet Union three decades earlier. Helping a national leader with solid domestic backing as a way of checking Soviet expansion in central Europe had been a reason then, but in the autumn of 1979 Amin had little backing and the Carter administration did not then see the Afghan situation as one of threatening Soviet expansionism. Although the United States tried to "explor[e] the possibilities for a less contentious relationship" with Afghanistan,[84] the country was not a high priority in American thinking. Worry about Afghanistan as a factor in Persian Gulf security would come later. Amin might qualify as a Tito in the sense of using Marxism for his own purposes, of converting it into a tool for national power. But, then, so would Stalin and Mao by that definition, but they did not have dominant power looming over them that they were so heavily dependent upon and so powerless to resist.

The Extent of Soviet Military Involvement

It simply was not physically possible for Amin's regime to divorce itself from Moscow. Soviets were running it. The Afghans had lost control of the essential levers of power to 1,500 or more Soviet officials in the civilian ministries and between 3,500 and 4,000 Soviet officers and technicians in the armed forces.[85] An estimated half of the 8,000 officers and noncommissioned officers of the Afghan army at the time of the coup had been purged for political reasons by October 1979.[86] When, in late October, a major offensive was launched by the army against guerrillas in Paktia province, on the Durand Line south of Kabul, Soviet military personnel commanded, ran logistics, and provided air power for the Afghan army. The offensive was a failure, however. In ten days newly supplied tanks, armored personnel carriers, MI-24 helicopter gunships, and other weaponry swept up to 40,000 refugees across the border while the guerrillas withdrew in the traditional insurgent way of not trying to stand against superior force. But when the offensive was over and the tanks returned to Kabul, the guerrillas reoccupied their old ambush sites and other positions.[87] As the Americans had found in Vietnam, it is possible for a strong anti-insurgency force to go anywhere it pleases, but it does no lasting good to sweep through an area, find few enemies to fight and thus few opportunities to reduce enemy combat strength, and then leave the area again to the enemy.

Paktia was one of the guerrillas' strongholds. Others running north along the Durand Line were Nangarhar province, whose capital is Jalalabad; Konarha and Laghman provinces, which make up most of the area known as Nuristan; and Badakhshan, which borders both Pakistan and the Soviet Union plus China at the tip of the Wakhan corridor. Another main area of resistance to the government was the mountainous central part of the country known as the Hazarajat. There were sporadic firefights in other areas, occasional uprisings against PDPA or Soviet activities, ambushes and guerrilla raids, and, beginning in early December, attempts to assassinate Afghan officials and Soviet advisers in Kabul. But in the autumn of 1979 the warfare had not reached the widespread extent that developed after the Soviet invasion.

Preparations for Intervention

General Pavlovskiy completed his study of the Afghanistan situation sometime in October and flew back to Moscow. What he reported to Defense Minister Dmitry F. Ustinov and other members of the Soviet politburo is not known, but it soon became apparent that the Soviet Union feared that the guerrillas in cooperation with disaffected Afghan army units might overturn the Amin government. During October the first steps were taken in the Soviet Union to prepare for a larger military role in Afghanistan than just sending in advisers, who had become commanders, and technicians, who were assuming larger logistical roles. Members of the Soviet Army reserve in Central Asia began to be called to active duty in order to raise two divisions based near the Afghan border to combat readiness.[88] These were mechanized infantry divisions that were normally maintained as shells with only 20 to 33 percent of their 13,000-man combat strength and with some but not all of their needed weaponry. The call-up and supplying of full military equipment to the divisions did not seem urgent, however; they did not reach full preparedness until early December. In November, a satellite communications ground station appeared at Termez when a military headquarters was established there and linked to the defense ministry in Moscow.[89]

The publicly expressed Soviet attitude toward Amin, never warm, became steadily cooler as the fruit trees in Kabul Valley turned golden and lost their leaves, and the winter winds began to sweep down from the Hindu Kush. By early December, Amin had almost become a nonperson to Soviet media, in the best tradition of a Beria or a Khrushchev. Tass marked the first anniversary of the friendship treaty by talking of the Soviet and Afghan peoples without mentioning the leaders of either, adding an unexplained reference to the treaty's providing for "conducting joint measures to insure the security, independence and territorial integrity of both countries."[90] The treaty in fact did not quite say that much. A few days later *Pravda* published a cheerful review of Afghan developments that attributed defense, economic, and social plans to vaguely anonymous organs of Afghan authority.[91]

But Amin could not be totally ignored. On 4 December, the eve of the treaty anniversary, Brezhnev and Kosygin addressed a message to him.[92] It was notable for two things. One was that the "cordial congratulations and friendly wishes," and the hopes of future successes, were all directed to the PDPA central committee and government units plus "the friendly Afghan people." There was no personal reference to the people's leader of the kind that such Soviet messages usually contain. Secondly, the message characterized relations as being "in the spirit of equality and revolutionary solidarity." Four such messages in Taraki's time had described relations of "comradeship and revolutionary solidarity."[93] Comradeship is a closer and more significant form of relations than equality in the Soviet scale of values.

As usual, however, Amin was not to be snubbed. He replied to his "dear comrades . . . esteemed comrades," saying he had "pleasure in sending sincere congratulations to you" as well as the Soviet organizations they headed. "Dear comrades," Amin concluded, "please accept best comradely wishes for health and new successes to you personally."[94] A few days later, Amin said the Soviet Union was fulfilling the treaty's provisions "very exactly and without deviation."[95] That is approximately what the Soviet Union, too, said about the treaty when its troops killed him three weeks later.

Chapter 7. The Correlation of Forces

If Soviet leaders had ever read Uncle Remus, they might have recognized in 1979 that they had gotten hold of an Afghan "tar baby". The years of cultivating a Communist party, in a country that Marx in his European economic frame of reference would never have recognized as being ready for Communism, had finally—if somewhat surprisingly—produced a regime to which the Soviets found themselves stuck.

A Kremlin student of the American involvement in South Vietnam should have noted some similarities with the increasing United States role there in the early and mid-1960s. Both Moscow and Washington had gone to the help of a government that was considered to be ideologically compatible, standing on a frontier against hostile manifestations of the rival ideology. Both provided aid and advice, both saw the aid absorbed without much visible effect and the client listening to the advice without changing his ways. Both sought ways to build up the client's base of popular support, but both saw those efforts sabotaged by a seemingly self-destructive urge to continue with narrowly rigid controls instead of broadening appeals.

The comparison should not, of course, be carried too far. There were important differences. While the governments in both Saigon and Kabul were guilty of torture and other human-rights abuses, South Vietnam was never accused of the large-scale executions that Afghanistan conducted. There were in the 1960s no "boat people" escaping Vietnam—they came after the Communist victory—but refugees began fleeing Afghanistan early in the Soviet involvement with Taraki. The PDPA regime practiced traditional Asian forms of coercion and terror with a greater rigorousness than the Saigon governments of the 1960s, reflecting the harsher cultural traditions and more violent history of the mountainous land than of the coastal and delta peoples. Afghan Communist leaders also showed less realism about what was possible and productive, not simply counterproductive.

The coercion that the Taraki and Amin governments used on their own people was not unlike what Stalin had practiced on the Soviet people in the 1930s. But the new rulers of Afghanistan lacked the preparation and the extensive system of supporting organizations that Stalin had built up. They did not have his thoroughness. Therefore, they had not insured that they would be able to bludgeon their country into submissiveness rather than just stirring it into rebelliousness.

The Soviet leaders of the 1970s, who as young men had made their careers by helping Stalin conduct his great terror in the late 1930s and stepping into the jobs of its victims, found their connection with Amin increasingly agonizing. The degree of Soviet control had not increased commensurate with the personnel, material, and prestige that Moscow had invested. For all their ability to dominate day-to-day operations of Afghan ministries and the armed forces through the advisers who had come to fill the role that traditionally belonged to colonial administrators, Soviet officials were unable to control the essential policies of the regime. They could not determine where Afghanistan was going, whether it was heading for some kind of smashup for PDPA rule or might jump the tracks of pro-Soviet Communism. They were being taken for a ride by Amin.

An obviously nettlesome awareness of this situation was shown by the Yepishev and Pavlovskiy missions to Afghanistan as well as the assignment of Safronchuk and other signs. But how to arrest the deteriorating situation? Kremlin leaders were faced with questions of what was politically and militarily possible inside Afghanistan, what was diplomatically possible in the face of the reaction that might be produced abroad by any greater involvement in determining Afghanistan's course. The aging Soviet leadership had shown itself in many ways both to be cautious about commitments, although increasingly willing to take risks abroad in places like Ethiopia, and to be determined to protect its concept of ideological, political, military, and economic interests with whatever assertiveness seemed necessary.

In the autumn of 1979, Moscow's perception of the problem presented by Afghanistan was shaped by the Soviet view of the world situation, of the Soviet role and power in the world, of relations with the West, as well as the view of the status of international Communism. It was also affected by domestic factors. The primary domestic one was the ethnic, linguistic, and religious similarity of Soviet Central Asian peoples to some of the peoples who were trying to reject a Communist regime south of the Amu Darya.

These factors not only affected the Soviet perception of the Afghan problem but also applied to the choice of methods for dealing with the problem. Little evidence was available to the outside world of the decision-making process in the Kremlin on such problems as Afghanistan; it is possible to study the background of Soviet thinking about other events; it is possible to understand the type of international problems that drew certain kinds of decisions from the closed and secretive circle of Soviet leaders.

Definition of "Correlation of Forces"

Soviet thinking about the world situation in which the Soviet Union has to operate, and which conditions its actions, is encompassed by one of the catch-phrases of the Leninist form of Communism: "the correlation of forces." As is the case with much of the Soviet terminology, the term seems to express an ideological approach to the real world and at the same time to be shaped by a shrewd appraisal of the way in which ideology has to be adjusted to world realities.

Correlation of forces is used by Kremlin spokesmen to refer to the relative strength of what they call socialism and capitalism. It has many aspects. One is political, involving the number of Communist countries in the world, their dynamism in international affairs, their prestige and self-confidence, as well as the strength and influence of Communists in other countries. Another is social, the Soviet view of class struggle and the influence that Marxist ideas have upon peoples throughout the world. A third aspect is ideological, concerning the extent of revolutionary forces as defined in the Soviet way of revolution leading to a Marxist system with a Leninist control imposed upon it—anything other than that system is by definition counterrevolution, and therefore bad.

Correlation of forces is also economic, primarily the industrial strength of Communist countries in relation to Western ones. It is the sheer weight of populations under Communist and non-Communist control, and the line-up of countries for, against, and neutral on Soviet policy. It is many things, usually trailing off into fuzziness in Soviet ideological writing so as to leave implicit all the factors that are meant.

But, over the years, it has come to mean one factor more than any other. That is raw military power. This aspect of the correlation of forces sometimes seems a bit embarrassing to Soviet ideologists. The claim that Communism is the wave of the future is supposed to rest on superior social and economic organization, not on the tips of bayonets. In the early days of the Soviet Union, when it was militarily weak, the always optimistic assessment of the changing correlation of forces in the world ignored that weakness and instead emphasized supposed support for the first socialist state by the downtrodden masses elsewhere and similar intangible things.

This began to change during World War II when the Soviet Union defeated Nazi Germany. It changed markedly in the 1970s when a steady buildup of Soviet military strength began to give Kremlin leaders some confidence that their country was equal to or perhaps in some ways even ahead of the United States in military power. It was this shift in military relationships rather than any political, social, economic, or other aspect of the world scene that most noticeably colored Soviet assertions in the 1970s about the changing correlation of forces.

Yet Soviet spokesmen try carefully to avoid simply defining the term in military ways. They seek a distinction between the correlation of forces and the conventional military concept of the balance of power. To link them would be to throw away the ideological basis for Soviet claims of moral authority in the world. This linkage would also create the risk of alarming the West, and therefore contributing to its rearmament. It is safe to brag about a change in a somewhat vague correlation of forces as a prideful assertion of superiority. But the military aspect of it has to be aimed at a more carefully selected audience that will applaud rather than react with concern. Since the change is represented as being historically inevitable and irreversible, it would be unwise to encourage efforts to reverse it.

Changed Definition in Action

By the 1970s the correlation of forces had changed sufficiently that Soviet leaders had begun to develop some self-confidence in the role they had long asserted for their country, that of a major world power. The 1972 "Basic Principles of Relations Between the United States of America and the Union of Soviet Socialist Republics," signed by President Richard M. Nixon and Brezhnev on the same day as the first Strategic Armaments Limitations Treaty (SALT I), recognized that "the security interests of the parties [are] based on the principle of equality."[1]

The new constitution adopted by the Supreme Soviet in 1977 contained three articles on foreign policy, a subject ignored by the 1936 "Stalin constitution" that it replaced. "The foreign policy of the USSR," it said, "is aimed at . . . consolidating the positions of world socialism, [and] supporting the struggle of peoples for national liberation and social progress." It also proclaimed "non-intervention in internal affairs" of other countries and "comradely mutual assistance with other socialist countries on the basis of socialist internationalism."[2] Those two provisions were in Afghanistan's case to come into conflict from a Western standpoint of what the words meant, but not as explained by Soviet and Afghan Communists.

The important fact was that Kremlin assertiveness in foreign affairs and the relative military strength on which it primarily depended had changed enough for the Soviet Union to take whatever action it felt necessary. For some time before the Communist coup in Afghanistan, Soviet leaders had—without referring directly to the military buildup of their country—been claiming that the correlation of forces had changed so much that the socialist system had become the dominant influence in international affairs.

"Socialism's positions in the world are steadily strengthening," Suslov, the chief Kremlin ideologist, said in a reiteration of this theme shortly after the invasion of Afghanistan. "The change in the correlation of forces in favor of socialism had created favorable conditions for the growth of the people's liberation struggle," Suslov asserted.[3] He avoided mentioning the military aspect. So did Brezhnev. Reporting to the Soviet Communist Party's congress in 1976, he said that "the switchover from cold war, from an explosively dangerous confrontation between the two blocs to détente, was related, above all, to the changes in the correlation of forces in the international arena."[4] Ustinov, the Soviet defense minister, also sought to place the emphasis on nonmilitary aspects. "The steady consolidation of the international positions, influence and authority of the Soviet Union and the entire socialist community," he said in 1980, "has led to profound changes in the correlation of forces in the world in favor of socialism."[5]

Karmal brought such generalized words down to the Afghan situation when he visited Moscow as president in October 1980. "The victory of the revolution in Afghanistan—a backward, semi-feudal and pre-feudal country—was made possible," he said, "thanks to the will and broad disinterested support of the hard-working people of our country, and the change in the correlation of forces in the international arena . . . . The historic victories of world socialism, led by the great land of the soviets, created the basic conditions necessary for this change in the correlation of forces."[6] This implied that Soviet power, not directly defined as military, stood behind the success of the Afghan revolution, but it was unclear whether Karmal meant the revolution in the sense of the April coup or in a more general way.

Military Buildup

The main component of the changed correlation of forces in the 1970s was a long, steady expansion of Soviet military strength. By the time of the Afghanistan invasion, it had continued for approximately two decades. The precise time at which the Soviet Union began the military buildup, which, as of 1982 showed no signs of slackening, has been the subject of some discussion among Western experts. It is variously dated from 1958 to 1965, with some subsequent variations in the rate of buildup as large items like new generations of intercontinental missiles were purchased. The earlier date is when Krushchev began to abandon his mid-1950s effort to save money on the military after a big Korean War-era weapons program. It is worth noting that Brezhnev was then Krushchev's Communist party secretary in charge of military industries as well as supervisor of the related portfolios of heavy industry and space programs. Brezhnev's career has been intimately linked to armaments, so that there is no surprise in the overriding priority given to the military within the strained Soviet economy during his tenure as party boss after 1964. That priority is never directly stated. The Soviet Union's own figures on the subject of military expenditures are generally regarded by Western specialists as deliberate disinformation. The announced Soviet military budget is considered by outsiders to be essentially a political signal, not a measure of the ruble costs of the Soviet armed forces and related military spending, nor does it give an accurate indication of the burden on the economy of that spending. It remained almost constant at around 17 billion rubles (about $25.5 billion at the 1981 official rate of exchange) for many years during which the numbers and technological complexity of Soviet weaponry increased greatly.[7]

Soviet sources have disclosed, however, that in 1970 the actual military expenditure was about 50 billion rubles and in 1972 some 58 billion. By the early 1980s, according to some estimates, it might have doubled the 1972 figure.[8] By 1971, as the United States began to reduce its Vietnam war effort, and possibly even earlier, Soviet military spending passed the United States level.[9] It continued to widen the gap even after the United States in the late

1970s started increasing its real, inflation-adjusted level of defense expenditures.

More significant than the amounts of money that the Soviets have spent on military power, however, have been two other aspects. One is the burden that the armed forces have placed on the Soviet economy and people; the other is the resulting ability of the Kremlin to project Soviet power into the world in fulfillment of the constitutional provision for consolidating socialist positions and supporting the Communist version of liberation struggles.

The burden that the small, closed Soviet leadership has over the years seen fit to place on their economy and their consumer public for the sake of military power is a measure of several things. The leaders represent military measures principally as a defensive reaction to the West's military effort and attitude, as a necessary protective counter to a dangerous world situation. Western analysts, on the other hand, regard the burden as a measure of the leadership's commitment to the long-term goal of a Communist world. That does not depend upon a Western judgment that the Soviet leadership intends to conquer the world by force; it is a more sophisticated assessment that military power has broad political implications aside from making it possible to take armed advantage of specific, narrow situations. By this way of examining the Soviet outlook, the military burden on the Soviet economy is a significant indicator of determination to preserve Communist power—including in new places like Afghanistan.

Until 1975, the CIA estimated that the Soviet Union was devoting between 6 and 8 percent of its gross national product to military purposes. That percentage was not much higher than the United States' proportion, which was running between 5 and 6 percent.[10] But in 1975 the CIA drastically revised its estimate after long argument within the United States intelligence community and the receipt of some new data from Soviet sources. It raised the estimate to an 11 to 13 percent burden on GNP. By 1979, with Soviet military spending continuing to grow 4 or 5 percent a year but overall economic growth slowing to only about 2 percent annually, the military burden on GNP had risen to an estimated 12 or 14 percent.[11] Some other estimates, most notably by a former CIA analyst, William T. Lee, and also by Chinese sources, run significantly higher than the CIA ones. They suggest that by 1979 the military growth rate was 8 to 10 percent and the proportion of Soviet GNP being devoted to military strength had reached 18 percent. Soviet statistics showed that long-term investment in economic growth was being sacrificed to military power, and the evidence of living standards in the Soviet Union showed that consumer interests were also being sacrificed.[12]

Guns before Butter

The point of importance in considering the Soviet attitude toward the problem in Afghanistan, then, is that Kremlin leaders had for some time been prepared to put a higher priority on the consolidation and expansion of the Soviet bloc and its realm of influence than upon the immediate or future improvement of material well-being of their own people. They were willing to sacrifice consumer comfort for world power. A related point is that the ideological justification for Soviet Communism is greater material prosperity for the people, more fairly distributed, but the practical result of the system at least in the 1960s and 1970s and going into the 1980s was to subordinate theoretical Marxist economics to military might. A rise in Soviet living standards that became evident in the late 1950s had probably halted by the late 1970s, and there were in the early 1980s signs of a decline.

The Soviet Union had become a country that was well adapted to generating armed strength, but that was the only thing at which it was noticeably successful. Its ideology was of declining appeal in the Third World; its model of economic development that had seemed to have a faddish pertinence to poor countries in the 1950s and 1960s had lost its appeal for almost all developing nations by the 1980s; its diplomacy was having decreasing success in projecting an image of Soviet peacefulness and Western imperialistic war-mongering. But its military power was increasingly able to bestride the world, influence distant situations, intimidate some countries and worry others, and, in places like Afghanistan, insure that a Communist regime once installed in power by whatever means would not be put out again, that the Marxist wheel of history would have a military chock put under it to prevent its rolling backward.

Stages of the Buildup

The thinking behind the long Soviet military buildup can be traced in Soviet military writings.[13] In the 1960s the predominant concern was developing strategic nuclear forces in order to attain strategic parity with the United States, which then had a lead in the ability to deliver nuclear weapons at long range. Once launched, the intensive Soviet development of strategic nuclear power continued virtually unchecked so that by the early 1980s it was in some ways superior to United States capabilities and in other ways catching up rapidly. That was typical of the Kremlin way: continuing to arm beyond the point of parity. The Soviets thus rejected United States military thinking that there is no rational point—and certainly no economic justification—in striving for superiority; that instead superiority has no utilitarian value and is likely simply to make for a more expensive arms race.

Once parity had come in sight in strategic forces, Soviet military thought turned more toward conventional forces in regional contexts: the balance of combined arms in Central Europe, along the China border, and in other areas. Those forces were also built up to a point of superiority. Still the improvement of them continued, because programs to make more and better tanks, like those to build missiles, are never stopped once they are started.

Finally, with confidence that the Soviet Union itself was adequately defended in both strategic counterforce and in conventional terms, the attention of military theorists began to focus on the projection of conventional power beyond the Soviet bloc. A major effort to develop equipment for that projection apparently was decided upon by the middle or late 1960s.[14] That was shortly after the Soviet Union found itself embarrassingly unable to counter with naval forces the United States blockade of Cuba during the October 1962 missile crisis and incapable of delivering more than a token amount of weapons and military equipment to the Congolese forces of Patrice Lumumba and Antoine Gizenga during the early 1960s' power struggles in the central African state that became known as Zaire.

Soviet military shipyards began building more of the kinds of naval vessels needed to establish an armed presence in distant waters—without slackening the production of missile-launching submarines for the strategic forces—and troop and freight ships. Aviation industries began building long-range transport aircraft capable of delivering troops and equipment throughout the Eastern Hemisphere with minimal dependence upon refueling facilities—without, again, slowing the output of combat planes and the expansion of helicopter production. In 1960 the Soviet Union had 160 surface warships and a sealift capability of 873 cargo vessels and tankers. Although the decision to invade Afghanistan did not directly involve naval power, it was made against the background of general military projection capabilities in which sea power had become an important component. At the time of the decision, there were 340 surface warships and 1,725 sealift ships.[15] The statistics obscure a general improvement in types of vessels to make those built in the 1960s and 1970s more capable of operating worldwide.

In 1960 the Soviet Union had no long-range military transport planes. Planes of the Aeroflot airline fleet that comprise part of the military airlift capability— troops arrived in Kabul in December 1979 on special flights of Soviet commercial airliners in addition to air force planes—were not well adapted by range or freight-carrying characteristics to serve military needs. There were in 1960 only 140 of the AN-12 turbo-prop military transports whose 460-mile range make them tactical rather than strategic airlift planes—a role they filled in the 1979 invasion by shuttling troops in from Soviet Central Asia. By that time there were 575 AN-12 transports. Some of the 150 strategic airlift planes in operation brought heavy weapons to Afghanistan—particularly the big AN-22 turbo-props that can carry 88 tons for 2,530 miles.[16]

As important as these specific tools for projecting power abroad was the Soviet strategic nuclear might and intimidatingly massive conventional strength. This nuclear and conventional capability provided an umbrella under which power could be employed for a particular goal with little fear that hostile military pressure at another point of an adversary's own choosing would force abandonment of that goal. No more would the Kremlin find itself in Stalin's situation in 1946 when he was forced by the implications of unmatched American nuclear power to withdraw Soviet troops from northwestern Iran and to see the collapse of the Communist government that he had installed in the Azerbaijani region of that country and the adjacent Kurdish separatist movement that he had encouraged. That was the one time since the Soviet Communist state had come of age militarily that it had to abandon a foreign Communist regime,[17] although there were later and different cases (as in Egypt) of withdrawing Soviet advisers from places where the regimes never were Communist as distinct from left nationalist. It was a whole new world by the time a Communist regime got into deep trouble in Afghanistan. The correlation of forces had changed.

Changes in Military Theory

With the acquisition of equipment for projecting Soviet conventional military power into parts of the world beyond the historically limited range of Russian foot soldiers came a change in the publicly voiced theory on the purpose of Soviet armed forces. This was noticeable by the early 1970s both in the speeches and writings of Soviet leaders, especially military ones, and in the indoctrination given to Soviet soldiers by Yepishev's political officers. Two American specialists on Soviet military doctrine, William F. Scott and Harriet Fast Scott, have traced the change in the two decades before the Afghanistan invasion.[18] The new outlook justified and explained the invasion in Marxist terms.

When in 1961 Soviet ability to intervene at a distance was small, a key textbook entitled *Marxism-Leninism on War and the Army* said that Communists "are mobilizing the people's masses to struggle to prevent a new world war, and also for prevention or suppression of local wars unleashed by the imperialists."[19] This emphasis on public opinion rather than force was a continuation of the mid-1930s effort to rally others against Hitler's Germany when the Soviet Union felt itself weak and threatened, and the late 1940s effort to marshal world opinion against nuclear weapons when the United States had a monopoly on them. In 1965, as examples of giving "every possible assistance, including military, to peoples struggling with the not-yet-disarmed imperialists," a Soviet commentator cited the provision of arms and advisers to Egypt, Cuba, Algeria, North Yemen, Indonesia, and North Vietnam.[20] This carefully avoided any commitment of Soviet soldiers as part of "every possible assistance."

But the gradual change was under way, most notably in successive editions of *Marxism-Leninism on War and the Army*. The 1968 edition defined the external function of the Soviet armed forces as protecting the socialist community—that is, members of the Soviet bloc—from "the danger of war coming from the imperialist camp."[21] An edition in 1977 redefined that function: "The international obligation of socialist states is to give support and aid to liberated countries in suppressing the imperialist export of armed counter-revolution."[22] Seemingly a widening of the defensive perimeter, this had a more offensive than defensive meaning when interpreted in the Soviet way of defining what are liberated countries and other terms. For instance, Afghanistan under Amin became a liberated country, and the rebellion of its people was explained as a manifestation of counterrevolution exported from Pakistan.

A turning point in the public expression of Kremlin thinking came in 1971 with a statement by Marshal Andrei A. Grechko, who was then the Soviet defense minister and soon after became a Communist party politburo member. The Soviet armed forces, he declared, "serve the noble cause of defending the entire socialist community and the worldwide historic victories of Communism." If that seemed deliberately vague, he made it clearer in 1974:

> At the present stage the historic function of the Soviet armed forces is not restricted merely to their function in defending our motherland and the other socialist countries. In its foreign policy activity the Soviet state purposefully opposes the export of counter-revolution and the policy of oppression, supports the national liberation struggle, and resolutely resists imperialist aggression *in whatever distant region of our planet it may appear.*[23]

Other Soviet military men elaborated this theme. "Greater importance is being attached to Soviet military presence in various regions throughout the world, reinforced by an adequate level of strategic mobility for our armed forces," a 1972 book said. It went on:

> In those cases wherein military support must be furnished to those nations fighting for their freedom and independence against the forces of *internal reaction* and imperialist intervention, the Soviet Union may require mobile and well-trained and well-equipped armed forces. In some situations the very knowledge of a Soviet military presence in an area in which a conflict situation is developing may serve to restrain the imperialists and *local reaction*, prevent them from dealing out violence to the local populace, and eliminate a threat to overall peace and international security.[24]

By including "internal reaction" among those whom Soviet forces might have to fight abroad, the authors clearly indicated that Soviet leaders envisaged the possibility of intervening in the Third World to help local Communists.

This led into a circular argument that was also expressed by another 1972 Soviet military writing: "The intensification and expansion of the international task of the Soviet armed forces also objectively conditions the need for their further strengthening. The situation requires increasing attention to questions of Soviet military construction."[25] Thus, the growing strength of the Soviet military machine made it possible to intervene "in whatever distant region of our planet," while the possibility of intervening became a justification for still further strengthening the machine. It was an argument to warm the hearts of the Soviet military-industrial complex, a very real factor in a closed system whose top man had long been associated with both political control of the armed forces and weapons production.

The two-hour political study periods supposedly held twice weekly for all servicemen began in the early 1970s to prepare them for the possibility of having to fight outside the Soviet bloc. The old emphasis on defending the motherland had long since been replaced by exhortation to defend the socialist community. It was broadened further to stress an international role. A textbook used for these study periods, *V. I. Lenin on the Defense of the Socialist Father-land*, edited by a deputy of Yepishev's, said in a 1977 edition that,

> in contemporary conditions, peoples conducting a just liberation struggle or defending their revolutionary gains have the possibility not only of resisting the aggression of the largest imperialist powers but also of defeating them by relying on the sure support of the Soviet Union, the other countries of socialism *and on socialist armies*. This increases the resolve of peoples to struggle and develop the initiative of revolutionary forces.[26]

An article addressed to servicemen by the Soviet defense ministry newspaper *Krasnaya Zvezda* ("Red Star") a few months after the Afghanistan invasion said that,

> Under the new historic conditions, the Soviet armed forces' international mission has broadened. . . . Strengthening the armed forces' combat might and increasing their combat readiness means fulfilling your patriotic duty to your people and motherland, serves the cause of defending the peoples of all the socialist community states, and means fulfilling an international duty.[27]

Soldiers then serving in Afghanistan were specifically told that they were fulfilling that international duty.

The political study textbook picked up a theme that had developed in the 1960s of praising the role of Soviet military men sent—ostensibly as volunteers—to fight for the Spanish republic against the Falangists in Spain from 1936 to 1938, for the Kuomintang against the Japanese in China from 1937 to 1939, and in other cases. The fact that Stalin had purged virtually all Communists who made it back to the Soviet Union after Generalissimo Francisco Franco's victory in Spain was conveniently ignored. The theme was later expanded. A Soviet diplomat disclosed in 1969 that during the Korean War almost two decades earlier Soviet pilots "downed dozens of American planes."[28] The Scotts suggested that one purpose of such disclosures was "to prepare both [Communist] party members and personnel in the Soviet armed forces for possible similar 'external functions' in the future."[29]

Reviewing the broader picture of Soviet military writings up to the end of the 1970s, they concluded that "the USSR is politically preparing the population and members of the armed forces for potential military activity overseas. . . . [They] are being psychologically prepared for the possibility of the actual involvement of Soviet military personnel in local wars. Further, . . . Soviet military personnel apparently are being trained in such actions." That was written before the Afghanistan invasion and the beginning of Soviet battlefield deaths fighting Afghan resistance.[30]

An additional interpretation can be read into the shifting Soviet line on foreign wars. It is a 1970s recognition in the Kremlin of the failure of attempts from the mid-1950s onward to convert Third World countries to Communism through either the appeal of local Communist parties or the Soviet penetration possible in aid programs. Therefore, it had become not only militarily possible but also politically necessary to seize upon any Communist foothold, however tenuous, and ensure its consolidation with armed might. While the ideologues still talked as if Marxism had an appeal that would for political reasons alone win over distant peoples, military men were dealing with the more realistic thesis that only a limited number of persons in any particular country could be converted and force would then be required to protect them. The appeal of Communism as preached from Moscow was waning, the world Communist movement was split into numerous factions that defied Soviet efforts to maintain control in the traditional Stalinist way that had benefited Russian nationalism, and the growing military might and confidence of the Soviet Union had become the answer for continuing to expand Kremlin influence.[31]

It has also become the answer for holding onto existing areas of Soviet influence. The same literature that recalled examples of Soviet military intervention in such non-Communist countries as Spain and China in the 1930s additionally cited the Soviet crushing of the Hungarian freedom fighters in 1956 and of the "Prague spring" liberalization in Czechoslovakia in 1968. The political study textbook, for instance, called these examples of helping the local people defeat counterrevolution.[32] The important distinction was not clearly made between sending small numbers of military men whose theoretical status of volunteers enabled the Soviet government to pretend there was no official intervention in places like Spain and sending the Soviet Army across borders.

Brezhnev Doctrine

The Western outcry over the armed suppression of Czechoslovak liberalization produced a statement in *Pravda* that became known as "the Brezhnev doctrine." It stated:

> There is no doubt that the peoples of the socialist countries and the Communist parties have and must have freedom to determine their countries' path of development. However, any decision of theirs must damage neither socialism in their own country, nor the fundamental interests of other socialist countries, nor the worldwide workers' movement . . . This means that every Communist party is responsible not only to its own people but also to all the socialist Communist movement.[33]

Seven weeks later Brezhnev personally elaborated on this. He said that,

> When external and internal forces hostile to socialism try to turn the development of a given socialist country in the direction of restoration of the capitalist system, when a threat arises to the cause of socialism in any country—a threat to the security of the socialist commonwealth as a whole—this is no longer merely a problem for that country's people, but a common problem, the concern of all socialist parties.[34]

Who would decide when damage might occur, when a threat might arise? The extensive consultations with Warsaw Pact allies before the Czechoslovak invasion, and the involvement of them in that invasion, indicated that the Kremlin wanted to spread the responsibility as widely as possible. The same pact pattern was followed in the winter of 1980–81 in the political discussions and military alerts around Poland. But there was never any doubt that the final decisions were being made by the Soviet Communist Party's politburo core group on foreign and security issues.

Phrased in terms of socialist countries, the Brezhnev doctrine was presumed in the West to apply only to the Soviet bloc, to those situations in which Communism was firmly and long established. The Afghanistan situation showed, however, the Soviet leaders' attitude that lay behind it to apply more broadly than to just East Europe and undoubtedly also to Mongolia.[35] The correlation of forces had changed since 1968. The Soviet armed forces had extended their reach far beyond East Europe or Mongolia. The doctrine could, therefore, be expanded. A basic assertion remained the same. As in the Hungarian and Czechoslovak cases, the claim was made in Afghanistan that the Soviet Army had been invited in by authorized local elements to help protect the legitimate government. This claim was difficult to sustain in all three cases, the most so in Afghanistan.

After the Afghan action, the doctrinal expansion was explained by a Soviet publication:

> What is the international solidarity of revolutionaries? Does it consist only in moral and diplomatic support and verbal wishes for success, or does it also consist, under justified, extraordinary conditions, in rendering material aid including military aid, all the more so when it is a case of blatant, massive outside intervention [by others]? The history of the revolutionary movement confirms the moral and political rightness of this form of aid and support . . . . Now that the system of socialist states exists, to deny the right to such aid would simply be strange. Under conditions where such an extreme necessity arises the Soviet Union acts in full accordance with the norms of peaceful coexistence enshrined in international enactments. To refuse to use the potential which the socialist countries possess would mean in fact avoiding fulfilling an international duty and returning the world to the times when imperialism would stifle any revolutionary movement with impunity as it saw fit. In this case, to fail to come to Afghanistan's aid would have meant handing over the Afghan revolution and peoples to be torn to pieces by the class enemies, imperialism and feudal reaction.[36]

So it had become a self-assigned duty of the Soviet Union to decide when to intervene in aid of revolutionaries who, in however shallow a way, could be identified as Marxists, however small and weak their local support, however rejected they were by "class enemies . . . and feudal reaction" aside from blaming foreign imperialism for the rejection. Another Soviet publication elaborated that "Non-interference is a good thing, but the principles of international law do not exist in a vacuum . . . History and politics cannot always be fit in legal formulas. There are situations when non-interference is a shame and betrayal. Such a situation developed in Afghanistan."[37]

Defense Minister Ustinov declared that it was the Soviet Union's "noble mission" to help "peoples struggling for their independence and sovereignty and for their revolutionary gains." That, he said, was what his troops were doing in Afghanistan.[38] What is in the Communist ideology the clinching argument— citing an appropriate quotation from Lenin—came in April 1980, at the height of the Soviet rebuttal to foreign criticism. Rather than "leave the Afghan revolution in the lurch, prey to the counterrevolution," a Soviet journal aimed at foreign audiences said, the Soviet Union

> proceeded from the behests of Lenin, who wrote back in 1915: the socialist state would if need be help the oppressed classes of other countries "using even armed force against the exploiting classes and their states." Lenin ridiculed the "recognition of internationalism in words, and its replacement in deed by petty-bourgeois nationalism and pacifism . . . in practical work."[39]

Pattern of Changing Attitudes

Changing Soviet attitudes on expanding Kremlin influence as well as holding onto existing areas of influence have been charted by Stephen S. Kaplan as showing an interesting pattern. His study of the use of Soviet armed forces for political purposes between June 1944 and August 1979 found that all but one of twenty-six cases of coercion to expand Soviet borders or authority occurred in the 1944–51 period. That was the period when Stalin was trying to benefit from World War II to broaden his control around the Soviet periphery. Military coercion in the Third World did not begin until 1957, and three-quarters of the forty-one incidents counted occurred between 1967 and 1979. Throughout the 1944–79 period, however, Soviet armed forces were periodically active in forty-three cases of coercion to maintain fraternal Communist regimes—thirteen times in East Europe to protect them from internal challenges, nine times also in East Europe to put down disloyalty and make them accept Soviet directions; and the remaining twenty-one cases because of external military or political trouble.[40] The Soviet intervention in Afghanistan might be included in all three of those categories, but the study's cutoff time came before that action. The picture Kaplan presents is of a power that had always been prepared to use its armed might for expanding and then holding onto its area of influence, but whose armed might had become increasingly useful for that purpose by the 1970s.

"Vietnam Syndrome"

The change in the correlation of forces, and the attitude that widened the application of the Brezhnev doctrine, had another major aspect besides the growth of Soviet military strength and political confidence. That was the perception in Moscow—and not just in Moscow, but in much of the rest of the world—of a change in the United States. United States military power remained great, especially in strategic nuclear terms. But the political will required to use that power, especially in terms of conventional forces, was thought to have declined. This was the "Vietnam syndrome" that developed from the failure of the United States to protect the Saigon regime, or friendly regimes in Cambodia and Laos, from North Vietnam and its Khmer Rouge and Pathet Lao comrades. As defined by a Soviet writer, "The 'Vietnam syndrome' implies Americans' condemnation of United States armed intervention in other countries and Washington's attempts to play the part of a world gendarme. . . . It also implies demands for a reduction in military expenditure and support for a policy of seeking agreement with the socialist countries."[41]

The Kremlin considered the United States to be both chastised and fatigued by its Indochinese war effort, shaken up and more cautious about becoming involved in foreign tests of strength. It was not that Vietnam had proven to the Soviets that getting involved in a counterinsurgency situation was necessarily a losing proposition. It was just that the United States had gone about it badly. "The experience of American aggression in Vietnam has indicated that, however strong a military presence may be from a military-technical standpoint, it will not of itself guarantee the achieving of political success," said the same 1972 Soviet book that said mobile forces may be required to restrain local reaction.[42] This was a point that Safronchuk was supposed to remember in 1979. But the important lesson that the Soviet Union thought *it* learned from what the Americans learned in Vietnam was that there was more latitude for Soviet maneuvers in the Third World without encountering meaningful American opposition.

Détente

This belief began to develop with the antiwar movement in the United States in the late 1960s. It was one of the elements in the development in the early 1970s of what became known as détente, accompanying a Soviet desire for more Western economic help for a troubled economy and a hope of slowing down Western military modernization while the Soviet arms buildup went rapidly ahead. "The purpose of détente was to make the process of international change as painless as possible," a Soviet commentator explained.[43] By change he meant the continued spread of Soviet-style Marxism.

There was a fundamental disagreement on what was intended by the 1972 Nixon-Brezhnev basic principles and other elements in the loose package that constituted détente. The United States was hoping for an end to Soviet pressures around the world, in such things as arming and encouraging forces seeking to disrupt the established order in the Third World, and for moderation in the direct use of the Soviet armed forces to make political changes. Henry A. Kissinger, who as Nixon's national security adviser shaped détente, wrote later that "we interpreted [it] as a denial of the Brezhnev doctrine," among other things.[44] Whether that was realistic at the time, and then conditions changed, or was simply an illusion perpetrated on the American public out of naiveté or, worse, for domestic political purposes, later became a subject of debate, often acrimonious.

Brezhnev made it clear at the 1976 Soviet Communist Party congress that détente would not restrict support for Communists abroad or those whose leftist leanings raised Kremlin hopes that, like Fidel Castro in Cuba in 1959, they might after their nationalistic victories be brought into the Communist camp. Brezhnev was under attack from Soviet ideological hardliners who feared the American hopes might be realized, that Soviet support for Third World revolutions would slacken as a result of détente. He replied,

> It is quite clear that détente and peaceful coexistence are concerned with interstate relations . . . Détente does not in the slightest way abolish, and cannot abolish or change, the laws of class struggle. Nobody can count on Communists' becoming reconciled to capitalist exploitation in conditions of détente . . . We do not conceal the fact that we see détente as a way to create more favorable conditions for peaceful socialist and Communist construction.

Using a favorite expression of Stalin's, Brezhnev went on that "life itself refutes" the reproach of unidentified hardliners who felt détente had frozen the world situation. "It is enough to recall the great revolutionary changes that have taken place in the world in recent years," he declared.[45] He apparently was referring to the Communist victories in Indochina after the 1972 détente agreements.

What might in retrospect be termed détente in East-West relations at the end of World War II was replaced by the Cold War. Most historians felt that the basic factor was an expansion of the area of Soviet control and Western resistance to it. The new détente of 1972 was similarly followed by continued Soviet aggrandizement. Again, as in the late 1940s, it took several years for the West to begin to react with any real alarm. Afghanistan more than any previous situation was found to be alarming. In the seven and a half years between the 1972 basic principles and the invasion of Afghanistan, the United States had seemed to the Soviet Union to be reacting weakly to Soviet activities in the Third World, western Europe reacting hardly at all. In 1973 the United States Congress had passed a resolution limiting the war powers of the president. Other congressional action and investigations had the effect of limiting presidential powers for using covert actions to influence foreign affairs in competition with Soviet overt or covert activities. Although the American withdrawal from Indochina was immediately followed by a show of force over the Cambodian capture of the freighter Mayaguez, that was an aberration, a postscript to the Indochina involvement. The Carter administration came to pride itself on not using United States soldiers in combat situations—while Soviet advisers and finally, in Afghanistan, ordinary soldiers were increasingly being injected into militarily hazardous situations that offered significant potential political gains for the Kremlin. Each time that hazard was braved without United States or other Western reaction, and the gain achieved, the way seemed open to seize another opportunity and try to exploit it. That was the road to Afghanistan.

Angola

The first important signpost was in Angola. The Soviet Union had been providing small amounts of military aid to the Popular Movement for the Liberation of Angola, or MPLA from its Portuguese initials, since 1964. The guerrilla war that this group and others in Angola and in other Portuguese "overseas provinces" fought against Lisbon's control finally led in 1974 to the collapse of Portugal's African empire. Until about the middle of 1975 Soviet aid to the MPLA was worth only some $54 million, but as Angolan independence neared, another $200 million to $300 million worth was put in. By that time the United States was involved. The CIA had been authorized by the Ford administration in January 1975 to provide $300,000 worth of covert support for a rival to the Marxist MPLA, the National Front for the Liberation of Angola, or FNLA, which was already receiving Chinese aid. The United States program was expanded in July to a $14-million program to arm FNLA and a third faction struggling for the succession to the Portuguese, the National Union for the Total Independence of Angola, or UNITA. UNITA also began receiving South African aid,[46] which automatically blighted it in the eyes of black African countries.

As United States and South African aid increased, so did Soviet involvement. A contest developed among the three Angolan groups for power when the last Portuguese administrator left. This turned into an East-West test of strength. Kissinger and the Ford administration had intended covert United States involvement to be a signal to the Soviet Union of American determination to resist in the post-Vietnam era Soviet expansionism under the guise of supporting local "wars of national liberation."

Instead, Moscow got the opposite signal. On 19 December 1975 the United States Senate, alarmed by the prospect of American involvement in another Third World guerrilla war, but also partly inspired by domestic American political considerations entirely divorced from Africa, voted to prohibit the spending of money for operations in Angola. The House concurred 27 January 1976. The MPLA won control of Angola's capital behind Cuban troops flown in by the Soviet Union.[47] Although the civil war continued, with UNITA holding much of the country, the Soviet Union had found little obstacle to helping a Marxist group into power in the era of détente. It had also demonstrated that its new airlift and shipping capabilities could operate effectively at the greatest distance from Soviet territory yet to have been profoundly influenced, aside from the different case of the already consolidated Cuban foothold. Soviet soldiers, who in 1975 had a book of military geography added to their recommended reading list, were told that the Angolan case was of great significance for all peoples "fighting today for national liberation."[48]

Horn of Africa

The next important signpost on the road to Afghanistan was in the Horn of Africa. Having defeated the Chinese in a 1960s aid competition in Somalia, the Soviet Union and such allies as East Germany had provided aid and advisers to Somalia in return for the use of military facilities at Berbera and other benefits. One of Somalia's neighbors—Ethiopia—with whom it had a territorial dispute over desert inhabited by ethnic Somalis, had received United States aid and advice for years. Ethiopia sent troops to fight alongside the Americans in the Korean War, and it leased a site for an important United States communications station.

The overthrow of Ethiopian Emperor Haile Selassie in 1974 began a period of change.[49] While the Ford administration in 1976 tried to lure Somalia away from the Soviets with offers of military aid, revolutionary Ethiopia was drifting away from the United States and beginning to explore Moscow's offers of arms. In February 1977, Colonel Mengistu Haile Mariam consolidated his control of the military junta in Ethiopia; in April he expelled the United States military mission and ordered the communication station closed; and in May he visited Moscow to sign a friendship declaration. Cuban advisers began to appear in Ethiopia. Renewed offers from the Carter administration of United States aid for Somalia led that country by late summer to invade the disputed Ethiopian territory, thinking it had American acquiescence. Although the United States then hastily withdrew its arms offer, a reversal of Soviet alliances was under way.

In November, as Soviet and Cuban aid to Ethiopia increased, Somalia broke its 1974 friendship treaty with Moscow and expelled Soviet and Cuban advisers. By early 1978, some 1,000 Soviet military advisers, hundreds of millions of dollars' worth of Soviet armaments, and about 15,000 Cuban combat troops— all rushed to Ethiopia by the Soviet strategic airlift fleet and followed up by seaborne supplies—had driven back the Somali invaders.[50] A Soviet general, one of Pavlovskiy's senior deputies and later his successor, commanded the operation. The Cuban Communist Party newspaper *Granma* reported that Cuban pilots, tank crews, artillerymen, and armored infantry brigades had taken part in the fighting.

The United States, which two years later ended up with a qualified agreement to use the Somali military facilities at Berbera, some of them built by the Soviets, proved as incapable of halting the Soviet action in Ethiopia as it had been two years earlier in Angola. Some United States officials talked of trying to blockade Ethiopia, throwing down the gauntlet to Moscow over the military projection of its power. But there was neither general acceptance within the administration, nor congressional backing, nor popular support for a confrontation with the Soviet Union over the Horn of Africa.

President Jimmy Carter's national security adviser, Zbigniew Brzezinski, sought to deter the Soviets by threatening to link progress on a new strategic arms limitations treaty, SALT II, to their restraint in the Horn. Carter disavowed this.[51] The administration also ruled out the use of United States grain sales to the Soviet Union as a source of leverage on Soviet policies in the Third World. As a result, as in Angola, Kremlin leaders found that a somewhat risky exercise of their new power projection capabilities had met with no significant resistance and a political gain had been achieved.

As in Angola, there was a question of how long that gain would last. Despite the continuing presence in Ethiopia of Soviet advisers and at least 14,000 Cuban troops, Mengistu resisted Moscow's pressure to establish a Marxist political party and allow some power to devolve from the junta to it.[52] This unwillingness to dilute personal power by trying to build a broader base of political support parallels Amin's resistance in the autumn of 1979 to Soviet advice in Kabul. The bloody terror by which both regimes consolidated their power, and the numerous ill-coordinated or entirely separate rebellions within the ethnic empires of Ethiopia and Afghanistan resulting from brutal attempts to rule primitive countries, are also strikingly similar. So are the Soviet roles, although proxy Cuban troops were used in one, real Soviet Army troops in the other one closer to home.

Regardless of the eventual outcome in Ethiopia, or in Angola, of whether the Soviets and their friends would have to pack up and leave as they did from Egypt, Somalia, and some other countries, the Soviet experience in moving into those two countries without encountering meaningful resistance from the United States or the world community as a whole was an important element in the thinking about Afghanistan in 1979.

South Yemen

Another was South Yemen, known formally as the People's Democratic Republic of Yemen. Although little noted in the world community, developments there in the late 1970s offer a striking parallel to later developments in Afghanistan, almost a testing ground for actions in Kabul.

When the British quit trying to hold South Yemen against Soviet-supported guerrilla warfare and gave it independence in 1967, the Soviets quickly switched from supporting one liberation front to cultivating the other one that had won control of the new regime. By 1969 the government had declared "scientific socialism" to be its ideology. Its Marxism alienated it from Arab neighbors whose aid was desperately needed. The bleak, impoverished land's only economic asset, the port of Aden, had been reduced in value by the closure in 1967 of the Suez Canal and the resulting sharp decline of shipping through the Red Sea and past Aden. South Yemen therefore turned to the Soviet Union, which was happy to establish a strategic foothold in Aden.[53]

Most Soviet aid was military. Armed forces that expanded to 23,000 men in a population estimated at only 1.8 million became dependent upon Soviet advisers for training, supervision, and technical support. Beginning in 1973 Cubans trained a separate 20,000-man Yemeni militia. The ruling National Front absorbed the local Communist party, the People's Democratic Union, in 1975. But the head of state, Salim Rubayya Ali, was less attracted by the rigid Soviet command system of politics and economics than the system then being advocated by China of Maoist popular spontaneity. He also responded to efforts by anti-Soviet neighbor Saudi Arabia to lure South Yemen away from dependence on Moscow. The Soviet expulsion in November 1977 from Somalia had, however, increased Moscow's stake in South Yemen at a time when Aden had become the key staging post for the Soviet Union's operations in nearby Ethiopia. The dry dock from Berbera was towed across the gulf to Aden, and other Soviet military equipment shifted, so that Aden became the main Soviet military facility on the Indian Ocean.[54]

On 26 June 1978, a week after Soviet planes had flown 5,000 Cuban troops into Aden from their successful offensive against Somalia, the South Yemeni militia with Cuban support attacked Ali's palace and the defense ministry. Cuban pilots flew air strikes against both places, and Soviet ships in the harbor bombarded the palace. Ali was captured, tried as a "leftist opportunist" who had attacked the "correctness of our relations with the socialist community, first of all with the Soviet Union," and immediately executed. The National Front's secretary general, Abd al-Fattah Isma'il, who believed in orthodox Leninist control, became the top man.[55]

The comparisons with the Soviet overthrow of Amin are strong. In both cases the president, although following generally Communist policies and heavily dependent upon the Soviet Union, came to be seen in Moscow as endangering Soviet interests by becoming increasingly independent. In both cases that man was killed by military action and a more acceptable Marxist installed in his place. In the Yemeni case, however, it caused little world outcry. There were three reasons. The most important was that the Soviet Army did not have to move across a border to impose its control. Another was the general obscurity of developments in Aden, a land whose Soviet ties had isolated it from its Arab neighbors and the Western world. News from Aden was secondhand and little noted, partly for the third reason, which was that the long-established Soviet and Cuban position there tended to erode outside interest in internal developments. South Yemen had been written off to the Communist world, almost like Eastern Europe, and therefore whatever internal changes occurred were considered to be just Communist business.

Those attitudes still held in October 1978 when South Yemen proclaimed itself a Marxist state—a step for an Arab Moslem country that was possible only because of the tight control system set up by the Soviet, Cuban, and East German advisers, complete with concentration camps.[56] In Moscow in October 1979, Isma'il signed a friendship treaty with the Soviet Union and agreed on extensive links between his National Front and the Soviet Communist Party[57]—

the kind of links that have also developed between that party and the Afghan PDPA.

Nevertheless, there occurred in April 1980 a Yemeni development that Karmal might take as a warning that loyalty to Moscow also needs to be accompanied by domestic results. Isma'il was ousted. He had failed to build up popularity at home for himself or for a regime that was publicly seen to depend upon the presence of between 12,000 and 25,000 Soviets, Cubans, and other Communist troops and advisers.[58] He had also failed to end the country's economic stagnation, which was increasingly being blamed on the Soviet Union, and he was mistrusted by Arab neighbors upon whom the Soviets hoped to shift the burden of supplying aid to South Yemen. By 26 April Ali Nasser Mohammed had in South Yemen acquired the same package of top titles that Karmal then held in Afghanistan: president, prime minister, and secretary general of the only political party.[59] More flexible than Isma'il in regional relations, he proved to be an equally trustworthy friend of the Soviets.

Lessons Learned

What lessons for future conduct in world affairs did the Soviet Union draw from the cases of Angola, Ethiopia, and South Yemen? Soviet media did not say. Instead, they emphasized the help that had been given to peoples fighting for what the Communists contend to be national liberation. In Suslov's February 1979 description of Afghanistan as a nation that had adopted "a socialist orientation" in the previous five years, he also named Angola and Ethiopia. Curiously, he did not name Cambodia and Laos.[60] The lessons for Moscow had to include the Vietnamese invasion of Cambodia without any Western reaction beyond words, only China reacting forcibly by bloodying Vietnam's northern border. On the other side of the ledger, faintly, was the effort by the United States, Belgium, France, and Morocco to repel Angolan-based rebels from invasions of Shaba province of Zaire.

From the overall picture of contention and strain in the Third World in the latter part of the 1970s, the lessons that some senior American officials thought the Soviets probably drew[61] were encouraging for further foreign adventures in a mix of political and military action that depended upon each new opportunity for expanding Soviet influence. In this view, the Kremlin learned that the United States was unwilling to become physically involved in halting the use of Communist military power to establish client states in new and distant parts of the world or to tighten the Soviet grip on old clients.

This was particularly true when Moscow used the fig leaf of proxy involvement to cover its own role in military action. The employment of Cubans, transported, armed, and financed by the Soviet Union, was a strong irritant to United States opinion because of the troubled American relationship with

Castro. But it was also a convenient excuse for United States opinion not to focus on these operations as in fact extensions of the kind of Soviet-backed aggression that the United States had fought in Korea and thought it was fighting when it began to get committed in Vietnam.

That proxy excuse would not be possible in Afghanistan. It was in the backyard of Soviet Central Asia, and the situation there was argued in Moscow as a danger to the Soviet Union—not a place to entrust to Cubans or other proxies. Perhaps the proxy cover was no longer so important. The cumulative effect of the earlier adventures was to have lowered the Soviet threshhold of sensitivity to foreign reactions by the time the Soviet Union sent the Soviet Army into a nation that it had never before occupied.

Two other developments in the late summer and autumn of 1979 affected Soviet thinking about American staunchness. One was the excitement in the United States about the presence in Cuba of "a Soviet combat brigade," some 2,600 Soviet soldiers with tanks and artillery. Although it had long been there, its discovery became a political issue in the United States. That caused the Carter administration to declare its presence unacceptable. But, after a few weeks, President Carter in effect accepted it on 1 October.[62] He also appealed for the episode not to affect ratification of SALT II, which he had been seeking unsuccessfully to push through a skeptical United States Senate. The next day the United States announced agreement to sell the Soviet Union twenty-five million metric tons of grain.[63] The message received by the Kremlin was that of United States vacillation and unwillingness to disrupt business as usual because of Soviet military activities abroad. After the invasion of Afghanistan, some United States officials said that the administration's backing away from the initially tough position on the Soviet brigade was, more than any other single episode, the most important influence in the Soviet leadership's decision that the invasion was an acceptable risk in terms of international reaction.[64]

The other development was the seizure 4 November of American hostages in Iran. In the first few weeks after the United States embassy in Tehran was captured by Iranian students, the Soviet Union indicated through broadcasts and press reports that it would not have been surprised if Carter quit abjuring the use of force in foreign affairs. After all, the Soviet Union would in the same circumstances have been very likely to use force. At the time the Afghanistan invasion was being mounted, then, Moscow was half-expecting an American military action next door. The United States Navy was gathering in the Arabian Sea, and there was talk of United States Air Force and ground forces' preparations. Perhaps the Kremlin would have liked the United States to strike quickly at Iran. That would have provided an American focus for Third World outrage that would reduce attention on Soviet action in Afghanistan, the way the British and French invasion of the Suez Canal area in 1956 had diverted world opinion from the Soviet crushing of the Hungarian freedom fighters. But even without a quick United States military action, the hostage situation served

Soviet interests. It meant that American opinion and officials were absorbed in the Iranian problem. So was much of the rest of the world. With others distracted, it would be easier, safer to move into Afghanistan.[65]

The way had been prepared by the changed correlation of forces, by the expansion of the Brezhnev doctrine, by Angola, Ethiopia, and South Yemen, by the Soviet brigade in Cuba, and by the American hostages in Iran. And by Amin, whose thwarting of Soviet plans for Afghanistan in the summer of 1979 was followed by an only partial compliance that seemed to the Kremlin to amount to defiance. It only remained for the Soviet leaders to evaluate all their own domestic factors, and the Afghan and international ones, and then decide what to do about the worrisome neighbor on their Central Asian border.

Chapter 8. The View from the Kremlin

As political and military support for the Kabul regime dwindled, starting with the Herat uprising in March and continuing through a summer and autumn of further army mutinies, rising popular opposition, and an increased refugee exodus, the Soviet Union and the United States each reacted to events in its own way. For Moscow that meant searching for some means of stabilizing and if necessary salvaging a deteriorating situation. This Soviet search was complicated by an apparent desire to keep a friendly and cooperative PDPA government in power in Afghanistan at the least cost in direct Soviet involvement or in provoking Afghan or foreign repercussions. But as the autumn went on and the situation worsened, the prospective costs kept rising.

Washington tried to monitor the obviously growing Soviet role in Afghanistan. In addition to observations from its embassies in Kabul and Moscow, the United States paid increasing attention to pertinent data from its routinely extensive collection of satellite reconnaisance and electronic intercept intelligence about Soviet activities. As it watched Soviet military moves, from the March alert of the strike force at Ferghana onward, the Carter administration searched for a way to turn its concern about the possible loss of Afghan sovereignty into some meaningful form of support for the independence and neutrality of Afghanistan.

This American search was complicated by more than just the distraction in its final period of the hostage problem in Iran. One complication lay in trying to coordinate attitudes with allies who lacked interest in the subject, leaving concern over Afghanistan pretty much up to the United States and thus turning it into a super-power issue. Another was a certain indecisiveness within the Carter administration on such issues that had not yet ripened into crises. Afghanistan was seen in its usual way as a small, remote country, no doubt of importance in East-West terms but traditionally viewed primarily as a gateway to South Asia. U.S. concern was not then focused on Afghanistan in relation to Iran and the Persian Gulf. The third complication might be called "the Pol Pot complex."

As the Afghan situation worsened, the Western world was already wrestling with a moral dilemma over Cambodia, or Kampuchea. It opposed on principle the Vietnamese invasion of Cambodia at the end of 1978 to replace with a puppet government the regime of Khmer Rouge leader Pol Pot. Since its 1975 defeat of the American-backed government in Phnom Penh, that regime had killed uncounted hundreds of thousands, perhaps millions, of persons in a brutal effort to remake the country. Opposing the Vietnamese aggression—a continuation of centuries' old imperialist expansion of the Tonkinese or northern Vietnamese—logically implied support for Pol Pot. China supported him, working through Thailand, America's closest associate in Southeast Asia. But his barbarities made it difficult for the United States to do so, leaving it in an equivocal position.

Just so was the awkward situation emerging in Afghanistan. Because Amin was different more in degree than in nature of brutality, his regime was not the kind that the Carter administration, with its emphasis on human rights, could readily support. Yet it seemed to be endangered by a Soviet takeover that the United States also could not support. This difficult situation plagued the United States, affecting both attitude and actions. Opposing Soviet imperialism became the dominant theme, but not without some misgivings. The United States did business with Amin, because he was the de facto leader of Afghanistan, but never welcomed his takeover with the kind of chilly greetings that Brezhnev and Kosygin sent.

Soviet Missions to Afghanistan

The Soviet search for solutions involved numerous missions to Kabul, just like the many American visits to Saigon during the war there. In each capital a web of connections was woven from the threads of training programs, economic support schemes, advisory arrangements, and other efforts to improve the client state's immediate situation and long-term prospects. In each case the insurrection-disrupted economy became more and more dependent upon outside financing while the local armed forces were increasingly armed and operated on the patron's model and even his direction. This is not to equate the Afghan and South Vietnamese political situations; they were strikingly different. But the mechanics of Afghanistan 1979 and Vietnam 1964 were notably similar.

From the Herat uprising onward, Soviet missions and American warnings against Soviet interference in Afghan internal affairs developed almost in parallel. The Kabul and Moscow media accusations of American, Pakistani, and Chinese involvement in rebellions against the Taraki government that accompanied blaming Iran for the Herat uprising, and the rushing of new Soviet weaponry, advisers, and technicians to Afghanistan immediately after the uprising, produced the first major United States warning. The State Department denied on 23 March 1979 any United States interference in Afghan internal affairs and added:

> We expect that the principle of noninterference will be respected by all parties in the area, including the Soviet Union. No useful purpose is served by false and provocative reports about outside interference—especially when they occur at the same time as increased Soviet activity in Afghanistan. We can only wonder at their intent. We would regard external involvement in Afghanistan's internal problems as a serious matter with the potential of heightening tensions and destabilizing the situation in the entire region.[1]

The Yepishev mission to Afghanistan came two weeks later. Just as Yepishev's visit to Czechoslovakia in 1968 was a major step toward the invasion of that country, so his mission to Afghanistan apparently was one of the decisive steps toward the December 1979 invasion. He found the Afghan armed forces weakened by defections, divided by Khalq-Parcham infighting, damaged by the purging of non-Communist officers and noncommissioned officers, and therefore in need of greater Soviet involvement.[2]

His visit was followed by a survey of the situation by a group of middling-ranked KGB officials. In addition to its foreign espionage duties, the KGB is responsible for suppressing dissent in the Soviet Union. In Afghanistan, the group presumably found missing the kind of political and police controls needed to do the thorough job that was done at home. During the approximate period of that visit, the State Department issued its second public warning. Occasioned by the Bala Hissar mutiny and the probable use of Soviet advisers to help suppress it, the statement warned against outside interference and said it would be regarded very seriously. A few days earlier, on 2 August, Brzezinski made a speech that his aides informed reporters had been cleared with Carter. The security adviser said the United States had exercised prudent restraint when its ally the shah had been ousted from Iran. "We expect others similarly to abstain from intervention and from efforts to impose alien doctrines on deeply religious and nationally conscious peoples," Brzezinski said.[3] Aides described this as a warning to the Soviet Union not to intervene to prevent the collapse of the Communist regime in Afghanistan in the face of popular opposition.

Such warnings, and later ones, were ineffectually vague. There is a good rule in diplomacy against making specific threats of what will happen if some undesired action is taken. Aside from creating their own reaction and likely exacerbating a situation, such threats give the antagonist a way of calculating the gains and losses of his prospective action so that he can decide whether it is worth going ahead. It is better to leave the losses uncertain enough to deter him by worry over how the ledger will eventually balance out. But the United States' vagueness did not leave much room for uncertainty. That had been removed by the lack of significant American reaction to earlier Soviet foreign adventures, especially in Ethiopia, and repeated White House assurances that such things as SALT II completion and ratification and as grain sales would not be thrown into the balance.

The vagueness had a more profound reason than diplomatic tactics, however. It was a result of senior American officials' failure to focus on the problem. In several earlier cases, from the Soviet action in Angola through the Soviet brigade in Cuba episode, State Department officials had drawn up lists of possible ways of bringing pressure against the Soviet Union to penalize it for what the United States considered to be violations of international norms of behavior. None had been studied very carefully or gotten beyond the list making stage. During the summer and autumn of 1979 officials did not even get that far on Afghanistan. The Carter administration simply issued warnings without thinking through what should lie behind them, what would be done if they were ignored. According to some senior officials involved in this, there was a positive reluctance to face the prospect of some United States action being needed if the warnings went unheeded and the momentum toward greater Soviet involvement in Afghanistan continued.[4] The warnings looked good on the bureaucratic record. They showed that the administration had not been unaware of the situation. But that was about all they were—a bureaucratic record.

And the overall record on this and other problems was so long that warnings were devalued. They were being issued constantly to the Soviets on a variety of subjects: Don't put on trial certain dissidents, don't use former American naval and air facilities in southern Vietnam, other things. As the Soviet Union went ahead and did these things, and nothing happened, each new warning seemed less important. There was an argument within the State Department about this. Some officials contended that, rather than hectoring the Soviets continually, the United States should reserve its warnings for major occasions. That way, they might be seen in Moscow as being individually more meaningful.

As it was, the Soviet attitude toward the repeated warnings about Afghanistan was summarized by a senior State Department official as being, "Bug off."[5] The special advisor on Soviet affairs to the secretary of state, Marshall D. Shulman, described the situation more elegantly: "The weight of our views was diminished by the frayed state of United States-Soviet relations and the fact that we had already invoked the prospect of damage to United States-Soviet relations and SALT on several other issues."[6]

Having heard it all before, Moscow did more than give a dusty answer. It counterattacked. American warnings about Soviet interference were met with Soviet accusations of American interference, and Chinese, Pakistani, and Egyptian as well. "On our part," Brezhnev said later, "we warned those concerned that if the aggression were not stopped we would not abandon the Afghan people at a time of trial."[7] Diplomatic messages were given to both the United States and Pakistan telling them to prevent guerrillas from crossing the Durand Line from camps in Pakistan.[8]

The Pavlovskiy mission probably was the decisive one. The then seventy-one-year-old general, who retired from the ground forces command a year after the Afghanistan invasion and was replaced by his deputy who had commanded the Soviet and Cuban offensive in Ethiopia in early 1978, was accompanied by about a dozen other generals and a large support team. They had had time to size up the growing opposition before Taraki's meeting with Brezhnev on 10 September. Pavlovskiy can be presumed to have reinforced the reports that Safronchuk and the KGB *residenta*, or station chief, were sending back to Moscow about the need for a fresh approach without Amin. But the denouement of the September effort to remove Amin presented a new and more perilous situation. With the flight of Watanjar and other officers with strong military backing from Amin's wrath, as well as Amin's unwillingness to do much more than pay lip service to Soviet advice, Pavlovskiy stayed on in Afghanistan for longer than he had needed eleven years earlier to plan the invasion of Czechoslovakia.[9] By the time his mission left in October, Shulman guessed later, it had come "to the conclusion that Amin had to be removed, that as long as he was there the regime was headed for disintegration."[10]

At the time Pavlovskiy was in Afghanistan his purpose was not clear to the United States. It did not bring the mission up in its diplomatic contacts with Moscow. Instead, Pavlovskiy was one element in the thinking that went into the continued American public warnings. On 19 September, responding to a press disclosure of the Soviet alert at Ferghana, the State Department said that "The United States is opposed to any intervention in Afghanistan's internal affairs."[11] Shulman made a similar statement 16 October.

By early December, American concern had deepened, although diluted by the hostage situation in Iran, as a result of intelligence reports on Soviet military moves. On 4 December the State Department summarized publicly what it knew of an increased Soviet advisers' "role in support of the Afghan military, especially in the area of command and control functions" and in planning and executing offensives against the guerrillas. Beginning on that day, in Washington and in Moscow, United States officials met six times with Soviet officials to express concern.[12] The last meeting was just a few hours before the Soviet overthrow of Amin became known. "The level of discussion was such that there could be no mistake about the authority and official character" of the United States warnings, Shulman told Congress later, but he described "these exchanges as unsatisfactory Soviet responses to our expressions of concern about their intentions."[13] On 19 December the United States notified a number of allied and friendly nations that its intelligence reports showed that a Soviet force of several divisions was preparing for combat in Afghanistan.[14] Three days later, after further press reports, the State Department sought to focus world opinion on the situation by telling reporters of the Soviet buildup north of the Amu Darya and expressing apprehension about the implications not only for Afghan sovereignty but also for the security of Pakistan and Iran.[15]

The Reasons for Soviet Intervention

The Soviet Union was by then long past the point of being affected by United States warnings or world opinion. Soviet explanations, offered after the invasion, of the situation before it, need to be taken with caution. But there is no reason to doubt that the Kremlin believed one key point: that the PDPA regime was in danger of collapse. The situation was naturally blamed primarily on outside intervention, although the role of domestic opposition was admitted when the black label "counterrevolutionary" was put on it. In what became an oft-used phrase, Soviet media explained that "an undeclared war" had been launched against the Kabul regime, with a general offensive impending, such as "to threaten the very existence of the Democratic Republic of Afghanistan as an independent and sovereign state."[16] Soviet help was needed "to prevent democratic Afghanistan from losing its gains," a Russian editor explained.[17] This, in Communist terminology, was a recognition that the 40,000 or so men left in the defection-weakened Afghan army; the 4,000 or more Soviet advisers, helicopter pilots, and technicians working with and commanding them; and the small Soviet garrison providing security at Bagram air base were not enough even to hold the situation, much less to turn it around. "By the end of 1979 the Afghan army was demoralized and was not capable . . . of preserving the integrity of the country," another Soviet writer said, and Soviet aid projects had to be halted because of security problems, areas sown to grain crops declined and food shortages occurred, and government work deteriorated.[18]

"The Afghan state was on the verge of disintegration," according to a deputy of Ponomarev's handling Soviet Communist Party relations with the PDPA. "To leave the Afghan revolution without internationalist help and support would mean to condemn it to inevitable destruction and to permit an access to hostile imperialist forces to the Soviet border."[19]

The Soviet politburo had to choose. It could abandon its support for a regime that under Amin was intractable and unsuccessful, cut its losses to prevent the disgrace of going down with him and the possible loss of thousands of Soviet lives if the guerrillas overwhelmed Kabul. Or it could plunge deeper into the developing Afghan quagmire. It is doubtful that pulling out was ever more of a real option than it was for the United States in Vietnam around 1964 or 1965. Except for Iranian Azerbaijan in 1946 and Chinese Sinkiang in 1943, the Soviets had never pulled out of a country under similar circumstances. In East Europe and Mongolia it had instead tightened up controls. The whole activist history of Soviet involvements abroad argued against quitting, against letting a Communist position once seized be relinquished, letting the wheel of history turn back.

But the ideological and bureaucratic momentum for going in deeper needed rationalizing. The Soviet leadership had a number of reasons for making the decision to send the Soviet Army into Afghanistan. Afterward, while defending its action to the world, it explained some of them. The explanations were separate from accounts of how events were supposed to have unfolded in the invasion period. The explanations were also probably separate from, or only part of, the actual thinking in the Soviet politburo. No inside, adequately informed account of that thinking had become available to the outside world more than two years after the invasion. The lack of any reliable version of the Soviet decision-making process on such older occasions as the Hungarian or Czechoslovak actions, or the involvements in Angola or Ethiopia, discouraged hope that the Kremlin would eventually yield its secrets on the Afghanistan decision. Nonetheless, from analysis of Soviet words and actions, not only in the immediate period of that decision but also in the broader framework that encompasses more general Soviet world concerns, an attempt can be made to assess the factors in politburo minds.

Defense

The dominant theme in Soviet explanations became the need to defend the security interests of the Soviet Union. This is a credible reason for incurring the costs of the invasion. The first rule of Communist power in Russia has always been protecting that power by whatever means are necessary. Soviet military literature talks of the need in earlier years to eliminate weak points in a nation's defenses by, for instance, taking over the Baltic states in 1940.[20] The Kremlin had always tried to avoid or eliminate instability or weakness on Soviet borders, almost seeming to prefer the predictability of a bordering Western ally like Turkey after World War II to the uncertainty of chaotic states like some in Eastern Europe before that war. As the Soviet Union grew stronger in the 1960s and 1970s, any uncertainty on its borders that caused military leaders concern over security requirements became less tolerable. The Afghan situation became intolerable.

The first authoritative Soviet account of the situation after the invasion, which was also the first official acknowledgment that the Soviet Army was in Afghanistan, set the theme. Under the pseudonym of Alexei Petrov, which is signed to authoritative articles, *Pravda* conceded on 31 December 1979 that there was local resistance within Afghanistan. This, in Communist terminology, was "by internal reaction, by forces that are losing power and privileges." But Petrov shifted the focus to what he said was an attempt of imperialism to take advantage of this. The fall of the shah had created cracks "in the notorious 'strategic arc' that Americans have been building for decades close to the southern borders of the Soviet Union," Petrov said in a harking back to the Dulles era. "In order to mend these cracks," the United States sought to bring Afghanistan under its control, but "our country made no secret that it will not allow Afghanistan's being turned into a bridgehead for preparation of imperialist aggression against the Soviet Union."[21]

Three days later *Pravda* elaborated that, "having lost their bases in Iran, the Pentagon and the U.S. Central Intelligence Agency were counting on stealthily approaching our territory more closely through Afghanistan."[22] Brezhnev's personal authority was given to this line in what was ostensibly an interview with him published ten days later by *Pravda*. He said there had been a "real threat that Afghanistan would lose its independence and be turned into an imperialist military bridgehead on our southern border."[23] Reporting six months after the invasion to the Soviet Communist Party's central committee, he claimed that plans "to create a threat to our country from the south have failed." Brezhnev added, "We had no choice but to send troops."[24] The central committee naturally announced that it "fully approves the measures taken" to repulse the creation of "a pro-imperialist bridgehead of military aggression on the southern borders of the USSR."[25]

With variations, these phrases were repeated endlessly in Soviet media and by such leaders as Defense Minister Ustinov and Foreign Minister Gromyko. One variation was that, "as long as an unstable situation exists near the USSR's southern borders," pressures could be brought to bear on them, and without the Soviet move "a state hostile to the Soviet Union would have existed" in Afghanistan.[26]

The shrillness of this line about possible Western aggression from Afghanistan against the Soviet Union increased as Western and Third World revulsion from the invasion became more obvious. The line can, therefore, be seen as an attempt to turn the condemnation of Soviet aggression around with a claim that the Soviet Army was only acting to prevent aggression by others. This had little impact in the outside world, which found the unsubstantiated contention to be unbelievable.

But as an indication of Soviet thinking the line remains significant. It overstates a real Soviet worry that dangers would be created by the replacement of a neutral if not friendly state on an ethnically and religiously sensitive part of the border by an antagonistic if not hostile state. The fact that the Soviet Union had itself undermined Afghan neutrality was irrelevant history. What concerned the aging, conservative Soviet leadership was a detrimental change. Kremlin planning had long accepted the existence of other antagonistic, even hostile regimes on the border, from Turkey to China, and had adjusted to the problems perceived to have been created by them. Adjusting to a hostile China in the 1960s had been difficult and, in terms of military movements, expensive. The Soviet leadership did not want to have to adjust again.

What was meant by "imperialist aggression" as a danger from a post-Communist Afghanistan? Soviet spokesmen never explained. But they seemed to have in mind more than just a traditional military invasion—which would have been totally illogical in that rugged part of the world remote from any potentially important enemy's logistical base. Occasional, terse Soviet references to religious and ethnic problems in the Central Asian republics and a handful of reports from the region about continued hostility to Russian colonial rule—for instance, a 1978 Tajik riot against Russians in Dushanbe—suggest a kind of danger that made the Kremlin more apprehensive about the Afghan border than any remote possibility of armies' attacking across it. A factor in the decision to keep Afghanistan from falling under the control of militantly anti-Communist Islamic leaders with ethnic and linguistic ties to Uzbeks, Tajiks, and other groups within the Soviet Union was, therefore, the feared vulnerability of the border republics to infection from outside.

The decision to invade Czechoslovakia had been strongly urged by the Communist Party boss for the bordering Soviet Ukraine, Pyotr E. Shelest, to quash reforms and concessions to ethnic minorities that threatened to cause unrest in his fiefdom by inspiring demands for similar reforms and concessions. It is not known if the party bosses in republics bordering Afghanistan—none of them a full politburo member with the power Shelest had—tried to bring such pressure on Moscow. It would not have been necessary. Russian sensitivity about the control of what are thought of as Moslem peoples was strong enough to keep the cross-border infection problem prominent in any considerations.

Despite more than half a century of atheistic propaganda, Islam remains strong in Soviet Central Asia. Even party officials have their sons religiously circumcised, pay brideprice money, are married by Islamic tradition, and have religious funerals. Moslem societies exist clandestinely.[27] The Shi'ite Moslem upsurge in Iran associated with the fall of the shah had already caused great concern across the border in Turkmenistan, where a religious revival appeared to be developing,[28] and Soviet leaders did not want to risk any further trouble from a successful upsurge in Afghanistan.

The KGB chairman for Soviet Azerbaijan, Major General Ziya M. Yusif-Zade, warned of the problem while typically trying to blame the United States. "In view of the situation in Iran and Afghanistan, the U.S. special services are trying to exploit the Islamic religion—especially in areas where the Moslem population lives—as one factor influencing the political situation in our country," he said.[29] Dupree reported meeting two Uzbeks who indicated that they had entered Afghanistan from the Soviet Union to join the fight against Communism.[30]

The preaching by Afghan guerrillas of jihad, a Moslem religious struggle that does not necessarily have the more common definition of "holy war," was bound to be heard across the Amu Darya. The *basmachi* fight had been well known and actively supported in Afghanistan, and it had provided folk heroes for Afghan Uzbeks and Tajiks. Despite Soviet efforts to isolate and insulate Central Asian peoples from outside information, the 1920 situation could hardly be expected not to recur in reverse. A deputy premier of Soviet Kirgizia was prematurely retired after noting to foreigners the proximity of Afghanistan and pointedly recalling that the Soviet Union had helped fight a locust plague there "that could have spread to us."[31]

Ideology and Military Concerns

Two other factors in the invasion decision might be distinguished as also being essentially Soviet internal reasons. One is ideological. As already suggested, ideology can in the Soviet Union be both a rationalization of reality and a force to shape events. Soviet media never made a significant effort to portray the Afghanistan action as being ideologically motivated, as protecting the advance of Communism. The official formulations of Afghanistan's socialist orientation, rather than routine listing as a member of the socialist community, might have made this seem unnecessary. Yet the point was made in Moscow that ideological considerations were involved. "Socialist internationalism obliged us to help the Afghan people defend the April revolution's gains," according to Victor V. Grishin, a politburo member and the Moscow city party boss.[32] Brezhnev's "interview" implied an ideological commitment by saying that failure to have acted "would have meant leaving Afghanistan a prey to imperialism, allowing the aggressive forces to repeat in that country what they had succeeded in doing, for instance, in Chile where the people's freedom was drowned in blood."[33]

This reference to the military coup d'etat that ousted the leftist and pro-Soviet Allende regime in 1973 became a recurring Soviet theme. It soon developed into the tougher formulation used in a 15 April 1980 speech that said the Soviet Union would not "permit the transformation of Afghanistan into a new Chile." The speech was made by the Soviet ambassador to Paris, Stepan V. Chervonenko.[34] As ambassador in Prague in 1968, he had joined with hardliners like Yepishev and Shelest to urge the crushing of Czechoslovak liberalism. Curiously, though, the available evidence suggests that the man usually considered to be the guardian of Soviet ideological purity, Suslov, was a moderate on how to handle the Czechoslovak problem, as he might have been on the Hungarian uprising. While dedicated to the long-term advance of Communism, he seemed to have been cautious in 1956 and 1968 about resorting to force; he might also have been in 1979.

The other internal factor was the influence of the Soviet armed forces in the Kremlin policy-making process. There is debate among Western specialists on Soviet affairs about how strong this influence is. But Brezhnev's background as a World War II army commissar and later as a party supervisor of the army and of military production, his close personal association with men like Yepishev and Ustinov, and other factors insured that military viewpoints were influential. It can be assumed, but not documented, that Soviet soldiers were both somewhat apprehensive about getting further involved in Afghanistan and reluctant to have to admit at least a partial failure there by withdrawing the advisers, commanders, and the technicians already deeply involved. Perhaps the latter consideration was stronger.

Soviet military writings suggest another consideration without directly linking it to Afghanistan. The 1972 Soviet military textbook already quoted says that in the West "particular importance is attached to such wars [as Vietnam] since they serve as unique [opportunities] for testing new models of combat equipment, for checking and improving upon the structure and organization of the armed forces, and, finally, for providing military personnel of NATO countries with combat experience. . . . This reserve of [American] combat-experienced personnel [from Vietnam] will endure for at least a decade."[35] Similar references indicate a positive jealousy in the idle Soviet Army over the American war. Afghanistan offered professional Soviet soldiers a chance to acquire some experience. Testing the new MI-24 helicopter gunship was the first obvious opportunity by April 1979, but soon others developed—many others.

Soviet Status

An external factor is related to ideological considerations. It is the need to be seen as supportive of Communist and pro-Soviet leftist governments in order to hold the loyalty and support of other such governments. Although the Kremlin relationship with East European countries would not be directly affected by the collapse of a Soviet-backed regime in Asia, the implications of Soviet weakness were not something that the conservative Soviet leadership was prepared to risk. And the more tenuous relationship with distant leftist regimes, such as Mozambique's, as well as relations with pragmatic or rightist but nonetheless cooperative regimes such as Libya's, were at least partially dependent on the maintenance of a Soviet reputation for providing needed support.

The prestige element in this was probably more important in Soviet eyes than in the opinions of foreign countries, but that did not reduce it as a factor in Soviet thinking about the Afghanistan problem. The staunchness of Soviet support for the world Communist revolution was being tested, and the politburo was not going to be found wanting. Its members' very long lifetimes of repeating Marxist slogans were against it. So was the memory of Khrushchev's being criticized for failing adequately to support Cuba in the 1962 missile crisis, a memory that argued against exposing any similar future vulnerability.

Access to Resources

Another external factor was more talked about in the West after the invasion. That factor was the historic Russian drive to control warm water ports and its contemporary significance. The importance of the area between the Soviet Union and the Indian Ocean had been accentuated by the existence there of the world's most productive oil fields. The nineteenth-century history of tsarist expansion into the Transcaucasian and Central Asian regions, and the grasping at Iran after World War II, made it easy to understand a motivation for moving into Afghanistan as a stepping stone toward other objectives. Brezhnev was quick to deny it: "Absolutely false are the allegations that the Soviet Union has some expansionist plans in respect of Pakistan, Iran or other countries of that area. The policy and psychology of colonialists are alien to us. We are not coveting the lands or wealth of others. It is the colonialists who are attracted by the smell of oil."[36] Yet the fact remained that the move into Afghanistan gave the Soviet air force a base 200 miles closer to the Straits of Hormuz, the entrance to the Persian Gulf through which sailed almost a third of United States oil supplies, two-thirds of Europe's, and three-quarters of Japan's. It put the Soviet Army at the Khyber Pass.

Offensive or Defensive?

This raised a point much discussed in the West: Was the move into Afghanistan primarily a defensive one to protect the Central Asian border and the Communist regime in Kabul, or was it an offensive one to advance the Soviet strategic position in the Middle East and South Asia? The slowness of the Soviet move, not surging across the Amu Darya as soon as the 1978 treaty provided a justification but waiting until Amin's regime was falling apart, argues strongly for a defensive move.

After examining the subject, the British House of Commons foreign affairs committee said it "heard no evidence that the invasion of Afghanistan was part of a Soviet grand strategy." But it also noted "the opportunistic trend of Soviet tactics."[37] Before that committee and United States congressional committees, various specialists argued both the defensive and offensive cases. The arguments, especially when made by those with little or no knowledge of the Afghan situation, sometimes sounded more based on personal attitudes toward Soviet Communism than on the case at hand.

Thus, a retired American diplomat expert on the Soviet Union, George F. Kennan, said that "in the immediate circumstances their [the Soviet] objective was primarily defensive"; while Richard E. Pipes, a historian and later a Reagan administration adviser on Soviet affairs, said the invasion was "clearly not designed as an end in itself . . . I see their entire design as offensive and not defensive."[38] Interesting in this context, although somewhat warped in its comparison to the Afghan situation, was a remark to an American by an unidentified "Russian arms-control official": "If Mexico, on your southern border, were suddenly in danger of being taken over by Communist infiltrators from Cuba, wouldn't you react? Of course you would, and we would understand."[39] A similar remark, which also applies to the question of ideology's role, has been attributed to Brezhnev. When assured in July 1968 that Czechoslovakia would remain socialist despite a liberalization away from Soviet forms of control, Brezhnev reportedly growled: "Don't talk to me about 'socialism.' What we have we hold."[40]

The defensive-offensive argument gradually subsided as the Soviet action receded in time, leaving the point as unresolved as it must remain so long as Kremlin records are unavailable. But perhaps the argument was meaningless. In the short term, the move into Afghanistan had a defensive quality; in the long term, it offered offensive possibilities even if they were not part of the original calculation. It could be viewed as tactically defensive, strategically offensive, without the two having to be posited as alternatives.

Other reasons for the Soviet leadership's feeling that it should send troops into Afghanistan can be adduced. These include such relatively minor ones as insuring against disruption of the flow of Afghan natural gas on which Soviet Central Asia had come to depend. Disruption of gas supplies from Iran because of the turmoil there had recently caused hardship in the Soviet Caucasus, so the problem was fresh in some Soviet officials' minds.

But, beyond such positive incentives for action, there were important negative considerations. One consideration was the costs that might be incurred by using Soviet troops—not proxies—outside the old established Soviet bloc. What would be the effect on relations with the United States? With other Western countries? With the Third World, including Afghanistan's Moslem neighbors?

United States Relations

The possibility of a serious effect on United States relations was heavily discounted by two lines of reasoning. One, largely unstated in Soviet public discussion but probably the dominant one, was the record of United States reactions to previous Soviet uses of military power abroad. American anger over the invasion of Czechoslovakia had not lasted too long, and Washington was then prepared to resume business as usual. The Angolan and Ethiopian actions had shown that in its post-Vietnam mood the United States was reluctant to get involved abroad. Nor was it willing to exert itself very strenuously to reinvigorate its ability to project conventional military power into the Third World. And the Carter administration had imposed upon itself limits that protected Moscow against the kinds of retaliation it had most reason to dislike, a halt to arms control negotiations that might mean pitting superior United States technology and economic strength against the Soviet Union in an uncontrolled arms race, and restrictions on grain sales to help bureaucratically and ideologically hobbled Soviet agriculture.

The other line of reasoning was that, within those American self-limitations, relations with Washington were already poor, did not seem likely to sink much lower in practical working terms regardless of action in Afghanistan, and were unlikely to improve soon even without such action. In its attempt to blame the United States for the worsened relations that came from a much sharper United States reaction than foreseen, Soviet media later argued that the Carter administration had set itself on a course of abandoning détente and increasing international tensions as early as the summer of 1977.[41] They cited the decision then to spend more on the United States armed forces, rather than less as Carter had promised in his 1976 election campaign; and the decision to prepare for armed protection of Western interests in such vital areas as the Persian Gulf, which led after much delay and the jolt of the Soviet action in Afghanistan to the creation on paper of the United States "rapid deployment force." Soviet media also cited the American abandonment of the 1 October 1977 declaration on the two powers' working jointly for an Arab-Israeli settlement after Egyptian President Anwar Sadat's November 1977 visit to Jerusalem and the resulting Camp David agreement that shut Moscow out of Middle East peace efforts.

But these were largely retrospective accusations. The Soviets had been irritated by these and other things, including the application of Carter's human rights campaign to their suppression of dissidents. At the time, however, Soviet leaders and media first began to accuse the West of abandoning détente upon the 31 May 1978 adoption by NATO of a fifteen-year plan to increase defense spending by 3 percent a year in real terms in order to counter Soviet military improvements. A policy statement published simultaneously by all major Moscow newspapers on 17 June 1978 reacted to that and to the tougher parts of a balanced speech by Carter at Annapolis 7 June 1978 on Soviet-American relations. The statement accused the United States of taking a course "dangerous to the cause of peace."[42] Brezhnev's personal spokesman later called the NATO decision "an aggressive act,"[43] and Gromyko said the United States seemed to be returning to, "if not a cold war, then something similar."[44]

From then on relations went downhill, past the 1 January 1979 establishment of normal United States relations with the Soviet Union's bête noire, China, with only a temporary upturn for the 18 June 1979 signing by Carter and Brezhnev of the SALT II treaty. A NATO decision to deploy in Western Europe 108 Pershing II missile launchers and 464 ground-launched cruise missiles, both medium-range weapons capable of delivering nuclear warheads to Soviet territory as a counter to Soviet SS-20 missiles and Backfire bombers,[45] was publicly argued by the Soviet Union to be a major step away from détente and toward worse relations. Not formally adopted until 12 December 1979, well after Soviet preparations for the invasion of Afghanistan were under way, this decision had been long known and attacked vehemently by Soviet media and leaders' speeches for several months. It had, therefore, already been taken into Kremlin account in judging what new Western reactions an invasion might produce.

In general, then, Soviet leaders seemed to feel that relations were already sour enough, and the West determined enough to try to begin matching the long Soviet military buildup, that there was little more to lose by any Western alarm at an Afghanistan takeover. Unlike the situation in August 1968, when the beginning of SALT negotiations was to have been announced the day after the Czechoslovak invasion and a world Communist conference was supposed to be held in November, nothing significant was pending in December 1979. The United States Senate was showing little sign of wanting to ratify the SALT II treaty. East-West relations were at an impasse. The Soviet politburo was willing to accept a setback in 1968 for the sake of what it had decided was a preemptive need to quash Czechoslovak deviation from the Leninist model, delaying SALT talks for what proved to be fifteen months and the world conference seven months. No such price was visible this time.

Third World Relations

Soviet relations with Third World countries were not so obviously troubled and therefore not already beyond seriously damaging by invading Afghanistan. Iran was absorbed in its internal affairs and its confrontation with the United States over the hostages. Pakistan was being accused of harboring guerrillas, and China and Egypt of helping them, along with the United States. Cuba was the titular head of the nonaligned movement, an asset in avoiding any criticism in the name of the movement itself. Soviet and Cuban actions in Angola and Ethiopia had drawn little fire from the Third World, and events in Aden had passed almost unnoticed. The Soviet calculation on Afghanistan, apparently, was that it too would pass. Anyway, in its new mood of exercising its military might abroad, the Soviet leadership seemed confident that any loss of good will among weak Third World countries would be more than offset by respect for its power and willingness to use it. A number of Third World countries had been awed into timid silence by unauthorized flights over them by the Soviet military airlift to Ethiopia in December 1977 and January 1978.[46] The Kremlin was accustomed to letting force speak for it in the Third World.

Who Made the Decision to Invade?

All these considerations had presumably been getting increasing thought in the Soviet Communist Party central committee's secretariat, in the foreign and defense ministries, in the KGB and the interior ministry during the autumn of 1979. There are conflicting reports whether the leadership went outside a small, tight group for advice, however. Reports credited by most Western officials say that the politburo did not repeat its practice before the Czechoslovak invasion of consulting Soviet specialists on the United States to get predictions of what the United States reaction would be.[47] This would indicate an assumption that the worsening relations with Washington had caused the leadership not to worry about any further damage in that direction. If true, it was a serious omission. The Soviet Union was in fact greatly surprised by the strength of the Carter administration's reaction—as were some Americans and West Europeans.

Contrary reports said that some Soviet "Americanologists" were consulted in advance and as a result were in disgrace afterward for having failed to predict accurately.[48] If any comprehensive effort was made to calculate reactions inside Afghanistan or in the Third World, there is no evidence of it. A few months later, a visitor to the putative main repository of expertise on Afghanistan and a number of other Third World and Middle Eastern countries—that is, the Soviet Academy of Science's Institute of Oriental Studies—found its Afghan specialists to be mainly historians and linguistics experts with little current knowledge of the country. A senior United States official involved in relations with Moscow observed later that Brezhnev had a conversational habit of gesturing as if to flick away some imaginary nuisance. The available evidence suggested to the official that Brezhnev and other key Soviet officials were so concerned with security and ideological interests in what they considered to be their backyard that they did not want to be bothered with taking into account foreign reactions. They simply flicked them away impatiently.[49]

Mechanics of Decision Making

The key officials in this kind of matter probably numbered six. This was an inner group of the fourteen-man politburo that was believed to be responsible for foreign and security questions, including military ones. Its members were Brezhnev, whose titles included Supreme Commander in Chief of the Soviet armed forces, KGB chairman Yuri V. Andropov, Gromyko, Kosygin, Suslov, and Ustinov. Ponomarev might also have participated because one of the Communist parties that he supervised was involved, but Kosygin might not have, because he had been ill and absent from public view since 17 October.

The central committee met 27 November. In theory, it makes important decisions. But Brezhnev had reduced it to a sounding board for politburo decisions, and the announcement of the 27 November meeting listed only domestic economic and budgetary matters as having been considered.[50] The committee approved the annual development plan and governmental budget for the following year. The Supreme Soviet then met from 28 to 30 November to formally enact the budget. This was the usual late autumn ritual. The defense budget was ritually reduced from 17.23 billion rubles to 17.1 billion, to show peaceful Soviet intentions.[51] Brezhnev "delivered a big speech" to the central committee that, as reported by Soviet media, made no reference to foreign affairs or Afghanistan.

In retrospect, it appeared that the crucial decision on Afghanistan—to prepare for a military takeover, subject to some final selection of that option once prepared—had already been made before the central committee met. The exact procedure is not clear because over the years various accounts have reached the West about how Kremlin decisions are made, and various theories have been developed from sparse information. One possibility is that Brezhnev's aides circulated among politburo members a memorandum on the Afghan problem, with possible actions to be chosen—and, while some members might not have felt strongly about preparing for an invasion, none had a strong reason to oppose it.

Another possibility is that the politburo's inner group met, discussed the situation, and decided on preparations shortly before the full politburo met on the eve of the central committee session, that is, on 26 November. Perhaps the whole politburo discussed it. That the decision was handled by the politburo inside the Kremlin walls—or in the central committee secretariat offices a few blocks away—is supported primarily by circumstantial evidence, although there was one report that seemed to confirm it, while needing to be taken with caution.

After an official of the Spanish Communist Party had visited Moscow to discuss the adverse repercussions among Western Communists of the Afghanistan invasion, the Spanish news agency EFE reported from Moscow that "reliable sources" there said the politburo decided 26 November "to reinforce the sending of troops" to Afghanistan. The report, which said Kosygin was in the hospital and missed the meeting, added that the decision was made after the politburo listened to a report from Puzanov, who had returned from Kabul five days earlier.[52]

The point that the politburo reportedly decided at that time only to send more troops, not to take all the steps that occurred a month later, is important and probably at least partially correct. The Soviet Army made preparations for the invasion of Czechoslovakia for some two months before the politburo actually decided to implement that option, and extensive preparations were made in the winter of 1980–81 to invade Poland without such a decision's being made then. The careful old men in the Kremlin believed in preparing for all possibilities while reserving final judgment as long as possible. In the Czechoslovak and Polish cases, Warsaw Pact allies were involved. That produced more secret consultations and public discussion of options within the Soviet bloc than were necessary with Moscow's sole decision on Afghanistan.

Thus, in late November 1979, the Soviet Union had decided that it could no longer tolerate the situation in Afghanistan. How was the basic decision reached? How were the various considerations weighed?

The tight, self-perpetuating Soviet leaderhip has a record of keeping secrets. As noted earlier, little has ever been revealed about how and why the Czechoslovakian invasion decision was made,[53] although at that time there was more diversity of opinion represented in the politburo than there was in 1979, after Brezhnev had eliminated a number of suspected rivals and brought in old friends and protégés. Before Khrushchev banished the "anti-party group" of rivals from the politburo (then called presidium) in 1957, he said that in politburo meetings Soviet leaders express "different points of view . . . . If on some question unanimity cannot be reached, the problem is decided by a simple majority vote."[54] That might not have changed much over the years, despite the fact that by 1979 only Suslov remained from the 1957 membership and Brezhnev's personal authority was greater. In poor health in November 1979, Brezhnev was generally regarded by outsiders as one who established a consensus more than one who tried to dictate policies to his key comrades.

In his first pronouncement after the invasion, Brezhnev said that "It was no simple decision for us to send Soviet military contingents to Afghanistan. But the party's central committee and the Soviet government acted in full awareness of their responsibility and took into account the entire total of circumstances."[55] He did not elaborate, but it was probably significant that he did not attribute the *decision* to the central committee or government, only the *action*. More than two months later, a Soviet broadcast in Dari to Afghanistan made a notable addition: "As Leonid Brezhniv declared, the decision to dispatch Soviet troops to Afghanistan was not an easy one for USSR due to the great financial cost as well as the international repercussions."[56] The question of cost was never officially elaborated, either.

Brezhnev's "no simple decision" statement can be interpreted as meaning that the leaders realized the complex implications of it. But it might also mean that there was considerable debate within the politburo, a division among key people about what to do despite later claims of leadership unanimity. No evidence has become available to substantiate the latter interpretation, and some Western officials later assumed that there probably had been general agreement on the need to eliminate Amin and his disastrous policies. Brezhnev was reported to have told the French Communist Party secretary general, Georges Marchais, as paraphrased by another member of the French party's politburo:

> They had weighed the pros and cons in the Soviet leadership; they had questioned the matter at length; they had had some hesitations; the Soviet leadership knew that there would be repercussions and consequences. But they went ahead. They did so because they could not do otherwise . . . .

[American intervention from Pakistan] was such that the democratic experience in Afghanistan was threatened. The Soviet Union, heeding the call of the revolutionaries and progressives, had to intervene to prevent a collapse.[57]

A member of the Soviet politburo for sixteen years before his ouster in 1976, Dmitry S. Polyansky, as ambassaor to Tokyo in early 1980 defending the invasion, said: "Decisions are made collectively, and in no case is a decision made individually. Questions are carefully discussed, but final decisions are made with unanimity. The decision on the dispatch of Soviet troops to Afghanistan was made in accordance with this practice . . . The debate on this question was not easy. But the final decision was adopted with unanimous approval."[58]

Addressing the first Soviet Communist Party Congress after the invasion, on 23 February 1981, Brezhnev reported on politburo work. Without referring to Afghanistan or any other specific matter—although it is possible to speculate that his remarks were made in reaction to disquiet about the Afghan decision—Brezhnev said:

> Questions submitted for the examination of the politburo have been carefully studied in advance . . . . In certain instances the politburo set up special commissions to study thoroughly and to make general conclusions about the things that have happened, as well as to take, as the situation demands, appropriate practical measures. In the preparation for sessions and during discussions different opinions were expressed—something which is quite natural—and numerous criticisms and proposals were submitted. However, all decisions were adopted in a *spirit of complete unanimity*.[59]

Whether there was a difference between unanimity and a spirit of unanimity was left unclear, but the wording was curious.

Despite this rallying around after the invasion had stirred up worldwide outrage, did all the key Soviet leaders in fact approve at the time the decision was made? The question cannot be answered, but some elements likely to have been involved in reaching a decision can be examined. The Stalinist Soviet Union in which one man's personal decisions were decisive had been replaced, in many Western specialists' opinions, by a bureaucratic state in which politburo members represent different interest groups. By this method of analysis, which is controversial, the invasion decision can be seen as a result of convergent interests. The armed forces, represented by Ustinov as well as Brezhnev, and the KGB, which is responsible for border security and controlling internal dissension in Soviet Central Asia as well as other areas, represented by Andropov, presumably would have had the security aspects of the situation uppermost in their minds. They would have been most urgently concerned with eliminating instability on the border with the possibility of a hostile government in Afghanistan supported by foreign powers antagonistic to the Soviet Union. Suslov, and Ponomarev if he was involved in the decision, would have been worried about sustaining a Marxist regime because its fall would have been a setback to

Communist efforts to win influence in other countries. There were reports later, on a not very authoritative basis and perhaps more speculations, that Gromyko's foreign ministry was reluctant because of problems that could be created in relations with truly neutral countries, but one diplomatic report said Gromyko personally favored proving to pro-Soviet neutrals that the Soviet Union honored its treaty commitments.[60] Kosygin, a normally cautious man who reportedly tried to play a pacifying role in the heated 1968 discussions of Czechoslovakia, was probably not directly involved in the 1979 discussions but was consulted.

This kind of analysis produces a count of five or six key people in favor of action and none actually opposed. But the analysis has to be more complex. For one thing, studies of the way decisions are made in any large, bureaucratic organization suggest that none of the main players acts because of a single simple reason. There are usually cross-currents of considerations. What is for one person a dominant reason might for another be only a secondary reason that reinforces his inclination to take the same action for another, different dominant reason. What influences one interest group most strongly might be a deterrent to another group. But in the politburo, competing interests might not be too strong on an Afghanistan kind of problem compared with, for example, competition for scarce domestic investment resources.

The system by which the Soviet politburo is renewed periodically—in Brezhnev's time only with old men replacing even older men, or replacing younger men who have been in effect purged—insures that its members share a community of interests. Gromyko might be no less sensitive to the need to prevent infection of Soviet Central Asia than Andropov, for instance; and Ustinov no less concerned than the foreign minister to maintain Soviet prestige in some distant leftist nation—where the Soviet ability to obtain naval or air facilities might be influenced by not abandoning the closer Marxists in Afghanistan.[61]

Another complexity is that factors which do not seem critical in making a decision might help make it easier to make. It is difficult to argue that the Soviet Union went into Afghanistan primarily because it wanted to exercise its long-inactive armed forces. It is also difficult, although perhaps less so, to argue that the primary reason was to advance on warm water ports on the Arabian Sea, on the Persian Gulf, and on the Indian subcontinent, despite the effort by some Westerners to make that argument. But it is not difficult to understand that these factors could have been seen as bonuses for a decision that had to be made mainly for other reasons. The distinction between defensive and offensive action blurs.

Add to all this the sheer momentum of the Soviet military buildup of advisers and equipment in Afghanistan, the confidence acquired from the tested ability to project the newly expanded Soviet armed forces into the Third World, the growing economic and administrative responsibility for keeping Afghanistan going and the vested interests that this generated, and the sense of moral commitment and prestige invested in backing a PDPA regime in Kabul. Subtract the negative factors and little is lost, because of the Kremlin view of the

United States lack of international vitality and unwillingness to conform to policies that the Soviet Union was advocating. Then the decision becomes understandable. It also comes to seem safe for those who made it. They included men who had used as one basis for toppling Khrushchev the charge of "adventurism" for sending missiles into Cuba in 1962 without adequate calculation of the risks. These were calculating men.

Something was to be done about Afghanistan. The military preparations, already afoot before the critical meetings of late November, speeded up after them. Now it was necessary to arrange a plausible, internationally acceptable way to increase the Soviet military role in Afghanistan in order to insure the survival of the form of PDPA control, if not the substance. The key to this was Amin.

Chapter 9. Invasion

Amin was, from the Soviet standpoint, a failure. So long as he remained in charge in Kabul there was no hope of consolidating the grip that Communism had gained on Afghanistan with the April 1978 coup. There was, instead, the danger of losing it, of having the country fall into a chaotic anti-Communist condition. Worse, it would be anti-Communism with strong Islamic overtones in a country bordering disaffected, colonially held and traditionally Islamic peoples of the Soviet Union. For a number of reasons, a coalition of interests, the Soviet leadership felt it had to continue the momentum that had been building since its original help to the new PDPA regime in May 1978. The logic of the situation, unsupported by any direct evidence, is that the leaders felt Amin had to go and the Soviet Army had to be used to insure that a feared collapse of Communist power did not occur. The massive popular rejection of the policies followed by Taraki as well as Amin, and the brutal methods used not only by Amin but also by a number of enthusiastic aides, must not be allowed to prevent the movement into the Soviet bloc of a sensitively located country. New men, new policies, new methods were needed, and a new military backbone had to be inserted in place of the unreliable Afghan army.

Justifying the Invasion

How could they make the substitutions under Amin's rule? His repeated statements that Soviet troops were not needed to protect Afghanistan made it difficult to send in the Soviet Army so long as he continued to be president. And he had done nothing more than listen seriously to repeated Soviet urgings for policy changes, so it was unrealistic to expect him to step aside voluntarily. What was needed was a way to push Amin out and bring in the Soviet Army under cover of a plausible story that the Afghans had done it themselves. But which Afghans? Amin had jailed, tortured, murdered, banished into exile, or otherwise eliminated just about everyone inside the country who might be expected to stand against him. The situation called for the invention of some group of Afghans who could be clothed in a claim of legitimacy, described as having removed their evil fellow-countryman, installed in power, and used to invite in Soviet help.

In Asia

The Soviet Union had plenty of accumulated experience in these matters. The union had in fact been put together by Russian Bolsheviks who held onto outlying parts of the tsarist empire by the same kind of methods that now seemed required for Afghanistan. In the Transcaucasian region, for instance, and in Bukhara, the Bolsheviks used small groups of local agents as their justification for sending in troops to consolidate Communist power and supervise accession of ethnically different peoples to a Russian-run state.

The first case of adding a country to the Soviet bloc that had not been part of the tsarist empire was in Mongolia, where the combination of an insignificant local group of Communists and internal chaos that the Bolsheviks feared might spill over the border provided an excuse for military intervention. A decade after the Red Army had put Sukhe Bator in power, it had to intervene again to keep his successors from being overthrown by a widespread popular uprising against policies that Mongolia had copied from Stalin's collectivization program, so the elements of the 1979 Afghanistan action had earlier occurred separately there.[1]

In Finland and the Baltic

When Stalin tried in 1939 to recapture Finland, a tsarist province that had only reluctantly been allowed by the weak Bolsheviks to escape in 1918, he set up a "Finnish People's Government" along the Soviet border headed by a veteran Comintern official, Otto V. Kuusinen. It signed a treaty with Moscow, and the Red Army tried to enforce its claim to be the legitimate government of Finland. It failed disastrously. After a three and one half month-long "winter war," the four million Finns forced the Soviets to abandon their effort after they suffered some 50,000 deaths and 150,000 wounded. The Kuusinen government evaporated, he to become in 1946 a member of Stalin's politburo. There was a murky affair after World War II in which Stalin tried again to dominate Finland, this time by burrowing from within more in the style that at about the same time in 1948 subverted Czechoslovakian efforts to maintain some degree of independence, but it too failed.[2]

The same technique of alleged appeals for help from Soviet protégés was used in 1940 to end twenty-two years of independence from Russian control by the Baltic states, Estonia, Latvia, and Lithuania. First the Soviets made a deal with Nazi Germany so that Stalin could do whatever he wanted with the states without German interference; then he forced them by stages to accept Red Army garrisons. The army supervised elections from which all non-Communist candidates were barred. Finally the resulting new national assemblies simultaneously on 21 July 1940 asked for admission to the Soviet Union. A key figure in the 1979 Afghanistan decision, Suslov, was personally responsible for the bloody purges, deportation of families, and crushing of local nationalism in Lithuania after it had been recaptured in 1944 from three years of Nazi control.[3]

In Hungary, Czechoslovakia, and Cambodia

More recent and better-known cases were in Hungary, Czechoslovakia, and Cambodia. Another central figure in the 1979 decision, KGB boss Andropov, was Soviet ambassador in Budapest when in 1956 the Hungarian people sought to escape Moscow's domination in the wave of destalinization touched off by Khrushchev's "secret speech" eight months earlier. Soviet Foreign Minister Dmitry T. Shepilov claimed that someone whom he could not identify had on 24 October 1956 telegraphed Moscow to send troops to Budapest to quell disturbances. The fact that the troops had arrived in Budapest at 2:00 A.M. that day made the timing even more curious than the lack of a signature on the supposed telegram, so that a United Nations special committee doubted that there had been any legal and formal request at all. Worse was to come.

After four days of intermittent fighting with Hungarian freedom fighters, Soviet troops withdrew. They had succeeded only in exacerbating the situation, alienating Communists, and rallying others to a genuine national revolution. Imre Nagy, who had become premier about the time the Soviet Army had arrived, became a symbol of nationalism although he always considered himself a Communist. He began trying to dismantle the structure of Soviet controls.

Janos Kadar, who became first secretary of the Hungarian Communist Party about the same time, struggled to control the situation for four days, then gave up and flew 1 November to Uzhgorod in the Carpatho-Ukraine, an area that Stalin had annexed from Czechoslovakia at the end of World War II to give the Soviet Union a common border with Hungary. There Kadar became premier of a Soviet-concocted "Hungarian Revolutionary Worker-Peasant Government." From a radio transmitter inside the Soviet Union that claimed to be a Hungarian station, Kadar's "government" proclaimed that Hungarian Communism had been endangered "through the increased influence of counterrevolutionary elements who edged their way into the movement." On 4 November Soviet Army units stationed in Hungary returned to Budapest, crushed the freedom fighters in street fighting, and installed Kadar in power. Nagy and his main associates were lured out of asylum in the Yugoslav embassy by Kadar's written guarantee of safe conduct and immunity from arrest, but the KGB abducted them; in 1958 first Moscow and then Budapest announced their trial and execution. The United Nations committee found that Kadar lacked the authority that he claimed in asking for Soviet military help and noted that broadcasts in the name of a Hungarian-based government in fact originated outside the country.[4]

The cast of principal Soviet characters for the Czechoslovak and Afghanistan invasions was practically the same. As Alexander Dubcek tried in the spring of 1968 to humanize the Leninist system that Soviet agents had imposed on Czechoslovakia since 1948, the Soviet politburo organized most Warsaw Pact countries to warn that "we cannot agree to have hostile forces push your country from the road to socialism." By mid-August Czechoslovak liberalization had become for Kremlin leaders a dangerously intolerable deviation from Soviet control that might infect not only other East European countries but also the Soviet Union itself.

A plan was made in Moscow to rally those still loyally pro-Soviet Czechoslovakian leaders. This group of presumed opponents of Dubcek was, if strong enough, to call a special meeting the evening of 20 August of the Czechoslovak Communist Party's presidium, or politburo. The group was supposed to depose Dubcek from the post of party first secretary and Oldrich Cernik from the premiership, replacing them with Moscow's supporters. East Germany's *Pravda*, named *Neues Deutschland*, had ready set in type an announcement that the new leaders had invited in Warsaw Pact armies to help it against revisionists and imperialist agents. But the anti-Dubcek majority did not materialize, and new leaders were not chosen.

A fallback plan, in case a presidium majority could not be gathered, was for a minority of pro-Soviet leaders in Prague to issue a public appeal for intervention. No such appeal was ever issued, largely because Dubcek loyalists kept control of the media for the first critical hours after the invasion began the night of 20–21 August. The Soviets fell back on a bogus Czechoslovak radio that actually was located in East Germany to broadcast claims of popular support for their action. On 21 August, Tass referred to "a request by party and state leaders . . . [for] immediate assistance, including assistance with armed forces."

The next day *Pravda* published the supposed text of an appeal by a group of members of the Czechoslovak party's central committee, the government, and the national assembly. But party and government leaders in Prague had already issued a statement saying, "The invasion happened without the knowledge of the president of the republic, of the chairman of the national assembly, the prime minister and the foreign secretary, of the Czechoslovak party and central committee." The Soviet subterfuge was unsuccessful. Opposition to the invasion was so solid that the pro-Soviet handful of leaders was unable to step forward. Reluctantly, Moscow had to quit mentioning the alleged appeal and to negotiate with Dubcek, who was not finally replaced with Soviet loyalists until the following April.[5]

The Soviet Union presumably learned at least two lessons from this and tested a useful trick. One lesson was that the Western outcry would not last long. The other was that the efficient disposal of an independent-minded foreign Communist leader requires the quick use of overwhelming force and the elimination of anyone who might be in a position authoritatively to deny the cover story. The trick was the removal of most ammunition and fuel from the Czechoslovak armed forces before the invasion, transferring them to East Germany on the excuse of need for military exercises there. The armed forces did not in fact resist the Warsaw Pact armies, because the Dubcek-majority presidium decided it would be hopeless. Afghanistan was different.

The invasion of Cambodia at the end of 1978 by Soviet-aided Vietnam, less than two months after Moscow and Hanoi signed a friendship treaty and exactly a year before the Afghanistan invasion, also used a cover story. Hanoi Radio announced on 3 December that a Kampuchean (Cambodian) United Front for National Salvation had been established in a supposedly liberated part of Cambodia and was rallying the people against the Pol Pot regime. The

Vietnamese invasion followed a three-week propaganda buildup for the front as representing the true interests of the Cambodian people, and the pretense was made for a time that it was the front's own army rather than Vietnam's that freed Phnom Penh from the barbaric regime. Vietnam installed in the Cambodian capital a puppet government headed by Heng Samrin, but it took some 200,000 Vietnamese troops to keep it in place. While Pol Pot had even less popular appeal than Amin, he escaped to continue resistance against an invader hated with the same kind of historic and racial antipathy that many of Afghanistan's peoples had for Russians.[6] The cover story that the change of government was locally decided, and foreign help then requested, was as unacceptable to a skeptical world watching Cambodia as later was the Afghanistan story.

In Afghanistan

The Soviet accounts of Afghan requests that the Soviet Army be sent to help the Kabul government were muddled. Amin's 9 September 1979 statement that "We are proud that we have not asked any foreign country to fight for us"[7] was reiterated a number of times by him, his foreign minister, Shah Wali, and other Afghan officials into mid-December.[8] After the invasion, Moscow said that it had been asked repeatedly to supplement military advisers and instructors with its own troops because of "growing counterrevolutionary attacks from outside" Afghanistan. Most versions said fourteen requests were made, but some said sixteen.[9] Some accounts said both Taraki and Amin made the requests beginning some time in 1978, others said beginning in March 1979, and one said only Taraki made such requests.[10] However, a Soviet commentator later said, "The situation in that period was not regarded as critical by the Kremlin."[11] It simply assured Kabul that it would provide adequate numbers of advisers and instructors and would train more Afghans in Soviet military schools. But when "a direct threat to the national independence, sovereignty and territorial integrity of [Afghanistan] developed as a result of aggressive actions" inspired by the United States and China, Karmal later explained, the Soviet leaders had to change their minds and send troops.[12]

Karmal's Account

Another muddled story was that Karmal had secretly returned to Afghanistan before the invasion and organized a majority of PDPA members against Amin. The evidence was that Karmal was flown into Kabul by the Soviets after they had killed Amin and secured control of the capital, but that was too demeaning. A more heroic account was needed. It apparently was fabricated.

After being ousted from the post of Afghan ambassador to Czechoslovakia in September 1978, and ignoring an order to return home and face conspiracy charges, Karmal was subsidized in exile in the way that the Soviet Union has for decades kept a wide variety of potentially useful foreign Communist leaders available for contingencies. His movements cannot be traced. One report said he moved from a Czechoslovak government hotel in Marienbad to Moscow in early 1979,[13] but other sources say he was still in Czechoslovakia in September 1979.[14] In speeches and interviews while president, Karmal said he entered Afghanistan from Pakistan into Paktia province south of Kabul[15]—an uncontrolled stretch of bleak, rugged border where guerrilla forces were strong— and lived underground in the capital. In different interviews Karmal gave his time of return as August 1979, before Taraki was overthrown by Amin, as late October, as mid-November, or as some vaguely later time closer to the invasion.[16] Rumors circulated in Kabul in October that Karmal was living disguised in the Soviet embassy,[17] where Watanjar and others were already believed to be hiding.

On his return to Afghanistan, Karmal later claimed, "Immediately, I organized, in cooperation with friends, the forces of resistance [to Amin] in the underground, naturally. We also established contact with the majority of members of the Revolutionary Council who were officially in the government, but who were our friends."[18] In the second week of December an overwhelming majority of both PDPA central committee and revolutionary council members exerted pressure on Amin to ask urgently for Soviet military assistance, and he was forced to comply, the post-invasion story said.[19] So, according to Karmal, Soviet troops entered Afghanistan beginning 17 December at the request of a government majority—that is, ten days before those troops killed Amin.

Karmal added that before 27 December a majority of the central committee and revolutionary council had tried Amin, decided to execute him, and elected Karmal to his three jobs of the committee's general secretary, the council's president and also prime minister.[20] This forestalled Amin's plans, variously described by Karmal's regime to have been plans to stage a 29 December anti-Communist crackdown by Amin in cooperation with resistance groups[21] and plans to flee abroad and live comfortably in the West on money "savagely plundered [from] our toiling people."[22]

It is difficult to sort this out. One problem is that Kabul Radio reported on 28 December that the PDPA politburo had met that day and unanimously elected Karmal as general secretary.[23] It also reported a revolutionary council meeting the same day that made Karmal president.[24] There was no mention then of his having been chosen for those posts earlier, secretly. That was a later story when the world began questioning his legitimacy.

A Soviet journal said that "throughout December 1979 Amin asked the Soviet ambassador four times that Soviet troops should be introduced into Afghanistan" because of pressure from "healthy forces" in the leadership.[25] Karmal said in January 1980 that Amin "did not ask the limited Soviet contingent for help. This request was made by the revolutionary council."[26] In March, Karmal said Amin was forced by committee and council majorities to make the request himself. He added then that this was done "without my personal knowledge concerning that request, and without an opportunity [for me] to bring influence to bear."[27]

This is strange. Did Amin ask for Soviet troops or were they requested behind his back? If a majority of PDPA leaders opposed Amin, why did they not simply vote him out of office? Perhaps they were afraid to oppose him because of his tight police control, but if so then how was Karmal able to operate underground in Kabul? The bitterness between Khalqis who dominated Amin's regime and the Parchami Karmal was so strong that it is difficult to believe that Karmal would not have been betrayed while trying to round up a majority against Amin. And if Karmal put together a majority, then why did he not know of the request for troops being made by that majority?

Karmal's statement about not knowing of the troop request, made in March 1980, is particularly curious. Despite his many other statements loyally supporting the Soviet Army presence in Afghanistan, it suggests that he wanted to avoid some of the blame for what had become by March an ugly situation with almost daily manifestations of popular hostility toward the Soviet invaders. But his foreign minister had claimed in January that Karmal "was in Afghanistan long before the turning point. He was informed of everything and was in charge of events."[28]

Soviet Activities

The Karmal account of secretly organizing Amin's downfall can be confidently disregarded in a search for what really happened in December. Attention should focus on what the Soviets were doing in Kabul. There were two key persons, in addition to Ambassador Tabeyev, Safronchuk, and others in the Soviet embassy. One was Viktor S. Paputin, a lieutenant general in the Soviet internal police and first deputy minister of the interior. The other was a shadowy Soviet general, apparently from the KGB, who was also reported in Kabul in the critical period before the invasion.[29] Circumstantial evidence, supported but not confirmed by later comments of Soviet sources in Moscow, indicates that one or both of them were given the assignment of quietly removing Amin from power, which meant killing him because he had shown that he was not a man to step down willingly.

What happened in Kabul in mid-December has to be hypothesized. No committee of the Supreme Soviet investigates the dirty tricks of the Kremlin's various secret services, nor does any Moscow newspaper probe into and publish disclosures on clandestine operations abroad. But the limited evidence and the logic of the situation combine to indicate that someone organized an attempt to remove Amin after the Afghans themselves had proven ineffectual for the job.

The Soviet politburo had apparently decided on 26 November that Amin had to be eliminated and the Soviet Army sent in. Wary of foreign reactions, and remembering criticism of unbelievable cover stories in the Hungarian and Czechoslovak actions, Soviet leaders wanted it handled discreetly. The outside world would readily believe that in Afghanistan, where two presidents had been killed in twenty months in what were generally seen as internal conflicts (and the four preceding kings murdered or overthrown), a third president with Amin's bloody reputation had also fallen to domestic forces. Then the way would be clear to install a more compliant leader who would publicly invite the Soviets to save him from his own people—while saying the danger was from across the Pakistani and Iranian borders.

The activities of Paputin and the shadowy Soviet general occurred against a background of Soviet military preparations. Not only were the military moves unreported but also there was no media campaign in the Soviet Union to prepare public opinion for the possibility of using troops in Afghanistan, and very little Soviet media coverage of the situation there.

Possibly the first direct combat involvement of Soviet forces (other than the use of Soviet helicopter gunships—ostensibly as part of the Afghan air force—and the roles of advisers) occurred in late November or early December in Badakhshan province. When its capital, Feyzabad, was seized by guerrillas, Soviet warplanes helped forces loyal to Amin.[30] They failed at that time to regain control.

On 29 November Soviet transports began flying more troops from the 105th Guards Airborne Division at Ferghana to strengthen the battalion that had arrived at Bagram in early July.[31] By 6 December there were three battalions there—about 2,500 men. Between 8 and 10 December a 600-man armored unit joined them, and ten days later it moved north to secure the highway through the Salang Pass tunnel that later became one of the two main overland routes for the invasion. Other Soviet troops from Bagram appeared at Kabul airport by mid-December. In Soviet Central Asia, further mobilizations were ordered to supplement the raising of the combat status of two divisions that had begun in October. Later reports told of unpreparedness by some reserve units in Tajikistan because corruption and bribery had allowed military equipment and spare parts to be diverted to fill civilian shortages.[32]

Between 11 and 15 December, transport planes gathered in the Moscow area and in the Central Asian area, and tactical fighter aircraft were shifted from bases deep inside the Soviet Union to bases near the Afghan border. Two other airborne divisions, part of the elite strike force of the Soviet Army, were placed on alert, the 103rd at Vitebsk in Byelorussia and the 104th at Kirovabad in Soviet Azerbaijan.[33] A Soviet combat battalion had been identified in Kabul by Western observers there by 12 December. The State Department announced it and gave another warning to the Soviet Union.[34]

Publicity in the West for the Soviet moves provoked denials. Amin said 16 December that Soviet forces had not been involved in fighting.[35] Two days later Moscow Radio issued a similar denial without saying if troops were actually in Afghanistan.[36] A Soviet broadcast to Iran on 22 December, however, said reports "that Soviet armed forces have been stationed on Afghan soil is a complete lie . . . . Soviet policy is based on complete equality and on respect for other states' sovereignty, territorial integrity and noninterference in their internal affairs."[37] The next day *Pravda* declared that "allegations that Soviet 'combat units' have been introduced in Afghan territory . . . represent the most transparent fabrications . . . with a sinister purpose" of isolating Afghanistan from its true friends. *Pravda* quoted Amin as having recently said that "The Soviet Union always displays profound respect for our independence and national sovereignty" and will never disparage it.[38] The falsity of *Pravda's* denial was obvious at the time and was later indicated by Karmal, who said that "the Soviet armed forces were in Afghanistan prior to" mid-December Western reports about them. He added that "their presence . . . was requested by the Afghan government of the time."[39] Despite the denials, the Carter administration told a number of countries on 19 December that the Soviet Army seemed to be preparing for combat in Afghanistan, as mentioned above. On 22 December State Department officials responded to press reports by briefing American reporters on the military buildup.

The presence in Kabul of the shadowy Soviet general became known to Western intelligence agencies after the fact as they tried to reconstruct what had happened, but a clear picture of his role never emerged. Paputin was easier to track. But he was a curious choice for the delicate task in which he was believed to have been involved. Paputin's limited amount of formal education was as a mechanic. After working as that and as a factory foreman, he became a career official of the Soviet Communist Party, an *apparatchik*.[40] Years of undistinguished jobs established personal contacts that paid off in the usual Russian way. Friends abruptly lifted him from the provinces into an important party post for the Moscow region. Seven years later, in 1974, his patronage ties within the party as well as his stolid dependability raised Paputin to a national position as first deputy minister of internal affairs, meaning a senior policeman. With that went a prestigious ranking as an alternative, or second-class, member of the party's central committee. Although he lacked experience in the police work of his new position, Paputin evidently had political reliability. He also had an Afghan connection. In 1978 his ministry began training the PDPA's new political police, the brutal force that Amin came to use in order to insure personal power.

Paputin arrived in Kabul about 29 November,[41] time enough after the 26 November Soviet politburo meeting to have received instructions. His visit was reported by Afghan media; the visit of the other general was never publicly mentioned, which might be seen as support for the idea that *he* was the real conspirator against Amin.

Starting 30 November, Paputin and an accompanying delegation held meetings with the Afghan deputy minister of the interior and his economic and planning directors on "bilateral cooperation and matters of mutual interest."[42] On 2 December Paputin met with Amin at his palace, the House of the People.[43] On 13 December Paputin left for home "after a series of friendly talks."[44] That was all that was officially reported about him. The talks dealt with Soviet aid for Afghan internal police work, Paputin's specialty. The reports from Soviet sources after Paputin's death imply that he returned unreported to Kabul later, but perhaps the other general was the key person who remained through the invasion.

Whoever it was, someone seems to have arranged an attempt on Amin's life. Paputin might have done so and, when it failed, returned to Kabul to try to pick up the pieces, but such jobs are more in the line of work for KGB officials than Soviet Communist Party *apparatchiks* like Paputin. A shooting occurred in the palace on 17 December.[45] Amin was reportedly wounded in a leg. His nephew Asadullah Amin, head of the intelligence service KAM, was more seriously wounded and was flown to the Soviet Union for medical treatment, thus removing from the scene Amin's top security aide.

Details of what happened are not clear; what is clear is that Amin realized that there was a plot to get him. He took defensive steps. In chess terms, Amin castled—he retreated from an obvious threat to a better-protected position. Gathering up a force of his most trusted Afghan guards, with eight tanks and some armored personnel carriers, he moved on 19 December to the Darulaman palace complex that King Amanullah had built seven miles southwest of the center of Kabul as a new capital.[46] He took up residence in a squarish Germanic building at the rear of the complex known as the Tajbeg Palace.

There was later speculation that Soviet advisers had prevailed on him to move for his own safety,[47] but this seems unlikely. The Soviets might have wanted him in a more isolated location once they realized that they were going to have to use troops to eliminate him. The House of the People was close to foreign embassies, and Moscow might have remembered the awkwardness of Nagy's escape to the Yugoslav embassy in Budapest twenty-three years earlier. It seems more likely, however, that Amin moved at his own initiative. Amanullah's old parliament building, the main Darulaman building now known as the People's Hall, was a headquarters for loyal troops, and the Tajbeg Palace uphill behind it was protected by them and the terrain.

Not wanting to take any chances, Amin ordered on 26 December that the 4th Tank Brigade at Pul-i-Charki east of Kabul immediately deploy to Darulaman to join his defenses, but its commander said later that he stalled.[48] That flouted order, issued as the Soviet airlift was delivering troops in Kabul, showed Amin's desperation. He reportedly looked dishevelled in an appearance on Kabul television 26 December, and some diplomats thought he looked strained in a photograph published the next day.[49] But if Amin was so desperately worried about a Soviet attack, why did he not tell the world in hope of bringing some international pressure to his aid? There was no such declaration, or even a public announcement of the reason for his move to Darulaman, only a brief announcement that the revolutionary council and prime ministry had moved and beginning 22 December all documents would be signed at the new location.[50]

Amin's desperation was obvious to Pakistan, although its government did not at the time understand the reasons. Afghan efforts to have Agha Shahi fly up from Islamabad for talks have already been mentioned, and so have their frantic nature toward the end. The Pakistani foreign affairs official's visit was finally announced on 17 December as beginning 22 December. When Shahi was preparing to leave that morning, however, the Pakistani air force informed him that snow had closed Kabul airport. Then Shah Wali, Amin's top deputy, telephoned from Kabul. He expressed great disappointment that Shahi could not come then and said he personally appealed for him to come as soon as possible. Kabul would be snowbound for a few days. Shahi had to go with President Zia to Saudi Arabia early on 24 December, then to visit Tehran; on return on 27 December he had to attend a nephew's wedding, so he and Wali finally agreed to postpone the visit until 30 December—by which time Wali was a Russian prisoner. What Amin and Wali hoped of Pakistan was never known to Shahi, who became a leader of the Islamic world's condemnation of the invasion.[51]

By the time Amin moved to the Tajbeg Palace, it must have been clear to Soviet leaders that their efforts to control the situation in Afghanistan had failed yet again. They had been unable to direct Afghan policy along the lines Safronchuk advised in the summer of 1979, they had failed to get rid of Amin and use Taraki as a more amenable leader in September, they had failed to rein Amin in during the autumn, and now they had failed to destroy him in a quiet, plausible way. If the military preparations up to then were only to prepare an option in case of necessity, or if they were made contingent on getting rid of Amin and being publicly invited in by an accepted successor, then it was time to decide on the next step. Events of the following week showed that a final decision was made in the Kremlin to use brute force where diplomacy and conspiracy had failed. Shulman suggested that "the climate in which the decision was made was one of intense emotionalism, one of anger, one of frustration."[52]

A logistical buildup on the Soviet side of the Amu Darya was completed by about 23 December, and so were the redeployment of transport aircraft and the preparations of airborne forces.[53] At 11:00 P.M. on 24 December troops of the 105th Airborne began to land at Kabul airport. Soon after, Soviet troops began flying into the Soviet-built military air bases at Bagram and at Shindand sixty-five miles south of Herat in the west, and the American-built airport at Qandahar in the south. The airlift into Kabul continued around the clock for two days.[54] "Afghans at the airport were shocked to see the Russians arriving in uniform and toting weapons," one Western witness reported. "I saw some weeping."[55] The estimated 400 military transports and Aeroflot planes that were involved discharged troops and armored vehicles without turning off their engines and then flew away for more.

By the morning of 27 December there were some 5,000 Soviet soldiers in Kabul. A Soviet lieutenant said later he thought it was just an exercise. Soviet advisers who by then were running Afghan army units told their troops that there was an exercise on. Repeating the trick used in Czechoslovakia, they ordered the Afghans to turn in live ammunition and take blanks for training purposes, and some batteries were removed from tank engines "for winterization."[56] Not all Afghan units around Kabul were emasculated, however. It was during this buildup that Amin asked unsuccessfully for additional tank protection, but he already had some loyal units at his side.

Despite the concern shown by his appeal for more Afghan protection, Amin continued with a show of normal activities. At 2:30 P.M. on Thursday, 27 December, a time at which government offices would be shutting down in devoutly Moslem countries as they prepared for the Friday day of prayers, Amin received at the People's Hall what Kabul Radio described as a courtesy call from the Soviet minister of communications, Nikolai V. Talyzin, who had arrived in Kabul 24 December "on an official and friendly visit."[57] That was Amin's last reported duty, and from his standpoint the last Soviet courtesy.

At about 7:00 P.M. an explosion knocked out the Kabul telephone system[58]— Soviet military planners were smarter and more experienced than had been the Saur revolutionaries, who had negligently allowed Daoud to try to coordinate his defense by telephone twenty tumultuous months earlier. Red tracer bullets rose in the sky around the interior ministry, headquarters of the internal police; by 7:15 Soviet airborne troops had captured it. An attack by Soviet tanks and armored cars on the Darulaman complex began about the same time,[59] but Afghan troops there fought valiantly and got some support from nearby army units.

While Amin was still holding out, a Soviet transmitter at Termez in Uzbekistan, where Marshal Sergei L. Sokolov of the Soviet general staff was directing operations from a special theater command headquarters, began broadcasting on the frequency of Kabul Radio.[60] Kabul was still transmitting normal programs. Overpowering it, Termez broadcast at 8:45 P.M. what Western intelligence analysts later said was a tape-recorded statement by Karmal.[61] According to a version given later by Tass, Karmal addressed his speech to those

> who up to the present have been subjected to intolerable violence and torture by the bloody apparatus of Hafizullah Amin and his minions, these agents of American imperialism . . . . The day of freedom and rebirth . . . has arrived. Today the torture machine of Amin . . . has been broken . . . . The central committee of the united People's Democratic Party and the revolutionary council of the Democratic Republic of Afghanistan proclaim true people's power . . . . We have once again raised the banner of national *jihad*, . . . a just war of the Afghan people for true democratic justice, for respect for the holy Islamic religion, . . . for implementation of the aims of the glorious April revolution.[62]

There was no mention of how Amin had been overthrown or of any Soviet involvement. Listeners in Tehran, who first reported the Termez broadcast—

which they took for the genuine Kabul Radio—to the world, said Karmal also praised Taraki as a "martyr of the revolution" and said that "we have returned to power,"[63] thus trying to don the mantle of his long-time PDPA rival, but this was not included in the Tass version. Tehran also heard a promise that "All democratic freedoms . . . will be guaranteed" and political prisoners will be released. A separate statement broadcast from Termez in the name of the Afghan revolutionary council and heard in Tehran announced support for Karmal, condemned "the bloody oppression of Amin," and called on the Afghan armed forces to remain "vigilant, disciplined and united."[64]

Some Afghan soldiers remained united with Amin's government and resisted the Soviet attackers. Fighting in downtown Kabul, especially around the Kabul Radio offices, continued until about 10:30 P.M.[65] By then, Soviet troops had destroyed two Afghan tanks guarding the radio station, killed a number of defenders, lost some tanks, and suffered significant casualties themselves, and finally seized the key radio facility. By 11:00 P.M. the central part of the city was quiet and under Soviet guard, but fighting continued at Darulaman into the early morning.

Before Kabul Radio could go on the air under new management, the international service of Tass had transmitted the alleged Karmal text around the world in Russian at fifteen minutes past midnight Kabul time. Tass said Karmal had made the address on Kabul Radio "on behalf of and on the instructions of" the PDPA central committee, the revolutionary council, and the Afghan government.[66] How these instructions had been given was not explained. Finally, at 2:40 A.M. 28 December, the real Kabul Radio broadcast a brief announcement that it said came from the revolutionary council's secretariat. Without any explanation of what had happened, it named Karmal, who was identified as general secretary of the PDPA central committee, as council president—and thus the president of Afghanistan. Named as vice-presidents were Sarwari, who had last been reported seeking sanctuary at the Soviet embassy, and Keshtmand, who had been in prison. Other members of the council presidium were Qadir, who had also been in prison, and Watanjar, who presumably had been under Soviet protection somewhere, plus Lt. Col. Gol Aqa.[67]

That was followed fifteen minutes later by an announcement in the name of the Afghan government:

> Because of the continuation and expansion of aggression, intervention, and provocations by the foreign enemies of Afghanistan and for the purpose of defending the gains of the Saur Revolution, territorial integrity, national independence and the preservation of peace and security, and on the basis of the treaty of friendship, good-neighborliness and cooperation dated 5 December 1978, the Democratic Republic of Afghanistan earnestly demands that the USSR render urgently political, moral, and economic assistance, including military aid, to Afghanistan. The government of the USSR has accepted the proposal of the Afghan side.[68]

Another twenty minutes later, at 3:15 A.M., came an announcement "by the revolutionary tribunal" whose composition and authority were never further identified:

> The revolutionary tribunal has sentenced to death Hafizullah Amin for the crimes he has committed against the noble people of Afghanistan. As a result of these crimes, many of the noble compatriots of Afghanistan, including . . . members of the civilian and military services, as well as representatives of the enlightened religious leaders, intellectuals, workers and farmers [were killed]. The sentence of the tribunal has been carried out.[69]

Amin apparently went down fighting, or was shot as soon as his defenses were overcome. The evidence from Westerners in Kabul, one of whom trailed the Soviet assault team toward Darulaman,[70] is that no Afghans were involved in the attack there, which ended in the middle of the night. But both Karmal's and Soviet spokesmen later insisted that Amin had been eliminated by Afghan action. "The fact that Amin was removed at the time the entry of the Soviet military contingent began is merely a coincidence," a Soviet commentator contended. "There is no causal connection between the two. The change of leadership on December 27 . . . was effected by the Afghans themselves, including some who were members of the party and government leadership under Amin."[71]

Another Soviet commentator reacted even more forcefully to the facts as understood by foreign governments:

> It is even asserted that Amin "was shot by the Russians." That is a lie. Amin was condemned and executed by Afghans, by the people's authorities against whom he had dared to raise a hand. The Soviet troop contingent was sent to Afghanistan not to interfere in the country's internal affairs but to help the Afghan government safeguard the security of [its] borders.[72]

No evidence was ever presented to support this contention, no inquiry permitted into events in Kabul 27 December. Asked later if others besides Amin had been "sentenced and executed in December," Karmal replied that, "During the 27 December *rebellion* some of his [Amin's] followers were killed—three or four people—because they were putting up resistance." About 200 men "who were involved in Amin's plot are in prison . . . being carefully interrogated" and will be given "humane and democratic" trials, Karmal added.[73] His use of the term "rebellion" showed the way the history of the December events was being rewritten.

On that cold night in December and into the next morning, scattered fighting continued in the Darulaman area and in a few other pockets around Kabul. The resistance to the Soviet takeover caused a death toll that was obvious to foreigners in Kabul to have been significant but was never officially announced. Diplomats' guesses of Soviet casualties began at 25 killed and 225 wounded and went upward, some much higher, while Afghan losses were presumed to have been considerably larger.[74] Among the coffins later seen being loaded onto

Soviet planes at Kabul airport was one that was given the honors due a general.

That was recalled by diplomats when *Pravda* reported on 3 January that Paputin had died 28 December.[75] The obituary for the fifty-three-year-old and presumably healthy police general was unusual. Unlike obituaries for two other deputy ministers of internal affairs published in the previous six years, it was not signed by senior politburo members, included no photograph, and was run on the back page.[76] It gave no indication where or how he died, not even the usual cryptic Soviet wording to indicate natural causes ("unexpectedly"), an accident ("tragically"), or combat ("heroically"). Two versions of Paputin's death soon began to circulate in Moscow.[77] One was that he had been killed in the attack on Amin's Tajbeg Palace, although why he would have been involved in an army action was unexplained. Another that became most widely circulated was that he had committed suicide because he had failed in his assignment to dispose of Amin quietly, without calling attention to the Soviet role.

Yet later reports said neither of these, that he had killed himself because of difficulties in Moscow that at worst had only been exacerbated by his Kabul trip. The later reports said Paputin had been under pressure from Yuri M. Churbanov.[78] Married to Brezhnev's daughter, Galina, the forty-four-year-old Churbanov had been getting rapid promotions in the interior ministry, becoming a deputy minister in 1977 and in late 1979 receiving unusual publicity for speeches around the Soviet Union. Two months after Paputin died, Churbanov was disclosed to have become first deputy minister,[79] and a year later he was made a nonvoting member of the Soviet Communist Party's central committee.[80]

It is impossible to tell where the truth lies, but a few points may be noted. One is that some senior Soviet officer may well have been killed in the stiff defense that Amin's guard put up, but it need not have been Paputin, who had no military experience to qualify him for the assault. Another is that some diplomats and others in Moscow, who had in the past received accurate reports from Soviet acquaintances, heard and believed the reports that Paputin committed suicide because of his failure in Kabul. A third is that a man of Paputin's background in political infighting would hardly have been likely to kill himself because Brezhnev's son-in-law wanted his job. The mystery remains.

The morning after the airborne troops had seized control of Kabul, two motorized rifle divisions began crossing the Amu Darya on pontoon bridges, while two more were mobilizing to cross soon after.[81] In addition to tanks and armored personnel carriers, they travelled in trucks made at the new Kama River truck plant.[82] The Nixon administration had agreed during the era of détente to provide the plant with specialized United States manufacturing equipment on condition that it would produce only civilian vehicles.

Since these four divisions had been brought up to combat strength with local reservists, some of whom were called up as late as 24 December, they had a high proportion of Uzbeks, Tajiks, and Turkmen.[83] The Soviet Union had abandoned by 1939 the practice of manning military units on a territorial basis, so the pre-callup manpower of the divisions presumably was more diversified, but still half or more of the infantrymen in these divisions might have been Soviet Central Asian Moslems. The airborne units, on the other hand, were predominately Russian, and as the normal ninety-day reserve callup period began to end, the rifle divisions received more Russian replacements.

But in the first month or two of the Soviet occupation, men from just north of the Amu Darya—who reportedly had been told they had come to fight pagans, not Moslems[84]—discovered common bonds with the Afghans, including common languages. A brisk business developed in selling the soldiers copies of the Koran, which is almost impossible to obtain in Soviet Central Asia. Soviet soldiers could be seen buying them in the marketplaces of Kabul, Herat, and Qandahar,[85] towns that the rifle divisions quickly garrisoned as they spread out to seize control of main population centers, airports, and communications lines.

With Soviet troops pouring into Afghanistan, expanding and consolidating their control, Moscow Radio reported at 2:30 P.M. Kabul time on 28 December the statement that had been broadcast from Kabul almost twelve hours earlier asking for aid, including military aid. The Moscow version was substantially the same as Kabul's, but six hours later Tass distributed the statement with an addition. It said Afghanistan had asked military aid, "which the government . . . *repeatedly requested* from the government of the Soviet Union."[86] Both versions concluded that "the Soviet Union has met the request."

Just who made it, and when, still presented a problem for the Kremlin, however. Its diplomats were instructed to inform foreign governments of the entry of Soviet troops into Afghanistan without mentioning that they had overthrown the government there. Ambassador Yuri M. Vorontsov in New Delhi called on Indian Foreign Secretary R. D. Sathe just before midnight 27 December to inform him that its troops had gone into Afghanistan to help "Afghan authorities . . . resist external aggression and interference." Vorontsov did not mention the coup d'etat then under way.[87]

Other Soviet ambassadors delivered notes the next day in a number of countries citing the 1978 treaty provision to "consult each other and take by agreement appropriate measures to ensure the security, independence, and territorial integrity of the two countries." The notes also cited Article 51 of the United Nations charter.[88] It recognizes "the inherent right of individual or collective self-defense if an armed attack occurs against a member of the United Nations, until the Security Council has taken measures necessary to maintain international peace and security." No proof of external attack was offered.

An interesting difference in the Soviet messages soon became apparent. Some governments were told that Amin had requested the Soviet troops on 26 December, although it was not explained why he would have done so if, as later charged, he were planning an anti-Communist crackdown 29 December; or why the request would have been made only well after they had begun to arrive. Other governments were told that the request was made by Karmal 27 December—at a time before Kabul Radio had announced his supposed selection as president.[89] The elaborate story of Karmal's having been inside Afghanistan earlier and organizing a majority of leadership survivors from Amin's repeated purges to turn secretly against him was concocted only later, after the initial Soviet explanations had met with disbelief.

Quoting Kabul Radio, Tass reported from Kabul twenty-four hours after the Soviet military action had begun there that the PDPA politburo had met 28 December and unanimously elected Karmal as general secretary.[90] This was some seventeen hours after Kabul Radio had at 2:40 A.M. identified Karmal as the party's general secretary in announcing the new revolutionary council presidium, including Karmal's presidency. Within an hour of its Kabul report, Tass reported that Brezhnev had sent a message to Karmal, whom it identified with the additional title of prime minister although there had not been any announcement of that. In contrast to the chilly "accept our greetings" on Amin's "appointment" in September, it said:

I heartily congratulate you on being elected as general secretary of the central committee . . . and to the senior state positions of . . . Afghanistan. On behalf of the Soviet leadership and myself personally, I wish you great successes in all your diverse activity for the good of the friendly Afghan people. I am sure that in the present conditions the Afghan people will succeed in defending the gains of the April revolution, the sovereignty, independence and national dignity of the new Afghanistan.[91]

Karmal replied to his "dear comrade" Brezhnev with "my profound and cordial gratitude for your very warm, fraternal congratulations in connection with my election. . . . I am convinced that with the fraternal aid and unchanging cooperation of the great USSR we will conquer and overcome all the difficulties which we have inherited from the past."[92]

There was another contrast in Brezhnev's message. It was with the one he and Kosygin had sent to Taraki after the April 1978 takeover. They said then that relations would develop on the basis of equality, good-neighborliness, respect for national sovereignty, and "noninterference in each other's internal affairs." There was no such mention when the Soviets installed their puppet in Kabul.[93] But when *Pravda* on 31 December published the first full, authoritative Soviet statement, it said the Soviet Union had decided to grant Afghanistan's

insistent request . . . [for] immediate aid and support in the struggle against external aggression . . . and to send to Afghanistan a limited Soviet military contingent that will be used exclusively for assistance in rebuffing the armed interference from the outside. The Soviet contingent will be completely pulled out of Afghanistan when the reason that necessitated such an action exists no longer.

Denying that the country was being occupied by Soviet troops or that the troops were involved in internal affairs, the article said that "patriotic forces in Afghanistan . . . rose not only against foreign aggression but also against the usurper. Relying on the support of the people, they removed Amin."[94] The term "usurper" showed that the Kremlin had never forgiven Amin for having seized power from Taraki, but the fact that neither Taraki nor Karmal was ever labeled a usurper showed it was in Soviet eyes all relative.

Aside from Karmal's own later conflicting claims of when he had returned to Afghanistan, he is not definitely known to have been in Kabul until 1 January, when he first appeared publicly there.[95] Some reports said that he arrived in a Soviet military plane around 2:00 A.M. 28 December,[96] which would indicate that he must have left Soviet Central Asia about the time the troops at Darulaman radioed that they had killed Amin; but President Carter said that "only several days later was the new puppet leader even brought into Afghanistan by the Soviets."[97]

Beginning 28 December, Kabul Radio began to carry speeches by Karmal that could have been taped elsewhere. In them, he sought to reassure the Afghan people of the moderation of his new regime. The speeches showed Karmal's oratorical skills from his parliamentary days more than a decade earlier, his emphasis then on moderation in moving toward socialism by establishing as broad a front as possible with non-Communist forces, and Safronchuk's policy of trying to rally wide support by playing down the radical leftist tendencies of the regime. In fact, beginning with Karmal's speeches the whole public relations effort of the Kabul government began to sound more and more like Soviet media. Within a few months the nature and tone of Afghan media material were almost exactly like those of Moscow or of some long-loyal Soviet ally, Bulgaria or Mongolia, for instance.

In his speeches from 28 December through a celebration 1 January of the fifteenth anniversary of the PDPA's founding, one of Karmal's themes was the freedoms lost by the Afghan people under Amin, "this bloodthirsty spy of U.S. imperialism, oppressor and dictator."[98] Those freedoms were now being returned. The new government, he said,

> will safeguard freedom and genuine inviolability of the person, freedom for political prisoners, genuine democracy, jobs for the unemployed, improved labor conditions for workers, land for peasants. The revolutionary council will ensure favorable and safe conditions for the return of those compatriots who as a result of the bloody oppression by the Amin regime have fled their motherland. The question of persons who have taken up arms against the government will be settled by political means. The revolutionary council will safeguard and protect the rights of all classes and democratic strata of society . . . [and] of all nationalities and peoples of Afghanistan, assure a genuine respect and guarantees for the sacred religion of Islam and the clergy, the lofty national traditions and customs, the family ties and personal property.[99]

Karmal promised "a total amnesty for all those political prisoners who have survived the bloody Amin regime."[100] He said the regime's main duty would be "to rectify harmful mistakes, to compensate for the damage inflicted, and to overcome the crisis."[101] Another main theme was the nature of the future government. "Our immediate task in the present conditions is not the introduction of socialism," Karmal declared, but the regime will try to strengthen and develop "the progressive social and political foundations" of the government, "bringing the anti-feudal national, democratic, anti-imperialist and anti-compradore revolution to final victory."[102] To achieve these goals, he said,

> At the first opportunity, a broad front will be created of all the national and democratic forces under the leadership of the People's Democratic Party of Afghanistan, the party of the working class and all working peoples. All democratic freedoms will be guaranteed, including the freedom to create progressive patriotic parties and people's organizations, freedom of the press, freedom of expression and assembly.[103]

In foreign relations, Karmal proclaimed "a peaceful foreign policy, a policy of positive and active neutrality."[104] He welcomed the overthrow of the shah in Iran, saying Afghanistan had no differences with that country and would try to improve relations. He called "for the elimination of all differences with the Pakistani leaders," but reiterated Afghan calls for self-determination for Pushtun and Baluch peoples in Pakistan. And he advocated "disinterested friendship" with China, "which is also our neighbor."[105]

Karmal appealed to Afghan soldiers "to defend fearlessly, no matter where you are, the great April revolution from all the schemes of the internal and external enemies." So long as there is outside interference in Afghan affairs, he said, we "shall ask for further assistance from the USSR and other peace-loving countries of the world . . . from Vietnam, victorious Cuba, Ethiopia, Angola and the victorious Palestinian Arab people and others."[106]

The first of Amin's political prisoners reported released were Keshtmand, Rafi, Qadir, Taraki's widow Nur Bibi Taraki, and Sarwari's wife, plus other PDPA members, religious leaders, and others.[107] Keshtmand was soon reported in Moscow for medical treatment because of the torture he had suffered in prison,[108] although there was an alternative report that he was hospitalized as a result of a 7 February shootout in the new leadership[109]—which included his chief torturer, Sarwari.

With those PDPA leaders released, and with Sarwari, Watanjar, and others who had been reported under Soviet protection in the autumn, reappearing in Kabul from unexplained places, the new leadership was assembled. Five of the seven PDPA politburo members were Parchamis, while two were Khalqis, and the party secretariat was composed of general secretary Karmal and one ordinary secretary from each faction. The PDPA central committee was predominately Parchami but also contained persons not previously associated with either faction, such as Qadir and Watanjar.[110]

The government announced 9 January that it had released about 6,000 political prisoners.[111] By July, Karmal was saying that 15,000 had been freed "in the first few hours" of his takeover.[112] Amnesty International said "independent sources in Kabul estimated that between 3,000 and 4,000 prisoners had been released from Kabul's Pul-i-Charki prison."[113] Since it was reported to have contained some three times as many persons in Amin's time, the amnesty seemed to have been selective. There were angry and occasionally violent scenes as relatives learned of prisoners' being deceased or still being held.[114] But the new regime did release a number of former government officials, politically neutral technocrats and others whom Amin had distrusted. It also began adding many new prisoners. They included Amin's deputy Shah Wali, who was still reported in Pul-i-Charki more that a year later, and seventeen others officially described as being "political prisoners who were closely related to Hafizullah Amin."[115]

Chapter 10. Consequences

The Soviet intervention in Afghanistan created a reaction that was swift and strong. It put the Soviet Union on the defensive before the outraged opinions of many countries. Surprised at the strength of denunciation, Soviet leaders reacted with tough defiance. Without yielding in their determination to hold Afghanistan within the Soviet sphere of direct and dominating influence, they launched a campaign to try to shift the blame to outsiders accused of supporting the Afghan resistance to Communist rule. The campaign met with little success, and the Soviet Union found itself unable to justify or explain away the cause of its widespread criticism. Not only the Western world but also the Third World condemned the invasion and the subsequent Soviet military occupation. In the United Nations, nations that normally tried to avoid being counted against Moscow—whose acquiescence in Soviet policies out of fear or self-interest the Kremlin had come to count upon—voted against the Soviet military presence in Afghanistan. Islamic nations condemned it. None had any effect on long-term Soviet intentions.

American Reaction

The worldwide reaction was led by the United States. "We are the other superpower on earth," President Carter said, "and it became my responsibility . . . to take action that would prevent the Soviets from [accomplishing] this invasion with impunity."[1] As soon as a picture of what had happened in Kabul emerged, Carter telephoned the leaders in Britain, France, West Germany, Italy, and Pakistan. All of them "agreed that the Soviet action is a grave threat to peace," Carter reported on 28 December.[2] Within a week Carter was calling it " an extremely serious threat to peace," explaining that this was "because of the threat of further Soviet expansion into neighboring countries in Southwest Asia and also because such an aggressive military policy is unsettling to other peoples thoughout the world."[3] By 8 January it had become "*the greatest* threat to peace since the Second World War," according to the president.[4] But on 15 January he made it only "one of the most serious threats to peace since the Second World War,"[5] and by 23 January Carter was telling Congress that "The implications of the Soviet invasion of Afghanistan *could* pose the most serious threat to peace since the Second World War."[6]

In condemning the Soviet action, Carter said it had caused "the overthrow of the established government and the execution of the president of that country[7] . . . . The Soviets claim, falsely, that they were invited into Afghanistan to help protect that country from some unnamed outside threat. But the president, who had been the leader of Afghanistan before the Soviet invasion, was assassinated —along with several members of his family."[8]

This was bitterly criticized by Soviet media and Soviet-controlled Afghan media. Reiterating the condemnation of Amin as a usurper, they denied that he was the legitimate president. Describing Taraki as the legitimate president "in accordance with the will of the people," Karmal asked about Amin, "Can a president who killed the head of state elected by the people be 'legitimate'?"[9] This conveniently ignored the fact that Daoud had gone though an elective process, questionable as it was, to ratify his seizure of power, but after Daoud was killed, Taraki had never submitted his rule to any form of referendum. Why had Carter not complained, Communist media asked, about Taraki's murder or the murder of "thousands of honest, innocent citizens" by Amin?[10] The United States had, in fact, earlier criticized human rights violations in Afghanistan, but the differences between internal affairs and the Soviet role was glossed over in the Soviet and Afghan media criticism. After ten days of this Communist propaganda campaign, the Afghan government press agency produced an open letter from Taraki's widow to Carter. Saying she was "angered and shocked," Nur Bibi Taraki accused Carter of "trying to protect this criminal and murderer Amin."[11] Karmal later added that the supposed American defense of Amin proved that he had been a CIA agent.[12]

The American reaction developed over a week that included the New Year's holiday weekend. On 28 December Carter sent Brezhnev a message calling for a Soviet troop withdrawal and saying that the Afghanistan action, "if not corrected, could have very serious consequences to United States-Soviet relations."[13] Brezhnev's reply was inadequate, Carter said 31 December.[14]

He claimed that he had been invited by the Afghan government to come in and protect Afghanistan from some outside third-nation threat. This was obviously false because the person that he claimed invited him in, President Amin, was murdered or assassinated after the Soviets pulled their coup. He also claimed that they would remove their forces from Afghanistan as soon as the situation should be stabilized and the outside threat to Afghanistan was eliminated. So that was the tone of his message to me, which, as I say, was completely inadequate and completely misleading.[15]

Asked if that meant Brezhnev were lying, Carter replied, "He is not telling the facts accurately." Carter went on, when asked about his earlier efforts to show good will toward the Soviet Union in hopes of its reciprocation, "My opinion of the Russians has changed most drastically in the last week than even the previous 2-1/2 years before that . . . . This action of the Soviets has made a more dramatic change in my own opinion of what the Soviets' ultimate goals are than anything they've done in the previous time I've been in office.[16]

Carter added later that "the Soviets have seriously misjudged our own nation's strength and resolve and unity and determination, and the condemnation that has accrued to them by the world community[17] . . . . They underestimated the courage and the tenacity of freedom fighters in that country, and they did not anticipate the world's quick and forceful response to their aggression."[18] After *Pravda* had accused the United States of "anti-Soviet hysteria reminiscent of the lamentable cold war times,"[19] Carter said that "We don't want to return to the cold war; we don't want to have a confrontation with the Soviet Union. . . . The Soviets have tried to mislead the world; they have failed."[20] As the bitter exchanges continued, Moscow media characterized Carter as "wicked and malicious."[21]

The Trigger Theory

The strength of the American reaction cannot be attributed to the Soviet intervention in Afghanistan alone. Moscow's move was more of a last straw that convinced Carter of the need to take a stronger stand against the Soviet Union. The Angola move had come before Carter's presidency, but he had agonized over Ethiopia and taken note of South Yemen. The Cuban episode three months earlier added to the administration's sense of frustration over Soviet actions, as did growing Soviet activity in Southeast Asia and support for Vietnamese aggression in Cambodia. Afghanistan seemed to prove the point that some officials had long been arguing: The Soviet Union is an aggressively expansionist power that is ignoring the supposed limitations of détente and understands only counterforce. A bureaucratic struggle had been going on in Washington over interpretation of a number of Soviet activities in the preceding few years—how aggressive they were, how inimical to United States interests, how the United States should deal with each new problem that touched on relations between Washington and Moscow. Afghanistan decided that struggle, at least for a time. Some officials who had believed in a tougher American policy of confrontation, and had often argued for retaliation, claimed to have been vindicated.

This became known in some Washington circles as "the trigger theory" about Afghanistan. The Soviets had only triggered the release of tensions that had been growing in superpower relations and within the Carter administration over how to handle them. Soviet media were quick to make this point, although twisting it to fit their own line. At the beginning of an election year, Moscow Radio's New York correspondent accused Carter on 2 January of "deliberately using events in Iran and Afghanistan to strengthen his position in the struggle for the presidency."[22] A government-authorized statement by Tass 6 January accused the United States of using the Soviet action as a pretext to worsen relations.[23] A few days later *Izvestiya* said that Brzezinski, who was "well-known for his extreme anti-Communism and morbid anti-Sovietism," had prevailed in the Washington struggle. Brzezinski's "line," the paper said, "which until recently scared many people in the United States with its extremism and fanaticism, has become . . . Washington's official policy."[24]

There was truth to this to the extent of the presidential security adviser's advocating a hard line—as Brzezinski was proud to acknowledge to friends, claiming credit for a policy reorientation that he had long sought. It was Brzezinski among top United States officials who was earliest with the harshest characterization of the Soviet action, calling it "a qualitatively new step involving direct invasion. . . . The naked use of military force to impose one's political will on a sovereign country and a sovereign government."[25]

But Soviet media missed or deliberately ignored the broader point of American concern about "the changed correlation of forces" and a long succession of events. The mood in America about relations with Moscow had been changing. Organizations like the Committee on the Present Danger, founded in 1976, were getting a wider hearing for their contention that growing Soviet power was becoming a grave threat to United States interests. By seeming to confirm in Afghanistan the aggressive nature of that power, Soviet leaders had intensified a trend. Perhaps they also contributed to the electoral defeat ten months later of Carter and the succession of a new president who believed in greater United States military strength and determination to confront the Soviet Union, thus affecting their long-term interests in a much more profound way than the Carter administration's immediate actions. It was significant, however, that the American attitude toward the Soviet Union had so changed that the Afghanistan invasion was absorbed into and affected that attitude without remaining for long a much-discussed subject. In the presidential campaign debate between Carter and Ronald Reagan on 28 October 1980,[26] for instance, Afghanistan was never mentioned, but both candidates assumed the need for greater military strength to resist the Soviet pressures.

The pressures that were feared the most were in the area of the Persian Gulf and its vital oil resources. Without contending that the Soviet move into Afghanistan was offensive in original purpose or intention, the Carter administration adopted the position that its results were very much offensive in a strategic sense. It was, Brzezinski said, "not a local but a strategic challenge."[27] Carter declared that

> our own nation's security was directly threatened. There is no doubt that the Soviets' move into Afghanistan, if done without adverse consequences, would have resulted in the temptation to move again until they reached warm water ports or until they acquired control over a major portion of the world's oil supplies.[28] . . . The Soviet Union has altered the strategic situation in that part of the world in a very ominous fashion.[29] . . . It places the Soviets within aircraft striking range of the vital oil resources of the Persian Gulf; it threatens a strategically located country, Pakistan; [and] it poses the prospect of increased Soviet pressure on Iran and on other nations of the Middle East.[30]

Such statements built up to a ringing statement in Carter's State of the Union address to Congress on 23 January that was inevitably labeled "the Carter doctrine": "Let our position be absolutely clear: An attempt by any outside force to gain control of the Persian Gulf region will be regarded as an assault on the vital interests of the United States of America, and such an assault will be repelled by any means necessary, including military force."[31] What this statement meant was unclear. It was rhetoric without analysis. Carter spoke without any detailed administration study of the policy implications or alternatives.[32]

Types of Responses

Thus, in a hasty, sometimes emotional way, the president had laid the basis for two types of American responses during the first month after the Soviet action in Afghanistan. One was a strengthening of the United States military position, with help if possible from allies far more dependent upon oil from the Gulf than the United States. The development of this response, with its increased defense budgets, its difficulties in preparing an effective "rapid deployment force" for the Gulf area, its problems in trying to work with those dependent allies as well as with vulnerable nations in the area, will not be pursued here. The other response was penalizing the Soviet Union for its aggression in the hope of deterring it from some future repetition and of thereby instilling confidence among friends and allies.

There was never any expectation that the penalties would cause a Soviet withdrawal from Afghanistan, although there was some initial hope that over time Kremlin leaders might decide that holding onto the country was not worth the costs. Shortly after the penalties were imposed, Secretary of State Cyrus R. Vance said that the Soviet Union "will continue to pay a heavy price as long as their troops remain in Afghanistan."[33] Five months after the invasion, however, Vance's successor as secretary, Edmund S. Muskie, expressed concern that Soviet censorship and denial of journalistic access to events in Afghanistan was so reducing Western media attention that "the public perception of the significance, gravity, and importance of the Soviet invasion will fade here, in Europe, and elsewhere around the globe, and our efforts to continue pressure on the Soviets—to continue to exact a price from them—may well begin to fade because of the lack of will."[34]

How to exert pressure? The Carter administration had failed during the long, closely monitored Soviet military buildup for the invasion to consider systematically what steps might be taken if the repeated United States warnings were ignored. It therefore had to focus hurriedly on the subject at a time when some key officials were off on Christmas and New Year's vacations. Once again, as in previous cases when Soviet actions seemed to have gone too far, lists were drawn up of ways to retaliate. But, whereas previously the lists had been put back into the files, this time Carter's opinion had "changed most drastically."

At the working level in the State Department, Soviet affairs specialists put on their lists every aspect of Soviet-American relations that might be changed. They even included some things they did not want changed because changes would hurt the United States more than the Soviet Union, such as closing new consulates and thus halting several years of hard work to open the first official American vantage point in the Soviet Ukraine, a consulate in Kiev. Carter said that the United States "has no desire, nor could we have effectively implemented military action, to drive the Soviet forces from Afghanistan."[35] Initially, he spoke only of making Moscow suffer "severe political consequences" for its actions,[36] but by 2 January this had been broadened. Meeting that afternoon with the National Security Council, Carter decided on both political and economic measures.[37]

SALT Delay

The first to be announced, the next day, was a request to the United States Senate to delay consideration of ratifying the SALT II treaty. "While the president continues to believe that ratification of SALT II is in the national security interest of the United States," his spokesman said, "he has concluded that the Soviet invasion of Afghanistan, in defiance of the United Nations charter, has made consideration of the SALT II treaty inappropriate at this time."[38] This was a sharp break with the administration's previous efforts to insulate SALT from the vagaries of Soviet-American relations. It was made all the more striking by Brzezinski's having argued three days earlier that SALT "should be pursued if it can be pursued, whether there are Soviet troops in Kabul or whether Soviet troops are marching back to Tashkent."[39] More than a foreign policy judgment, it represented a domestic political decision that the already doubtful prospects for ratification of the controversial treaty had been further damaged and that it would be better to wait than to have the treaty rejected by the Senate. Some other aspects of arms control negotiations with the Soviet Union that the Carter administration had started with great optimism in 1977 but had soon become stalemated, such as trying to restrict military forces in the Indian Ocean and limit conventional arms sales to Third World countries, were in effect abandoned.[40]

The Six Sanctions

In an address to the nation 4 January, Carter announced six ways in which the United States would attempt to penalize the Soviet Union, separate from his decision on SALT, so that it would not "commit this act with impunity."[41] One lesson learned from history "at great cost is that aggression, unopposed, becomes a contagious disease," Carter said. "The response of the international community to the Soviet attempt to crush Afghanistan must match the gravity of the Soviet action."

The first step he listed was a delay in opening new consular facilities. That meant the United States lost its seven-person Kiev outpost. The Soviets simply had to forego a seventeen-person consulate in New York City, where they already had a huge staff for United Nations business as well as commercial representation.[42]

Second was a deferment of most cultural and economic exchanges then under consideration. A 1973 General Agreement on Contacts, Exchanges and Cooperation had expired on 31 December 1979. Negotiations for a new agreement had been under way well before that. The new one was expected to be completed in the new year, with retroactive effect to the old one's expiration. Under a succession of such agreements, scores of Soviet researchers had obtained access to leading United States technological institutes, among other places. Americans had, by contrast, found themselves severely restricted in the Soviet Union—a sore point for years with some United States critics of the agreements. There was no effort to expel those Soviets already in the United States under the expired agreement, but Carter halted negotiations on a new one.[43]

His third step was a severe restriction on trade. Carter said he had directed "that no high technology or other strategic items will be licensed for sale to the Soviet Union until further notice." Later a lasting ban was put on such things as high-capacity computers and oil drilling equipment. With the CIA predicting a future oil shortage in the Soviet bloc, the drilling equipment ban was controversial. Some Americans contended that it would only increase the likelihood of a Soviet move toward the Persian Gulf oil fields and therefore was unwise and potentially counterproductive. Brzezinski had argued against selling the equipment in 1978 but lost; after Afghanistan his view prevailed. But fifteen months later specialists on Soviet economics at the United States Congressional Research Service concluded that "Restrictions on high technology exports have largely had the effect of shifting Soviet orders to other Western suppliers. . . . The short-term impact on the Soviet economy appears to be negligible."[44]

The fourth step listed by Carter was a curtailment of Soviet fishing privileges in United States waters. This reduced possible Soviet catches from 435,000 metric tons annually to 75,000 metric tons, cutting some 4 percent from the Soviet worldwide catch. Moscow tried to make this up by shifting its long-range fishing fleet to other waters.[45]

Fifth was denial of seventeen million metric tons of grain that the Soviet Union had obtained authorization to buy in the United States in order to build up Soviet livestock herds. Under a five-year agreement signed in 1976, the United States had promised to sell the Soviet Union up to eight million tons of grain a year and to consider further sales. After a bad harvest in 1979, Moscow asked for twenty-five million tons. It had initially been approved, and the Soviet grain trading agency Eksportkhleb had already contracted for almost twenty-two million, when Carter cancelled the approval for everything over the eight-million basic agreement. "After consultation with other principal grain-exporting nations," he said, "I am confident that they will not replace these quantities of grain by additional shipments on their part to the Soviet Union." The consultations turned out to have been only very hasty and incomplete, however, and Carter too optimistic that political principle would prevail over the profit motive. Other nations, most notably Argentina, did replace the American grain. At some inconvenience and higher cost, "The Soviets were able to replace most of the embargoed grain from other sources," the Congressional Research Service study concluded. American farmers, rather than Soviet consumers, came to be seen as the main losers from the embargo.[46] This made it a United States domestic political issue. On 24 April 1981, after argument within his new administration, President Ronald Reagan lifted the embargo.[47] Within months, the Soviet Union, suffering in 1981 from its third poor harvest in a row, resumed large-scale purchasing of American grain.

Carter's sixth step was a warning of a possible United States withdrawal from the 1980 summer Olympics in Moscow if there were "continued aggressive actions" by the Soviet Union. The United States did boycott the games, and it claimed to have "helped to persuade 59 other countries to take similar action."[48] But the Olympics went on, seventy-nine countries (including Puerto Rico) participated, and "the administration could only be dissatisfied at the level of support for the boycott on the part of its traditional allies in Western Europe," the CRS study said.[49]

It concluded that Carter's sanctions might have had political benefits, but

> the economic punishment to the USSR was quite limited . . . . While many nations supported the Olympic boycott, no other nations followed fully the U.S. embargo and restrictive actions. This illustrates the difference between the United States and the other Western allies, which generally supported the political aspects of the sanctions while not supporting the principle of economic punishment adopted by the Carter administration.[50]

Carter had, in sum, adopted virtually everything on the lists of possible United States reactions, including some items that middling-ranking officials had put on them without seriously expecting acceptance—or even wanting it, as in the case of giving up the Kiev consulate. The mood of Soviet-American relations had been sharply altered. Only a few minor suggestions, such as slashing the United States embassy staff in Moscow and forcing a cut in the much larger number of Soviet citizens in Washington, were not adopted. The Afghan situation was later cited as the reason for steps in other fields, including the president's call 8 February for draft registration.[51]

It could be argued that Carter's strong language and strong actions were both results of earlier frustrations in dealing with the Soviet Union. By adopting angry positions in times of previous difficult relations, by calling the Soviet brigade in Cuba unacceptable, for instance, the administration had devalued the rhetoric of reaction. In previous difficulties, the administration had looked for some form of leverage to get the Soviets to adhere to the Western interpretation of détente rules, but it had failed to find anything effective while it held out SALT and grain sales as untouchable.

On SALT there was a curious reversal of thinking. Before the Afghanistan action, United States officials had thought Soviet leaders considered SALT too important to risk by committing open and blatant aggression, while Soviet officials thought the Carter administration considered it too important to link to Soviet actions. But the Afghanistan problem became too urgent in Soviet minds to leave unresolved, thus breaking any linkage that might have existed in Moscow between SALT and foreign actions. The United States, however, found the Afghanistan action too egregious to exclude SALT from the repercussions. SALT, and grain too, became an administration hostage to superpower relations, as SALT had already partially become a Senate hostage.

The Soviet reaction to the American reaction developed quickly. First came *Pravda*'s saying that the United States violation of agreements between the two countries "can only serve to further complicate economic development for the United States and its allies which is already weakened by a series of severe crises."[52] Then the Tass statement on 6 January declared that, "If the White House decided to influence in some way the Soviet Union, its foreign policy, this is a hopeless undertaking. Such attempts flopped in the past and they will flop now."[53] Moscow Radio said mysteriously that Carter had "obviously underestimated the possibility of Soviet retaliation."[54]

This culminated in Brezhnev's statement in *Pravda* 13 January. After accusing the United States of having embarked in 1978 "on a course hostile to the cause of détente," and explaining the "no[t] simple decision" to send the Soviet Army into Afghanistan as a result of what he said were external aggression there and a threat to the Soviet border, Brezhnev said Carter's steps "show that Washington again, like decades ago, is trying to speak to us in the language of the cold war." Reversing the situation as seen from the United States, he contended that

> the arrogation by Washington of some sort of a "right" to "reward" or "punish" independent sovereign states raises a question of a principled character. In effect, by such actions the U.S. government deals a blow at the orderly international law system of relations among states. . . . The world is increasingly forming the impression of the United States as an absolutely unreliable partner in interstate ties. . . . These actions of the U.S. administration will not inflict on us the damage obviously hoped for by their initiators. . . . They will hit back at their initiators, if not today then tomorrow.[55]

Brezhnev specifically promised that, despite the grain sales restrictions, "the plans of providing the Soviet people with bread and bakery products will not be lessened by a single kilogram."[56] This deliberately missed the point Carter had made that the withheld "grain was not intended for human consumption but was to be used for building up Soviet livestock herds."[57] Feed for livestock was already in critically short supply in some parts of the Soviet Union,[58] and the American restriction had a significant impact on Brezhnev's long-term commitment to increase the small amount of meat available to Soviet consumers.

Brezhnev's politburo deputy Andrey P. Kirilenko said a month later that "The next nationwide task is to win the battle to maintain the livestock population and prevent a decrease in the production of meat, milk and other livestock products."[59] But the battle went poorly in 1980, when grain harvests were again low and herds had to be reduced. The restriction of United States grain and technology sales to the Soviet Union cut trade between the two countries about 50 percent in the first nine months of 1980, while Soviet trade with the West overall increased 26 percent.[60]

Carter's economic steps gave new life to the Soviet internal debate over emphasizing autarky or seeking the benefits of foreign trade.[61] Kosygin's successor as premier, Nikolai A. Tikhonov, tried to resolve this argument by his speech to the Soviet Communist Party's twenty-sixth congress in February 1981. His government wants "stable, mutually advantageous" trade with the West, Tikhonov said. Ignoring Afghanistan, he continued:

> It is not our fault that, for example, trade with the United States is declining or in a state of stagnation. This is the result of the U.S. policy aimed at using trade for unseemly political ends alien to the interests of equitable international cooperation. As for the Soviet Union, we are also ready to develop economic relations with the United States on an equitable and mutually advantageous basis.[62]

This was seen by some American officials as an admission by Moscow that the Carter restrictions had hurt and that the Soviet Union was eager for the new Reagan administration to lift them.[63]

In addition to the penalties, Carter announced 4 January that, "Along with other countries, we will provide military equipment, food, and other assistance to help Pakistan defend its independence and its national security against the seriously increased threat it now faces from the north."[64] The Pakistani government had on 29 December expressed grave concern over the "external military intervention" in the bordering nation, saying it had "far-reaching negative consequences" and calling for a Soviet withdrawal.[65] Two days later Brzezinski publicly affirmed the 1959 United States commitment to "take such appropriate action, including the use of armed force, as may be mutually agreed" in case of aggression against Pakistan—subject to American "constitutional procedures," which meant congressional approval.[66]

As a professional soldier, President Zia knew that the United States could provide little direct military support on his mountainous northwest frontier, however. He wanted weapons and related help to build up his own well-trained but somewhat antiquated 400,000-man army. When the United States offered $100 million in military aid for each of two years, and an equivalent amount of supporting economic aid, he scorned this as "peanuts."[67] The Reagan administration took up the subject a year later and finally, on 15 September 1981, completed agreement with Pakistan on $3.2 billion in aid over six years beginning 1 October 1982, if Congress provided the money. Half of this was to be military aid, half economic. In addition, Pakistan would buy forty F-16 jet fighters for $1.1 billion, if it could scrape up the money.[68]

The key question about the United States aid and about any F-16 financing Pakistan might get from rich Arab friends was whether Pakistan could be made secure enough against Soviet pressure and even retaliatory cross-border raids for it to be able to give active support to the guerrillas inside Afghanistan. Zia had denied Afghan and Soviet charges of helping Kabul's opponents in the period before the invasion, and he reiterated the denials after it.[69]

European Reaction

West European governments generally criticized the Soviet Union, but there was some reluctance to react as strongly as the United States did. A British parliamentary committee noted "inadequate consultation among alliance members before it was decided to impose sanctions . . . . Had there been consultation, the possibility of sanctions' proving effective would have been strongly questioned and the differing interests of the allies on the use of sanctions would have emerged."[70] In a period of economic recession, few Western nations were eager to restrict their trade with the Soviet Union; West Germany increased its exports there by 31 percent in the first nine months of 1980 while boycotting the Olympic games.[71] Many Europeans were more eager to continue arms control talks with the Soviet Union in hope of preventing a breakdown of détente and limiting the arms race than they were to punish Moscow for violating the spirit of détente. There was a musty echo of 1938 in this unwillingness to relinquish hopes for good East-West relations "because of a quarrel in a faraway country between people of whom we know nothing."[72] A United States House subcommittee report declared that "the reactions of the allies have been found wanting."[73] There was no more than the usual continuing controversy in Western Europe about building up defenses. The situation in Afghanistan had some little effect on the discussions, but there were differences over whether to try to project European power into the Persian Gulf or to make a greater effort to facilitate American military efforts there. And there were the old disagreements over the proper balance between negotiating with an adversary and confronting him.[74]

While Moscow emphasized the deep roots of détente in Europe, seeking to separate NATO allies from the United States position, the allies as a whole condemned the Afghanistan action but limited their reactions to largely symbolic acts.[75] They also began seeking diplomatic means of easing the problem, including formulas for a Soviet troop withdrawal. Soviet efforts to influence the European reaction went beyond media campaigns and ordinary diplomatic contacts. The Soviets were reported to have warned Scandinavian nations such as Sweden, which had been outspokenly critical of United States actions in Vietnam, not to criticize the Afghanistan invasion.[76] This was seen by some Europeans as outright intimidation, and a Finnish newspaper suggested that there was a double standard in the mildness of the general world reaction to the Soviet action.[77]

Third World Reactions

In the Islamic world and in other Third World countries, there was a wave of protests against the Soviet Union. Most of these were countries with which Moscow had tried over the years to claim similar interests and sympathetic understanding. It continued to try, and over time the protests began to subside, while the United States sought diplomatically to encourage the outrage.[78] Among Islamic countries, those not directly involved in the Arab-Israeli conflict showed the strongest and most lasting concern about Moslem Afghanistan. Islamic reaction focused quickly on an extraordinary meeting of foreign ministers on 27 to 29 January 1980 in Islamabad, Pakistan, to consider the invasion. Thirty-five nations strongly condemned "the Soviet military aggression against the Afghan people," called for "the immediate and unconditional withdrawal of all Soviet troops . . . [who] should refrain from acts of oppression and tyranny against the Afghan people," and said Moslem countries should not recognize the Karmal government. They also set up a three-man committee headed by Pakistan's Agha Shahi to seek a peaceful solution to the Afghan problem.[79] A summit meeting of the Islamic Conference in Islamabad in May somewhat softened the January stand against dealing with Kabul,[80] but criticism continued of what Saudi King Khalid later called "the imperialistic invasion of Moslem Afghanistan."[81]

The damage done to the Soviet position in the Islamic world was shown by a boycott by most important Moslem countries of an international Islamic conference held in Tashkent in September 1980.[82] Organized by the most important of four boards that supervise Moslem affairs in the Soviet Union—all the boards are controlled by the Soviet Communist Party secretariat—the conference was part of a regular effort to use compliant Soviet Moslem leaders to further Soviet foreign policy objectives. Delegations that ignored the boycott appeal by the secretary general of the World Moslem League and attended the conference got into a dispute with the Soviet hosts over a final declaration that echoed Kremlin foreign policy lines. When the delegates tried to insert an amendment calling for the withdrawal of all foreign troops from Moslem countries and noninterference in their internal affairs, the hosts abruptly ended the conference without adoption of the declaration. In subsequent months, there was a noticeable decline in statements by Soviet Moslem leaders on foreign affairs, publicity directed abroad about the life of Soviet Moslems, and Soviet exchanges of religious delegations with Moslem countries.[83]

The Soviet Union also had trouble in other Third World countries and organizations. The nonaligned movement, with Cuba as the chairman as a result of having hosted the September 1979 summit conference—Taraki's last big public event—was especially agitated by the Soviet action against one of its founding members. Cuba initially tried to use its role to moderate criticism of

Moscow, but it soon found even the usual monthly meetings at the United Nations of the movement's coordinating bureau too awkward to hold because many members wanted to discuss the continuing Soviet military presence in Afghanistan.[84] When the movement's foreign ministers met in New Delhi in February 1981 to consider the worsening international situation, India produced a draft resolution that did not call for the withdrawal of foreign troops from Afghanistan. A Pakistani amendment was adopted that expressed "particular concern" over Afghanistan and "urgently called for a political settlement on the basis of the withdrawal of foreign troops and full respect for the independence, sovereignty, territorial integrity and nonaligned status of Afghanistan."[85]

India had been sensitive to Soviet attitudes since the invasion, avoiding the condemnation of most other countries in the region and giving more credence to the Soviet explanation of protecting Afghanistan from external aggression. But as months passed with Soviet troops digging in rather than showing signs of withdrawing, India became increasingly critical in a quiet way intended to avoid exacerbating its relations with Moscow.[86] Indian military leaders were concerned, in the tradition of the British Indian army, about the strong Russian force in the mountains above the South Asian plains, but they were also worried about the situation's leading to increased Pakistani military power.

Iran protested to Moscow that the "Soviet military intervention" into its neighboring country was an act against all Moslems and called for the Soviet Union to "immediately remove its army from Afghanistan."[87] Another neighbor of Afghanistan's, not nonaligned, produced some of the harshest attacks on the Soviet Union. China charged that, "From pulling the strings and using surrogates, their [the Soviet] method has escalated to . . . armed occupation of a sovereign country and change of its government by violent means. They have extended the use of the 'theory of limited sovereignty' from their 'community of nations' to a nonaligned and Islamic country of the third world."[88] Accusing the Soviet Union of having supported Daoud's coup in 1973 and Taraki's in 1978, China said the Soviets then became very dissatisfied with Amin and eliminated him with an excuse of fulfilling a treaty obligation that "can fool no one."[89] The tough United States reaction was applauded in China.[90]

The worldwide reaction came together in the United Nations. A draft resolution submitted by nonaligned members of the Security Council was vetoed by the Soviet Union on 8 January 1980.[91] An emergency session of the General Assembly was then called, using the procedure developed at the time of the Korean War for bypassing a Security Council veto on matters deemed to be of serious and immediate danger to international peace and security.

The assembly met seven times from 10 to 14 January and passed a resolution saying peoples should be able to choose their own governments, calling for the immediate, unconditional and total withdrawal of foreign troops from Afghanistan, urging all parties concerned to help the voluntary return home of Afghan refugees, and appealing for humanitarian relief for the refugees. The vote was an unusually overwhelming defeat for the Soviet Union, 104 to 18, with 18 abstentions.[92] Only countries beholden to the Soviets or to their close allies opposed the resolution, and a number of usual supporters of Moscow abstained, while 11 countries were absent, some because their positions were particularly awkward, such as Libya and Romania. On 20 November 1980 the regular assembly session repeated the call for immediate withdrawal of foreign troops from Afghanistan by an even larger majority, 111 to 22, with 12 abstentions, and a similar vote a year later was 116 to 23, with 12 abstentions.[93]

In addition to Romania, which had a history of refusing fully to accept Soviet foreign policies, for instance on China and Arab-Israeli problems, Moscow encountered resistance from some other Communist countries and from some Communist parties in the West. Only staunchly loyalist Bulgaria, Czechoslovakia, and East Germany gave the Afghanistan action immediate and full support. Hungary and Poland, both apparently worried about détente as well as new precedents for Soviet intervention, were slow and circumspect in their endorsement of the action and the Karmal government.[94] Cuba, torn between loyalty to Moscow and its attempt to stay ahead of nonaligned opinion, muted its reaction to the action itself and focused its fire on the United States reaction.[95] North Korea tried to balance its relations with the Soviet Union and China by an equivocal stand, but when forced to be counted at a February 1980 meeting of Communist parliamentarians it refused to support a resoluton expressing solidarity with Karmal's regime and implicitly backing the invasion. Mongolia, Vietnam, Laos, and Cambodia dutifully endorsed the action and its resulting regime. Yugoslavia and Albania criticized them. The Communist parties of Belgium, Britain, Italy, Spain, and Sweden criticized the Soviet use of force, earning them rebukes from Moscow, while support was given by the French, Portuguese, and other parties.[96]

Confronted with widespread hostility to its action, the Soviet Union mixed tough defiance with efforts to reassure world opinion—without making concessions on the basic point of keeping its troops in Afghanistan. It had never expected approval, a Soviet journal said, from "imperialist circles, Beijing, [and] reactionary forces in the East. . . . It also took into account that these actions might lead to temporary confusion, misunderstanding amid its friends in progressive circles. That exactly, unfortunately, happened. . . . A number of Communist parties, some nonaligned countries took a negative stand." But, the journal concluded hopefully, the world was now learning better, "acquiring a sober view of the situation" after being deluded by Western propaganda.[97]

A sterner tone was used by other Soviet voices. A West German reporter was told by a Soviet official "who represents the interests of his country in Washington not only as a diplomat" that, "If the rules we had with the Americans are no longer applicable, then we shall play our way indeed. If we are not treated as equals, then it will be necessary to remind the Americans to do that."[98] Commenting on Carter's State of the Union message, *Pravda* said American leaders "obviously are unwilling to make their policy in keeping with the United States' real weight in the present-day world." There is a new correlation of forces, the Communist party newspaper said, and attempts "to somehow influence the Soviet Union and its foreign policy . . . will suffer a fiasco."[99] *Izvestiya* commented that "it is time the United States learned to behave rather more modestly."[100]

Kosygin linked the United States reaction to Soviet military policy. "No one must be left in doubt that the Soviet Union will not allow any disturbance of the balance of forces *which has come about in the world* to the detriment of its security," he said.[101] This implied that any impetus given to American defense efforts by the Afghanistan invasion and apprehension about the Persian Gulf would not be allowed to cut into the military advantages that his country had been working long and expensively to develop.

This tone of Soviet comments did not change, but as the world began to grow accustomed to the Soviet presence in Afghanistan the need to argue the situation receded. In January, 16 percent of all the official statements, speeches by leaders, press comments or radio talks from Moscow were about Afghanistan. By late April, four months after the invasion and three months after the United Nations vote and Carter's State of the Union message, only 1 percent of Soviet commentary was on the subject.[102]

Soviet reassurances were aimed primarily at consumers of Persian Gulf oil. Within weeks of the move into Afghanistan and the resulting United States apprehension about security of oil supplies, Soviet spokesmen like Gromyko began denying any designs on the Gulf. The Soviet Union had "never claimed other people's oil resources, nor had it ever declared oil-containing areas a 'sphere of its vital interests'," an authoritative *Pravda* byline said.[103] The Soviet Communist Party secretary responsible for propaganda, Mikhail V. Zimyanin, denied on the second anniversary of the Saur Revolution that the Soviet Union had any "wish to lay hands on the petroleum resources of the Persian Gulf and to gain access to the warm southern seas . . . The Soviet Union does not harbor any aggressive intentions against either Iran or Pakistan."[104]

In the tradition of Soviet peace offensives intended to allay foreign fears without changing any realities or making any significant concessions, Moscow launched a proposal for Persian Gulf security. Brezhnev opened the way by saying 22 February that it "is understandable" that the United States was talking "about the necessity of insuring the safety of U.S. oil supply routes."[105] A week later a Tass commentary suggested that a European energy conference might consider oil route security and "appropriate guarantees [of] equal commercial access" to Gulf oil.[106] This implied more than just an interest in reassuring industrial nations dependent on that oil; it also was a Soviet bid to be included for the first time in both security and sales of Gulf oil, which CIA projections said the Soviet bloc would need within a few years.[107]

On a visit to India in December 1980, during which he defended the Soviet role in Afghanistan against an increasingly cool Indian attitude, Brezhnev proposed a Gulf security plan. Saying that "the USSR has no intention of encroaching upon either Middle East oil or its transportation route," he offered to agree with other powers that none would establish military bases in the Gulf region, deploy nuclear weapons there, employ or threaten the use of force or interfere in internal affairs, draw local states into military alliances, and other points.[108] This was spurned in the West as an effort to block defense efforts for the region while in no way hindering the Soviets, who always denied that places like Aden were military bases or that sending troops into foreign countries was interference in internal affairs. Also, the proposal ignored the looming presence of Soviet forces in Afghanistan, the immediate cause of Western concern over the Gulf. Brezhnev made a gesture of dealing with this last criticism by offering in February 1981 to include "the international aspects of the Afghan problem" in Gulf security discussions.[109] By excluding "internal Afghan affairs," however, he made it clear that Soviet forces would not withdraw as part of a Gulf plan.

Chapter 11. Quagmire

The arrival of the Soviet Army in Afghanistan transformed the situation there militarily and also politically. In neither way was the result what Soviet leaders had apparently hoped to achieve. Instead of restoring order, settling the people down to compliant acceptance of Communist rule, and enabling Afghans to direct their own affairs in a way agreeable to Moscow, the Soviet military intervention had opposite effects. In the first few years of occupation, areas of disorder that were lost to Kabul's control widened, while the people resisted Communist rule by force of arms or by obstructing daily matters with silent hatred or by fleeing from the country. Those Afghans anointed by Moscow proved unable to compose their internal differences or win over their compatriots enough to run their own affairs. What had probably seemed to the Soviet politburo like a limited military action became an endless problem. The Soviet troops who had been supposed to clear up the trouble became a major source of trouble. Their presence spread and intensified the conflict from essentially a civil war among Afghans into primarily a national war of resistance to foreign invaders and their local puppets.

Afghan Army Resistance

Before the intervention, the Afghan army had been withering away from defections because it was expected to fight under Soviet advisers against fellow countrymen. Once the Russians were seen to be assuming direct control like a would-be conquering army—Russians, a traditional enemy of Central Asian Moslems, not just some vaguely multi-ethnic Soviets—the collapse of the Afghan army was accelerated by massive refusals to fight for a Russian-installed regime. At the same time, parts of the country that had tried to ignore Kabul, or had offered little active opposition up to December 1979, were inflamed by the new situation.

This greatly extended the areas of sporadic guerrilla attacks. The moral stature of men in the resistance was greatly increased. They came to be known as *mujahideen*, a term with Moslem religious connotations. Its emotional content might best be translated as "freedom fighters." The Soviets applied the derogatory term *basmachis* or a local word for enemies, *dushman*. Support for the *mujahideen* also increased as some Moslem countries, the United States, and others began cautiously channeling limited amounts of small arms and other military equipment to them.

What had been a steady stream of refugees before the Soviets arrived, some fleeing into Iran but most of them crossing the Durand Line mountains to

Pakistan, became a flood in the first year of the Soviet occupation. By the end of that year, total refugees reached possibly as much as one-eighth of Afghanistan's original population; after two years, perhaps one-fifth and still increasing. Politically, the new regime sought to rally popular support with new policies but found instead that the fact of its Soviet sponsorship poisoned the atmosphere for national reconciliation.

Even the initial attempt by Karmal to establish a broad government including both Parchamis and Khalqis, as well as persons not in the PDPA, met with little success. The old personal rivalries between the two PDPA factions, newly embittered by the killing of Amin, reasserted themselves as another weakening factor in a regime that already lacked capable Afghans who could play a constructive role in building a new, Soviet-style country. What became known as the second phase of the Saur Revolution, and was advertised as a new beginning that would overcome the problems and mistakes of the Taraki and Amin periods, was plagued by somewhat different but far worse problems than had been the first phase.

Soviet military force in Afghanistan numbered some 85,000 men within a few weeks of the initial movements. Another 30,000 supported them from just north of the border.[1] The first objectives, after destroying Amin's regime and installing Karmal's, were seizing control of the main towns, key communications and logistical points, and the main transportation arteries. The Soviet plan seemed to have been for the Soviet Army to provide the security that had become uncertain in Amin's time, releasing the Afghan army to pursue the guerrillas into the hills. As soon as the Soviet movements began, however, some Afghan military units fought against the invasion, and over time many other units or significant numbers of their members defected to the resistance or simply faded away to their villages. Precise numbers are not available, but Western intelligence estimates said that an Afghan army of about 100,000 men before the 1978[2] coup had by the end of the first year of the Soviet occupation dwindled to perhaps 30,000 men, of whom only 10,000 to 15,000 could be used as effective fighting troops. After two years, the numbers were believed to be even smaller.[3] Some units were ineffective because they were disgruntled and therefore untrustworthy in Soviet eyes.

This situation exploded periodically in revolts of Afghan units. After the first round in January 1980, others occurred sporadically. One of the largest reported—such reports were always secondhand and it was not possible to verify them fully—was by the Afghan 14th Armored Division stationed at Ghazni. When a Parchami officer was sent from Kabul in July 1980 to replace the Khalqi commander, the troops mutinied, and thousands fled to join the resistance when Soviet forces tried to restore discipline. Also in July, a revolt, or perhaps a plan for a coup, was reported quelled by Soviet troops at the big Pul-i-Charki armored center near Kabul, and another uprising at the center was reported in October. Most of the Afghan soldiers who successfully deserted took their weapons with them, providing the main source of armaments for the *mujahideen*. By late summer, Soviet advisers who ran the remaining Afghan army units withdrew from their possession such weapons as anti-tank and anti-aircraft rockets in order to prevent their being used against Soviet units.[4]

Resistance in Rural Areas

During the first year of resistance to the Soviet occupation, a conflict that had before December 1979 been primarily centered in the eastern part of the country, with a few pockets elsewhere, spread to almost every part of Afghanistan. All twenty-six of the country's provinces[5] were mentioned in reports of guerrilla action or local uprisings at one time or another.

Roads became unsafe for government or Soviet vehicles as *mujahideen* sometimes ambushed them, forcing them to travel in armed convoys; even then they were not always immune from attack. The resistance was able to collect its own road tax on some of the main arteries, including at times the road from Kabul to Qandahar. The road from Kabul to Jalalabad and the Khyber Pass was so frequently controlled by guerrillas that most official movement between the capital and Jalalabad was by air. The vital overland route from Kabul to the Soviet border through the Salang Pass tunnel was heavily guarded by Soviet troops, in apprehension of the tunnel's being sabotaged, but repeated offensives during 1980, 1981, and 1982 up the Panjshir Valley just east of the tunnel failed to clear it of *mujahideen*. That valley was one of many areas into which Soviet and Afghan forces found it impossible to penetrate except briefly in force, and, upon withdrawing, found the resistance closing up around them again, preventing any lasting hold on the countryside.

As much as 90 percent of the country was estimated by Western specialists to be out of government control. Kabul and Moscow media complaints about the wrecking of schools and health centers—targets because they were used as centers for population control and indoctrination—and the destruction of bridges, power transmission lines, and other facilities seemed to confirm such estimates.[6] Karmal gave an assessment of the situation, using Communist labels for the resistance, without even blaming outside interference as being anything more than a help to domestic opposition. In a Kremlin speech in October 1980, he said that security is a problem.

> The enemies of the Afghan revolution are resorting to methods of terror, banditry, brigandage on the roads, gangsterism, the upsetting of normal life and the natural economic and social links in parts of Afghanistan. They are trying to prevent . . . the practical implementation of [the PDPA's program]. They are scaring and robbing the population, are killing members of the party and workers of state organizations, and are destroying material riches.[7]

The official line emphasized the outside element of American, Chinese, and other external enemies as the cause of what the government considered rebellious activity but the *mujahideen* considered patriotic defense against a foreign army and its local puppets. The fact that the rejection of the Karmal regime and its Soviet backers was essentially indigenous could not be hidden, however, and various formulas had to be concocted to explain it. Most emphasized the "counter-revolutionary" nature of the opposition, as if that label alone were sufficient to condemn it, but no public analysis of its strength and persistence was offered.

Resistance in the Cities

That strength and persistence were most noticeably manifested in the towns, particularly Kabul. The capital had always been the main political center, and its students had been recruited in the 1960s and 1970s by the PDPA as the most vocal public element. After the Soviet invasion, students resumed that political role, but this time against the PDPA, while other groups that had been politically silent were aroused to protest against the regime and its alien backers. Shopkeepers and other urban residents defied curfews in the early months of the occupation to send up from the flat-topped roofs of Kabul, Herat, Qandahar, and other towns a night-long chant of "Allah e Akbar!" ("God is great!") in opposition to Soviet atheism.[8]

These demonstrations, which Soviet troops tried to intimidate into silence by bursts of automatic weapons fire, were encouraged by resistance groups but apparently spread with spontaneous enthusiasm. Some were urged by clandestine leaflets that began appearing within a week of the Soviet intrusion. One that circulated in Kabul in February 1980 said:

> In the name of Allah, "Do not accept the orders of the infidels, wage *jihad* against them" [a quotation from the Koran]. . . . The Moslem people and the *mujahideen* of Afghanistan, with the sublime cry of "Allah e Akbar," will bring down their iron fist on the brainless head of the infidel and Communist government. *Mujahideen* Moslems, remember that our weapons are the weapons of faith. These are the strongest and most effective weapons in the world. Even the most modern weapons will be unable to resist ours. That is why, if we resist Soviet imperialism's Communist infidel government we will be victorious and it will suffer a crushing defeat. . . . The only path to happiness is faith in the *jihad* and martyrdom![9]

Another leaflet that reportedly penetrated into Soviet camps asked the soldiers there why they were fighting in Afghanistan. "We are victims of the aggression of your government; we are fighting for our freedom from the yoke of Communism and our right to choose our own leader," it said.[10] In addition to leaflets, students in Kabul were able for a time to publish an underground newssheet named *Falah* ("Deliverance").[11]

In Kabul, a city swollen to more than a million persons[12] as villagers sought refuge from army attacks intended to root out *mujahideen*, major demonstrations occurred in February, April, May, early June, and late June of 1980, and further outbursts of public opposition continued into 1981.[13] On the second anniversary of the 1978 coup, protests by students—even elementary school children participated—were met with gunfire by Afghan troops and PDPA militia backed by Soviet helicopter gunships. Unconfirmed reports said at least fifty persons were killed and several hundred wounded, but some estimates said 600 or more, and officials said 620 had been arrested. Many male students were summarily conscripted; women took up the cause.[14]

This was followed by student agitation in Herat, Qandahar, Shindand, and Jalalabad. The former leftist ideological appeal to Afghan young people had been replaced with nationalism; the arrival of the modern manifestation of the Marxist state, Soviet soldiers and administrators, had blighted the former appeal of international Marxism for students and renewed their sense of Afghan patriotism. Herat and Qandahar were especially rebellious, with the former reported to have been out of Soviet control during an upsurge of urban guerrilla warfare in early August and the latter on several occasions in late 1980 and early 1981. Similarly violent outbursts against Karmal and the Soviets were not reported from towns north of the Hindu Kush, but reports of widespread rural guerrilla warfare there suggested better Soviet control rather than greater popular acceptance.

The Soviet Army sought to control the towns with massive force, ringing them with armor and roadblocks in efforts to keep *mujahideen* and their weapons from getting in, but the flood of refugees from the villages made this difficult—and, anyway, the enemy was already inside the gates, consisting of most of the ordinary people. A Russian soldier could not walk through an Afghan bazaar without risking a knife in the back. During the daytime, the Afghan army and militia were supposed to maintain urban security, but Soviet soldiers always guarded main government buildings, communications centers and other key buildings, and at night heavily armed Soviet Army patrols operated through the curfew hours. Resistance groups warned non-Communist foreigners, including diplomats, to leave Afghanistan. Many did.[15]

While trying to maintain their grip on the towns, Soviet forces evolved tactics for dealing with *mujahideen* in the mountains. It had been almost three decades since the Soviet Army had last fought guerrillas, putting down the post-World War II resistance to Moscow's control of the Ukraine, Lithuania, and some adjacent areas of mainly flat and forested terrain, although Soviet advisers had seen the problem in Angola, Ethiopia, and other places. In those three decades regular Soviet military units had been configured primarily for combat with heavily armed conventional armies. There were also some special troops, KGB units and militia forces trained to deal with urban uprisings. Few Soviet soldiers were prepared for the unusual problems of combating popularly supported guerrillas.

Soviet Tactics

The divisions sent into Afghanistan at the end of 1979 were equipped with the full complement of weaponry needed for meeting a NATO force on the plains of central Europe. Much of it, such as missiles for artillery and for antiaircraft purposes, was useless for hitting guerrillas, and the heavy tanks might intimidate urban residents but could not get into the roadless areas where the *mujahideen* were strong. In some of the initial campaigns against the guerrillas—continuing operations in Badakhshan that had begun before 27 December and beginning operations in March 1980 in the Konar River valley running northeast from Jalalabad into Nuristan—Soviet commanders attempted fairly conventional tactics. They used road-bound armor and supporting helicopters and jet fighter-bombers.[16]

These proved unsuccessful. The *mujahideen* faded into the mountains and reappeared in surprise attacks or ambushes. The Soviet Army had proven what the United States Army had shown in Vietnam, that heavily armed troops with control of the air could go anywhere the terrain permitted, but, as in the Paktia offensive in October 1979, as soon as they withdrew the guerrillas resumed control in virtually the same strength as before.

Soviet commanders began, therefore, to develop new tactics that emphasized mobility, the ability to airlift troops to choke points in valleys, and other advantages of their superior firepower and mechanization.[17] They began wide-spread use of chemical warfare—the Soviet units had arrived with the full equipment for this that is standard issue in the Warsaw Pact.[18] There had been evidence of Soviet-supplied chemical warfare agents' being used by Vietnamese forces fighting continuing resistance in Laos and Cambodia in the previous few years, with numerous deaths reported although not all gases had been clearly lethal. In Indochina both non-lethal riot control agents as well as deadly gases seem to have been employed.

The United States said in September 1981 that evidence from Southeast Asia had enabled it to identify three lethal agents. They were mycotoxins of the trichothecene group, little-known poisonous substances produced by living organisms. "The possession and use of toxins is a violation of both the 1925 Geneva Protocol and the 1972 Biological Weapons Convention," Under Secretary of State Walter J. Stoessel, Jr., said, "as well as the rules of customary international law of armed conflict."[19] No physical evidence had been obtained from Afghanistan, where areas of reported gas attacks were less accessible, a senior State Department official said. But, he added, reports from that country were similar to those from Laos and Cambodia in "describing a yellow or dirty brown cloud being used with exceptionally unusual and rapid hemorrhagic deaths associated with vomiting and diarrhea."[20]

Some reports of gas attacks had begun coming out of Afghanistan even before the Soviet invasion. In August and September 1979, warplanes that presumably were equipped and controlled by the Soviet Union made gas attacks in the Panjshir Valley to stave off guerrilla threats to the nearby Salang tunnel road. In 1980 signs of Soviet use of nerve gas were found, especially in Badakhshan, and by 1981 there had accumulated evidence of the use of mycotoxins—a weapon the Soviets had apparently tested in the North Yemen civil war in the 1960s and again in Indochina, always choosing areas remote from detection and world denunciation.[21] The United States government concluded in 1982 that lethal chemical and toxin agents had been used in Laos since 1975, in Cambodia since 1978, and that "Soviet forces have used a variety of lethal chemical warfare agents, including nerve gases, in Afghanistan since the Soviet invasion."[22] Soviet and Afghan media, as well as Vietnamese, denied these charges and countered with accusations of American chemical warfare.[23]

Another specialized weapon used in Afghanistan was the small anti-personnel mine. Large numbers of them, some disguised as rocks or as attractive toys, were strewn from the air along the numerous mountain trails across the Durand Line beginning in mid-1980 in an attempt to interdict support from Pakistan.

A further change in Soviet tactics was the use of terror. At first the Soviet Army sought out *mujahideen* to fight, although it showed no concern for protecting bystanders, many of whom were killed in indiscriminate use of heavy firepower. But soon Soviet frustration at being unable to come to grips with the elusive guerrillas caused a shift to trying to destroy the popular base of support for the resistance. Under Soviet advice, the Afghan army had used terror against opposition villagers in a number of cases from late 1978 onward.[24] That was reported by enough independent accounts to seem reliable, although first-hand evidence could not be obtained. For instance, in April 1979 Afghan troops accompanied by Soviet officers massacred the inhabitants of Kerala village, according to people who escaped. This episode and other reported ones were denied by Soviet and Afghan media,[25] who accused the *mujahideen* of conducting a "white terror" in answer to charges of "red terror,"[26] but a continuing flow of independent accounts left no doubt in Western specialists' minds.

The Soviet Army began razing villages in areas of ambushes, killing many inhabitants and driving the rest out as refugees; it started destroying crops in areas it could not control in order to deny the guerrillas food; and it used napalm and bombs on remote places suspected of being *mujahideen* strongholds.[27] Such methods could eventually sap the strength of the resistance, but there was no sign of that up to mid-1982. Instead, Soviet brutality seemed to insure that the pacification of the country would not be achieved within the foreseeable future.

That meant the Soviet Army was likely to be in Afghanistan indefinitely fighting a war that had no end in sight. Not that there had ever been much doubt about its staying for a long time. As the normal 90-day callup periods of

Soviet Central Asian reservists began to run out, the first army units to enter Afghanistan began to fill up with regular troops, a higher proportion of them Russians, and tours of duty were set at two years. The Tajbeg Palace in which Amin had been killed was renovated as a Soviet command headquarters; permanent quarters were built for Soviet troops in some places and the better Afghan military quarters taken over in others; permanent fuel and ammunition storage facilities were constructed at key locations; mobile field communications were replaced with permanent systems; the pontoon bridges across the Amu Darya used in December 1979 by the mechanized infantry divisions were replaced when the first permanent bridge was opened 12 May 1982—at least one bridge had been planned before the invasion as a primarily economic development—and plans were made to build the first railroad into Afghanistan to facilitate logistical support for the Soviet Army.[28]

The long-term presence of Soviet troops in Afghanistan was given formal status. In a sense, so retroactively was the invasion, during a visit to Moscow 13 and 14 March 1980, by Afghan Foreign Minister Shad Mohammad Dost. He discussed with Gromyko "practical problems pertaining to the temporary stay of the limited Soviet military units in Afghanistan."[29] Announcements in Kabul and Moscow on 4 April disclosed that they had signed an agreement or treaty "on conditions for the temporary stay" of these units. The announcements were of its ratification by both governments. The text was kept secret.[30]

This contrasted with the publicized signing in October 1968, two months after the "Prague spring" was crushed, of an agreement for the supposedly temporary stay of Soviet troops in Czechoslovakia—some 60,000 of whom were still there eleven and a half years later when the Afghan agreement was made. The Czechoslovak agreement, which might have been the model for the Afghan one, specified that the Soviet troops' presence in that country "does not violate its sovereignty," exempted Soviet forces, equipment, and supplies from normal national immigration and custom controls, gave Soviet troops some exemptions from local laws and from control of their military construction or operations, and generally established a kind of extraterritoriality that the Soviet Union had criticized Western nations for exercising in colonial areas.[31]

On 22 June 1980, "the command of Soviet military contingents now staying in Afghanistan" announced that "some army units whose stay . . . is not necessary at present are being withdrawn" to the Soviet Union.[32] This was a political gesture, not a military reduction. Some 10,000 men went home with 108 tanks, three missile batteries, and other heavy equipment that was useless in Afghanistan. They were replaced with infantrymen, more helicopter gunships, and other weaponry better adapted to the irregular warfare. The total number of Soviet troops in the country remained at about 85,000 by United States estimates, or nearer 100,000 by European intelligence estimates.[33] The Soviet high command was unable to reduce its troops substantially without risking exposing towns, airfields, and other key points to *mujahideen* attacks because there was virtually no Afghan army to rely on.

Efforts were made to build up the depleted Afghan army, first by pay raises, reenlistment bonuses, and other incentives,[34] later by tightening conscription laws and impressing youths into service. Neither approach was very successful. An unpopular regime found it difficult to get and to keep recruits for a nasty kind of warfare that few could support out of conviction.[35] Both Soviet and Afghan Communist leaders seemed to realize that the only long-term hope for building a stable Afghan government depended on establishing a wide enough base of support that military security might be turned over to Afghan forces, rather than having the constant aggravation of using a foreign occupying army to keep the regime in place.[36] Perhaps that was why conscription efforts were intensified, the draft age was lowered to twenty, and soldiers discharged before 22 October 1978 were called back to one year's active duty in August 1981 if still under thirty-five years old.[37] None of this produced a viable Afghan army, however. Into the third year of Soviet occupation, with the Soviet Army more obviously engaged in roles that the Afghan army could not or would not fulfill, there was no sign of the Soviet military force's being able to relax and let its local levies do the job.

Soviet Stranglehold on Publicity

Kremlin authorities tried to hide from the Soviet public the fact that the Soviet Army was doing virtually all of the fighting in Afghanistan. The original formula used to explain the intervention, that Soviet troops had gone to help repel outside aggression, was maintained for the early months, during which Soviet media were curiously silent on what the troops were doing—even *Krasnaya Zvezda*, the defense ministry newspaper. When articles finally began to appear, they depicted the soldiers as providing medical aid to grateful villagers, helping plant trees and improve public buildings, and generally acting as good neighbors.[38] Articles for the Soviet Army's sixty-second birthday in February 1980 that were published in Ashkhabad and Tashkent newspapers under the bylines of two different generals used identical words to report that "The laboring people of Afghanistan feel great warmth for the Soviet soldiers . . . who are performing their noble international mission with a feeling of high responsibility."[39] On the same occasion in 1981, Ustinov talked of their "patriotic and international duty" and added that soldiers' "martial valor and everyday military labor are inscribing glorious new pages in the history of the Soviet armed forces."[40] This implied combat experience.

Well into the third year of the Afghanistan action, routine speeches by Soviet military leaders or speeches by other members of the Soviet leadership that touched on military matters dealt with the confrontation with the United States, NATO, and China, but virtually ignored Afghanistan, as if the public were not supposed to be reminded of it. One Soviet civilian leader who commented on Afghanistan more than most was Ponomarev, who apparently kept responsibility for working with the PDPA even after the country was drawn into the Soviet bloc and that responsibility might have been transferred to the Soviet Communist Party secretariat's section for bloc party relations. In a speech 4 February 1980, Ponomarev denied that any "clashes are taking place between Afghans and our soldiers, as all kinds of 'voices' unscrupulously and long-windedly claim"[41]—a reference to reports by Western radios that were widely known inside the Soviet Union. Other officials reiterated such denials,[42] thus tending to confirm reports from foreigners in the Soviet Union of growing concern there about casualties in Afghanistan. Occasional mentions began to appear in Soviet media of Soviet Army involvement in combat. The bluntest statement was by Karmal in a 19 October 1980 speech on Soviet nationwide television: "In spite of their small numbers, the Soviet soldiers courageously, selflessly and devotedly are fulfilling their international debt and are rendering aid in the repulsion of the undeclared aggression. . . . We are profoundly grateful . . . and we shall always preserve the memory of their courageous heroism."[43]

Despite official efforts to insulate the Soviet public, however, the word spread that Russian boys and those from other Soviet ethnic groups were dying in a foreign land fighting a hostile population. Awkward questions began to be raised in the regular neighborhood and party cell meetings at which Communist agitators spread the official line and dealt with matters too delicate to be discussed in the open media.[44] Ustinov felt it necessary to deliver a sharp public lecture on the need for unquestioning army obedience to Communist Party decisions,[45] thus implying that intervention in Afghanistan was causing grumbling in the ranks. Soviet Army psychologists, who had had little more to do than alleviate the sense of isolation felt by conscripts assigned to barracks in East Europe away from local peoples, began to encounter problems with soldiers who came home from Afghanistan distressed or even guilty about having oppressed a free, religious people.[46] They also encountered Central Asians unsettled by having seen the Koran after years of only hearing atheistic propagandists' versions of it. Some soldiers from non-Russian ethnic groups were particularly upset by *mujahideen* leaflets saying they were

> in Afghanistan as soldiers of an imperialist occupation army. You are fighting against . . . peaceful people who have never done you any harm. With your hands you are serving the political system in the USSR that has deprived men of basic democratic freedoms, has created a new ruling class of oppressors and exploiters. . . . You are shedding your blood and the blood of innocent Afghans in order to colonize a foreign country. . . . Your dead friends are sent home in sealed coffins and their families are told that they have been killed during maneuvers.[47]

During the second year of what had for the Soviets become a nasty little war, authorities in Moscow found it increasingly difficult to ignore public opinion. More explanation and defense of the Afghan adventure was needed. This proceeded on two tracks: generally favorable publicity about the nature of military service there, and carefully separate accounts of the widespread and persistent nature of guerrilla activities.

Soviet newspaper reports on the troops in Afghanistan became increasingly frequent and cautiously more realistic. Articles referred to both patriotic and internationalist duties of Soviet soldiers, thus combining the themes of defending the motherland's own borders and of helping a friendly people who were portrayed as being under attack for having chosen Communism. Descriptions of helping Afghans plant trees gave way to accounts of helping them fight the *mujahideen*. Occasionally, details were given of the deaths of Soviet soldiers while helping the Afghan army.[48] There was, however, a deliberate avoidance of depicting the kind of operations by the Soviet Army itself that constituted the bulk of the fighting, thus preserving the illusion of just helping an ally. Reports of Soviet soldiers' winning such awards for bravery in combat as the title of Hero of the Soviet Union or Order of the Red Star did not dwell on the nature of the combat involved.[49]

"It is hard to serve in Afghanistan," admitted the newspaper most specifically aimed at Soviet citizens of draft age, *Komsomolskaya Pravda*, because of the tense military situation and the severe terrain, "lack of water, heat, lifeless mountain slopes, deserts."[50] But, the paper assured an anxious mother who had written to it, her son was defending "peace on earth, happiness, and the motherland's tranquillity."[51] Other reports depicted the loneliness of duty there in an apparent effort to encourage letters from home.[52] These reports fit with reports reaching United States officials that the stress and loneliness of service in Afghanistan, a country in which various kinds of narcotics were plentiful, was by early 1981 beginning to cause a heroin addiction problem for Soviet soldiers that was similar to, and for the same sorts of reasons as, the drug problem of American soldiers in Vietnam a decade earlier.[53]

When the Soviet press began to admit that a few Soviet soldiers were dying in Afghanistan, it also made it clear that the struggle there was not subsiding. Articles began to appear in the summer and autumn of 1981 giving extensive listings of areas where the *mujahideen* had been active and describing roads as usually unsafe.[54] The message was clear: Soviet soldiers had to be expected to remain in Afghanistan for some time to come. One late summer article even admitted that half a year earlier, in February 1981, Herat had been temporarily taken over by guerrillas;[55] in standard Soviet media control style, this admission appeared only in a report describing how the problem was solved and how everything was now all right.

The number of Soviet troops killed in the ongoing war was kept secret. Near the end of the third year of the Soviet occupation, Western diplomats in Pakistan estimated total Soviet killed and wounded at between 10,000 and 15,000. China published a much higher estimate of 16 Soviet deaths a day, or more than 5,000 a year.[56] Another 5,000 to 10,000 soldiers reportedly contracted diseases like typhoid and hepatitis during the first year, partly because they ignored the Soviet Army's instructions on boiling water and taking other prophylactic steps.[57] Many of the Soviet wounded were reportedly taken to Eastern Europe or to Soviet Black Sea resorts for treatment in order to keep them away from the general knowledge of the Soviet public.[58] Coffins of bodies returned for family burial were sealed because the *mujahideen* often mutilated their victims, in traditional Central Asian style. After some months, there were reports that many of the Soviet dead were being buried in Afghanistan to avoid public outcry over burials at home. Their wooden coffins were encased in metal containers made in the Jangalak industrial complex built at Kabul as a Soviet economic aid project in the early 1960s.[59]

After one of the most recent occasions on which Soviet troops had died in combat, the clash with China in March 1969 over the Ussuri River island of Damansky, or Chenpao. The thirty-one Soviet dead became national heroes. Some received medals posthumously. They were publicized as having died defending the motherland against what is for most Russians a very real sense of a "yellow peril." But Soviet casualties in the air defense of Egypt in 1970 against Israeli attacks were not publicized, nor Soviet losses in advisory roles in Angola or Ethiopia. Afghanistan was originally in the second category. For the first year or so of the war there, the deaths of Soviet soldiers were not publicly explained as their defending a national border the way the Ussuri heroes had done. Afghanistan thus fit into the pattern for foreign expeditions rather than the one for motherland defense. The cautious beginning of admissions of a few deaths—a very few, only hinting at the scope of casualties—during 1981 seemed less a shift toward emphasizing a defensive role than an unavoidable justification of what the Soviet people already knew, vaguely or with personal sorrow.

The attempt to conceal the human costs of Afghanistan from the Soviet people was intended to prevent the military role there from being questioned by the public. This was one of the more important ways in which the Soviet leadership sought to avoid the kinds of problems that arose in the United States over the Vietnam war. Some parallels between the two experiences have already been noted. But important differences arose: the Soviet Union handled information differently, and the overall geographic and political situation created differences. Afghanistan was not to be allowed to become the Soviet Vietnam if the Kremlin could avoid it.

Public frustration with Vietnam had eroded American determination to persist there. The tight Soviet control of news from Afghanistan, broken only by the "voices" of foreign broadcasts and the inevitable rumors, kept the Soviet public from being able to focus clearly on the frustrations of involvement in that country. Soviet media did not report the daily action; the ambushes were not on television, nor the retaliatory destruction of villages and killing of women and children in the process; in fact, the war was scarcely reported at all, officially almost ignored. The denial of access for foreign reporters meant that the rest of the world was also unable to focus on the brutal nature of the war in graphic terms. Secondhand accounts filtering through diplomatic sources or intelligence channels lacked the emotional impact that the Vietnam war had had on the world—and they could more readily be denied than eyewitness reports. There was, therefore, little foreign pressure from international outrage, almost none of the angry demonstrations in neutral and Third World countries that had marked the American involvement in Vietnam.

In addition, the Soviet public did not know the cost of Afghanistan any more than it knew the cost of the overall military establishment. It had no way to relate the action there to its chronic consumer shortages or other domestic problems—just as it was not told how much it cost to subsidize Cuba or, increasingly, Vietnam.

Control of the Soviet public's perception of Afghanistan was facilitiated by the geographic and political factors. Afghanistan was next door, easily accessible, not the tremendous logistical expense that distant Vietnam had been for the United States. Afghan resistance lacked any clear direction, any strong centralized control to give it military cohesion, such as Hanoi had provided in its long struggle to control all of Vietnam. Neither did the *mujahideen* have the constant additions of fresh army troops, the safe havens in which to build up and prepare with full local backing, or the massive flow of weapons that North Vietnam provided for the war against South Vietnam. Lacking these, the Afghan resistance was a weaker challenger to a tougher, less inhibitedly brutal Soviet military effort. Though the fires of hatred and defiance of Russian Communist control burned more fiercely in Afghanistan than the passions ever aroused among the majority of South Vietnamese, insuring that resistance would last a long bitter time, at least the Soviet determination to outlast it would not be sapped by the pressures that Vietnam created in the United States.

Refugees

A difference between Vietnam and Afghanistan noted earlier is that the flood of refugees from Vietnam came after the war was over rather than during it. The similarity behind this is that both the "boat people" and the Afghans fleeing across the Durand Line or the Iranian border were escaping Communist totalitarianism imposed by different if not completely alien peoples: the Tonkinese establishing their control over Annamese and Mekong delta peoples of Vietnam, and Russians over various ethnic elements of Afghanistan. During the first year of the Soviet occupation, approximately one million refugees crossed into Pakistan.[60] As food shortages grew in Afghanistan, and Soviet Army operations devastated more villages, the number more than doubled in 1981.[61] Near the end of the third year, Pakistan said it had 2.7 million Afghan refugees in its territory; estimates by the office of the United Nations High Commissioner for Refugees ran only a little lower. The number in Iran was uncertain. The confused governmental situation and an unwillingness to work with United Nations officials left refugees in Iran both uncounted and less aided than in the organized camps in Pakistan. "We do not know how many refugees there are or where they live," a senior official of the Iranian interior ministry said in October 1981—but he went on to estimate 1.5 million, ten times as many as the lowest available estimates.[62]

Allowing for the uncertainty of the figures, it appeared that up to one-fourth of Afghanistan's people had become refugees abroad after three years of Soviet occupation. They placed a heavy burden on Pakistan and Iran. In Pakistan's tribal areas, refugees and the several million head of livestock that they brought with them competed for scarce water resources and grazing land. This caused some tension with Pakistani Pushtuns and Baluch despite those people's general sympathy and traditional sense of hospitality for tribal or ethnic kin.

The Karmal government tried to lure the refugees home. It offered a "general amnesty, especially [to] those whose hands have not been soiled with the blood of their countrymen."[63] Those who accepted the amnesty were promised the return of land confiscated under the land reform decree, up to legal limits, or equivalent new land if theirs had been distributed to others.[64] These moves had no noticeable effect. Although the refugee flow began to slacken as areas of Afghanistan close to the Pakistani and Iranian borders became depopulated, there continued throughout 1981 a steady trickle of departing Afghan professional men, government officials, and others whose talents were needed but who refused to work for the Soviets. Diplomats, representatives to international organizations, Olympic athletes, shopkeepers, farmers, nomads—all types of people fled, most silently, some with ringing statements of defiance or pitiful tales of despair.

Resistance Groups among the Refugees

The refugees provided the base for expanding the groups that had been set up in 1978 to oppose Communist rule in Afghanistan. By the time of the Soviet invasion, at least six groups were operating from Peshawar, and half a year later a Soviet newspaper counted twenty-two in Pakistan and ten more in Iran.[65] The National Rescue Front announced in June 1978 faded away, but by the following month the first important group to begin armed opposition to Taraki had become the _Hezb-i-Islami Afghanistan_ ("Afghanistan Islamic Party").[66]

Formed in 1968 by Moslem traditionalist students in Kabul to oppose modernization and leftist trends, it had ties with the fundamentalist Moslem Brotherhood that operated throughout the Middle East. The party fought in Kabul streets against Parchamis and other leftists during the constitutional period, and it opposed King Zahir Shah's policies that had made possible the development of Marxist movements as well as the modernizing trend away from strict Islamic traditions. With ties to Khomeini's Iran and to Saudi Arabia, the well-financed party sought in the early 1980s to establish an orthodox Moslem state in Afghanistan. It would put the veil back on women. Its leader, who was a founder of the party, was Gulbuddin Hekmatyar, one of the few Pushtuns in the Peshawar exile leadership. A strong-willed leader who made extravagant claims, Hekmatyar pursued a goal of fundamentalism in personal terms that made him refuse to cooperate with other resistance groups.[67]

A breakaway group using the same name, *Hezb-i-Islami Afghanistan*, was headed by Mohammed Younus Khales.[68] Dr. Syed Burhanuddin Rabbani, a Tajik from Badakhshan who had in 1978 organized the National Rescue Front, headed *Jamaat-e-Islami Afghanistan* ("Afghanistan Islamic Society"), another fundamentalist organization, with mainly Tajik and Uzbek support.

A more Westernized group, advocating secular democracy for an Afghanistan freed of Soviet control, was *Payman-e Ettehad-e Islam* ("National Islamic Front"). Its leader was Sayed Ahmed Gailani, a liberal specialist on Islamic law from an Afghan landholding family claiming descent from the great prophets and caliphs. Impressed by Taraki's promises of reforms, Gailani was his adviser for two months before going into opposition. Dressed in stylish European clothes, Gailani stood out among the bearded *mullahs* in Peshawar, and he traveled widely on a Saudi passport to publicize his cause.

Other groups included the *Jabha-ye-Azadire Afghanistan* ("Afghan National Liberation Front"), headed by Sibghattula Mojadeddi, another man of aristocratic background who once ran a Libyan-financed Moslem center in Copenhagen, and *Harakat-e-Enqelab-e-Islami* ("Movement for the Islamic Revolution"), led by Mohammed Nabi Mohammadi, a rival of Mojadeddi's for the religious inheritance of a *mullah* best known for opposing King Amanullah's reforms.[69] While the Peshawar groups were predominately Sunni Moslem, Shi'ites looked to their co-religionists in Iran for support. A Hazara leader, Mohamed Asif Mohseni, led one Iran-based group variously known as the Afghanistan Islamic Movement Association or the Afghan Islamic Revolution Freedom Front. Another such group was Hoseyn Sadeqi's *An-Nasr* ("Victory").[70]

None of these or the several other *mujahideen* factions conformed to the pattern of typical late twentieth-century "national liberation front" programs in anything more than opposing foreign domination. The usual front sought popular support with promises of social reform and economic progress, even if this was only a ploy by cynical men who sought power without knowing how to implement their promises. The Afghan resistance was more personal than ideological. It was a bundle of often competing messages that emphasized religious, ethnic, and other deeply ingrained ties; that played on the traditional desire to avoid the domination of a centralized government in Kabul; and that preached hatred of Khalqi brutality, a rejection of Parchami subservience to foreigners, and a xenophobic outlook focused on Russians. It was in many ways a throwback to nineteenth-century resistance encountered by European colonial powers in their attempts to impose change on parts of Africa and Asia.

The personal nature of various factions was a key element in an inibility to unite in one coordinated movement to face the Soviets and to appeal for outside help. The old rivalries that made cooperation between Khalq and Parcham so difficult were mirrored in the resistance. The old tribal and ethnic conflicts that plagued Karmal's regime also had their effects on the *mujahideen*. Competition for foreign support, particularly from conservative Middle Eastern oil states, was another complication for the resistance.[71] Yet another was competition for localized support inside Afghanistan. The combination of all these sometimes led to armed clashes between guerrilla bands.

Although some of the Peshawar leaders' pictures were pasted on the walls of mosques in Kabul and their proclamations circulated in Afghan towns, it began to appear by late 1980 that guerrillas inside the country took weapons and other supplies—but few orders—from the Peshawar organizations, As the struggle continued and bickering went on in Peshawar, there was a growing tendency within Afghanistan for the old clan, tribal, and ethnic divisions of the country to be submerged in new, informal forms of cooperation among *mujahideen* groups. From this could emerge a kind of all-embracing nationalism that the old Afghan empire had never known. It was still too early to be sure of such a development in the third year of resistance to Soviet rule, but the example of the growth of Algerian nationalism out of the long independence struggle with France was suggestive. Perhaps, however, the opposite was equally valid: that the experience of maintaining their own regional and ethnic defiance of Kabul, especially among long-downtrodden peoples like the Hazaras, would erode the tenuous links that generations of royal rule had created in Afghanistan and leave the country more divided than ever.

Attempts to unify the various resistance groups based in Peshawar were made repeatedly. An imitation of the traditional *loya jirgah* was held in Peshawar on 13 May 1980 in an attempt to rally all elements of the resistance. Every province and tribe was said to have been represented. But the main groups were unwilling to submerge themselves in a council that was appointed.[72] Talk of setting up an exile government, or establishing a government in *mujahideen*-controlled territory inside Afghanistan, came to little because of factiousness and also because of Pakistani caution about hosting an exile regime. In Rome, former King Zahir Shah quietly tended his garden, not seeking any influence in the new situation but "at the service of his people and his nation" if called, Abdul Wali said.[73] While nostalgia for his reign was reportedly strong among many refugees, some of the exile leaders opposed him, making it difficult for the king to emerge as a unifying figure.[74]

By late 1982 three elements were discernible among *mujahideen* groups. One loosely coordinated the Islamic fundamentalists, with Hekmatyar as the strongest and most uncooperative leader. Another brought together those known by contrast as liberals for their more modern, Westernized attitudes. Some independent Afghans led by Abdul Rahman Pazhwak, who had been president of the United Nations General Assembly in 1966, tried unsuccessfully throughout 1982 to negotiate a statement of principles that could form the basis for a coalition of these two elements. A third element sought to bypass the Peshawar groups and unify the main *mujahideen* commanders inside Afghanistan, although such a new alliance would have trouble tapping the Peshawar groups' sources of money and weapons.[75]

Foreign Support for the Resistance

The resistance groups routinely denied that they were receiving guerrilla training and weapons from foreign sources,[76] although the evidence of plentiful money for some Peshawar organizations made it difficult to deny any form of external support. In general, they insisted that they were receiving from Afghan army defectors or capturing from the Soviet Army whatever weaponry they needed, and training was provided by former Afghan soldiers—some of them originally trained in the Soviet Union.[77] President Zia repeatedly asserted that Pakistan was not permitting the training or equipping of guerrillas on its territory and would not allow them to use it as a sanctuary for attacking across the Durand Line.[78]

There was overwhelming evidence otherwise. The denials were politically motivated. The resistance groups could not admit foreign support without compromising their position as directing an indigenous revolt. To the extent that they had no real influence on most of the guerrilla activity going on inside Afghanistan and coordinated internally by the growing contacts among separately organized *mujahideen* bands there, there was nothing to compromise, but the whole movement was in danger of being tainted.

Zia was in an awkward position. He and other Pakistani generals saw an advantage in the Soviet Union's not being able to consolidate its grip on Afghanistan and thus pose a greater threat to move on into their country. For that reason, a strong resistance benefited Pakistan. But helping make it strong risked provoking the Soviet Union, and Pakistan was apprehensive of that. Its leaders remembered Soviet encouragement and support for India's detaching East Pakistan in 1971 and setting it up as independent Bangladesh, as well as Soviet collusion with Afghanistan in helping some Baluch who sought more autonomy or even independence for Pakistani Baluchistan. If these were reasons for acting against the Soviet Union across the Afghan border, they were also reasons for caution. The Soviet Army occasionally reinforced them by sending helicopter gunships across the Durand Line to shoot up Pakistani outposts in remote areas and refugee camps that were suspected of being guerrilla training centers. In September 1981 Pakistan complained to the United Nations that Afghanistan—meaning the Soviets more than the Afghan military—had "committed as many as 62 violations of Pakistani territory and 271 violations of its air space since April 1978."[79] In only a few cases did armed clashes occur between Pakistani forces spread thinly along the border and the Soviet or Afghan raiders across it; usually, the raids were on unprotected places.

Within less than a year of the 1978 Kabul coup, a network of camps inside the Pakistani frontier was training guerrillas. Visitors found Pakistani soldiers involved in some camps, although the government insisted they were there only to guard refugees. Few healthy men were seen in refugee camps, only women, children, and old or sick men. The men were training separately and walking across the maze of border trails to fight inside Afghanistan.[80] The Kabul regime, both before and after the Soviet intervention, sought to depict this situation as foreign aggression and attribute to it the entire responsibility for guerrilla activity, ignoring locally generated resistance and the local support that was given to men operating from Pakistan.

Both Kabul and Moscow media began by early 1980 saying there were twenty military camps and fifty strongpoints in Pakistan where Pakistani, American, British, Chinese, Egyptian, Israeli, and other instructors trained guerrillas. By later 1980 the standard citation had risen to thirty camps. Occasionally references were also made to between five and eight camps in China's Sinkiang province and eight in Iran.[81]

Attempts were made to relate this training to specific publicized examples of opposition to the Karmal regime. Thus, Karmal said the first major Kabul uprising against him and the Soviets, on 21 and 22 February 1980, was "a limited rebellion" that occurred after "The foreign enemies infiltrated about 6,000 bandits, murderers and terrorists into our country."[82] Beyond producing a handful of Pakistan-trained *mujahideen* on Kabul television, the authorities were never able to substantiate their charges that such outbursts were of foreign inspiration rather than expressions of local hostility, and promises of full documentation for charges of external aggression were never fulfilled. But Soviet intelligence did provide Moscow media with detailed reports of arms shipments into Pakistan that were said to be for the *mujahideen*, including ships' names, cargoes, and transshipment arrangements for American and Chinese supplies.[83]

Aside from Pakistan's delicate position, many Moslem nations made no secret of their material as well as moral support for the Afghan resistance. Iran presented a particular problem for Moscow, which was trying to keep some influence with the openly anti-Communist Khomeini regime at the same time it looked ahead to the possibility of a leftist surge there after the ayatollah died. Neither Moscow nor Kabul media mentioned Iran's role so often as the role of other countries, and Karmal made several gestures toward improving relations with Iran.[84] But Tehran not only concurred with the Islamic Conference's boycott of the Kabul government but also included *mujahideen* leaders in its delegation to the May 1980 meeting of the conference.[85] A Tehran newspaper reported that Khomeini's revolutionary guards were training Afghan guerrillas in southeastern Iran;[86] the Soviet press said there was a training center at Mashhad in northeastern Iran;[87] *Pravda* said that, despite the break in Iranian-American relations over the hostage problem, the CIA was able to work with Afghan guerrillas in Iran by using Pakistani agents sent from Peshawar;[88] and *Izvestiya* publicized a report that two *mujahideen* organizations based in Iran "maintain links with CIA agents in Iran. . . . Iran's authorities have lost the capacity to control the situation in Iranian cities and settlements bordering Afghanistan."[89]

Among Arab nations, Egypt was the most open with its backing for Afghan guerrillas. President Anwar Sadat talked publicly during 1980 about sending weapons to them "until the Afghans liberate their country," and he offered to train them in Egypt, where Daoud had sent Afghan officers for training in the mid-1970s.[90] Shortly before he was assassinated, Sadat said in an interview broadcast 22 September 1981 that the United States had contacted him soon after the Soviet invasion. It "told me, 'Please open your stores for us so that we can give the Afghanis the armaments they need to fight,' and I gave the armaments," Sadat said. "The transport of armaments to the Afghanis started from Cairo on U.S. planes." Sadat said he supplied Soviet-made weapons that he had obtained before he broke with Moscow in 1972.[91]

It was in the tradition of covert intelligence operations for the United States to turn to these stocks for weapons whose use in Afghanistan would not be readily distinguishable as not resulting from the defection of Afghan army units with their weapons. The *mujahideen* particularly needed small, hand-held anti-aircraft missiles for defense against helicopter gunships. Sadat reportedly supplied them with his old Soviet missiles and received in return new United States versions—although Pakistan let few of the missiles through to the guerrillas, apparently for fear of stirring Soviet retaliation if so deadly a weapon were used.[92]

Sadat's candid remarks confirmed what anonymous officials in Washington had been telling a few reporters since shortly after the invasion.[93] But the Carter administration's interest in helping anti-Communists in Afghanistan did not begin with the invasion. The United States had supplied some medical supplies and communications equipment to *mujahideen* groups, with which it had established contacts in Peshawar and possibly elsewhere, as the Soviet role in Afghanistan was building up before the invasion. Soviet media saw a United States hand behind an organizational meeting of Afghan groups in November 1979 to seek greater cooperation among them because it was held in Munich, a center for American-financed broadcasting to the Soviet bloc.[94] After the invasion, the Soviet embassy in Washington distributed material that said Carter "was the main inspirer and organizer of intervention in" Afghanistan by those helping the *mujahideen*.[95] Visits of guerrilla leaders to Washington seeking help were publicized by Soviet media, and an American committee to aid Afghan refugees was labeled by Moscow as a CIA front. Moscow Radio said camps to train Afghans in guerrilla warfare were set up in Carter's home state, Georgia.[96]

About the same time he decided on the public measures to penalize the Soviet Union for its invasion, Carter decided that the United States had "a moral obligation" to help the resistance, according to other officials.[97] On 9 January 1980 the Senate Select Committee on Intelligence was briefed by the CIA on plans for covert aid to the *mujahideen*; there were no congressional objections, a measure of the new mood in a Congress that had blocked aid to an anti-Communist faction in Angola in 1975. The United States worked out cooperation with a number of countries in addition to Egypt.[98]

Other Arab countries provided mainly money, some separate from any United States arrangement. There was a tradition in Saudi Arabia, the Gulf states, and some other Middle Eastern Moslem nations of funding and supporting Moslem peoples fighting for autonomy or independence from non-Moslem rule, for instance, in the Eritrean rebellions against the Amharic Christian empire of Ethiopia. Support for Afghan guerrillas against atheistic Soviet control was, therefore, not an unusual policy. Some of these countries had strong financial influence in Pakistan and used it to encourage Zia to allow the transshipment of limited amounts of weapons despite his apprehension about provoking the Soviets.

China was also active, although parallel to rather than in cooperation with the United States effort. Its main newspaper, *Renmin Ribao*, declared on 13 March 1980 that it was a "bounden duty for all countries [to provide] energetic support and assistance" to the resistance in Afghanistan as well as in Cambodia.[99] Independent sources reported that it was doing so, although its aid through Pakistan was a little better concealed than its aid through Thailand to Pol Pot's guerrilla war against the Vietnamese army and its puppet regime. British anti-tank missiles turned up in *mujahideen* hands after the Thatcher government had talked of unspecified support.[100]

Whatever the United States effort, it was enough to provoke Moscow into focusing most of its criticism for outside interference on Washington. However, aid was not enough to threaten the Soviet Army with a major defeat. That it was severely limited was indicated by the attitude of the new Reagan administration in early 1981 that more should be done. President Reagan expressed on 9 March 1981 his personal willingness to supply the guerrillas,[101] and he revived Carter's idea of providing aid that would give Pakistan confidence enough to let supplies through. Reagan's statement provoked Kabul and Moscow into saying that the mask had been torn off "U.S. secret operations in Afghanistan [that] began soon after the 1978 revolution,"[102] but no evidence was offered that the internal fight against Communism and Soviet domination was of foreign origin in addition to receiving some foreign aid.

Foreign help for the resistance raised several questions. One that disturbed some Westerners was whether the Afghan people should be encouraged to resist an occupying army that showed no scruples about using terror to suppress any sign of opposition, levelling whole villages in retaliation for ambushes, killing women and children in frustration at being unable to catch *mujahideen*. Was outside help only an invitation to genocide? Was it moral for the West to ask Afghans to sacrifice themselves because of an increasingly strong Western determination to stand up to Soviet aggression? Should the United States and other countries try to fight the Soviets to the last Afghan?

Such questions tended to be dismissed quickly by most Afghans in touch with the outside world. All they asked was help in carrying on their proud tradition of resisting any outside control, of maintaining their independence as they had historically tried to maintain it against invaders. They could and would fight without any outside assistance, Afghans insisted—and proved it continually, according to reports from Afghanistan. This attitude partially answered a related question: Would the resistance become dependent on foreign help and vulnerable to collapse—with even worse Soviet massacres—if for foreign political reasons that help were suddenly withdrawn, for instance in some new bout of détente? The example some observers had in mind was the intensification of Kurdish resistance to the Iraqi government in northern Iraq in 1974 with cross-border help from Iran and a backup involvement of the CIA. Resistance collapsed when in 1975 the shah made a deal with Iraq and cut off help to Iraqi Kurds. The apparently spontaneous and primarily locally generated fight against Kabul's representatives and the Soviet Army in numerous pockets all over Afghanistan seemed to argue against this possibility, although the exile organizations in Peshawar became vulnerable as they grew bloated and corrupt with Arab oil money.

Another interesting question was whether the shoe was now on the other foot. During the buildup in the early and mid-1960s of Soviet aid to Hanoi's effort to win control of South Vietnam, Soviet officials argued to diplomats and foreign journalists in Moscow that a popular revolt was under way in that country. The Soviet Union was not responsible for that opposition to the Saigon government and its American backers, they contended. It was only providing what people wanted in order to fight for their independence, which surely was moral and right, the argument went. Its hollowness was shown by Hanoi's admissions after its victory in 1975 that North Vietnam had always run the war in the south, rather than its being primarily a local fight, and by the exodus of refugees from the resulting regime.

Soviet spokesmen were forced to redefine terms when it came to Afghanistan. They were unwilling to accept the Afghan resistance as that of a people wanting to fight for their independence, and therefore deserving help, although the lack of centralized direction and inspiration there compared with Hanoi's control in the 1960s made the case for foreign aid incomparably more justifiable. The Communists did not completely abandon their stance, however. The Karmal government, under Soviet direction, began helping domestic opponents of Zia's government in Pakistan. Denouncing the Pakistani regime as "lackeys of reaction and imperialism," Afghanistan provided a haven for opponents of it.[103] This presented an initial possibility simply of bringing pressure on Zia to restrict the passage of weapons to the *mujahideen*. In the long run, it raised the possibility of trying to replace his military-based government with a leftist regime that might accommodate itself to Soviet control of Afghanistan.

While always making it clear that Soviet troops would not leave Afghanistan until the survival of Karmal's regime was guaranteed, the Soviet Union sought to counter Western denunciations of the invasion with peace formulas, and Western diplomats also searched for ways to resolve the problem. In his initial statement on the subject, in *Pravda* 13 January 1980, Brezhnev said Soviet troops "will be fully withdrawn from Afghanistan once the causes that made the Afghan leadership request their introduction disappear." Those causes he defined as outside interference.[104] In a speech 22 February, he reiterated that and added that the United States and Afghanistan's neighbors should "guarantee . . . a complete cessation of all forms of outside interference."[105] That came shortly after foreign ministers of the European Common Market had adopted a proposal to guarantee the neutrality of Afghanistan if Soviet troops were withdrawn, thus satisfying the publicly expressed Kremlin concern about the security of its border, and Carter had independently talked of a neutrality guarantee.[106]

The gap between these two kinds of guarantees was huge. The West had in mind something like the 1955 guarantee of Austria's neutrality that ended the post-World War II occupation by American, British, French, and Soviet troops and enabled Austria to choose its own government. But Moscow had never installed a client Communist regime in Vienna, so it gave up little. Afghanistan was different; it had been drawn into the Soviet orbit already. The guarantee that Soviet leaders had in mind would insure that Afghanistan would stay within the orbit because the Karmal government would survive.

This was another matter of definition: Since the Kremlin insisted that the only opposition to Karmal was externally motivated, any resistance to his rule had to be outside interference. The price that the Kremlin demanded for a troop withdrawal was, therefore, a Western underwriting of the Karmal regime, a guarantee not simply against outside inteference but against the free choice of people inside the country. That was impossible for anyone to give, as the Kremlin well knew. Its peace plan was not a serious step toward seeking a way to pull the Soviet Army out of Afghanistan. It was a way of fending off Western proposals for a withdrawal.

Such proposals were stalemated by the Afghan government's announcement on 14 May 1980 of what became for several years its—and the Soviet—position on a settlement. Kabul proposed talks with Iran and Pakistan on normalizing relations, meaning halting any help for guerrillas, and the return home of refugees under an amnesty. "Practical measures should be taken to prove that armed interventions . . . are being halted," with guarantees from the United States "regarding the banning of subversive activities against Afghanistan," the announcement said. If effective guarantees were received, then the question of a Soviet troop withdrawal could be resolved, it said.[107] Brezhnev welcomed this "concrete program,"[108] which Western governments presumed had been written in Moscow.

But both Iran and Pakistan refused to grant the Karmal regime the legitimacy of dealing officially with it, and Western nations scorned the idea of guarantees as unrealistic. There followed various other proposals as diplomats refused to believe that this was an intractable problem, United Nations officials tried to keep alive some hope of a settlement, and the Soviets and their Afghan protégés periodically denounced Western plans while offering minor variations of their own that kept the central essential point of preserving Communist power in Afghanistan.[109] The stubborn reality of Kremlin attitudes made any agreement unlikely so long as overall Soviet power remained intact.

Karmal's Problems

In the early months of Karmal's leadership, there were peculiar signs that even the Soviets were uncertain about dealing with him and might have been thinking of replacing him. In placing Karmal in power, Kremlin leaders presumably thought he was capable of rallying some support on the basis of his Parchami ties and his background as a relatively moderate Communist. The overwhelming popular rejection of him as a stooge of the Russians, shown for the first time in full force by the 21–22 February riots in Kabul, apparently caused doubts in Moscow about keeping him. And Karmal seemed to have severe self-doubts. He looked shaky on his few public appearances, held official meetings at night rather than during normal working hours, was reportedly rejected by his own father—Daoud's old general—because he was "surrounded by Russians,"[110] and in June 1980 diplomatic reports said he was prevented from committing suicide by his chief Russian aide[111]—a report he later denied.[112]

A routine message of greetings from Brezhnev and Kosygin on the second anniversary of the Saur Revolution was noticeably cool toward Karmal personally, almost as cool as the last similar greeting to Amin.[113] The Soviet Union seemed to be considering replacing Karmal with someone else who might make a fresh start at winning popular support. Qadir made trips around the country for speeches that could have been a testing of him as an alternative leader, but he too was compromised by working for the Soviets—probably anyone would have been—and in one case was driven from a speaking platform by rotten fruit.[114]

Eventually Safronchuk and other Soviet officials in Kabul seem to have advised Moscow that no improvement on Karmal could be found, no other leader who could combine loyalty to the Soviet Union with an acceptable appeal to the Afghan people because the two were irreconcilable. The Kremlin therefore decided to stick with Karmal. There is a parallel with Janos Kadar. He had served immediate Soviet purposes in the crushing of the Hungarian freedom fighters. For some time afterward, however, Moscow acted as if there were uncertainty about his suitability for long-term leadership. Finally he became acceptable to both his sponsors and his subjects—to remain more than a quarter century in power.

The sign that Moscow had decided to stick with and accept Karmal, without his having been accepted by the Afghan people, was his being invited to pay an official visit to the Soviet Union in October 1980. Most of the top Soviet leaders concerned with the Afghanistan problem—Brezhnev, Andropov, Gromyko, Tikhonov filling in for the sick Kosygin, Ponomarev, Ustinov's deputy Marshal Nikolai V. Ogarkov, Tabeyev—met with Karmal and his main deputies in the Kremlin.[115] The Soviet leaders seemed to have given him a sharp lecture on the need to do better, if not a severe tongue-lashing for the shortcomings of his regime. This was indicated by the stiff criticisms Karmal gave his own officials on return home, described below. It was also indicated by the characterization in the official statement on his visit of talks' having been held "in an atmosphere of cordiality, comradely *frankness* and full mutual understanding."[116] In his admissions of mistakes in speeches while in Moscow, and in his abject manner in praising Brezhnev, Karmal seemed intent on proving that he had learned his lesson and would loyally do better in the future.[117]

In the Kremlin Karmal said he was proud that "we enjoy firm support and immense internationalist aid" from the Soviet Union and its Communist party.[118] One particular kind of aid he described on return to Kabul. "At our request, the USSR has sent experts and advisers for nearly all areas of government and for the ministries and administration of Afghanistan," he said.[119] Maximum advantage should be made of them, so that Afghans learned technical expertise and methods of organization and work, Karmal added, but some Afghans simply wanted to leave everything up to the Soviets.

This was an understandable tendency because reports showed that Soviet advisers so dominated affairs that little was left to the few trained and capable Afghans. In his 4 February speech, Ponomarev had tried to pretend otherwise to a Soviet audience: "The Soviet Union is not interfering in Afghanistan's internal affairs in the slightest. . . . Its government itself determines its own national policy. Exclusively Afghan citizens work in the whole structure of state and administrative power organs that is operating in a completely sovereign fashion from top to bottom."[120] This was so patently untrue that the otherwise full account of Ponomarev's speech broadcast to Afghanistan in Dari omitted that last sentence.[121]

From Safronchuk, who worked in the foreign ministry next to Dost and who along with eight Russian colleagues either wrote or cleared all outgoing cables, throughout the other civilian ministries and the armed forces, Soviet citizens were in charge and usually did the work rather than directing Afghans to do it. Usually they were Russians, with Central Asians used for their linguistic abilities but rarely in senior positions. Karmal was reportedly protected by Soviet bodyguards, and his doctor, cook, and chauffeur were Russians, while his Afghan guards carried empty weapons. The number of Soviets involved in running Afghanistan was not known to the outside world, but in mid-1980 British estimates were that it "may now run into tens of thousands." Sections of Kabul became Soviet colonies, with Afghans employed as servants.[122] Outside the capital, Soviet advisers seemed to fill the role that traditionally was filled by colonial officers. A blond, crewcut adviser to the governor of Konarha province was reported by a Western journalist who encountered him there to be empowered to intervene in political, administrative, logistic, and military affairs.[123]

With the effective takeover of Soviet advisers, an effort was begun to Russify the country. English was dropped from the compulsory curricula of schools. When the United States was the main provider of educational aid, English had been seen as the opening to the outside world. Now, Russian became compulsory.[124] The adaptation of Soviet textbooks for Afghan use that had begun under Taraki was intensified. The number of Afghans being educated in the Soviet Union jumped from 4,000 at the end of 1979 to 7,000 in early 1981, in addition to numerous others going there for specialized training courses.[125] This was the beginning of a long-term effort to develop new Afghan leaders who would reliably run a Soviet satellite country.

Finding reliable Afghans to back up Karmal was difficult. One reason was the widespread antipathy toward his Soviet sponsors. Another was the old distrust and hatred from Khalqis—who had dominated the government under Taraki and Amin—for Parchamis who became dominant under Karmal. When Karmal returned from the Soviet Union in November 1980 (he had spent nineteen days there, first on the official visit, then "for a brief rest and a course of treatment"[126]) he began passing along to PDPA members the lectures he had received there. He told party activists that more sincere efforts were needed for party unity because of the difficult tasks facing them and also because of "the great trust and all-round assistance" of the Soviets.

Henceforth the assessment of party membership and the appraisal of the activities of party and government cadres will not depend on previous service or relationships ... [nor on] an instance of heroism or other service. ... [It will depend on] their active struggle for the realization of the objectives of the Saur Revolution and the struggle against the counterrevolution ... on the successful fulfillment of the duties which the party puts forward in the political, economic, and social fields. The pursuance of eternal friendship and solidarity with the Leninist Community Party of the USSR and friendship between our countries and our peoples are the basic measures and yardsticks for the appraisal of the work of every member of the party from top to bottom, and of party and government officials from top to bottom.[127]

In other words, Afghans would be judged primarily on being good Soviets. Karmal went on that some Afghans in "high and responsible posts" had been guilty of "factionalism, bribery, repression, suffocation, law breaking, threats and oppression, promises and other unsuitable activities outside their authority." This will not be tolerated, he declared.[128]

He, and presumably also Soviet officials in Kabul, had in fact been complaining for some months. In April 1980 Karmal said it was necessary to eliminate "lawlessness, disobedience, embezzlement, bureaucracy, pilferage of public property, chauvinism, and so forth,"[129] and in July he said that "until now the PDPA has not succeeded in changing the decadent, old, strangulating and repressive government. ... The administrative machinery of our government is antipeople."[130] Karmal was speaking to a young, inexperienced party. Most of its members were less than thirty years old.[131] As noted earlier, brighter and more talented Afghans had tended to go into business, the professions, and government service under the monarchy or Daoud, while the Marxist factions attracted youths who had less hope of succeeding in those fields. In public statements,

Karmal tried to rally all PDPA elements, Khalqi as well as Parchami. Taraki and Amin had emphasized that theirs were Khalqi regimes; Karmal dropped those labels and talked only of the PDPA as a whole.[132] But the internecine conflict would not go away.

The inclusion of both Khalqis and Parchamis in Karmal's leadership group when he was put in power, presumably done by Safronchuk and other Soviet advisers, created a tense situation. Part of the apparent Soviet coolness toward Karmal in the initial months might be attributable to his inability to serve as a conciliator within the party, aside from his failure in this role for the country as a whole. The agreement that legalized the presence of Soviet troops in Afghanistan caused in April the first reported outburst of a long-tense situation, with Khalqis even more opposed than Parchamis to an arrangement that they knew might keep Karmal in power, aside from their nationalistic opposition to Russian control.[133] By mid-summer, many of the assassinations of government officials were being attributed to PDPA factional rivalry rather than to the *mujahideen*, and there were unconfirmed reports of Khalqis covertly helping the guerrillas or deserting the regime to join them.[134] A curious case in June of poisonous, but not lethal, gases being used in Kabul schools and public institutions, and the poisoning of water supplies, was initially blamed on guerrillas but later said to have somehow resulted from Khalqi-Parchami infighting. A young PDPA member told a Hungarian journalist of attending party meetings with a member of the other faction who had torn out his fingernails during Amin's persecution of Parchamis. Qadir was reported to have been shot by a Khalqi on 14 June and had to be flown to the Soviet Union for medical treatment.[135]

In an apparent effort to crack down and establish control, the government announced on 8 and 14 June the execution of a number of former Khalqi officials.[136] They included Assadullah Amin, Hafizullah Amin's nephew who had been brought back from hospitalization in the Soviet Union for the wounds received in the 17 December 1979 shooting at the House of the People; a brother of the late president, Abdullah Amin;[137] those already mentioned as being involved in Taraki's murder; and former ministers of communications, border affairs, and planning. A number of other Khalqis were reported to be among the estimated 3,000 to 9,000 political prisoners being held in Pul-i-Charki prison in late 1980. Guards at the prison included Soviet troops, and Soviet advisers were present during interrogations under torture.[138]

These actions against the Khalq faction seem to have worsened rather than improved the situation. They further weakened the regime. On 19 July 1980, wearing his prime minister's hat, Karmal presided over a cabinet meeting that approved a 15 July PDPA central committee decision to restructure the government so as to increase his own administrative power—or that of the Russians around him.[139] This gave his Parchami comrades better control of personnel matters, and it stripped the interior ministry headed by Khalqi official Gulabzoy of most of its power. Gulabzoy had been the last Khalqi leader left in a major position, except for the more quiet and noncontroversial Ziray, who along with the Parchami Keshtmand became one of Karmal's two top deputies.[140]

The other major, and controversial, Khalqi had been Sarwari, the torturer of Keshtmand and many others. He left for Moscow in June as the factional showdown began, ostensibly for medical treatment but according to some accounts because Karmal demanded that the Soviets remove him. Without returning to Kabul, he arrived on 15 August in Ulan Bator to become Afghan ambassador to Mongolia[141]—the place to which Khrushchev had banished Molotov when he defeated the "anti-party group" in 1957. The assignment stirred speculation in Kabul as well as abroad that Sarwari, who had always been presumed to be a Soviet favorite, perhaps inaccurately, and who was the nominal leader of the Khalqi faction after the demise of Taraki and Amin, was being kept available by Kremlin planners for some future contingency in which Karmal might have to be replaced. Apparently sensing such a contingency, Sarwari reportedly returned to Kabul in May 1981 when a governmental reorganization was being considered. But instead of returning to power, he was stripped of his PDPA politburo membership by a Central Committee session on 11 June 1981.[142]

That session made changes that presumably had been worked out in advance by Afghan leaders and their Soviet advisers, and later the same day the Revolutionary Council formally enacted them. The council was expanded so that for the first time it included persons not in the PDPA. Also, without announcing Karmal's resignation from the job, Keshtmand was appointed as chairman of the council of ministers, or prime minister.[143] The Afghan leadership was thus brought into conformity with what had in 1977 become the Soviet pattern and was used in several Soviet bloc nations: the Communist party leader was also chief of state, but the government was headed by a less important, trusted party technocrat. There was no indication that Karmal had lost to Keshtmand, who also headed the State Planning Committee, whatever real power that Soviet control allowed him. When Amin took the prime ministership from Taraki in March 1979, leaving Taraki with the party and state titles, real power was in the process of shifting. Circumstances were different in 1981.

Despite these various changes, however, or because of them, the bulk of Khalqis remained disaffected. The United States State Department said it heard credible reports of major military coup plots by Khalqi officers in June, July, and October 1980, [144] again in early February 1981,[145] and later. All were quelled by arrests, probably indicating more an efficient Soviet intelligence network than any competence of the again-renamed Afghan intelligence organization, which under Karmal had become the Government Intelligence Service, or KHAD.

But neither the danger of military subversion nor the broader aspects of Khalqi-Parchami conflict could be eliminated. Karmal told "political activists" in the army in August 1981 that

the destiny of our homeland and of the Saur Revolution depends on the unity and coordinated work of all party members. To forget this basic principle . . . is an explicit treason. . . . In most of the party organizations, these demands of the party [for an end of factionalism] have not been observed, and a number of members of the party, due to their links with previous factions—this faction and that faction—have not stopped their lies, allegations, and slanders.[146]

Bringing the administration under control, so that Russian rule could operate from behind a screen of unified and cooperative Afghan officials, was one of Karmal's tasks after he was installed in power. Another was revising the policies of Taraki and Amin that had alienated so many of the Afghan people. In fact, alienation from the government in Kabul was now based less on government policies than on its Soviet sponsorship. This was something Karmal could not affect, but he and his Soviet advisers set out to try to reduce or remove the domestic policy causes of opposition to the regime.

An early, obvious necessity was placating Moslem religious leaders and trying to overcome Moslem hostility to the PDPA. "The Amin clique regarded clergymen as bitter enemies," Karmal said, "and encroached on the religious rights of believers."[147] Karmal's brother, A. Mahmud Barialay, who became an important official of the party, said that in "the first phase of the revolution" the regime had been "impatient and often used force against religious leaders, whom it regarded without exception as opponents of progress." But in the second phase, he said, we realize "that the thinking of the predominately illiterate population is still being formed mainly by the *mullahs*."[148] The use of force had included the persecution and torture of Islamic leaders, the new government said as part of its condemnation of Amin, and he "massacred them in an unprecedented savage manner so that mosques . . . were emptied of noble scholars and spiritual leaders, [which] led to nationwide mourning over the tragedy that befell the clerical community."[149]

That was only a slight exaggeration for polemical purposes. Part of the Afghan Marxist creed since the early 1960s had been the charge that conservative *mullahs* helped the British to overthrow Amanullah and stood against modernization. One of the most prominent and honored clerics, Hazrat Shor Bazar Mojaddidi, and some 120 of his followers were killed by a government raid on his compound in Kabul in February 1979 as the PDPA tried to break religious opposition,[150] and there were numerous similar cases. Partially as a result of oppression, but also spontaneously because of the permeating cultural and social influence of Islam separate from any clerical role, religion was at the heart of the resistance. "It was under the banner of Islam that the counterrevolution developed" in Afghanistan, observed a leading Soviet specialist on the religion and spokesman on the country, Yevgeniy M. Primakov.[151]

Karmal sought to reassure Moslem feelings. He made a declaration in January 1980 guaranteeing freedom of religion, and he later told the Afghan people that "the date of 27 December represents the intervention of God Almighty. That the USSR is helping us is also an act of God."[152] In suppressing the February demonstrations, which had been proclaimed by handwritten leaflets circulated from mosques calling for "*jihad* against the unbelievers," the regime reportedly imprisoned a number of religious leaders, but publicly it took steps to avoid antagonizing Islamic feelings.[153] Party "theses" issued by the PDPA for the second anniversary of the 1978 coup promised "full freedom and rights of Moslems, the clergy, and noble and patriotic *ulemas*. . . . Their religious activities in the social, economic and cultural spheres will be supported."[154]

The government also issued its "basic principles," which filled the gap until a new constitution was written, that promised "resolutely following the sacred religion of Islam."[155] The principles included a new national flag with the old colors of the royal flag, black, red, and Islamic green, and religious symbolism in the state emblem on it. Over Khalqi protests, this replaced the all-red flag adopted by Taraki that had inflamed traditionalist passions, but that flag was retained as the PDPA banner. Other symbolism included an avoidance of Communist terminology, which *Pravda* noted had been "incomprehensible to simple people . . . [and] not only undermined the masses' enthusiasm but also their trust in the leadership."[156]

Karmal denied calling himself a Marxist after he took power.[157] The regime talked of "the social development of society" as its goal rather than Communism or socialism.[158] At repeated meetings with leaders of Afghanistan's estimated 320,000 *mullahs*, Karmal insisted upon the benign intentions of his government and sought their support. A religious conference that Karmal addressed 1 July 1980 at the House of the People turned hostile, however, with a number of the 800 theologians and clerics who attended denouncing the Soviet occupation. A *mullah* who supported the regime was booed down.[159] Nonetheless, the conference was announced by the official media as having adopted a resolution approving the government's actions and calling on all Moslems to cease resistance to it. The conference also approved a government proposal to establish a "chief board on Islamic questions" attached to the revolutionary council plus a "supreme council of the *ulemas* and clergy of Afghanistan."[160]

This conference was the first attempt to bring a religion that lacks a clerical hierarchy—none for Sunni Moslems, only an informal one for the Shi'ite minority of Afghans—under some bureaucratic control. It imitated the Soviet pattern of trying to channel and control Moslem activities. It also began an attempt, in imitation of Soviet practices, to obtain the appearance of religious sanction for government policies. The new Council of *Ulema*, for instance, urged Afghan men to obey military callups by quoting the Koran to contend that fighting for the Karmal regime was "accomplishing the injunction of God."[161]

The development of new Moslem institutions as a way of trying to manipulate one type of interest group, religious leaders, was part of a broader pattern of seeking to win favor or influence with the various constituent elements of Afghan society, many of them overlapping. In some areas this entailed the simple expedient of buying support. The most notable example was in dealing with Pushtun tribes. The tradition of a ruler in Kabul paying for tribal support was well-established. Using what could only have been Soviet-supplied money, Karmal's minister for frontier and tribal affairs, Fayz Mohammed, set out to divide up the various tribal and clan elements in eastern Afghanistan, buying loyalty where possible. In September 1980 he was killed by tribesmen whom he had gone to bribe.[162] The word coming out of the hills later was that the *pushtunwali* injunction of *melmastia*—the tribal code's provision of hospitality—did not apply to stooges of Russian infidels.[163]

Karmal's promise in his initial policy statement as president to create "a broad front . . . of all the national and democratic forces" under PDPA leadership[164] was followed by the inclusion of three ministers in his first cabinet who were not PDPA members.[165] This was widely publicized. So were the appointments in succeeding months of deputy ministers and other officials from outside the party.[166] Their numbers were small, however, and their power weak, not only because the PDPA was clearly designated to make policy and control the government but also because of the omnipresent Soviet advisers. In a few cases, prominent figures from pre-Communist governments were lured from retirement, but some of them did not long remain in Karmal's regime, and some former leading officials went into exile rather than being pressed into serving a system they detested as a veil for Russian colonialism.[167]

Talking to a Bulgarian journalist less than a month after coming to power, Karmal compared his proposed front with the Fatherland Front organized in Bulgaria on Communist initiative during World War II.[168] It was both an inaccurate and a revealing comparison. In Bulgaria, and Hungary and Romania as well, the destruction of Nazi German influence by the Soviet Red Army was followed at Moscow's instigation by genuine coalition governments. The Communist parties were in minority positions, and they cooperated with democratic parties on short-term programs under conditions of free speech and political activity. That did not last long. What became known as "salami tactics" were applied. Internal Communist and external Soviet pressures reduced non-Communist parties to inferior positions. In some cases their true leaders were banished and Communist stooges installed instead. After a period of bogus coalition, the fronts became monolithic organizations under Communist direction with non-Communists only for window dressing. Police and military power had enabled the Communists to overcome other political elements despite numerically small popular support.[169] Karmal did not have to go through these stages. His minority group already had power. What he wanted was a front to create the appearance but not the substance of a broad-based, popular government. For that, the example of Mao's China would have been more appropriate. A political front was created there after power had been captured militarily, and non-Communist parties were brought in without any pretense of their having real authority.[170]

Before a full-scale national front could be established in Afghanistan, constituent elements had to be created. In his 16 October Kremlin speech, Karmal explained that party and state leaders were busy organizing meetings of various social, economic, ethnic, tribal, and religious groupings. This was, he said, "one of the stages along the road to forming a new structure for organizing the masses." He added that it was "important at this stage of the national-democrat-ic revolution to expand the national fatherland front to support the party and government in carrying out the socioeconomic transformations."[171] No question, then, of giving non-Communists a real voice in policy. It was, instead, a matter of trying to co-opt a wide range of people into what had already been decided by the PDPA under Soviet guidance. "It is the law of the revolution that the party of the working class and all toilers of the country have the historic mission of leading the broad national fatherland front," Karmal told a Kabul meeting of teachers, doctors, writers, journalists, and other "groups of intellectuals."[172]

By the summer of 1980 efforts were under way to build the kind of loyally supportive trade union movement that the Soviet Union had long used to control its own workers—not the kind that developed in Poland in 1980 with the founding of Solidarity. The PDPA politburo said on 16 August that the first task of unions was "the explanation of party and government policy to the workers, [and] the organization of workers . . . for the defense of . . . the revolution," with only the final task being "the defense of workers' interests and rights."[173] By 7 March 1981, when the first congress of Afghan trade unions began, unions had 160,000 members "under the political leadership" of the PDPA, Karmal said in opening the congress.[174]

In September 1980 more than 600 delegates held the first meeting of the Dem-ocratic Organization of the Youth of Afghanistan, which was modeled after the Soviet Young Communist League, or Komsomol.[175] All of its members were required to belong to "public order teams" that were supposed to back up mili-tary and militia units in guarding against guerrillas and urban unrest.[176] Camps for children were established on the model of the Soviet Pioneer camps,[177] which are indoctrination centers as much as vacation spots. Also in September, organi-zational meetings were held for a union of artists and for a journalists' union. Both groups were told that it was their duty to "propagate the lofty aims of the revolution" and show its irreversibility as well as to expand cooperation with the Soviet Union.[178]

In October, a union of writers was created; in November, the Democratic Women's Organization of Afghanistan held its first conference; and in Decem-ber, a central council of agricultural cooperatives, claiming to represent 190,000 farmers, met with the purpose of "insuring [that] peasants take active part" in the front. Delegations from equivalent organizations in the Soviet Union and other Soviet bloc countries attended these meetings, and media accounts of PDPA messages to them and of proceedings were indistinguishable from the kind of publicity that accompanied such organizations' conferences in Moscow.[179]

After "the entire structure of public organizations [had] in effect been created from scratch," as *Pravda* noted,[180] a conference of "Afghan national and patriotic forces" was held on the first anniversary of the Soviet invasion, 27 December 1980, at the Revolutionary Council's headquarters in Kabul, Salam Khanah Palace.[181] Without discussion, the conference accepted a list read by Nur of forty-four PDPA leaders and some nonpolitical figures as members of a commission. The commission would prepare a founding congress of the National Fatherland Front, decide which tribal representatives, social and economic organizations, religious leaders, and others to admit to the front, and draft a charter.[182] "The PDPA, as a political vanguard force, is included in the front," Karmal told the 2,000 delegates. "Our party, which legally possesses the power of the state and government, regards . . . [the] NFF as the best form of the organization of the masses of the people."[183] The delegates dutifully adopted a declaration saying the purpose of establishing the NFF "is to mobilize, in pursuance of PDPA policy, . . . all noble people of Afghanistan to take active and conscious part" in achieving official goals.[184] Karmal promised that, after the NFF's founding, national elections would be held, but he said that "those so-called parties which are operating from outside Afghanistan" would not be recognized.[185]

The founding congress was originally scheduled to be held by or shortly after 21 March 1981.[186] But there were problems rounding up support from a hostile, or at best apathetic, populace.[187] After a long silence on the subject, the 11 June 1981 PDPA and Revolutionary Council meetings that made party and governmental changes also cleared the way for the NFF congress.[188] So, almost two years after Moscow had begun urging the PDPA to use a front for trying to broaden its appeal, and Soviet media had publicized PDPA decisions in favor of a front that the Afghans themselves did not mention, the congress finally was held.

It took only one day, 15 June, to run through a well-rehearsed procedure. The 940 delegates approved a "fundamental statement" read by Karmal,[189] elected Ziray as chairman of the NFF national committee,[190] and adopted a constitution that said the PDPA was "the guiding force of the National Fatherland Front and the whole society of Afghanistan."[191] The constitution added:

> The basic task of the NFF is that, following the general policy line of the PDPA, vast masses of the people be attracted to participate actively and consciously in constructing democratic and progressive Afghanistan and in observing respect for the sacred religion of Islam, the specific historical, spiritual and national customs and traditions of all nationalities and tribes of the country, and to propagate and explain on a broad scale the policy of the PDPA, the Revolutionary Council and the Government of the DRA.[192]

The NFF's "patriotic duty," it also said, was to "protect and expand the valuable treasures of friendship and cooperation between the peoples of Afghanistan and the Soviet Union.[193]

In following months there was little sign of the NFF's serving its intended purposes. It became nothing more than a propaganda device, apparently not even an effective one. Those who had been delegates to the congress or became NFF officials—in many cases, minor government functionaries masquerading as regional leaders, in place of popularly accepted leaders who wanted nothing to do with it[194]—became targets for *mujahideen* assassination. There was no further talk of elections, which would have been impossible to conduct among more than a small fraction of the population.

Thus, a start was made toward rectifying mistakes of the Taraki and Amin periods and building a new base under the PDPA regime installed by Soviet tanks. "A very severe process is taking place," Primakov said on the first anniversary of the invasion. "It is quite difficult, but it is a process of stabilizing the situation."[195] How stable it was becoming was doubtful, however. Equally doubtful was the regime's degree of success in convincing the people that hated policies were being revised. The *mujahideen* resistance continued, the exodus of refugees accelerated. There was no sign of popular trust in the professions of Karmal and his officials that Islam would be respected and that the regime would honor individual rights. There was too much evidence otherwise.

The new facade of the NFF appeared to foreign observers to be an empty shell. If filled by anything, it was by the Soviet Army, the only real authority in the country. But by creating it, the Karmal government and its Soviet backers were better able to make the pretense that Afghanistan was returning to normal under a domestically supported political structure. So long as censorship and denial of foreigners' access to most of the country made reports of true conditions mainly secondhand, and the loudest denials of normality came from Peshawar guerrilla groups or Afghan exiles abroad, whose statements were often discounted as exaggerations, the pretense could be loudly proclaimed by Communist media to be the reality.

Costs of the Invasion

The appearances of normality were expensive. Since it was part of the pretense to insist that the Afghan economy was functioning fairly well, and since the Soviet Union always keeps secret the costs of its foreign adventures and the burden of sustaining clients from Vietnam to Cuba, there was no reliable figure on how much the takeover of Afghanistan cost Moscow in initial expense or recurring costs. China estimated the daily cost in 1981 at $3 to $4 million for military supplies, gasoline, and related expenses alone.[196] One Western estimate of the economic cost, separate from Soviet Army expenses, was some $600 million for the first half of 1980,[197] and another estimate was a much higher daily cost of $10 to $12 million,[198] but both must be taken as guesses.

The important fact was that the Soviet government's economic planning organization, Gosplan, had obviously been given the assignment of sustaining Afghanistan. An official of the Academy of Science's Institute for Oriental Studies, which was headed by Primakov, commented that in economic terms Afghanistan had become another backward republic of the Soviet Union whose deficits and development expenses had to be met from Moscow.[199]

The dislocations caused originally by land reforms, the disruption caused by the resistance, and the destruction of crops and other measures taken by the

Soviet Army in fighting the *mujahideen* meant that normal trade was virtually halted. Soviet-held cities were cut off from agricultural and other supplies from the countryside. Customs tolls and road taxes, normally the financial basis for government, were estimated by former officials who went into exile to have dropped 80 percent.[200] The Soviet Union had to fill the gap in goods and money. The Afghan official supervising the economy, Keshtmand, said in 1980 that "We would not have survived" without Soviet economic as well as military aid.[201] Speaking in 1981 as prime minister, he said that "We obtain all vital materials and means for the defense of the revolution—that is, food, arms, equipment, oil and other material goods—from the USSR."[202]

Keshtmand depicted an economy paralyzed by the guerrilla war, despite other officials' claims of good harvests. "A number of industrial institutes in the country, for example coal mines, some factories and mines . . . were not exploited at all or are partially exploited," Keshtmand said.[203] Governors and other provincial officials are "dutybound to revive economic activity in their regions," he added, and "research and extraction work on oil and gas" must also be revived.[204] Gas was particularly important to the Soviets. It was the only immediate economic return from Afghanistan of any consequence. A second gas field in the Sheberghan area, at Jarquduq, began producing shortly before the invasion, and the Soviet Army made sure that the pipelines from it and from the Khvaja-Gugardag field across the Amu Darya were protected from the kind of guerrilla attacks that frequently cut the military fuel pipeline that was laid into Afghanistan. Soviet import statistics showed a quadrupling in value of gas from 33.7 billion rubles in 1978 to 134.9 billion in 1980.[205] Although some of this apparently was a result of Soviet agreement to raise the price it paid as a bookkeeping offset to Afghan debts—Afghan exiles contended that the price was still only half the world level[206]—gas was a significant return to Moscow for its long investment in aid for Afghanistan.

But gas could not pay for everything the country needed in its disrupted condition. "The Soviet Union provided a number of indispensable commodities free of charge and imposed foreign trade terms exceedingly favorable for Afghanistan," Keshtmand said in 1981.[207] Diplomatic reports said free distribution of Soviet-supplied food, soap, shoes, clothing, kerosene, and other items was done on a coupon system apparently intended to benefit supporters of the regime,[208] a system similar to that used by Vietnam in Cambodia. Karmal, who said 80 percent of the aid being received in late 1980 was from the Soviet Union, reported that Soviet help had made possible pay raises for government employees, apparently another way of trying to insure loyalty.[209] With only India among non-Communist nations continuing its aid program for Afghanistan, the remaining aid came from East European countries that were accustomed to being coerced by Moscow to help support its clients. In June 1980 Keshtmand told the Soviet bloc's economic organization, the Council for Mutual Economic Assistance, in which Afghanistan was given observer status, that "the economic and moral aid of socialist countries is of special importance to us" because of guerrillas' "creating numerous economic problems for us."[210] Czechoslovakia, East Germany, and Hungary led the list of East European countries providing help.[211] Foreign aid merely kept the economy going, but could not prevent it from sliding backward in some economic terms as guerrillas targeted particularly vulnerable infrastructure projects in remote areas such as power plants and transmission lines. Meanwhile the Kabul government tried to continue with land reforms and other rural changes in areas it could control. In addition to agricultural cooperatives, into which theoretically independent farmers were pushed, the Soviet model was used in establishing state farms on which workers are salaried employees. Six new ones were set up in 1980, bringing the total to eight of a planned twenty or twenty-five.[212] At the same time the first four of a network of machine and tractor stations were established to provide mechanized services for cooperative farms, thus duplicating Stalin's system for gaining economic and political control over nominally independent farmers through the leverage of providing vital services. Although only 25 percent of state capital investment was put into agriculture, compared to 50 percent in industry,[213] Soviet planners in Kabul apparently felt it necessary to devote resources as well as political effort to seeking a better grip on the countryside. Rural influence was also sought by a revival in 1981 of Taraki's abortive land reform program. While indirectly admitting that land reform had up to then been less sweeping or successful than had previously been claimed, the new decrees were more openly political than the program had previously been. Land became a tool with which to try to win the support of religious groups, enlist persons willing to fight for the regime, and lure back those in opposition to it.[214]

Chapter 12. Soviet Afghanistan

The future is bleak for the Afghanistan that has through the centuries proudly fought to maintain its independence and its separate ways. At a cost in human lives that probably will never be counted, and at a cost in crushed individual freedom that cannot be measured statistically, Afghanistan might as a future part of the Soviet bloc achieve faster material progress than it had been likely to attain on its own. That would, however, be a distant future. The present prospect is not progress. It is death and destruction as the Soviet Union tries to break the resistance of the Afghan people and bend them to its imperial will.

The Soviet military occupation that began in 1979 has led to policies of a new colonialism in Afghanistan. Today's conditions are much different from the nineteenth-century colonialism that was resisted on more equal military terms. But this is not so new a colonialism for Russians who have practiced it before in other places, both before and after the Bolshevik Revolution. They have practiced it with tenacity. A number of factors in the situation that has developed in Afghanistan since the occupation began point to a Soviet determination to retain, consolidate, and solidify control. The Soviet Army came to stay in Afghanistan, however long it takes to insure the permanency of Soviet-influenced Communism there.

Some of the reasons for this determination are similar to the reasons that produced the occupation in the first place. One is geography. More than a century of Russia's concern about any instability or hostility just across its frontier, and search for opportunities to establish influence across that frontier, insure that the present involvement is not ephemeral. A historic thrust has reached a new stage, one that cannot readily be abandoned. Because Afghanistan lay on its border, the Soviet Union committed its personnel, material, and prestige there to a degree that it has cautiously avoided doing in more distant Third World countries.

The strong commitment is itself a reason for staying in Afghanistan. If the 1978 rise to power by a Soviet-cultivated PDPA was unexpected or even unwanted—an unproven "if"—nonetheless it meant unavoidable decisions in the Kremlin. Help was needed, it was given, and Soviet prestige became involved. The unrealistically ideological approach of the PDPA toward governing started a process that by its own momentum and logic culminated in the Soviet invasion. Once the PDPA government had been propped up with Soviet bayonets, it became doubly difficult to withdraw support. One reason was that a collapse of Communist rule in Afghanistan then would have been even more obviously a Soviet failure and setback than before the invasion. Another was that, whatever its claim to indigenous roots in 1978, by 1980 the PDPA regime had come to be seen by most Afghans as a Soviet surrogate. That made it all the more hated and all the more unable to survive on its own.

Soviet advisers have tried to press Afghanistan into the mold of Moscow-style Communism that eventually brought peace and stability in the similar areas of Soviet Central Asia. This deepening and intensification of the Soviet pattern for control is a third element of determination. Karmal, in a puppet position that gave him no choice, heeded Soviet advice in a way that the two previous PDPA presidents had not done. He adopted policies devised in Moscow, but they had an internal contradiction. They were intended to de-emphasize but not actually deny the Communist nature of the regime in an effort to soften policies that had proven antagonistic to the Afghan people. But they were also intended to remake the country eventually in a way that would insure a Communist nature in Leninist control terms if not in theoretical Marxist economic terms.

Implementing these policies of control created a fourth reason for the Soviets to remain. That is the development of strong ties between the Soviet Communist Party and the PDPA. The Afghan party was rebuilt in the Soviet image. This meant a virtual takeover of the party under the guise of Soviet advice that paralleled the way Soviet advisers came to run the Afghan government and army. Although not stressed immediately after the invasion in institutional ways, presumably to avoid unnecessarily antagonizing Moslem and Third World countries, it also meant the gradual absorption of Afghanistan into effectively full membership of the Soviet bloc.

A fifth reason is the well-demonstrated reluctance of the Soviet leadership, and especially of the aged group of men who made the decision to seize military control of Afghanistan, to admit to having made mistakes and to reverse policies. It would have been better to have let the PDPA regime collapse of its own self-inflicted wounds in 1979 than to have gone in half-heartedly. But once the earlier Soviet commitment to Communist rule in Afghanistan had been turned into an international issue, backing out would show an intolerable weakness. If Khrushchev got into trouble for being unable to sustain an unwise commitment of missiles in Cuba in 1962, the potential for pressures by Communist party and military officials on the Soviet politburo would be greater here. The compulsion to sustain a Communist regime that contributed to the invasion decision in 1979 was all the stronger once the choice came to seem to be one between that ideological imperative and yielding to foreign pressure. There could be no admission of a mistake, however bad the original calculations of either the internal problems to be tackled in Afghanistan or the foreign reaction.

Perhaps the Soviet leaders would have been willing to retreat if offered a plausible way of having their PDPA regime in Afghanistan and going home too. This best of both worlds hope lay behind the 14 May 1980 proposals. While these proposals were unacceptable to neutral and Western nations alike, how to negotiate the Soviets out of Afghanistan became a subject of much speculation in the West. The speculation sometimes ignored the basic factors that had gotten them in. Diplomats began to fabricate diplomatic solutions,

Afghan specialists abroad began to spin out complex analyses of possible settlements, and Moslem countries talked vaguely of the Afghan resistance's driving away the Russians. There was an air of unreality about much of this. Partly, it was ignorance of both Afghanistan and the Soviet Union. Partly, also, it suggested a sort of psychological defense against admitting the truth about long-term policies and attitudes that led to the invasion, as if the Soviet action had been only a momentary emotional thing that could be undone when calm returned.

There were suggestions of the "Finlandization" of Afghanistan. They ignored the reality that the Soviet Union tried several times to reestablish tsarist control of Finland and only finally allowed it a carefully nonantagonistic form of neutralism when those attempts failed. The Red Army never had to retreat from Finland and take with it local puppets and Soviet overseers who had been running its government. Other suggestions of an Austrian peace treaty type of neutrality ignored the power balance in Central Europe ten years after World War II that led to an East-West compromise there. Such a balance did not exist in South Asia. Nothing comparable to the North Atlantic Treaty Organization stood on the other side of Afghanistan, only a politically and militarily weak Pakistan. Yet other speculation ignored the absence of a stable, coherent alternative to a Soviet-directed Afghan government. There was no unified force in sight that could provide the stability which would have to be built into any solution, that could insure tranquillity on the Soviet border. The first three years of the Soviet attempt to control Afghanistan only proved the essential ungovernability of the country. Communists in Kabul feuded. Resistance groups carried on their traditional tribal conflicts. The split in the resistance between Moslem fundamentalists and westernized Afghans was exacerbated by competing efforts to rally foreign support.

The Soviet Union had several reasons to stay in Afghanistan for however long it took to insure the country's permanent place within the Soviet bloc. It had no reasons beyond the tolerable pain of the guerrilla war to abandon its effort. The world can therefore take at face value two basic Soviet statements about Afghanistan made after the invasion. Expressed in the special language that defines terms sometimes to suit Marxist ideology, sometimes to suit the Soviet nation's foreign policy, they have clear meanings. They have been often repeated in various ways, but Brezhnev summarized them clearly in his Kremlin dinner speech welcoming Karmal in October 1980. "The revolutionary process in Afghanistan is irreversible," Brezhnev declared in one key expression of Soviet determination. The second one, its corollary, was that the Soviet Union and its supporting Communist and leftist allies will back "the Afghan people and its government." He went on, "We will firmly stand on guard of the security interests of both our states and will do our internationalist duty to the Afghan people and to its government headed by Comrade Babrak Karmal."[1]

By "revolutionary process," Brezhnev meant the establishment of a Leninist system of rigidly centralized control by a small group of Afghan leaders willing to accept Soviet tutelage. Any attempt to challenge that small group, no matter how broad the support for a challenge or how much of a majority it represented, would by definition be "counterrevolutionary" and therefore unacceptable. It would be resisted by the political, economic, military, and security police resources of the Soviet Union. Although the public justification for the Soviet Army's being in Afghanistan was to protect the country against external aggression, it was not a challenge from outside that worried the Soviet leadership. It was the resistance by the Afghan people to changes pressed upon them without the approval of public opinion, in a primitive land where opinion tended to be expressed not by polls but by guns. Afghan resistance later challenged foreign rule through local front men. The attitudes expressed by Brezhnev meant that the Soviet Army would go home only when an Afghan Communist regime subservient to Moscow was secure from rejection by its own neighbors.

Such security might eventually develop in a crushed country. It was not in sight in the early 1980s. Nor could it readily be assumed possible to achieve for a long time after that. Even if *mujahideen* resistance were reduced to occasional knifings of Soviet soldiers in Afghan bazaars or ambushes on isolated roads away from any villagers whom the Soviets might be expected to kill in retaliation, even if ordinary people were cowed by policies of retaliation so massive as to amount to preventative terrorism, it was unlikely to be possible for a PDPA government to do without the ultimate guarantee of a Soviet military presence.

By the time of the Afghanistan ocupation, the Soviet Army had been present in Eastern Europe for three and a half decades. Still it remained there, for several reasons. One was to insure Soviet interests. It provided a guarantee of Communist power, and it gained a buffer between Soviet territory and Western Europe. These benefits could be achieved relatively easily. Eastern Europe lacked Afghanistan's traditions of harassing and rejecting conquerors or of fighting to a draw one of the world's greatest imperial powers, Britain. Also, in Eastern Europe and in economically modernized countries in general, the mutual interdependence of integrated economies makes it almost impossible for pockets of resistance to sustain themselves. In a country like Afghanistan almost self-sufficient villagers still know how to grow their own food and make their own shoes. Czechoslovakia was too dependent on trade to sustain its living standards without economic linkages that the Soviet Army could easily have broken. The lower living standards of rural Afghanistan are less vulnerable, the people therefore better able to operate in individual defiance of Soviet power. Compared to the relative ease of holding Eastern Europe between brief flareups of trouble in 1953, 1956, 1968, and the Polish problem from 1980 onward, the Soviet Army could not simply sit in barracks in Afghanistan. What Brezhnev called "our internationalist duty" required fighting against hostility that endangered the Kabul regime.

As suggested already, the Soviet record of withdrawing troops from foreign countries in which their presence has helped establish regimes friendly or even subservient to the Soviet Union is a limited one. The cases have varied. The

Soviet Army has gone home when under pressure of superior military force, as in Iranian Azerbaijan. It has left when a Communist regime has become so solidly entrenched that Soviet interests are assured without the continued presence of a guaranteeing guard, as in North Korea. And it has withdrawn when a greater overall gain is seemingly offered by relinquishing control in a limited area, as in Sinkiang—although the gain was lost in the Sino-Soviet split. In none of those places did the Soviet Army have to combat any significant amount of local resistance. There was, therefore, no element of decision involving any immediate cost of staying and fighting either a conventional or a guerrilla war. Afghanistan was a new experience.

It also obviously was and is a costly one. If the Soviet government is as bureaucratically muddled on this cost as it seems to be on others in an overloaded administrative structure, it probably lacks a clear sense of Afghanistan's price. The United States government never fully appreciated the cost of its Vietnamese involvement in immediate, hidden, and latent ways, including the inflationary effect. The number of Soviet military deaths in Afghanistan can be counted, while being kept secret. They might well be considered acceptable as the price for actual combat experience, something the Soviet Army had with minor exceptions lacked for more than a generation. Whatever grumbling is heard inside the Soviet Union about the Afghan war, that conflict logically would be the place to be for patriotic and ambitious military men. West Point graduates knew that not just one but two tours of duty in Vietnam would enhance their careers. Similarly, Soviet military men who had been under fire, while stationed in Egypt during the 1970 duels between Soviet air defenses and Israeli warplanes, were regarded as being superior to untested troops.

But the financial costs cannot be counted so readily as casualties. Building new military facilities in Afghanistan was an obvious expense. It would be extra expense, however, only to the extent that scheduled military construction inside the Soviet Union had not been shifted across the Amu Darya. Military operations against the *mujahideen* have their costs, but to some extent they have probably replaced maneuvers and therefore been partially covered out of planned expenditures. The key question is the incremental cost of holding Afghanistan, the cost at the margin. In the absence of any figures available to the outside world, the subject should be viewed in this way. In such a way, it might not seem to Kremlin leaders so great as a simple counting of the 100,000 or more Soviet troops in Afghanistan in late 1982 would suggest.

Another kind of cost seemed to have surprised the Soviet Union. It was unprepared for the strength of the world-wide condemnation of its move into Afghanistan. As has already been indicated, it is doubtful that an advance knowledge of the international outcry would have deterred Soviet leaders from their decision. Their probable failure to conduct the kind of extensive consultations with their foreign affairs experts that were normal for major foreign moves showed that the problem in Afghanistan in the autumn of 1979 was considered too critical to allow its solution to be influenced by diplomatic considerations. The Soviet politburo was prepared to ride out whatever storm resulted from an action that had come to seem essential. The lack of any meaningful change in policy of Afghanistan after that storm had burst confirms this, in addition to showing a determination not to show any sign of national weakness by yielding to world pressure.

That pressure was not so great as it might have been. Verbal condemnation of the Soviet Union was not followed in the outraged Moslem world by any significant action to try to penalize the aggressor. While the Moslem world had little leverage it could use, the lack of a cohesive religion-based reaction was emphasized by a continued enhancement of Soviet ties by such Moslem nations as Syria and Libya, who did not allow Afghanistan to become a major cause of concern. Trade of many Western countries with the Soviet Union increased in the first year of the Afghanistan occupation. The United States lead in trying to penalize the country that it labeled an aggressor found few followers, and American efforts to use the invasion as a strong new reason for building up the military power of the Western alliance had little effect in Europe. The 1978 NATO decision on increasing defense spending in real terms, which Soviet media sometimes cited as the beginning of a deterioration of East-West relations long before the Afghanistan action, was not being implemented by most alliance members after that action. The United States was moving toward trying to strengthen its military capabilities, especially in projection into regions near Afghanistan. The invasion gave that new impetus. But the Kremlin's move was less costly in terms of causing changes in the military balance to Soviet detriment than it was in diplomatic terms.

Accepting the various costs, the Soviet design for Afghanistan is to develop a new cohesion around a Communist party that follows Soviet advice. The party is intended to exercise tightly centralized control of all aspects of national life that can be reached from Kabul with the help initially of the Soviet Army and at some future time with a new, loyal Afghan army. The Soviet policies that led to the invasion and those adopted after it all point unmistakably in that direction. The Kremlin is now seeking in Afghanistan a safe, reliable border bulwark.

It is a difficult quest because the initial excesses of the Taraki government blighted chances for a gradual consolidation of the power seized in the 1978 coup. The Soviet advisers to the Karmal government had to backtrack from those excesses in an attempt to establish a foundation of institutions on which a civilian-based power could be built instead of having it rest solely on the modern version of bayonets. This is different from the way Communist power was developed and loyal Soviet satellites created in Eastern Europe after the Red Army had moved in beginning in 1944. There, a methodical process of establishing a power base first added local police control to the operations of Soviet troops and political police. Then, some non-Communist political factions were discredited and others neutralized by working from inside to eliminate their leaderships. Finally, the originally small Communist parties that had been harbored by Moscow during the war emerged into the appearance of local power. It was an appearance that was used on Soviet advice to begin implementing policies intended so to change the countries of Eastern Europe that there would never be any future question of rejecting Communism or going against Soviet wishes. The important point is that these major changes—in the economy as well as political structure—came after the consolidation of power.

But in Afghanistan the PDPA had tried to carry out major changes before it had a firm grip on power. The result was to create opposition that it could not handle, despite a form of official terrorism. That terrorism only made the situation worse. Once an overwhelming majority of the population had been antagonized and driven into opposition, use of the preferred Soviet technique of co-opting support from non-Communist factions before beginning the imposition of Leninist and Stalinist changes in the political structure and economy had been foreclosed. It became necessary to try to undo some of the damage of the initial excesses while reaching out for support to people who had been alienated by them. This would be a difficult, lengthy process, even without Afghanistan's historic antipathy to foreign influence.

Rather than an East European comparison, the situation in Afghanistan was more like what faced Bolshevik leaders in Central Asia in the *basmachi* period around 1920. Initial policies of the Tashkent Soviet had alienated Moslems of Turkestan. In two stages, in 1920 and again after most *basmachi* resistance had been broken at the end of 1923 (though it continued in isolated pockets for many years), officials from Moscow implemented new policies. Some reversed earlier policies. Food was sent into the area for distribution under controls intended to keep it from the guerrillas, manufactured goods made available to ease shortages and keep prices down, and Moslem traders once again allowed free commerce after a period in which it had been forbidden. Concessions to Islamic feeling included making Friday the day of rest, restoring to mosques and religious boards property that had been confiscated by the state, and allowing the return of Islamic *shariat* courts. In Bukhara, a congress of Moslem clergy was held in 1924 to denounce the *basmachi*. This last step was part of a more subtle attack on the power of religion to become a rallying point for resistance to the infidel Russians. It was an effort to draw religious leaders away from the oppostion, to deny the *basmachi* the emotional support of conducting a *jihad*, as the amir of Bukhara had proclaimed in 1919.

The overall effect was to allow the Uzbeks, Tajiks, Turkmen, and other Moslem peoples of Central Asia to return to their traditional way of life and thus dissuade them from supporting the *basmachi* resistance to Russian threats to their traditions. It was less a resistance to Marxist economic or political theory as practiced by the Bolsheviks than a desperate defense of their whole Islamic culture against impositions and abuses. The new policies and the use of force to quell remaining resistance brought enough order to Central Asia for the Russian officials there to begin building new political structures. Local people who had fled from any involvement with the Bolsheviks were brought into the government. Unified opposition by the traditional leadership of wealthy and educated men thus was broken up. A new generation was trained to appreciate the benefits of adherence to the large new Soviet state and had vested interests in the material progress offered by it. Then, gradually, as the Russian grip became stronger, further policy changes were made. Religious property was divided into several categories and the state assumed control of much of it. Such stages of gradual encroachment into traditional ways led to collectivization, the abolition of Moslem trading rights, and other steps to reclaim what had been lost in order to quell the *basmachis*. Central Asia had been broken to Soviet rule. Russians were in the role of colonial masters carrying out an enlightened economic policy of modernization for the benefit of local people as well as the greater good of the central power. Which of these two motives predominated can be debated without any gain from an answer. The point was that political control came before everything else.[2]

The parallels with Afghanistan are already clear from the policies at the beginning of the Karmal era that were outlined in the previous chapter. The approach used north of the Amu Darya six decades ago and being used south of the border river now is to take one step backward after two steps forward had encountered severe problems. Some of Karmal's statements about the Taraki and Amin periods echoed the Soviet blame on the Tashkent Soviet for "not considering the native peculiarities" and for doing "little to ameliorate the situation created by nationalist, bourgeois agitation for autonomy and the counterrevolutionary activity of the inspired *basmachi*."[3] By emphasizing the continued role of *shariat* courts, encouraging private trade while trying to build up the government's economic role, creating organizations of Moslem clergy, workers, intellectuals, and other elements, and in many other ways, the same sort of approach is now being tried in Afghanistan that was pursued in the old tsarist Turkestan.

The fact that PDPA regimes had attacked the clergy, intellectuals, and other groups during the first twenty months of the Afghan revolution meant, however, that many of the bridges used by the Russians in Central Asia to reach the local people had already been burned in Afghanistan. It became necessary for the Karmal government to develop a new generation of leaders and experts for a country that has been drained of most of the talented people trained over the last few decades. The rejection of the new Soviet system by a sizeable part of the better-educated youths, shown by Kabul demonstrations, leaflets and "night letters," and by the evasion of military service, meant that there was a very limited reservoir of enthusiasm to be tapped in training a new generation.

Even the proverbial village lads on whom ideologues of left or right have traditionally depended for malleable material to serve their cause could not readily be used in Afghanistan. The message spread through the *mullahs* to them has usually been one of hostility toward the regime. Schools with PDPA teachers that were supposed to counter that influence have for exactly that reason been *mujahideen* targets. Kabul's educational system reached very little of the country by 1981. There will be in any society some who are willing to serve those in power. Afghan youths sent to the Soviet Union by the Karmal government for education might prove loyally willing when they return. But in Afghanistan it was likely to take many years to reach and convert a generation to acceptance of the country's new status in the Soviet bloc.

Perhaps it would not be possible even in a number of years. There is an interesting, if not predictive, parallel in the Chinese experience in Tibet. After the Dalai Lama fled from Lhasa in March 1959, the Chinese government stepped up its program of taking youths from Tibet to eastern China for education and training as technicians and administrators of their homeland. But years in Han Chinese surroundings while receiving Maoist indoctrination and education failed to overcome the strong cultural influence of the Tibetan blend of religion with secular authority. Few of the students proved willing to put Chinese interests ahead of peculiarly Tibetan ones. Many of them rebelled against both their educations and their Chinese tutelage. It therefore was impossible for the Chinese to rely on this cadre as a whole to carry out Peking's policies rather than bending toward their own traditions.[4]

Unlike Afghanistan, Tibet has a figure of recognized leadership, the Dalai Lama living in exile in India, around whom the emotional rejection of Chinese ways can focus. This is doubtlessly a significant difference. But the parallel is important because of the strong grip held on average people of both lands by cultures based on religions that traditionally have a strong, even dominant influence on secular affairs. Both Islam and Tibetan Buddhism absorb their believers in a world view that is difficult to understand in modern political terms. Neither is readily permeable by normal politics. The persistence of religious beliefs in Soviet Central Asia, even among educated Communist officials, testifies to the emotional pull of the Islamic cultural system as much as the strength of the religion itself in Western terms of defining what constitutes religion.

This emotional pull would continue to be felt in Afghanistan for internal reasons. It would also be felt because Islam provides a basis for leaders in Peshawar or elsewhere outside of Soviet reach to direct a message to the Afghan people. Soviet Central Asia was only little disturbed by the existence of outside forces preaching resistance to the Russians in the 1920s, much less providing very significant support to the *basmachi*. The Afghan support then was minor. The 1980s were different. Nor was the co-opting of Moslem leaders in the old tsarist empire disturbed by large numbers of them having been killed beforehand and most others alienated. This again was a modern difference in Afghanistan. By comparison, the Chinese launched a frontal assault on the Tibetan religious hierarchy. They emptied the monasteries. This did the Chinese no good in trying to curb the resistance of a strong culture based on religion. Similarly, the Taraki-Amin attack on uncooperative Moslem clerics failed to crack Islamic opposition. Instead, it inspired that opposition to greater defiance.

There was another example of the effects of outside pressures upon the Tibetan form of Buddhism, however, that pointed in a different direction. It also provided a model for the future of Afghanistan that in some ways was more pertinent than that of Soviet Central Asia, which had already been part of the tsarist empire when its resistance to Communism began. The example was Mongolia. What happened after a Communist regime was installed there in 1921 by the Red Army was of significance in the Afghan context. Tibetan Buddhism of the Dalai Lama's sect had become established among the Mongols only in the sixteenth century. According to one interpretation, its introduction was a Chinese scheme to sap the threateningly martial vigor of the Mongols by tying up much of their manpower in monasteries.[5] Whether a Chinese scheme or not, Buddhism attained a strong popular position in Mongolia that proved debilitating for a formerly warlike society. The development of firearms that enabled China's settled society better to withstand assaults by nomadic warriors than in Genghis Khan's time, and the reorientation of Chinese military concerns from the nomadic hinterlands toward the seacoast whence came the modern European-based dangers, added to the effects of Buddhism in reducing Mongolia to a depressed backwater province of China. Outer Mongolia, the part farthest from the Manchu empire's capital at Peking, was the most neglected and depressed.

The Bolsheviks extended their control into a degenerate society: diseased, ignorant, living at the mercy of the elements. Chinese merchants dominated the Mongol herdsmen; there was no Mongol middle class; much of the Mongol Buddhist hierarchy was sunk in drunken sloth. As a result, the Mongolians lacked a cohesive national leadership, even a modern sense of nationhood. In the Mongolian case, without the rallying point of a Dalai Lama, Tibetan Buddhism had not adapted to changing circumstances enough to withstand or absorb outside pressures. Outer Mongolia therefore offered little resistance to Soviet influence in nationalistic, intellectual, or religious terms.

Also, just as some of the Soviet influence in Afghanistan was exercised by Soviet Tajiks, Uzbeks, and other ethnically and linguistically similar peoples—to the extent that the Russians trusted them—so the Soviet Union had an opening wedge in Mongolia. Outer Mongolia was inhabited predominately by the Khalka branch of the greater Mongol family. The tsarist empire already included Buryat Mongols from the trans-Baykal area just north of Outer Mongolia and Kalmyk Mongol settlers on the lower Volga. Except for dialect differences, they could mingle easily with the Khalkas. Working as representatives of the Comintern, which meant on orders from Moscow, Buryat and Kalmyk Mongols played the leading role in running Mongolia in the 1920s. During that period most of the small original group of Khalka Mongols who had turned to the Bolsheviks for help, thus providing the excuse for what became Soviet Russia's first colony, were liquidated. They had not proven reliable and trustworthy in following the twists of policy coming from Moscow.

The hardest policy twist in Mongolia came between 1929 and 1932, a period roughly comparable to the Taraki reforms period. Imitating Stalin's attempt to get a grip on Soviet agriculture, the men controlling Mongolian policy tried without planning or preparation to collectivize the livestock herding that was the mainstay of Mongolia's economy and to nationalize other economically vital forms of private enterprise such as transport and retail trade. The result was not only an economic disaster but also rebellion. A simultaneous assault on the remaining Buddhist lamas as being class enemies compounded the resistance to the government. It was unable to deal with the armed uprisings that developed. In June 1932 the Red Army entered Mongolia again, this time to use armored cars and planes against horsemen with rifles. Some of the rebellion's leaders were lamas and survivors of the old Mongolian nobility, providing a basis for Soviet propaganda that the rebellion was only a defense of feudal rights over the common people. But it was essentially a popular resistance to a threat to traditional ways and to economic survival, rather than a religious or social upheaval. Members of the Communist party and its youth league as well as poor herdsmen had risen in revolt. As a result, the Stalinist policies were labeled a "leftist deviation" and were sharply modified, still under Stalin's influence. New Soviet advisers arrived, new Khalka Mongols were put into leadership positions. The Soviet Communist Party took over direct supervision instead of Moscow's working through the Comintern. Mongolian administration became an appendage of the Soviet bureaucracy: the local party, the security services, and the army all were run as provincial branches of the Russian system.

In addition to the Mongolian rejection of a Soviet system, which is comparable to the resistance of the Afghans, there is an instructive parallel in the strategic situation that faced Stalin in East Asia when he reacted so forcefully to the rebellion. The Japanese army had seized all of Manchuria in the three months after the 18 September 1931 "Mukden incident." This brought to the Mongolian border the only military power in Asia capable of threatening Soviet interests. Mongolia was a power vacuum, unable even to govern itself or maintain internal order. A leading Western historian of Mongolia, Charles R. Bawden, has found no indication that the Mongols asked for Red Army intervention to put down the rebellion or sought the more direct control of Soviet "advisers" that followed. It was more likely, he wrote,

> that Stalin realized the potential dangers to Soviet security of a feeble Mongolia, riven by civil war, lying on her flank with Manchuria and Inner Mongolia precisely at a time when Japanese aggression was most to be feared. . . . It was most probably not out of any love for the task itself, but simply to secure her own flank, that the USSR undertook in 1932 to analyze the reasons for Mongolia's frenzy of error, to force upon an allied government the odium of publicly eating its own words at the direction of a foreign political party, and to saddle herself with trouble beyond her own borders: she simply could not tolerate the collapse of society and administration in Mongolia.[6]

If this sounds remarkably similar to the Afghan situation, with the approach of United States military power to a hostage-holding Iran in place of the Japanese in Manchuria, there were differences. The rebellion in Mongolia was quickly crushed, the people having no tradition of guerrilla warfare and showing no stomach for prolonged resistance. For the next decade and more the Soviet controllers of Mongolia concentrated on building up an army there to help the Soviet Army resist Japanese probes. It was not an army to fight fellow Mongols; therefore it was not hard to recruit or subject to defections. There was in this period little effort to develop the economy. Khalka Mongol was given a cyrillic alphabet and Russian became the main foreign language, cutting the country off from both its Mongolian script heritage and the more numerous Mongols under Chinese control.

In the 1950s Mao's China was allowed by Moscow to share the burden of beginning to develop the Mongolian economy. That did not last long. The Sino-Soviet split led to purges in the early 1960s of those Mongolian leaders suspected by the Soviets of being pro-Chinese. Moscow even arranged the purge of those who simply aspired to a neutrality that would enable Ulan Bator to play Moscow and Peking off against each other for Mongolia's own benefit. It wanted no repetition of what had occurred with a nearby Soviet-established regime, in North Korea, which had not so long been under Soviet tutelage that a whole generation could be educated to Soviet purposes. Mongolia was a land that lacked an Afghan-type history of resisting foreign influences and that had long known Chinese control; its people were accustomed to being dominated by larger and stronger neighbors—the way Eastern Europe also accepted outside domination fairly readily following World War II because of a long history of it. Soviet domination of Mongolia was an alternative to control by China, which had through colonization reduced the Mongols to a minority in Inner Mongolia. The new generation educated under Soviet auspices accepted its colonial assignment of fulfilling orders from the metropolitan center, Moscow. Although several divisions of the Soviet Army have been stationed in Mongolia since 1966, they are there to confront the Chinese rather than the docile Mongolian people. The Mongolian army is a minor element in this confrontation.

Afghanistan is more like Tibet in a tradition of rejecting outsiders than Mongolia in accepting foreign control, although all three have historically had periods of projecting their military power far beyond their present politically defined areas. Afghanistan is also more like Tibet in having a strong, still vital cultural sense that resists foreign influences and makes indoctrination difficult. But perhaps the most pertinent parallel comes back to Soviet Central Asia. There Russians brought a Moslem population under control. They were mainly lowland Uzbeks and valley Tajiks, not mountain Pushtuns, but the Islamic nature of the cultural obstacle to a Communist system was the same as in Afghanistan. The less fierce, less proudly independent peoples who were already in the tsarist empire did not put up the resistance of the Afghans. After one generation had been purged, with the original leaders of Moslem Bolshevism sent to die in Stalin's labor camps, a new generation was educated to accept the fact of life under Russian domination. This experience there and in Mongolia is what the Soviet Union is now trying to duplicate under the much more difficult conditions of Afghanistan.

It is also trying to accomplish what is more recognizable in terms of American experience as "Vietnamization" of the war in Vietnam in the early 1970s. Turning the war over to a local army is a far different situation in Afghanistan than in Vietnam, however. The United States was working with a large, broad-based local army that, however corrupt and inefficient, had a significant degree of popular support. It was seen by a sizeable proportion of the Vietnamese population as a protection against a foreign threat. Contrary to the standard propaganda line from Kabul and Moscow, the threat to the PDPA regime in the early 1980s did not come primarily from across the border; it was indigenous. There was no broad-based local army, despite press-gang efforts to build one. The Soviets had the advantage of their colonial levies not having to face a strong conventional army from a well-organized and determined government with a secure base across a political demarcation line, as the Americans did in Vietnam. Instead, they had the problem of raising those levies from among a hostile population and keeping them loyal and willing to fight.

It was one thing to organize bureaucrats who could sit at desks in Kabul and shuffle papers to give the appearance of an Afghan administration in front of Soviet control. It was a much different thing to organize Afghan soldiers to go out and fight other Afghans. It even proved difficult to rely on the Afghan army for routine security maintenance because its loyalty was suspect. The Soviet Army had to take over much of that routine job, particularly in Kabul. By the end of the second year of the Soviet occupation, the Afghan army had faded from being a significant factor in an essentially Soviet confrontation with the resistance. The Americans were seen by far more South Vietnamese as their partners in a common effort than ever Afghans have seen Soviets that way.

The examples of Uzbekistan, Tajikistan, and Turkmenia, as well as the case of Mongolia, show that the Russian rulers of the Soviet empire can convert different peoples to roles that fit them into the overall pattern of the Soviet Union, its political structure, its military preparations, its centralized economic system. Mongolia has in practical terms long since become simply another Soviet republic. Its retention of a separate status of an independent nation, belonging to the United Nations, is no more real than the separate United Nations' memberships of Soviet Byelorussia and the Ukraine that were created in a political deal when the world organization was founded. It is significant that the Soviet Union never sought to change the de facto absorption of Mongolia into a de jure status by formally annexing it, the way Tannu Tuva was absorbed. The China complication might have been the main reason, but there was little point in provoking the criticism of old-fashioned, obvious imperialism that would have resulted when all the benefits of control already had been assured. Nor was the Soviet Union interested in tidying up sub-ethnic boundaries by detaching from predominately Khalka Mongolia the northern fringe occupied by Buryats and adding it to the Buryat Autonomous Soviet Socialist Republic.

The temptation to clarify ethnic lines might be greater across the Amu Darya. So are the problems. There has never been an irredentist movement among Uzbeks, Tajiks, or Turkmen north of the river or northwest of Afghanistan. Before the Bolshevik takeover the sense of nationalism was not well-enough developed for it; after that, the Russian interest in isolating each people from any pan-Islamic or pan-Turkic pulls prevented it. Soviet absorption of those ethnic groups from a dismembered Afghanistan would not bring a stable, secure boundary. It would be more likely to exacerbate relations with the Pushtuns who lie beyond them, making control over a rump Afghanistan state even more difficult. A Soviet recognition of the inadvisability of tampering with Afghanistan's borders was indicated by the 16 June 1981 treaty on the Wakhan corridor border. Any larger attempt to submerge the entire present-day Afghanistan into the Soviet Union would be self-defeating. Again, it would provoke cries of imperialism for no practical gain. Why lose a vote in the United Nations and in the nonaligned movement when it can be manipulated from Moscow? The growing ties of the Afghan economy to Soviet centralized planning, the control of Afghan administration, police, and military by Soviet advisers, the direction of Afghan education and media by Soviet specialists—all these are the reality of Soviet republic status without the international political liabilities of further hardening foreign hostility to the Soviet role.

Hostility will remain inside Afghanistan for the indefinite future. It is not the kind of country to settle down to acquiescent rule by foreign puppets. Even if it were isolated from any outside influence, cut off from foreign material or moral support for the resistance, it would continue to struggle against the combination of Russian domination and strong centralized control from Kabul. This struggle took violent form when possible, obstructive noncooperation when outright opposition was not possible. Afghan history testifies to such refusal to be conquered. So do events since April 1978 and the inability of Karmal to win popular support since December 1979. Yet Russian history and the record of Soviet policy also indicate that the Kremlin leadership would not back away from the effort needed to maintain control of Afghanistan. After almost three years of Soviet occupation, the price did not seem from outside observation to be so high as to cause a change in Soviet determination to hold on for a long process of taming the country. There was no great pain to be alleviated by withdrawing, no major benefits to be gained by giving up, and many penalties, from Moscow's standpoint.

The price could be raised by greater outside aid to the *mujahideen* than leaked through the land mines on paths across the Durand Line or evaded other Soviet efforts to isolate Afghanistan. The limited commitment of aid made by President Carter in January 1980 grew into covert programs involving a number of nations that made the resistance more effective than it would otherwise have been. It was, however, very limited aid. The self-imposed isolation of Iran from the Western world made it impossible to organize significant support for the *mujahideen* through that country, although Iran itself gave some help. China's forty-seven-mile border with Afghanistan was easily controlled by Soviet troops. That left only the Durand Line with Pakistan for overland supplies to the guerrillas. Pakistan's vulnerability to Soviet pressure and retaliatory cross-border strikes caused its government to be wary of becoming a channel for enough aid to seem threatening to Soviet interests. The program of United States military and economic aid for Pakistan agreed upon in 1981 was a step toward easing this problem, but it could not solve it.

Yet it was only right that the non-Communist world should help those in Afghanistan who chose to fight. It was not for outsiders to make a determination that the cause was hopeless, that greater resistance would only cause greater suffering for the Afghan people. So long as they asked for support against Soviet imperialism, it should be given. But it had to be given with the recognition that the prospect of driving the Soviets out of Afghanistan was very dim and distant. It was conceivable that other factors could cause them to leave, although none was on the horizon in the early 1980s. Guerrilla resistance alone was not sufficient.

Instead of yielding to local opposition, the reaction in Moscow was likely to continue to be one of using the outside aid as an excuse for the Soviet presence there. Whether increased foreign involvement would actually justify in Soviet minds the line that help was being given against external aggression, it contributed to Soviet use of that line abroad as a justification. It also helped reinforce the feeling that Afghanistan had to be held as a buffer against foreign influence. Although more aid to the resistance can cause escalating costs for the Soviets to hold the country, it is difficult to foresee a level of expense at which the costs would outweigh Soviet apprehension of abandoning Afghanistan. Moscow had no intention of leaving it to a far worse form of chaos than the Soviet Army went in to prevent. So meeting increased resistance with increased Soviet force has a logic for Moscow, despite the avoidance of putting many more troops into Afghanistan during the first three years. To paraphrase the classic statement from the Vietnam war about a Mekong delta village in the 1968 Tet offensive, the Soviets might have to destroy Afghanistan in order to save it.

And the conflict might not be limited to Afghanistan alone. There have already been warning incursions across the Pakistani border. Too much military pressure inside Afghanistan would tempt the Soviets to try to push the buffer farther out, to plunge into Prince Gorchakov's 1864 dilemma: to go into new "difficulties and sacrifices" or to "deliver [the] frontier over to disorder." The record in Soviet times is even more clear than in tsarist times of choosing the horn of that dilemma calling for new "difficulties and sacrifices"—and new buffers under Communist influence if not direct rule. In the building of a coalition of interests in the Soviet Union for a policy decision, the motive of protecting a new client state in Afghanistan could coincide nicely with a Soviet desire to acquire a port on the Indian Ocean at some Baluchi harbor like Gwadar.

Russian and Soviet power has historically thrust forward until it met some military or political reason for stopping. There have been only occasional exceptions of withdrawing because of Russian internal reasons. Those exceptions could recur, but the world could not count on a collapse of the Soviet state as the hope for its gigantic armed forces to cease being a danger. Nor could it count on external reasons around Afghanistan. The political factors that checked the Soviets in Scandinavia after World War II, the military factors that held them in Central Europe and in Turkey and Iran during the same period, the political factors that caused a withdrawal from Sinkiang in 1943, and the power that blunted aggrandizement in Korea—these did not exist in the region around Afghanistan in the early 1980s. The Afghan people were left almost alone to face those who would subjugate them in a new form of colonialism. There were no political or military pressures to help them, only small shipments of weapons for them to use at great risk. It would take the Soviet Union a long time to consolidate its hold on such a defiant country.

The Soviet determination to do it was clear. Also clear was the lesson for other weak countries within easy reach of Soviet power, that lack counterbalancing forces to protect them—such as Iran under Khomeini. Many of the same factors that thrust Soviet power into Afghanistan already existed or were clearly visible possibilities in Iran in the early 1980s. The long growth of Soviet influence in Afghanistan that led to a military takeover and attempt to remake the country in the image of Soviet Central Asia or Mongolia could not be lightly ignored. For the Afghan people, the Soviet attitude meant a dark future. For many other peoples on the periphery of Soviet power, it meant a worrisome future.

Notes

Chapter 1. Country of Conflict

1. Nicholas V. Riasanovsky, *A History of Russia* (New York, 1963), p. 250; R. C. Majumdar, H. C. Raychaudhuri, and Kalikinkar Datta, *An Advanced History of India*, 2nd ed. (London, 1960), pp. 635–42; Firuz Kazemzadeh, "Russia and the Middle East," *Russian Foreign Policy: Essays in Historical Perspective*, ed. Ivo J. Lederer (New Haven, 1962), p. 490.

2. The term was originally applied to the competition of British and Russian intelligence agents in the Central Asian area between their two empires, but it came to apply more broadly to the struggle over Afghanistan, with Persia and Tibet as sideshows. Capt. Arthur Connolly seems to have coined the term before he visited Bukhara on a British mission in 1841, was seized by Emir Nasr Allah, thrown into a vermin-filled pit for several months of agony, and finally beheaded. Rudyard Kipling popularized the term. See Seymour Becker, *Russia's Protectorates in Central Asia: Bukhara and Khiva, 1865–1924* (Cambridge, 1968), p. 15, and note on pp. 348–9.

3. Majumdar et al., *Advanced History*, pp. 754–60.

4. The complete text of Gorchakov's memorandum is in W. Kerr Fraser-Tytler, *Afghanistan: A Study of Political Developments in Central and Southern Asia*, 2nd ed. (London, 1953), pp. 319–23.

5. Lewis M. Alexander, for the Geographer, Bureau of Intelligence and Research, Department of State, *International Boundary Study No. 26: Afghanistan-USSR Boundary* (Washington, 1963) [hereafter cited as *Boundary Study No. 26*].

6. United Nations *Treaty Series*, Vol. 31 (New York, 1949), pp. 147–68. The Russians until 1946 claimed without treaty justification that the Amu boundary was on the southern bank; see Roman T. Akhramovich, *Outline History of Afghanistan After the Second World War* (Moscow, 1966), p. 69. The 1946 treaty did not establish rights to river water, a significant point in view of irrigation needs in the area; see Neil C. Field, "The Amu Darya: A Study in Resource Geography," *Geographical Review* 44, (October 1954): 528–42.

7. Alexander, *Boundary Study No. 26*.

8. This was the length used in standard Soviet and Afghan references in the early 1980s; e.g., Foreign Broadcast Information Service, *Daily Report, South Asia* [hereafter *FBIS/SA*] (Washington, 7 July, 1981), p. C1, which uses the equivalent 2,384 kilometers. Alexander, *Boundary Study No. 26*, uses 1,281 miles, or 2,061 kilometers, based on imprecise map measurements.

9. The Geographer, Bureau of Intelligence and Research, Department of State, *International Boundary Study No. 89: Afghanistan-China Boundary* (Washington, 1969). In the same series, see also *No. 64: China-USSR* (1966), and *No. 85: China-Pakistan* (1968). On the Chinese-Soviet border dispute, upon which depended part of the Afghan border, see John W. Garver, "The Sino-Soviet Territorial Dispute in the Pamir Mountains Region," *The China Quarterly* 85 (March 1981): 107–18; Moscow Radio, 16 June and 18 September 1981, in FBIS, *Daily Report, Soviet Union* [hereafter *FBIS/SU*], 17 June and 21 September 1981, p. D1; and *Beijing Review*, 3 August and 14 September 1981, 7 and 21–23.

10. The Geographer, Bureau of Intelligence and Research, Department of State, *International Boundary Study No. 6: Afghanistan-Iran Boundary* (Washington, 1961).

11. J. R. V. Prescott, *Map of Mainland Asia by Treaty* (Melbourne, 1975), pp. 177–87. Prescott quotes a local proverb about the Durand Line that, when Allah created the world, he dumped the rubbish on the Northwest Frontier of India and Baluchistan.

12. For the full text of the 1893 agreement, see C. U. Aitchison, *A Collection of Treaties, Engagements and Sanads Relating to India and Neighbouring Countries, Vol. XIII, Containing the Treaties &c., Relating to Persia and Afghanistan* (Calcutta, 1933), pp. 256–57 [hereafter cited as *Treaties*].

13. Louis Dupree, *Afghanistan* (Princeton, 1980), p. 560. This was only about a tenth of Afghanistan's nomads. On the same day, 8 February 1980, *Pravda* quoted Afghanistan's minister of border affairs, Fayz Mohammad, as saying there were 3 million nomads (*FBIS/SU*, 13 February 1980, p. D6), while Tass news agency reported that the minister of agriculture and land reform, Fazl Rahim Mohmand, had told a French journal the number was 2½ million (*FBIS/SU*, 11 February 1980, p. D1).

14. James F. Spitler and Nancy B. Frank, "Afghanistan, A Demographic Uncertainty," *International Research Document No. 6*, (U. S. Department of Commerce, Bureau of the Census, Washington, September 1978); James Trussell and Eleanor Brown, "A Close Look at the Demography of Afghanistan," *Demography* 16 (February 1979): 137−56.

15. Babrak Karmal said "more than 15 million"; see *Pravda*, 29 January 1980, in *FBIS/SU*, 1 February 1980, p. D2. Basil G. Kavalsky, "Afghanistan, the Journey to Economic Development," an excellent but unpublished World Bank study completed in 1977, says (p. 62) the best estimate in 1977 was 14 million. Harvey H. Smith, and others, *Area Handbook for Afghanistan*, 4th ed. [hereafter cited as *Area Handbook*] (Washington, 1973), quotes (p. xxxv) a United Nations estimate for mid-1972 of 17.9 million and a population growth rate possibly 2.3 percent, which would if continued give a 1980 population of more than 21 million. Even estimates of the number of villages range from 13,000 to 20,000.

16. Estimates of different Afghan ethnic groups are, except as noted below, from Dupree, *Afghanistan*, pp. 59−64, citing "official Afghan estimates" of 1967 "and interpolations from my own estimates"; Leon B. Poullada, "The Pushtun Role in the Afghan Political System," *Occasional Paper No. 1*, The Afghanistan Council of The Asia Society (New York, 1970), p. 2, citing unpublished studies of the Afghan Ministry of Planning; and Smith, *Area Handbook*, pp. 63−79.

17. The number of Baluch in Pakistan is uncertain, or at least too politically sensitive to be published officially. The 1961 Pakistan census showed Baluchi as the mother tongue for 982,512 residents of West Pakistan; similar figures were not later issued. However, Selig S. Harrison, *In Afghanistan's Shadow: Baluch Nationalism and Soviet Temptations* (New York, 1981), p. 1, gives the Pakistani Baluch population as 3.65 million, with another 1 million in Iran. The 1970 Soviet census showed 13,000 Baluch in the Soviet Union, but they were being assimilated by Turkmen, and the 1979 Soviet census did not list them.

18. All 1979 Soviet population figures are from Ann Sheehy, "The National Composition of the Population of the USSR According to the Census of 1979," *Radio Liberty Research*, RL 123/80, 27 March 1980.

19. The low estimate for Turkmen in Afghanistan is from Dupree, *Afghanistan*, while the high one comes from M. G. Aslanov, E. G. Gafferberg, N. A. Kisliakov, K. L. Dadykhina, and G. P. Vasilyeva, "Peoples of Afghanistan," in *Narody Perednei Asii*, ed. Kisliakov and A. I. Pershits (Moscow, 1957), as translated by Mark and Greta Slobin in *Afghanistan, Some New Approaches*, ed. George Grassmuck and Ludwig W. Adamec, with Frances H. Irwin (Ann Arbor, 1969), p. 75.

20. Aslanov et al., "Peoples of Afghanistan," p. 35 in Grassmuck, *Afghanistan*, writing in 1957 says there were some Hazaras in the Soviet Union and in Iran, but gives no details. Soviet census reports did not list them.

21. Donald N. Wilber, ed., *Country Survey Series: Afghanistan* (New Haven, 1956), pp. 60−71; Dupree, *Afghanistan*, pp. 66−74; Smith, *Area Handbook*, p. 81.

22. Mountstuart Elphinstone, *Account of the Kingdom of Caubul* (London, 1815), p. 253, quoted by Olaf Caroe, *The Pathans: 550 B.C.−A.D. 1957* (London, 1958), p. 278; Poullada, "The Pushtun Role," pp. 6−7. Describing the Pathan, or Pushtun, character, Caroe lists daring, hospitality, insufference, jealousy, factiousness, aversion to cruelty, manliness, contempt for hypocrisy, love of beauty, vainglory, personal loyalty, and lack of inhibitions; see his p. 493.

23. Kavalsky, "Afghanistan," pp. xiv and 77−81; Smith, *Area Handbook*, pp. 60 and 110; Wilber, *Country Survey*, pp. 316−17. The incidence of malaria, especially in the Hindu Kush foothills, rose in the 1970s as mosquitoes made a comeback after post-World War II DDT spraying ended—as was true in many parts of South Asia.

24. Kavalsky, "Afghanistan," p. 81; Smith, *Area Handbook*, p. vii.

25. Information Department, Ministry of Foreign Affairs, *Undeclared War: Armed Intervention and Other Forms of Interference in the Internal Affairs of the Democratic Republic of Afghanistan* (Kabul, 1980), p. 65; *Izvestiya*, 17 January 1981, p. 4, in *FBIS/SU*, 22 January 1981, pp. D4−5; Fred Halliday, "Afghanistan: The Limits of Russian Imperialism," *New Statesman*, 5 December 1980, p. 11. The Afghan government said more than 1,500 schools had been destroyed by mid-1982; see Moscow Radio, 9 July 1982, in *FBIS/SU*, 12 July 1982, p. D1.

26. There were rumors that the Soviets made major oil strikes in northern Afghanistan years before the Communist takeover, but Soviet geological teams did not tell the Kabul government.

27. A French oil company was forced by Soviet pressure on the Afghan government to abandon promising drilling near the southeastern border with Pakistan in the mid-1970s, according to the head of an American geological team then in Afghanistan, John F. Shroder, Jr.; his report to the Middle East Studies Association, Washington, D.C., 7 November 1980.

28. Smith, *Area Handbook*, p. 24; *Business Week*, 29 September 1980, p. 62; Shroder report.

29. Vice President (later Prime Minister) Sultanali Keshtmand, interviewed in Nicosia newspaper *Kharavyi*, 3 February 1980, in FBIS, *Daily Report, Middle East & North Africa* [hereafter *FBIS/ME*], 4 February 1980, p. S9. Keshtmand, who was also minister of planning at the time, said that "Some $600 million to $700 million are needed to exploit these deposits. We have already signed an agreement with the Soviet Union" to develop them over a period of five or six years, he added, but nothing happened in the first few years after that. In the 1970s the Soviets developed a major copper deposit in Mongolia rather than exploit their own reserves in colder, less accessible places.

30. Smith, *Area Handbook*, p. 24.

31. *Business Week*, 29 September 1980, p. 62.

32. Ibid., and Shroder report.

33. Amanullah changed his title in 1923 from amir to padshah, or king, a title that his father Habibullah had occasionally used; see Dupree, *Afghanistan*, p. 450.

34. From a letter by the treaty's chief British negotiator, A. Hamilton Grant, foreign secretary of India, to the dubious chief Afghan delegate, Ali Ahmad Khan; see Aitchison, *Treaties*, 13: 286–88, for the treaty and letter.

35. Edward H. Carr, *A History of Soviet Russia: The Bolshevik Revolution, 1917–1923*, Vol. 3 (Pelican ed.; London, 1966), pp. 240–42.

36. Ibid.; *Pravda*, 19 August 1981, p. 1, in *FBIS/SU*, 27 August 1981, pp. D1–2.

37. Ibid.

38. Carr, *Bolshevik Revolution*, Vol. 3, pp. 240–42. See also Vartan Gregorian, *The Emergence of Modern Afghanistan: Politics of Reform and Modernization, 1880–1946* (Stanford, 1969), pp. 231–32, and Gunther Nollau, and Hans Jurgen Wiehe, *Russia's South Flank: Soviet Operations in Iran, Turkey, and Afghanistan* (New York, 1963), pp. 95–96.

39. From a Bolshevik resolution on the nationalities question adopted 12 May 1917, as quoted by Alvin Z. Rubinstein, *The Foreign Policy of the Soviet Union* (New York, 1960), pp. 352–54. According to David Klein, "The Basmachi—A Case Study in Soviet Policy Toward National Minorities," unpublished manuscript in the Department of State library, Washington, D.C., 1952, which gives the text of the resolution, p. 65; the meeting was held 7–12 April 1917.

40. Geoffrey Wheeler, *The Modern History of Soviet Central Asia* (London, 1964), pp. 92–95; Olaf Caroe, *Soviet Empire: The Turks of Central Asia and Stalinism* (London, 1953), pp. 89–91; Richard Pipes, *The Formation of the Soviet Union: Communism and Nationalism, 1917–1923* (rev. ed.; Cambridge, 1964), pp. 83–84; Klein, "The Basmachi," pp. 6–7. The February 1917 revolution in Petrograd halted official investigations of how many died, but in Turkestan alone Russian dead and missing approached 4,000 while in the Steppe just to the north killing of settlers was greater. A Soviet estimate is that between 1914 and 1918 the population of Turkestan dropped by 1,230,000, presumably mostly from the retaliatory killings by Russians, and another estimate suggested that some 300,000 persons from the Steppe fled into China.

41. Klein, "Basmachi," pp. 6–14; Pipes, *Formation*, pp. 86–93; "The Basmachis: The Central Asian Resistance Movement, 1918–1924," *Central Asian Review* 7, 3 (1959): 236; Wheeler, *Soviet Central Asia*, pp. 103–7; Caroe, *Soviet Empire*, pp. 99–104.

42. Becker, *Russia's Protectorates*, pp. 265–69, 289–95; Klein, "Basmachi," pp. 13–14.

43. The nearest comparable resistance was in the Ukraine. Although Soviet power was established there by 1920, some armed opposition continued. World War II enabled Ukrainian nationalists to rearm themselves for a guerrilla struggle against Moscow that was not finally crushed until 1952. In ethnic, religious, cultural and terrain terms, the 1920–22 uprising of Moslem peoples in the Daghestani-Chechen region of the Caucasus mountains against Soviet rule—continuing a long history of opposing Russian control there—was more similar to Central Asian resistance.

44. Pipes, *Formation*, pp. 178–79; Klein, "Basmachi," p. 16; "Basmachis," p. 235; Alexandre A. Bennigsen and S. Enders Wimbush, *Muslim National Communism in the Soviet Union: A Revolutionary Strategy for the Colonial World* (Chicago, 1979), p. 213. Although it had been used before 1917 to refer to bands of raiders or marauders in Central Asia, the term seems to come from a Turkic word meaning "to oppress." Hence, the *basmachi* could originally have had the connotation of oppressed people fighting for their rights.

45. *Bol'shaya Sovetskaya Entsiklopediya*, quoted by Klein, "Basmachi," p. 17. That was the 1927 edition; the next edition took the opposite view that it had been a short-lived rebellion of reactionary landlords and other feudal elements, since it had become ideologically unwise to admit popular opposition to the Communist Party—which is supposed to express the popular will.

46. Yu. A. Polyakov and A. I. Chugunov, *Konets Basmachestva*, (Moscow, 1976), p. 36, quoted

by Martha B. Olcott, "The Basmachi or Freemen's Revolt in Turkestan 1918–24," *Soviet Studies* 33 (July 1981): 355.

47. Pipes, *Formation*, pp. 178–79. See also Klein, "Basmachi," p. 18; "Basmachis," p. 237.

48. A. N. Lapchinskiy, "The Organization and Use of Airborne Landing Parties," in A. B. Kadishev, ed., *Problems of Tactics in Soviet Military Works, 1917–1940* (Moscow, 1970), pp. 352–54, says that the first Red Army use of airborne forces—possibly the world's first—was "in the desert during the struggle with the *basmachi*" in the early 1920s when an armed reconnaissance party was put down "in the Saksaul brush country." This citation provided by William F. Scott and Harriet Fast Scott. *Sovetskaya Voennaya Entsiklopediya*, Vol. 2 (Moscow, 1976), p. 287, says that in the spring of 1929 armed troops were landed by planes at Garm, Tajikistan, which was then under *basmachi* seige (during a revival of resistance caused by Soviet collectivization policies); cited in "The Soviet Military Air Transport Force," *Radio Liberty Research*, RL 385/81, 1981.

49. Novosti Press Agency, *The Truth About Afghanistan; Documents, Facts, Eyewitness Reports* (Moscow, 1980), pp. 24–25. Soviet media sometimes accused not only the British but also the U.S. consul at Tashkent and "the rest of the high-ranking foreign diplomats" as having "participated in organizing" the *basmachi*. "The counter-revolutionaries were trained by British army officers." See Moscow Radio, 4 July 1981, in *FBIS/SU*, 10 July 1981, pp. R2–4.

50. The half-million estimate is in David C. Montgomery, "The Uzbeks in Two States: Soviet and Afghan Policies Toward an Ethnic Minority," in William O. McCagg, Jr., and Brian D. Silver, eds., *Soviet Asian Ethnic Frontiers*, (New York, 1979), p. 160. But some Western anthropologists who worked in northern Afghanistan in the 1960s and early 1970s calculated the number as only a tenth of that.

51. This is the date given by Gregorian, *Emergence*, p. 232. Other sources vary. Novosti, *Truth*, p. 23, says it was signed on 24 February 1921. Carr, *Bolshevik Revolution*, 3: 291, says it was agreed in Kabul in September and signed in Moscow on 28 February. Afghan media seem to have settled for 28 February 1921; see *Kabul New Times*, 1 March 1981, p. 2, in *FBIS/SA*, 1 April 1981, p. C5. Amanullah's government did not ratify it until August 1921, delaying because of displeasure over Soviet crushing of Bukharan independence.

52. Novosti, *Truth*, p. 23; Gregorian, *Emergence*, p. 232. Peter G. Franck, *Afghanistan Between East and West* (Washington, 1960), p. 8, says the Soviets never provided the promised gold subsidy, but Grigorii S. Agabekov, *OGPU: The Russian Secret Terror* (New York, 1931), p. 46, says it was delivered in the summer of 1924 by a new Soviet minister to Kabul.

53. Carr, *Bolshevik Revolution*, 3: 288; see also Alec Nove, *An Economic History of the USSR* (London, 1969), p. 83.

54. Edward H. Carr, *A History of Soviet Russia: The Interregnum, 1923–1924* (Baltimore, 1969), pp. 174–81, 229n; Louis Fischer, *The Soviets in World Affairs*, Vol. 1 (London, 1930), p. 448; M. R. Masani, *The Communist Party of India: A Short History* (London, 1954), p.22.

55. Percy Molesworth Sykes, *A History of Afghanistan*, Vol. 2 (London, 1940), p. 298; Fraser-Tytler, *Afghanistan*, pp. 204–6; Dupree, *Afghanistan*, pp. 448–49.

56. Quoted by Ludwig W. Adamec, *Afghanistan's Foreign Affairs to the Mid-Twentieth Century: Relations with the USSR, Germany, and Britain* (Tucson, 1974), p. 108; see also pp. 88–98; Nollau and Wiehe, *Russia's South Flank*, p. 102.

57. Amanullah was the first king to be received by the Bolsheviks, who spied on him, according to Agabekov, *OGPU*, p. 162. Fraser-Tytler, *Afghanistan*, p. 209, says the Soviets promised him munitions and thirteen more airplanes. The United States, which had not established diplomatic relations with Kabul, rebuffed his efforts to visit Washington; see Leon B. Poullada, "Afghanistan and the United States: The Crucial Years," *The Middle East Journal*, 35 (Spring 1981): 178–90.

58. Fraser-Tytler, *Afghanistan*, pp. 210–17; Dupree, *Afghanistan*, pp. 451–54; Gregorian, *Emergence*, pp. 258–66.

59. Adamec, *Afghanistan's Foreign Affairs*, pp. 160–62; Fraser-Tytler, *Afghanistan*, p. 218; Agabekov, *OGPU*, pp. 165–68. Agabekov says the Soviet foreign ministry favored supporting Amanullah for his anti-British outlook but the secret (political) police preferred the plebeian Tajiki, and the Communist Party politburo made the decision. Agabekov apparently repeats such things at fourth-hand, however, and is a dubious source.

60. British historians writing on Afghanistan are as chary of mentioning Nadir Kahn's Indian connection as the Soviets are of mentioning the Ghulam Nabi expedition. See Fraser-Tytler, *Afghanistan*, pp. 220–22; also Gregorian, *Emergence*, pp. 281–86; Dupree, *Afghanistan*, pp. 458–60.

61. Sykes, *History of Afghanistan*, 2: 327–28; Dupree, *Afghanistan*, pp. 474–76, notes conflicting accounts of the assassin's ties to Ghulam Nabi.

62. See footnote 6. The agreement set the border at the *thalweg*, the conventional river boundary

line for international treaties since its apparent first use in an 1887 British-Russian agreement on a Kushk River stretch of Afghanistan's northwestern border. Despite Soviet readiness to accept the *thalweg* principle with Afghanistan, Moscow refused for decades into the early 1980s to clarify its river borders with northeastern China by accepting the same principle.

63. Stalin added to the Soviet Union all or part of Finland, Estonia, Latvia, Lithuania, Poland, Germany, Czechoslovakia, Romania, Mongolia (Tannu Tuva earlier detached from Mongolia), and Japan. Turkey and Iran were enabled by Western pressure to resist his designs, and China thwarted efforts to detach some of Inner Mongolia.

64. Dupree, *Afghanistan.* p. 512.

Chapter 2. The Cold War in Afghanistan

1. Department of State, *Foreign Relations of the United States, 1948, Vol. 5, the Near East, South Asia, and Africa, Part 1* (Washington, 1975), pp. 488−90 (hereafter cited as *Foreign Relations, 1948*).

2. Franck, *Afghanistan*, p. 36; Wilber, *Afghanistan*, pp. 247−48.

3. Kavalsky, "Afghanistan," p. 109. See also Franck, *Afghanistan*, pp. 36−39 and 48−49; Wilber, *Afghanistan*, pp. 223−37; Dupree, *Afghanistan*, pp. 482−85. For the pejorative Soviet version see Novosti, *Truth*, pp. 29−30; also Akhramovich, *Outline History*, pp. 40−42.

4. Department of State, *Foreign Relations, 1948*, 5/1:490.

5. Department of State, *Foreign Relations of the United States, 1949, Vol. VI, The Near East, South Asia and Africa*, (Washington, D.C., 1977), p. 1779; Franck, *Afghanistan*, pp. 38−41. Poullada, "Afghanistan and the United States," pp. 181−82, says Morrison-Knudsen, "which had considerable political influence" in Washington, supported the full loan application, but the bank approved only the Helmand project part, "thus assuring M K's construction profits."

6. Agency for International Development, "U.S. Overseas Loans and Grants, 1979," (Washington, 1979); AID, "Congressional Presentation, FY '81" (Washington, 1980).

7. *New York Times*, 9 August 1946, quoted by J. C. Hurewitz, *Middle East Politics: The Military Dimension* (New York, 1969), pp. 300−301.

8. Records of the British chiefs of staff, quoted by Elisabeth Barker in a letter to *The Economist*, 19 July 1980, p. 4.

9. Louis Dupree, "An Informal Talk with King Mohammad Zahir of Afghanistan," *American Universities Field Staff Reports, South Asia series* (hereafter *AUFS/SA*), 7, 9 (1963).

10. Department of State, *Foreign Relations, 1948*, 5/1:491−93.

11. See, for example, letter from the 1951−53 deputy chief of the U.S. mission in Kabul to *The Economist*, 2 August 1980, p. 4.

12. *Foreign Relations, 1949*, 6:1,777; Department of State, *Foreign Relations of the United States, 1950, Vol. V, The Near East, South Asia and Africa*, (Washington, 1978), p. 1,449.

13. *The Declassified Documents 1979 Collection* (Washington, 1979), no. 33A. The study concluded that Afghanistan should not be included in a program then being developed by the Truman administration to spend $75 million for overt and covert support of countries around China, where Communists had come to power in 1949. The program developed into, among other things, training and logistical support for the guerrilla resistance in Tibet to Chinese control. The Tibetan situation in the 1950s and early 1960s had strong similarities with the Afghan situation after 1979 and presented some of the same possibilities for outside support of guerrillas. Although kept secret at the time, details of U.S. aid to Tibetan guerrillas that became known later closely paralleled some aspects of American aid to the Afghan resistance that were reported in 1981.

14. Poullada, "Afghanistan and the United States," p. 186.

15. *Declassified Documents 1978 Collection*, no. 377A.

16. Department of State, *Foreign Relations of the United States, 1951, Vol. VI Asia and the Pacific, Part 2* (Washington, 1977), p. 1,965. A State Department policy statement dated 21 February 1951, on which the advice to Truman was based, said that "Afghanistan continues to maintain toward the USSR an attitude of cautious correctness combined with firm resistance to Soviet efforts at penetration. . . . So far, Soviet pressure has not been severe nor has Soviet influence in Afghan territory contiguous to the Soviet Central Asian Republic [sic] been extensive." Ibid., pp. 2,005−10.

17. Poullada, "Afghanistan and the United States," pp. 186−87.

18. Dupree, *Afghanistan*, pp. 485−90; Fraser-Tytler, *Afghanistan*, pp. 306−10; Caroe, *Pathans*, pp. 435−36; Grassmuck et al., *Afghanistan*, p. 277.

19. Afghan Information Bureau, *Pakhtunistan: The Khyber Pass as the Focus of the New State of*

Pakhtunistan: an important political development in Central Asia (London, 1952?), p. 8. See also Arnold C. Fletcher, *Afghanistan: Highway of Conquest*, (Ithaca, 1965), p. 254–55. Different Afghan-financed publications give differing definitions of the new nation.

20. E.g., on 31 August 1979; see *FBIS/ME*, 5 September 1979, p. S1.

21. *Foreign Relations, 1950*, 5:1,447–48; Fletcher, *Afghanistan*, p. 255; Dupree, *Afghanistan*, pp. 491–93.

22. Louis Dupree, "Afghanistan's Big Gamble: Part II, The Economic and Strategic Aspects of Soviet Aid," *AUFS/SA*, 4, 4 (1960), p.3.

23. *Foreign Relations, 1951*, 6/2:1,952–53 and 1,960.

24. *Foreign Relations, 1950*, 5:1,448.

25. *Foreign Relations, 1951*, 6/2:2,012.

26. Daoud warned 30 December 1953 that it would create "grave danger to security and peace in Afghanistan"; see Grassmuck et al., *Afghanistan*, p. 281.

27. William J. Barnds, *India, Pakistan, and the Great Powers* (New York, 1972), pp. 92–102.

28. Mohammad Ayub Khan, *Friends Not Masters: A Political Autobiography* (London, 1967), p. 116.

29. Keith Callard, *Pakistan: A Political Study* (London, 1957), pp. 321–22.

30. Dupree, *Afghanistan*, pp. 497–99.

31. Poullada, "Afghanistan and the United States," pp. 184–85.

32. Marshall I. Goldman, *Soviet Foreign Aid* (New York, 1967), p. 115; Franck, *Afghanistan*, p. 55. The grain elevator in Kabul became a landmark known as a symbol of Soviet friendship. Less known was the fact that American aid wheat kept it supplied for years. The Afghan army had to be required to eat the Western-style bread from the bakery because Kabul residents refused it in favor of traditional unleavened Moslem Middle Eastern bread.

33. Joseph S. Berliner, *Soviet Economic Aid: The New Aid and Trade Policy in Underdeveloped Countries* (New York, 1958), pp. 10–24; Roger E. Kanet, "Soviet Attitudes Toward Developing Nations Since Stalin," in Roger E. Kanet, ed., *The Soviet Union and the Developing Nations* (Baltimore, 1974), pp. 27–28; Elizabeth Kridl Valkenier, "Soviet Economic Relations with the Developing Nations," in ibid., pp. 215–16; Valkenier, "The USSR, the Third World, and the Global Economy," *Problems of Communism* 28 (July–August 1979): 19–20; Morton Schwartz, "The USSR and Leftist Regimes in Less-Developed Countries," *Survey* 19 (Spring 1973): 209–44.

34. Rubinstein, *Foreign Policy*, pp. 395–97.

35. Ibid., p. 383.

36. Richard Lowenthal, "Soviet 'Counterimperialism'," *Problems of Communism* 25, (November–December 1976): 52–63; Valkenier, "The USSR, the Third World," pp. 17–33; Central Intelligence Agency, "Changing Patterns in Soviet-LDC Trade, 1976–77" (Washington, D.C., 1978). The head of the Soviet foreign aid program since 1958, Semen A. Skachkov, wrote in 1982: "The economic effect of giving technical assistance to foreign countries is increasing. Our country obtains necessary products for the money received as payment for that assistance and as repayment for credits. This sum averages 3.5 billion rubles annually just from enterprises and projects built with the USSR's assistance"; see *Pravda*, 1 July 1982, p. 4, in *FBIS/SU*, 14 July 1982, pp. CC8–11.

37. Central Intelligence Agency, "Communist Aid Activities in Non-Communist Less Developed Countries, 1979 and 1954–79" (Washington, 1980), p. 17.

38. Ibid., p. 13.

39. Ibid., pp. 16, 20, 34–35.

40. Franck, *Afghanistan*, pp. 55–58; Goldman, *Soviet Foreign Aid*, p. 115.

41. Dupree, *Afghanistan*, p. 539; Franck, *Afghanistan*, pp. 56–57; Novosti, *Truth*, p. 31.

42. N. A. Bulganin and N. S. Khrushchev, *Speeches During Sojourn in India, Burma and Afghanistan, November–December 1955* (New Delhi, 1956), p. 175. Earlier on that tour, Khrushchev had endorsed Indian rejection of self-determination for Kashmir, whose main part was held by India and disputed by Pakistan; see ibid., p. 86. SEATO was guilty of a similar inconsistency, supporting Pakistan's call for self-determination for Pushtunistan but rejecting it for Pushtunistan, although the legal position was technically correct for SEATO because Kashmir remained before the United Nations as its status legally undecided while the Durand Line had treaty validity; see Callard, *Pakistan*, pp. 321–22.

43. Nikita S. Khrushchev, *Khrushchev Remembers* (Boston, 1971), pp. 560–62.

44. Goldman, *Soviet Foreign Aid*, pp. 115ff; Franck, *Afghanistan*, p. 57; Dupree, *Afghanistan*, pp. 508–9, 645.

45. Franck, *Afghanistan*, p. 57. Both the amount of gas that the Soviets, who controlled the meters, drew from the Afghan system that they built, and the price they paid, became controversial.

Iran, which was later similarly tied into the Soviet gas pipeline network, complained that it was underpaid; the Soviet-controlled Afghan press after the invasion denied any unfairness to Afghanistan; see *Kabul New Times* in *FBIS/SA*, 21 April 1980, pp. C1–2, and 25 April 1980, pp. C2–3.

46. On 4 February 1980; see *FBIS/SU*, 7 February 1980, p. D5.

47. Goldman, *Soviet Foreign Aid*, pp. 122–23. A World Bank mission in 1971 found otherwise. It said some Communist and Western aid projects "have been dictated as much by strategic or ideological considerations as economic ones," and were hard for Afghanistan to administer and operate; see Kavalsky, "Afghanistan," p. 36.

48. Louis Dupree, "The Mountains Go to Mohammad Zahir: Observations on Afghanistan's Reactions to Visits from Nixon, Bulganin-Khrushchev, Eisenhower and Khrushchev," *AUFS/SA*, 4, 6 (1960): 8ff.

49. Poullada, "Afghanistan and the United States," p. 187.

50. Fletcher, *Afghanistan*, p. 261.

51. Airgram no. A-71, U.S. Embassy, Kabul, 26 June 1971, "Policy Review: A U.S. Strategy for the '70s."

52. Uri Ra'anan, *The USSR Arms the Third World: Case Studies in Soviet Foreign Policy* (Cambridge, 1969), pp. 30n, 76–77; Adam B. Ulam, *Expansion & Coexistence: The History of Soviet Foreign Policy, 1917–1967* (New York, 1968), p. 586.

53. International Cooperation Administration, "Soviet Bloc Economic Activities in the Near East and Asia, as of November 25, 1955"(Washington, 1955), in *The Declassified Documents Retrospective Collection* (Washington, 1976), 3F.

54. Akhramovich, *Outline History*, pp. 109–10, gives the text of the *loya jirgah* approval.

55. Franck, *Afghanistan*, p. 58. Franck does not give a specific source for dating the agreement to July, nor does Poullada, "Afghanistan and the United States," cite sources other than his own personal knowledge from diplomatic service in Kabul at the time for saying, p. 189, that it was agreed upon in the December 1955 Khrushchev and Bulganin visit but not announced until 25 August 1956. It is possible that the Soviet leaders made preliminary soundings but it took another seven or eight months to work out the details.

56. Report of the U.S. Joint Chiefs of Staff dated 15 November 1956, in *Declassified Documents 1978*, no. 371B.

57. International Institute for Strategic Studies, *The Military Balance, 1977–1978* (London, 1977), pp. 55–56.

58. "Note by the Executive Secretary to the National Security Council [James S. Lay, Jr.] on U.S. Policy Toward South Asia," 7 December 1956, in *Declassified Documents Quarterly Catalog* 5 (January–March 1979): no. 44B.

59. Security Assistance Agency, Department of Defense, "Fiscal Year Series, 1979"(Washington, 1979), p. 71. Some U.S. officers who trained and who went to school with Afghan officers reported that these Afghans were particular purge targets after the Communists came to power.

60. "Expansion of Soviet Influence in Afghanistan and U.S. Countermeasures," 11 May 1956, in *Declassified Documents 1980*, no. 280B; report by the Operations Coordination Board, National Security Council, dated 28 November 1956, in *Declassified Documents 1981*, no. 76B. See also Franck, *Afghanistan*, p. 72.

61. *Declassified Documents 1978*, no. 65B.

62. E.g., *Pakistan Times*, Lahore, 13 December 1959, cited by Dupree, "Afghanistan's Big Gamble," p. IV–80.

63. Dupree, *Afghanstan*, pp. 513–14.

64. W. R. Polk, "Elements of U.S. Policy Toward Afghanistan" (1962), in *Declassified Douments 1978*, no. 65B. Alternative spelling of Qandahar as in original.

65. Kavalsky, "Afghanistan," pp. 236–37.

66. Former diplomats interviewed in Washington, D.C., in September 1981.

67. E.g., Polk, "Elements of U.S. Policy"; *Declassified Documents 1977*, no. 110B; *1978*, no. 380A; and *Declassified Documents 1980*, no. 280B; conversation 21 July 1961, between Afghan Ambassador Mohammed Hashim Maiwandwal and President John F. Kennedy, summarized by memorandum in *Declassified Documents 1977*, no. 110A. Among those interviewed on this subject in Washington, D.C., in 1980 and 1981 were former U.S. diplomats and Defense Department officials as well as former Air Force personnel.

68. Poullada, "Afghanistan and the United States," pp. 185–86.

69. Patrick J. Reardon, "Modernization and Reform: The Comtemporary Endeavor," in Grassmuck et al., *Afghanistan*, p. 161; Dupree, *Afghanistan*, pp. 539–46; Fletcher, *Afghanistan*, pp. 275–76.

70. Louis Dupree, "The Decade of Daoud Ends: Implications of Afghanistan's Change of Govern-

ment," *AUFS/SA*, 7, 7 (1963); Fletcher, *Afghanistan*, p. 276. The Soviets flew out perishable Afghan fruit, supposedly to Soviet consumers but sometimes for resale at a profit in Europe.

71. Meeting 27 September 1962, summarized in *Declassified Documents 1977*, no. 110B.

Chapter 3. Royalists and Communists

1. Text of the announcement in Dupree, *Afghanistan*, p. 554.

2. "A Correspondent"[Henry S. Bradsher], "Afghanistan: Change in Kabul," *The Economist*, 8 June 1963, p. 1006.

3. Dated 13 March 1963, and made public 24 May 1977 (with deletions).

4. Hasan Kakar, "The Fall of the Afghan Monarchy in 1973," *International Journal of Middle East Studies* 9 (May 1978): 211–12; Fletcher, *Afghanistan*, pp. 262–63; Richard S. Newell, *The Politics of Afghanistan* (Ithaca, 1972), pp. 170–71.

5. Hurewitz, *Middle East Politics*, pp. 303–4; Nollau and Wiehe, *Russia's South Flank*, p. 111.

6. Reardon, "Modernization and Reform," p. 153. There was no reason to assume that the elections were much more democratic.

7. Dupree, *Afghanistan*, pp. 494–97; Akhramovich, *Outline History*, p. 45–52; Wilber, *Afghanistan*, pp. 108–9; Smith, *Area Handbook*, pp. 208–9; Fred Halliday, "Revolution in Afghanistan," *New Left Review*, 112 (1978): 17.

8. Louis Dupree, "Afghanistan's Slow March to Democracy: Reflections on Kabul's Municipal Balloting," *AUFS/SA*, 7, 1 (1963).

9. Smith, *Area Handbook*, pp. 192–200; Dupree, *Afghanistan*, pp. 565–87; Newell, *Politics*, pp. 101–9.

10. From the Taraki subtribe of the Ghilzais, the largest Pushtun tribe in Afghanistan. A subtribe or regional name is commonly used as a family name by Afghans.

11. Political Department of the People's Armed Forces, "Biography of President Nur Mohammed Taraki" (hereafter cited as "Biography of . . . Taraki) in A. M. Baryalai, ed., *Democratic Republic of Afghanistan Annual* (Kabul, 1979), pp. 7ff; Hannah Negaran (pseudonym), "The Afghan Coup of April 1978: Revolution and International Security," *Orbis* 23 (Spring 1979): 93–113; Halliday, "Revolution in Afghanistan," pp. 21–22; Louis Dupree, "Red Flag over Hindu Kush, Part 1: Leftist Movements in Afghanistan," *AUFS/Asia* [hereafter *AUFS/A*], 44, 6 (1979).

12. Aslanov, "Peoples of Afghanistan," p. 29.

13. *Literaturnaya Gazeta*, 17 May 1978, p. 9, in *FBIS/SU*, 23 May 1978, pp. J1–2.

14. Interview with U.S. government official who declined to be identified.

15. Political Department, "Biography of . . . Taraki."

16. *Literaturnaya Gazeta*, 17 May 1978, p. 9, in *FBIS/SU*, 23 May 1978, pp. J1–2.

17. Dupree, *Afghanistan*, p. 495; Akhramovich, *Outline History*, pp. 53–63; Negaran, "The Afghan Coup."

18. He was interviewed in Washington, D.C., in November 1980 on condition that he not be identified, because of relatives still in Afghanistan.

19. Telegram no. 3372 from U.S. Embassy, Kabul, 30 April 1978.

20. *New York Times*, 12 November 1953, p. 9. Taraki left in Kabul a wife whom he had married in 1942; they had no children; see U.S. Embassy telegram no. 3372, 30 April 1978.

21. *New York Times*, 12 November 1953, p. 9.

22. Political Department, "Biography of . . . Taraki," p. 9.

23. *New York Times*, 12 November 1953, p. 9.

24. Interview with the former colleague cited in Note 18.

25. *New York Times*, 17 December 1953, p. 6 (from Karachi).

26. Political Department, "Biography of . . . Taraki," p. 12.

27. U.S. Embassy, Kabul, telegram no. 3372, 30 April 1978.

28. Negaran, "The Afghan Coup"; also Dupree, "Red Flag, Part 1," p. 6.

29. U.S. Embassy, Kabul, telegram no. 3372, 30 April 1978. This information was also omitted from Taraki's official biography after he came to power, which said that from 1953 to 1963 he "primarily did odd jobs to eke out a living," with a hostile government intelligence service forcing him out of every good job he found; see Political Department, "Biography of . . . Taraki," p. 14.

30. Dupree, "Red Flag, Part 1," p. 6.

31. Tanjug news agency, Belgrade, from Kabul, 6 May 1978, in *FBIS/ME*, 9 May 1978, pp. S1–3 (which quotes Taraki as saying he wrote about a dozen novels; other sources say he published more than thirty, but this count apparently includes short stories).

32. Halliday, "Revolution in Afghanistan," p. 22.

33. Interviews with former colleague and other Afghans who declined to be identified.

34. Political Department, "Biography of . . . Taraki," p. 17.

35. Ibid.

36. Alexandre Dastarac and M. Levant, "What Went Wrong in Afghanistan," *Le Monde Diplomatique*, (February 1980): 6-7, in *Near East/North Africa Report*, No. 2093, Joint Publications Research Service, Arlington, Va., 21 March 1980.

37. Biographical material issued by the U.S. Department of State on 27 December 1979.

38. Ibid.; *Der Spiegel*, Hamburg, 30 June 1980, pp. 113-18, in FBIS/SA, 1 July 1980, p. C2.

39. Andreas Kohlschuetter, "Points of the Compass: The Day of the Kabul Rising (& After); In Afghanistan," *Encounter* 55 (August-September 1980), 68-79; State Department biographical material; Reardon, "Modernization and Reform," p. 170.

40. Kohlschuetter, "The Kabul Rising"; Dastarac and Levant, "What Went Wrong"; Reardon, "Modernization and Reform," p. 170. See also P. Demohenko and L. Mironov, "The Revolution's Difficult Steps," *Pravda*, 14 January 1980, p. 6, in *FBIS/SU*, 16 January 1980, pp. D10-12.

41. In conversations with leftist colleagues and others, interviewed in Washington, D.C., who declined to be identified.

42. The foreign adviser, who declined to be identified, was interviewed in Washington, D.C.

43. State Department biographical material.

44. Kakar, "The Fall of the Afghan Monarchy," p. 203.

45. Biography in *Kabul Times*, 28 March 1979.

46. *New York Times*, 14 July 1979, p. 19.

47. *Broadway*, 8 November 1979.

48. Interviews with exiled Afghans.

49. Interview with an Afghan who declined to be identified.

50. *Kabul Times*, 28 March 1979.

51. Kabul Radio, 13 November 1979, in *FBIS/ME*, 19 November 1979, pp. S1-3. One version of Amin's becoming a Marxist is that he was "radicalized while attending study-work camps at the University of Wisconsin," according to Louis Dupree, "Red Flag Over the Hindu Kush, Part 2: The Accidental Coup, or Taraki in Blunderland," *AUFS/A*, 45 (1979): 50. Dupree does not specify the date, but the context suggests Amin's second period in the United States. A similar version says 1963; see Nancy Peabody Newell and Richard S. Newell, *The Struggle for Afghanistan* (Ithaca, 1981), p. 61. Neither cites a source. There is no reference to this in Amin's official biography, and the statement that he established contact with Taraki in 1958 seems to argue against 1963. The U.S. Federal Bureau of Investigation, which tries to monitor Communist activities among foreign students in the United States, said in answer to a query that neither its Washington headquarters' files nor its Madison, Wisconsin, field office had any record of Communist recruitment of Afghans in the United States during the 1950s or early 1960s, or of Communist activities at any student conference in Wisconsin in 1963 (letters to the author from FBI Assistant Director Roger S. Young, 10 and 25 February 1981). The lack of FBI data does not, of course, disprove that Communists proselytized among the Afghan students, and the University of Wisconsin had a long history of Marxist activity, especially among foreign students.

52. Afghan exiles interviewed in Washington, D.C.

53. *Kabul Times*, 28 March 1979; interviews with Afghans and former U.S. aid officials in Kabul.

54. The Editors, "How the CIA Turns Foreign Students into Traitors," *Ramparts* (April 1967), p. 3.

55. Interview with an American adviser to the Associated Students of Afghanistan in the United States.

56. *Kabul Times*, 28 March 1979.

57. Hafizullah Amin, "Afghan Youth Movement," in Mohammed Yassin Nassimi, ed., *Yearbook of the Associated Students of Afghanistan in the United States* (np: 1964), p. 9.

58. *Broadway*, 8 November 1979.

59. Political Department, "Biography of . . . Taraki," p. 20.

60. Kabul Radio, 8 January 1980, in *FBIS/ME*, 9 January 1980, pp. S4-5; Kabul Radio, 15 March 1980, in *FBIS/ME*, 17 March 1980, pp. S1-2; Tass from Kabul, 16 January 1980, in *FBIS/SU*, 17 January 1980, pp. D1-2.

61. Kabul Radio, 2 August 1978, in *FBIS/ME*, 17 August 1978, pp. S1-4.

62. Biography of Nur Ahmad Nur Panjwa'i in Afghan government note to U.S. Embassy, Kabul, sent in airgram no. A-58 to State Department, 26 June 1978.

63. *Asiaweek*, 9 June 1978, pp. 7-9; Kuldip Nayar, *Report on Afghanistan* (New Delhi, 1981), p. 2n. An Indian writer, P. R. Chari, director of the Institute for Defense Studies and Analysis in New

Delhi, asserted that an "underground Communist movement, with pro-Soviet linkages, had operated in Afghanistan during World War II" and surfaced again in 1965. But there is no available evidence of a wartime movement, or of a tie between it and the PDPA. Taraki apparently was talking about the development of a more vague radical tendency. See *Asiaweek*, 3 August 1979. The U.S. State Department said there was "no overt or clandestine indigenous Communist organization in Afghanistan" in 1951; see *Foreign Relations, 1951*, 6/2:2,005.

64. In Dari, obtained privately by the author, cited hereafter as PDPA secret history.

65. PDPA constitution in airgram No. A-60 from U.S. Embassy, Kabul, 3 July 1978.

66. PDPA secret history.

67. Ibid. See also Ghatur Attar, "Das Volk an der Macht," *Anti-Imperialistische Informationsbulletin* (May−June 1978), quoted by Halliday, "Revolution in Afghanistan," pp. 22−23. Halliday, p. 23n, gives a different list of central committee members and alternates from the PDPA secret history, and Dupree, "Red Flag, Part 1," p. 7, gives the same list as Halliday, but both seem to have included persons who were only added to the committee after its founding.

68. Interview with unidentified "Afghan Marxist" published in *Pakistani Progressive*, March−April 1980, reprinted in *MERIP Reports*, 89 (July−August 1980): 21; Kavalsky, "Afghanistan," p. 17; Ye. M. Primakov, in *Voprosy Filosofii*, 8 (1980): 60−71, in *FBIS/SU* Annex, 6 October 1980, pp. 1−12.

69. *New York Times*, 9 September 1979, p. 3; Halliday, "Revolution in Afghanistan," p. 24. The pragmatic position that PDPA leaders did not need to be workers contrasts with the Soviet disillusionment with bourgeois leaders in the Third World after 1960s setbacks. Prof. Rostislav A. Ulyanovskiy, deputy chief of the Soviet Communist Party's section for Third World countries and a chief formulator of policy on the subject, wrote in 1971 that the working class is "the vanguard of the socialist forces, and no other class can replace it in that function"; see Ulyanovskiy, "The Third World—Problems of Socialist Orientation," *International Affairs* 9 (1971): 30, quoted in Schwartz, "The USSR and Leftist Regimes," p. 230.

70. Louis Dupree, "Constitutional Development and Cultural Change, Part VIII: The Future of Constitutional Law in Afghanistan and Pakistan," *AUFS/SA*, 9, 10 (1965), p. 6.

71. Interview in Washington with a former deputy premier of Afghanistan, an educator, who declined to be identified.

72. Dupree, "Constitutional Development."

73. Interviews with former U.S. Embassy political officers in Kabul, who declined to be identified.

74. Airgram no. A-71 from U.S. Embassy, Kabul, 26 June 1971. A number of later PDPA leaders said they had joined the party as students. One said he joined the French Communist Party while a student in France—where Communists had for decades been even more active than American Communists in recruiting students from colonial and underdeveloped lands, such as Chou En-lai and Ho Chi-Minh.

75. Telegram no. 3372, U.S. Embassy, Kabul, 30 April 1978.

76. Nayar, *Report on Afghanistan*, p. 107n.

77. PDPA secret history.

78. Dupree, *Afghanistan*, pp. 590−95; Louis Dupree, "The Chinese Touch Base and Strike Out: Observations on China's Relations with Pakistan and Afghanistan," *AUFS/SA*, 10, 11 (1966); Louis Dupree, "Afghanistan: 1966; Comments on a Comparatively Calm State of Affairs with Reference to the Turbulence of Late 1965," *AUFS/SA*, 10, 4 (1966); Reardon, "Modernization and Reform," p. 178.

79. Reardon, "Modernization and Reform," pp. 186−87.

80. PDPA secret history.

81. *Khalq* statement, in Taraki's translation, privately obtained by the author.

82. Ibid.

83. Ibid.

84. PDPA secret history.

85. Dupree, "Red Flag, Part 1," p. 8; Dupree, "Afghanistan: 1966"; Dupree, "Afghanistan: 1968, Part III: Problems of a Free Press," *AUFS/SA*, 12, 6 (1968): 11−12.

86. PDPA secret history.

87. Eliza Van Hollen, "Soviet Dilemmas in Afghanistan," State Department Special Report no. 72, Washington, D.C., 1980, describes the Parchamis as always having been closer to the Soviets. The report of a visit by Taraki to Moscow after the split, given by an Afghan who declined to be identified, might have been a confusion with the forty-two-day visit in 1965, before the split, reported from U.S. Embassy, Kabul, biographic files by telegram no. 3372 on 30 April 1978.

88. PDPA secret history.

89. Ibid.

90. Ibid.

91. "Conversations with the Readers: With regard to the Khalq Party of Afghanistan," *Tariqust Al-Shaab* (Baghdad) 841, 23 June 1976.

92. Negaran, "The Afghan Coup."

93. Van Hollen, "Soviet Dilemmas."

94. Dupree, "Red Flag, Part 1," p. 8.

95. U.S. State Department, *World Strength of Communist Party Organizations*, 24th annual report, 1972 edition (Washington, 1972), pp. 89–90. Ulyanovskiy wrote in 1982 that "Toward the end of the 1960s the total membership of the PDPA comprised only several thousand people," but between 1965 and 1973 the party was able to organize more than 2,000 meetings, demonstrations, and strikes. See his "The Afghan Revolution at the Current Stage," *Problems of History of the Soviet Communist Party*, no. 4 for 1982, in *USSR Report, Political and Sociological Affairs*, no. 1279, Joint Publications Research Service, 20 July 1982, p. 9.

96. Robert G. Neumann, "Afghanistan," *The Washington Review of Strategic and International Studies* (July 1978): 116.

97. Dupree, Afghanistan, pp. 614–15.

98. "Labour Press Service," Release LPS/09A/80/E, New Delhi, 10 September 1980; Halliday, "Revolution in Afghanistan," p. 27.

99. A policy statement identified as NSCIG/NEA 69–23, as cited in a "formulation [that] varies only slightly" from the original, in airgram no. A-71 from U.S. Embassy, Kabul, 26 June 1971.

100. Ibid. Emphasis in the original.

101. See, for instance, airgram no. A-13 from U.S. Embassy, Kabul, 27 February 1978, entitled "Annual Policy Assessment: Additional Submission," Part Two; airgram no. A-66, U.S. Embassy, Kabul, 5 June 1972, enclosure 1, p. 6.

102. Kavalsky, "Afghanistan," pp. 42–47 and p. 592; *The Economist*, 19 December 1970, p. 43.

103. Kakar, "The Fall of the Afghan Monarchy," pp. 209–11; Smith, *Area Handbook*, pp. xix-xx; *Hong-Kong Standard*, 16 November 1972.

104. *New York Times*, 7 June 1973, p. 16, and 17 July 1973; Richard S. Newell, "The Government of Mustafa Shafiq: Prelude to Disaster," report to Middle Eastern Studies Association, Washington, D.C., 7 November 1980.

105. A. H. H. Abidi, "Irano-Afghan Dispute over the Helmand Waters," *International Studies* 16 (July–September 1977): 357–78. Babrak Karmal led a demonstration against Moosa Shafiq's agreement with Iran on the waters problem that was one of the largest such public turnouts on a political issue ever seen in Kabul.

Chapter 4. Daoud's Republic

1. Louis Dupree, *Asia Society Occasional Paper*, (Spring 1976): 5; Dupree, "A Note on Afghanistan: 1974," *AUFS/SA*, 18, 8 (1974).

2. Newell, "The Government of Mustafa Shafiq."

3. Mohammed Daoud, "The Republic of Afghanistan: Statements, Messages, and Press Interviews of the National Leader and the Founder of the Republic," No. 1 (Kabul, 1973), p. 2, quoted by Kakar, "Fall of the Afghan Monarchy," p. 213.

4. Interviews with Afghans and with former U.S. diplomats in Kabul.

5. Biographical material issued by State Department, 27 December 1979.

6. For instance, Kakar, "Fall of the Afghan Monarchy."

7. Interviewed by the author at the United Nations, New York, 10 October 1980, on condition that he not be identified.

8. *FBIS Trends in Communist Media* [hereafter *FBIS Trends*], 3 May 1978, p. 3.

9. Tass from Kabul, and Moscow Radio, both quoting Daoud, both 25 July 1973, in *FBIS/SU*, 26 July 1973, pp. B9–10. The Soviet Union became the first nation to recognize Daoud's new government, on 20 July 1973, and by 26 July its leaders had sent a message expressing "confidence that the genuinely good-neighborly relations of friendship and all-round cooperation existing between the Soviet Union and Afghanistan will further successfully develop." See Tass from Moscow, 20 July 1973, in *FBIS/SU*, 20 July 1973; and 27 July 1973, in *FBIS/SU*, 30 July 1973, p. B13; also *Pravda*, 31 July 1973, in *FBIS/SU*, 3 August 1973, p. B10.

10. Dupree, "A Note on Afghanistan: 1974."

11. Robert G. Neumann, "Afghanistan Under the Red Flag," in Z. Michael Szaz, ed., *The Impact of the Iranian Events Upon Persian Gulf & United States Security* (Washington, 1979), pp. 128–48.

12. *New York Times*, 1 August 1973, p. 13, and 29 April 1978, p. 9; Dupree, *Afghanistan*, p. 759.

13. Dupree, "A Note on Afghanistan: 1974"; Kabul Radio, 25 July 1973, in *FBIS/ME*, 26 July 1973, p. M1.

14. Delhi Radio, quoting Kabul Radio, 17 July 1973, in *FBIS/ME*, 17 July 1973, p. R1; Kabul Radio, 17 July 1973, in *FBIS/ME*, 18 July 1973, pp. M1–2.

15. Dupree, *Afghanistan*, p. 753; Tass from Kabul, 19 July 1973, in *FBIS/SU*, 19 July 1973, p. B2.

16. Tass from Rome, 24 August 1973, in *FBIS/SU*, 27 August 1973, p. J1.

17. Henry S. Bradsher, "Kabul Remains Shaky After July Coup," *Washington Star-News*, 24 November 1973, p. B-back; Dupree, "Red Flag over Hindu Kush, Part 1: Leftist Movements in Afghanistan," *AUFS/A*, 44 (1979): 12–13.

18. Halliday, "Revolution in Afghanistan," p. 29.

19. *Novoye Vremya*, 17 October 1980, pp. 14–15. In a speech on 11 May 1981, Karmal said that, "It was the uprising of the progressive forces of the Afghan army that caused the monarchy to be overthrown in 1973." See Kabul Radio, 11 May 1981, in *FBIS/SA*, 12 May 1981, pp. C1–4.

20. Delhi Radio, 25 July 1973, in *FBIS/ME*, 25 July 1973, p. R1.

21. Bradsher, "Kabul Remains Shaky." In the first few months after the coup, reports circulated in Kabul that Karmal and his main deputies in Parcham, identified at the time as Khyber, Sulaiman Laiq, and Anahita Ratebzad, "formed a kind of subcommittee of the . . . Central Committee, which passed on all senior appointments in the" government; see airgram No. A-24 from U.S. Embassy, Kabul, 30 April 1975, entitled "'The Left' in Afghanistan." In retrospect, it seems unlikely that this was ever true; Daoud never allowed anyone else that much authority.

22. Neumann, "Afghanistan Under the Red Flag," pp. 7–8; Dupree, *Asia Society Occasional Paper*, p. 5; Halliday, "Revolution in Afghanistan," p. 29.

23. U.S. Embassy airgram No. A-24, 30 April 1975.

24. Dupree, *Asia Society Occasional Paper*, p. 6.

25. Kabul Radio, 12 May 1978, in *FBIS/ME*, 15 May 1978, pp. S1–4.

26. PDPA secret history.

27. U.S. Embassy airgram no. A-24, 30 April 1975.

28. Telegram no. 539 from U.S. Embassy, Kabul, 28 January 1974.

29. Bradsher, "Kabul Remains Shaky." Within the first day of the downfall and death of Daoud in 1978, Radio Kabul in broadcasts apparently under military control accused "the rotten republican regime" of "giving electric shocks, pulling out fingernails, pouring boiling oil on naked bodies, and other unseen tortures." But the PDPA civilians in control, the new regime soon far outdid Daoud in such practices. For the accusation, see telegram no. 3279, U.S. Embassy, Kabul, 28 April 1978; later PDPA practices are described in subsequent chapters.

30. *New York Times*, 21 August 1974, p. 7, and 10 December 1976, p. 6; *Pravda*, 13 January 1975; Dilip Mukerjee, "Afghanistan under Daud: Relations with Neighboring States," *Asian Survey* 15 (April 1975): 302–3.

31. Telegram no. 539, U.S. Embassy, Kabul, 28 January 1974.

32. Halliday, "Revolution in Afghanistan," p. 30; Dupree, "The Democratic Republic of Afghanistan, 1979," *AUFS/A*, 3 (1979).

33. Kavalsky, "Afghanistan," pp. 379–80.

34. Airgram no. A-41, U.S. Embassy, Kabul, 24 May 1978. The clandestine circular, or "night letter," that circulated in Kabul before Daoud completed his 1977 constitution was an apparent leftist attempt to influence the writing of the document—without effect. It is unclear which PDPA faction wrote it, but internal evidence suggests Parcham. Its text is in the U.S. Embassy airgram.

35. David Chaffetz, "Afghanistan in Turmoil," *International Affairs* 56 (January 1980): 19–20.

36. Interviews with former U.S. diplomats in Kabul.

37. British Broadcasting Corp., *Summary of World Broadcasts, Far East*, 28 August 1973, pp. C2/1-5.

38. Kavalsky, "Afghanistan," pp. 36–37, 47–48, 202, and 592–95.

39. Interview with *Die Zeit*, Hamburg, 9 June 1978, in *FBIS/ME*, 9 June 1978, pp. S1–5.

40. James Philips, "Afghanistan: Islam versus Marxism," *Journal of Social and Political Studies* 4 (Winter 1979): 306–7; Theodore L. Eliot Jr., "Afghanistan After the 1978 Revolution," *Strategic Review* 7 (Spring 1979): 59.

41. Airgram no. A-26, U.S. Embassy, Kabul, 24 March 1976.

42. Airgram no. A-28, U.S. Embassy, Kabul, 17 April 1974.

43. Apparently first published by Halliday, "Revolution in Afghanistan," pp. 30 and 43, and repeated and elaborated by Selig S. Harrison, "The Shah, Not Kremlin, Touched Off Afghan Coup," *Washington Post*, 13 May 1979, pp. C1 and C5, and later articles by Harrison, including "Dateline Afghanistan: Exit Through Finland?", *Foreign Policy* 41 (Winter 1980–81): 163–87, and by others.

44. See Halliday, whose other writings include strong attacks on the shah's domestic and foreign policies.

45. U.S. Central Intelligence Agency, "Iran's International Position (NIE [National Intelligence Estimate] 34-61)," Washington, D.C., 1961, released 6 April 1978.

46. Interviews with retired U.S. officials. See also Mohammed Reza Pahlavi, *Answer to History* (New York, 1980), p. 133.

47. Abidi, "Iran-Afghan Dispute," pp. 373–74.

48. Mukerjee, "Afghanistan Under Daud," p. 311.

49. Telegram no. 778, U.S. Embassy, Kabul, 5 February 1975; Dupree, "Afghanistan 1977: Does Trade plus Aid Guarantee Development?", *AUFS/A*, 11, 3 (1977). The U.S. Embassy in Kabul observed that "Afghan administrative and technical capabilities are often insufficient, unaided, to make completely workable a 'you perform and we will respond with support' procedure [by foreign suppliers of aid. There are] administrative systems and institutional weaknesses, such as technical skills shortages (and therefore training needs), and project design/management deficiencies (and therefore the need for professional advice as well as training)." Such problems made the Afghan development ambitions based in Middle Eastern oil money completely unrealistic. See telegram no. 468 , U.S. Embassy, Kabul, 19 January 1977.

50. *Kabul Times*, 1 May 1975; Kabul Radio, 1 May 1975, in *FBIS/ME*, 2 May 1975; p. R4; Tehran Radio, 30 April 1975, in *FBIS/ME*, 1 May 1975, pp. R1–2.

51. Dupree, "Afghanistan 1977: Does Trade"; Amin Saikal, *The Rise and Fall of the Shah* (Princeton, 1980), p. 200.

52. *The Economist* Intelligence Unit, "Quarterly Economic Review: Pakistan, Bangladesh, Afghanistan," 4 (1975): 21.

53. *Krasnaya Zvezda*, 23 January 1980, p. 3, in *FBIS/SU*, 29 January 1980, pp. A16–17.

54. Philips, "Afghanistan," pp. 306–7.

55. *Far Eastern Economic Review*, 23 June 1978, p. 32.

56. Eden Naby, "The Ethnic Factor in Soviet-Afghan Relations," *Asian Survey* 20 (March 1980): pp. 243–44.

57. Eliot, "Afghanistan After the 1978 Revolution," p. 59; Halliday, "Revolution in Afghanistan," p. 31; see also Naby, "The Ethnic Factor."

58. This change by Moscow, and its granting economic aid to Pakistan, was rewarded by Pakistan's closing American military operations in Peshawar, where U-2 pilot Francis Gary Powers took off for his ill-fated 1 May 1960 flight across the Soviet Union and where the United States operated an extensive array of electronic devices to monitor Soviet missile tests and other events.

59. A. G. Noorani, "Soviet Ambitions in South Asia," *International Security*, 4 (Winter 1979–80): 41.

60. See Soviet and Afghan reports on the visit in *FBIS/SU*, 4–12 June 1974.

61. Tass, 5 June 1974, in *FBIS/SU*, 6 June 1974, pp. J1–3.

62. *The Economist*, 3 August 1974, pp. 29–30; *Economist* Intelligence Unit, "Quarterly Economic Review," 4(1975): 21.

63. *FBIS/SU*, 9–17 December 1975. Podgorny was accompanied by a Soviet deputy defense minister, Army General Ivan G. Pavlovskiy, who returned to Afghanistan in August 1979 for two-month visit that prepared the way for the Soviet invasion.

64. *Izvestiya*, 11 December 1975, pp. 1–3, in *FBIS/SU*, 17 December 1975, pp. J1–3.

65. Tass, quoting *Izvestiya*, 12 December 1975, in *FBIS/SU*, 17 December 1975, p. J3.

66. Tass, 15 April 1977, in *FBIS/SU*, 18 April 1977, pp. J1–3.

67. Tass, 12 April 1977, in *FBIS/SU*, 13 April 1977, pp. J3–5.

68. Tass, 12 April 1977, in *FBIS/SU*, 13 April 1977, pp. J5–9.

69. Ibid.

70. Tass, 15 April 1977, in *FBIS/SU*, 18 April 1977, pp. J1–3.

71. Tass from Kabul, 16 April 1977, in *FBIS/SU*, 18 April 1977, p. J4.

72. Interviews with former Afghan officials and with other Asians, including senior officials of neighboring countries.

73. Ibid.

74. Interviews with American officials.

75. Dubs to House International Relations Committee's subcommittee on Asian and Pacific affairs, in *Department of State Bulletin*, 78, 2014 (May 1978): 50.

76. Philips, "Afghanistan," p. 307.

77. See *FBIS/ME*, 5 April 1978, pp. C2–3. The Saudis "expressed readiness to study some of the development projects in Afghanistan with a view to taking part in some of these projects." After a brief visit to Kuwait, another rich Arab state that gave money to Moslem countries, Daoud went to Egypt. In a Cairo speech 6 April 1978, he "denounced the policy of racial discrimination and imperialism of certain states and deplored the deteriorating situation in the Horn of Africa as a result of this detested policy," according to Cairo Radio's indirect quotation; see *FBIS/ME*, 7 April 1978, p. D3. Although vague, this could have been interpreted by the Soviets as another attack on them.

78. Included in the PDPA secret history.

79. Ibid.

80. *DRA Annual*, 1979, p. 22. Some secondary sources say Amin began recruiting in the armed forces in 1967. If he did that early, which is doubtful, there were no signs of success. If true, however, the postdating in the official record would indicate a desire to cover up initial recruiting failures.

81. Ibid., p. 23. See also Taraki speech 1 August 1978, in *FBIS/ME*, 17 August 1978, pp. S1–4.

82. PDPA secret history.

83. Ulyanovskiy, "The Afghan Revolution," in *USSR Report*, no. 1279, 20 July 1982, p. 9.

84. PDPA secret history; Halliday, "Revolution in Afghanistan," pp. 30–31.

85. Airgram no. A-41, U.S. Embassy, Kabul, 24 May 1978.

86. *Tariqust Al-Shaab*, no. 740, 22 February 1976.

87. Statement obtained privately by the author from a copy circulated by hand but not known to have been published.

88. *Tariqust Al-Shaab*, no. 841, 23 June 1976. This article, which gave the Parchami version of PDPA history, has been erroneously cited without direct quotation as "an unprecedented appeal for Communist unity in Afghanistan," which it is not; see Harrison, "The Shah, Not Kremlin," (which mistakenly dates the article as March 1976) and Harrison, "Dateline Afghanistan," p. 166.

89. Negaran, "The Afghan Coup."

90. *The Socialist*, (Sydney, Australia) 24 November 1976, p. 6.

91. Ulyanovskiy, "The Afghan Revolution," in *USSR Report*, No. 1279, 20 July 1982, p. 9.

92. Ibid. Ulyanovskiy's article did not say where the conference was held, and Afghan officials had only said that unity was achieved in July 1977 without giving any details; see *DRA Annual*, 1979, p. 23.

93. Babrak Karmal, *World Marxist Review*, 23, 4:53; N. K. Krishnan, "Prospects of Democratic Advance in Afghanistan," *Party Life*, 22 May 1976.

94. Krishnan, "Prospects of Democratic Advance."

95. *DRA Annual*, 1979, p. 23; note to the author from a senior Indian Communist, who declined to be identified, in January 1981.

96. Interview with N. K. Krishnan, conducted for the author by R. Ramanujam in New Delhi, March 1981.

97. Note from the Indian Communist official cited in note 95 (not Krishnan).

98. Ibid.

99. Ibid.

100. Halliday, "Revolution in Afghanistan," p. 31, says that a veteran Pakistani Communist living in exile in Kabul, Ajmal Khattaq, mediated between Khalq and Parcham. He seems to have had little success.

101. Interviews with Afghans and Western officials. See also Nayar, *Report on Afghanistan*, p. 36.

102. This is the estimate of Dupree, "Red Flag Over the Hindu Kush, Part V: Repressions, or Security Through Terror Purges, 1–IV," *AUFS/A*, 28, 3 (1980): 3. See also *New York Times*, 9 September 1979, p. 3. Ulyanovskiy, whose estimate of several thousand members in the late 1960s has been cited above, and who claimed "more than 60,000" members in 1982, does not give an estimate for 1978; see his "The Afghan Revolution," in *USSR Report*, No. 1279, 20 July 1982, p. 18. Amin claimed in 1979 that there were 15,000 members before the coup; see *FBIS/ME*, 17 December 1979, p. S2. Some Western diplomats in Kabul at the time accepted estimates of 5,000 to 10,000 for the two factions combined.

103. *The Economist*, 2 August 1980.

104. *DRA Annual*, 1979, p. 26.

105. Dupree, "The Democratic Republic of Afghanistan, 1979."

106. Neumann, "Afghanistan Under the Red Flag"; Dupree, "Red Flag Over the Hindu Kush, Part 2: The Accidental Coup, or Taraki in Blunderland," *AUFS/A* 45, 4 (1979).

107. *New York Times*, 5 December 1977, p. 2.

108. The idea that SAVAK agents—some say 250 of them—were helping Daoud suppress his domestic Communists has become firmly implanted in periodical literature on the 1978 coup without any evidence being offered. It is part of the assumption that the shah destabilized Afghanistan and deserved much of the blame for the Communist takeover. An extensive inquiry into the subject, however, with key Iranian officials of the period, Afghan officials, Western diplomats then in Kabul and Tehran, and current and former Western intelligence officers in a position to know about SAVAK's operations, failed to find any substantiation. Many of these sources, in fact, deny SAVAK was working with Daoud. There is no doubt that the Iranian embassy in Kabul contained a sizeable number of SAVAK agents, and others worked elsewhere in Afghanistan, but that was a normal projection of the shah's concern over what was happening in a neighboring country about which he had always been nervous. He and Daoud had too many doubts about each other to become too closely linked. Nor was Daoud, who had been running his own political police operation off and on for a quarter-century, the kind of man to ask for outside help in his internal affairs. Equally unconvincing are published reports that the Soviet KGB killed Khyber as part of a plan to provoke trouble that would overturn Daoud.

109. Kabul Radio, 12 May 1978, in *FBIS/ME*, 15 May 1978, pp. S1–4.

110. Kabul Radio, 1 January 1980, in *FBIS/ME*, 2 January 1980, p.S2.

111. Interview with former Afghan official; Karmal, *World Marxist Review*, 23, 4:53.

112. Telegram no. 108913 from the State Department to U.S. embassies in a number of Asian and African countries, 28 April 1978; Dupree, "Afghanistan Under the Khalq, " *Problems of Communism* 28 (July–August 1979): 34; Feroz Ahmed, interview in *MERIP Reports*, 89 (July–August 1980): 13.

Chapter 5. The Saur Revolution

1. *DRA Annual*, 1979, pp. 43–49. Taraki's own version is in *FBIS/ME*, 22 May 1978, pp. S1–2.

2. Ibid.

3. Ibid.; and Dupree, "Red Flag Over the Hindu Kush, Part 2." Dupree gives what is essentially the official account, adding some information to it but not differing from or questioning it.

4. Interviews with exiled Afghans who declined to be identified. Dupree, "Red Flag, Part 2," says that "the number three man in Daoud's primary intelligence unit was a long-time Khalq mole," but he does not offer this as an explanation for the delay in taking Amin to prison; instead, he simply implies incompetence.

5. This account is based on *DRA Annual*, 1979, pp. 51ff; Dupree, "Red Flag, Part 2"; Kabul Radio, 12 May 1978, in *FBIS/ME*, 15 May 1978, pp. S1–4; Havana Radio, 21 May 1978, in *FBIS/ME*, 22 May 1978, pp. S1–3; Tanjug from Kabul, 6 May 1978, in *FBIS/ME*, 9 May 1978, pp. S1–3; *New York Times*, 3 May 1978, p. 1, and its magazine, 4 June 1978, p. 50; *Asiaweek*, 9 June 1978, pp. 7–9.

6. Kabul Radio, 12 May 1978, in *FBIS/ME*, 15 May 1978, pp. S1–4. Dupree, "Red Flag, Part 2," p. 13, quotes Amin as having said on 21 March 1979 that thirty-four "party comrades" and sixty-seven "anti-revolutionaries" were killed in the coup. A resistance leader, Prof. Sibghattulah Mojadeddi, said more than 10,000 soldiers, police, republican guards and civilians died within the first thirty-six hours, and twenty-nine members of Daoud's family were executed; see his statement in New York City 25 May 1979, reproduced in *Newsletter*, Afghanistan Council, The Asia Society [hereafter Afghan Council *Newsletter*], New York, 3 June 1979.

7. Dupree, "Red Flag, Part 2."

8. *DRA Annual*, 1979, pp. 27–28.

9. *Die Zeit*, 9 June 1978, in *FBIS/ME*, 9 June 1978, pp. S1–5.

10. Havana Radio, 21 May 1978, in *FBIS/ME*, 22 May 1978, pp. S1–3.

11. Kabul Radio, 27 April 1978, in *FBIS/ME*, 28 April 1978, p. S1, and 1 May 1978, pp. S1–2.

12. *DRA Annual*, 1979, pp. 29 and 56.

13. Telegram no. 3234, U.S. Embassy, Kabul, 27 April 1978.

14. Telegram no. 3242, U.S. Embassy, Kabul, 27 April 1978; Kabul Radio, 29 April 1978, in *FBIS/ME*, 1 May 1978, pp. S1–2. The text of the policy statement given here is from a Kabul Radio broadcast on 29 April that said the statement had been issued on 28 April, but the U.S. Embassy reported hearing it on 27 April. The embassy's version of the statement is a slightly shorter and somewhat garbled one, but it clearly is the same statement taken down by embassy personnel rather than FBIS's professional monitors (or, in this case, probably the BBC's and then passed to FBIS).

15. Kabul Radio, 27 April 1978, in *FBIS/ME*, 28 April 1978, p. S1.

16. Kabul Radio, 28 April 1978, in *FBIS/ME*, 1 May 1978, pp. S1–2.

17. Ibid.

18. See *FBIS/SU*, 1 and 2 May 1978, pp. J1–2.

19. *International Affairs* (Moscow)(March 1979): 47; Ghulam Muradov in *Oriental Studies in the USSR (No. 3), Afghanistan: Past and Present* (Moscow, 1981), p. 196.

20. *DRA Annual*, 1979, p. 59.

21. Telegram no. 3380, U.S. Embassy, Kabul, 30 April 1978 (emphasis added).

22. The message from the Afghan embassy in Washington to the State Department on 3 May 1978, requesting diplomatic recognition in what seems to be only a slightly different translation of the same original note, says, as did the later history, that "in its first session on the 30th of April 1978" Taraki was elected, rather than using the *dated* 27 April form; see embassy message no. 157, in State Department registry no. 7808922. Replying, the State Department said that the U.S. embassy in Kabul informed the foreign ministry there on 6 May 1978 that the United States would maintain diplomatic relations with the Democratic Republic on the assumption that it "will continue to honor and support the existing treaties and international agreements in force between our two states," which is a standard formulation; see registry no. 7808922.

23. Kabul Radio, 4 May 1978, in *FBIS/ME*, 4 May 1978, p. S1.

24. Kabul Radio, 9 May 1978, in *FBIS/ME*, 10 May 1978, p. S1.

25. Kabul Radio, 11 May 1981, in *FBIS/SA*, 12 May 1981, pp. C1–4. The text of the original coup announcement is in Dupree, "Red Flag, Part 2," but his and other published accounts ignore the soldiers' policy statement and do not question who was initially in charge.

26. Kabul Radio, 30 April 1978, in *FBIS/ME*, 1 May 1978, p. S1; see also Moscow Radio in *FBIS/SU*, 1 May 1978, pp. J1–2; and Tanjug from Kabul, 4 May 1978, in *FBIS/ME*, 5 May 1978, p. S1–2.

27. Moscow Radio, 2 May 1978, in *FBIS/SU*, 2 May 1978, p. J1. This report on the new Afghan leadership seems to have been the only time Soviet media mentioned Karmal's name until the Soviet invasion twenty months later, when he was suddenly discovered to be the true leader of the PDPA. Until the coup, Amin had not been a member of the PDPA politburo, but during party meetings sometime between 27 April and 1 May he was elected to the politburo "with full interest," Taraki said later, thus moving into the third-ranked position as an apparent reward for his coup services; see Taraki's address to the party central committee meeting 27 November 1978 in *DRA Annual*, 1979, p. 572. Dupree counted eleven of the twenty-four new cabinet members as having worked for the government at the time of the coup and six as having at previous times served in prison; see his "The Democratic Republic of Afghanistan, 1979."

28. Kabul Radio, 9 May 1978, in *FBIS/ME*, 10 May 1978, p. S1.

29. Dupree, "Red Flag, Part 2."

30. *Kabul Times*, 4 August 1979.

31. Alexander Bovin, "Apropos the Afghan Revolution," *Moscow News Weekly*, No. 16, 1980, p. 7. See also Oleg Golovin in *New Times*, as reported by Tass 19 March 1980, in *FBIS/SU*, 21 March 1980, pp. D1–3, as an example of creating a legend out of whole cloth.

32. Kabul Radio, 4 May 1978, in *FBIS/ME*, 4 May 1978, p. S1.

33. Tanjug from Kabul, 4 May 1978, in *FBIS/ME*, 5 May 1978, pp. S1–2.

34. Kabul Radio, 25 May 1978, in *FBIS/ME*, 8 June 1978, pp. S2–3.

35. *Die Zeit*, 9 June 1978, in *FBIS/ME*, 9 June 1978, pp. S1–5.

36. *Washington Post*, 7 November 1978, p. A17.

37. *DRA Annual*, 1979, p. 657; Kabul Radio, 10 November 1978, in *FBIS/ME*, 1 December 1978, p. S2.

38. Interviews with U.S. government officials.

39. Interview with a senior U.S. diplomat in Kabul at the time.

40. House of Commons, "Afghanistan: The Soviet Invasion and Its Consequences for British Policy" (London, 1980), p. 6; *Washington Post*, 6 May 1978, p. A15.

41. *FBIS Trends*, 3 May 1978, p. 2.

42. Tass from Moscow, 6 May 1978, in *FBIS/SU*, 8 May 1978, pp. J1–2. Taraki said 7 September 1979 that "at the dawn of the success of the revolution, our comrade Brezhnev and Jimmy Carter both were equally surprised"; see Havana Radio, 8 September 1979, in *FBIS Latin America Report*, 10 September 1979, pp. AA7–8. The Libyan foreign secretary, who rushed to Kabul to find out what was happening, was assured by Taraki that "the revolution was not externally inspired and did not receive any outside help"; see *FBIS/ME*, 10 May 1978, pp. S4–5.

43. Telegrams nos. 3372 and 3381, U.S. Embassy, Kabul, both 30 April 1978.

44. *FBIS Trends*, 3 May 1978, p. 2.

45. Tass, 3 May 1978, in *FBIS/SU*, 4 May 1978, p. J1. Taraki's and Amin's replies were not reported by Moscow until 10 and 11 May; see *FBIS/SU*, 17 May 1978, p. J1.

46. Moscow Radio, 1 May 1978, in *FBIS/SU*, 2 May 1978, p. J1.

47. *Pravda*, 6 May 1978, p. 5, in *FBIS/SU*, 9 May 1978, pp. J1–2.

48. *Izvestiya*, 13 and 23 May 1978, p. 3, in *FBIS/SU*, 18 and 25 May 1978, pp. J1–3; Moscow Radio, 15 and 16 May 1978, in *FBIS/SU*, 17 and 18 May 1978, pp. J1–3.

49. Tass, 19 May 1978, in *FBIS/SU*, 19 May 1978, p. J1.

50. Ibid.

51. Afghanistan Task Force, Foreign Affairs and National Defense Division, The Library of Congress, Congressional Research Service [hereafter CRS], "Afghanistan: Soviet Invasion and U.S. Response," issue brief number IB80006, as updated 13 June 1980, and 22 December 1980, p. 3.

52. Dupree letter in *New York Times*, 20 May 1978, p. 18.

53. *Washington Post*, 8 May 1978, p. A16.

54. Recounted by a key State Department official involved in Afghan affairs at the time, who declined to be identified.

55. *New York Times*, 4 August 1978, p. 4.

56. Zia's relations with Taraki were related by a senior Asian official directly involved in them, who was interviewed on condition that he not be identified.

57. Telegram no. 4062, U.S. Embassy, Tehran, 30 April 1978.

58. *Indian Express*, (Bombay) 7 May 1979, quoted by Noorani, "Soviet Ambitions," p. 43; *Far Eastern Economic Review*, 8 September 1978, in Afghan Council *Newsletter*, Fall 1978.

59. Interviews with U.S. government officials with access to reports from Kabul.

60. Louis Dupree, "Red Flag Over the Hindu Kush, Part V: Repressions, or Security Through Terror Purges, I–IV," *AUFS/A*, 28 (1980): 3–4.

61. Airgram no. A-58, U.S. Embassy, Kabul, 26 June 1978; memorandum from Peter Tarnoff, executive secretary of the State Department, to Zbigniew Brzezinski, national security adviser, dated 29 June 1978 (recommending acceptance of Nur as ambassador).

62. Agence France-Presse [AFP] from Kabul, 5 July 1978, in *FBIS/ME*, 6 July 1978, p. S1.

63. Kabul Radio, 11 July and 21 August 1978, in *FBIS/ME*, 27 July and 23 August 1978, pp. S1 and S3.

64. Kabul Radio, 8 July 1978, in *FBIS/ME*, 8 and 21 July 1978, both p. S4.

65. *Pravda*, 19 January 1980, p. 5, in *FBIS/SU*, 23 January 1980, p. D1. The word "cadre," which originally was a collective term for a skeleton organization of people, especially in an army, was used by Nur in its Soviet usage of individual officials, especially in a Communist party.

66. Tehran Radio, 20 July 1978, in *FBIS/ME*, 21 July 1978, p. S1. See also Amin's denial that a Parcham party had ever existed, on Kabul Radio, 27 September 1979, in *FBIS/ME*, 28 September 1979, p. S2.

67. Kabul Radio, 2 August 1978, in *FBIS/ME*, 17 August 1978, pp. S1–4.

68. Kabul Radio, 17 August 1978, in *FBIS/ME*, 18 August 1978, p. S1. From the Khalq-Parcham split in the summer of 1978 "until the end of 1979 around 10 mass purges were carried out in the army," according to Ulyanovskiy, "The Afghan Revolution," in *USSR Report*, no. 1279, 20 July 1982, p. 14.

69. Kabul Radio, 18 and 23 August 1978, in *FBIS/ME*, 21 and 24 August 1978, p. S1.

70. *Washington Post*, 7 November 1978, p. A17; Dupree, "Red Flag, Part V," p. 5.

71. *DRA Annual*, 1979, pp. 6, 566–73, 1,338, 1,341–61; Kabul Radio, 27 November 1978, in *FBIS/ME*, 13 December 1978, pp. S1–7.

72. *DRA Annual*, 1979, p. 6.

73. Kabul Radio, 27 November 1978, in *FBIS/ME*, 13 December 1978, pp. S1–7.

74. *DRA Annual*, 1979, p. 6.

75. Ibid., pp. 572–73.

76. Telegram no. 9163, U.S. Embassy, Kabul, 16 November 1978; interview with a former senior official of a nearby country. The official, who declined to be identified, met Taraki in Kabul shortly after the coup and again in the autumn of 1978. Amin, as foreign minister, was present both times. The first time Amin was very deferential toward Taraki and would not even sit down in Taraki's presence, but the second time Amin acted casual if not disrespectful toward Taraki.

77. *New Times* (the English version of *Novoye Vremya*), quoted by Tass, 19 March 1980, in *FBIS/SU*, 21 March 1980, pp. D1–3.

78. *New York Times*, 9 May 1978, p. 13.

79. *Asiaweek*, 1 September 1978, in Afghan Council *Newsletter*, Fall 1978; Amnesty International.

"Violations of Human Rights and Fundamental Freedoms in the Democratic Republic of Afghanistan" May 1979 [hereafter cited as "Violations of Human Rights"].

80. Tass from Kabul, 15 May 1978, in *FBIS/SU*, 17 May 1978, p. D1.

81. Kabul Radio, 25 May 1978, in *FBIS/ME*, 8 June 1978, pp. S2–3.

82. Tass from Kabul, 26 April 1980, in *FBIS/SU*, 28 April 1980, p. D3.

83. House of Commons, "Afghanistan," Appendix 1; *Washington Post*, 29 May 1978, p. A12.

84. Alexandre Bennigsen, "Soviet Muslims and the World of Islam," *Problems of Communism*, 29 (March–April 1980): 47.

85. Zalmay Khalilzad, "Afghanistan and the Crisis in American Foreign Policy," *Survival* 22 (July–August 1980): 154.

86. AFP from Islamabad, Pakistan, 1 June 1978, in *FBIS/ME*, 2 June 1978, p. S2; *New York Times*, 1 July 1978, p. 4.

87. Kabul Radio, 2 August 1978, in *FBIS/ME*, 17 August 1978, pp. S1–4.

88. Tass, 5 December 1978, in *FBIS/SU*, 6 December 1978, pp. J3–10.

89. David Chaffetz, "Afghanistan, Russia's Vietnam?," Afghanistan Council Special Paper no. 4, The Asia Society (Summer 1979), p. 8.

90. Interviews with Afghanistan specialists of the American Anthropological Association, 5 December 1980, Washington, D.C.

91. Budapest Radio, 11 December 1980, in *FBIS/SA*, 12 December 1980, pp. C1–2.

92. Kabul Radio, 12 May 1978, in *FBIS/ME*, 15 May 1978, pp. S1–4.

93. Kabul Radio, 13 June 1978, in *FBIS/ME*, 6 July 1978, p. S2.

94. *Die Zeit*, 9 June 1978, in *FBIS/ME*, 9 June 1978, pp. S1–5.

95. Kabul Radio, 7 January 1980, in *FBIS/ME*, 9 January 1980, p. S2.

96. *DRA Annual*, 1979, pp. 76–77; interviews with Afghans; *Kabul Times*, 6 August 1978, in Afghan Council *Newsletter*, Fall 1978.

97. Dastarac and Levant, "What Went Wrong."

98. Eden Naby, "The Ethnic Factor in Soviet-Afghan Relations," *Asian Survey*, (March 1980): 244. Naby notes that the Shi'ite Hazaras were ignored as a separate language group. "Choices of which ethnic groups to cultivate have been based on political rather than cultural or demographic factors," she says.

99. Wheeler, *Modern History of Soviet Central Asia*, pp. 194–95.

100. *DRA Annual*, 1979, pp. 80–85; Dupree, "Red Flag Over the Hindu Kush, Part III: Rhetoric and Reforms, or Promises! Promises!," *AUFS/A*, 23 (1980).

101. *Izvestiya*, 12 July 1980, p. 5, in *FBIS/SU*, 17 July 1980, pp. D1–3.

102. H. Beattie, "Effects of the Saor Revolution in the Nahrin Area of Northern Afghanistan," report to the American Anthropological Association, 5 December 1980, Washington, D.C.

103. Kabul Radio, 2 August 1978, in *FBIS/ME*, 17 August 1978, pp. S1–4; *Washington Post*, 7 November 1978, p. A17.

104. Thomas Barfield, "Afghans Fight Old Battles in a New War," *Asia* (March/April 1980): 12–15, 46–47.

105. *DRA Annual*, pp. 86–87; Dupree, "Red Flag, Part III."

106. Nancy Hatch Dupree, "Revolutionary Rhetoric and Afghan Women," report to the American Anthropological Association, 5 December 1980, Washington, D.C.; interviews with anthropologists. The paying of brideprice, or the reverse in the payment of a large dowry, has been considered a handicap to economic and social modernization in many Third World countries, but it has proven impervious to law or exhortation. More than half a century after Soviet power was consolidated in Central Asia, "bridemoney . . . still exists. . . . We cannot fail to be alarmed at the fact that not only elderly but also young people support the absurd custom," the main newspaper of Tajikistan, *Kommunist Tadzhikistana* (Dushanbe), said 31 October 1980, in *FBIS/SU*, 12 November 1980, p. R3.

107. Kavalsky, "Afghanistan," pp. 89–90 and 127–31; Dupree, "Red Flag, Part III."

108. *DRA Annual*, 1979, pp. 88–96.

109. Akhramovich, *Outline History*, pp. 8–9; Feroz Ahmed in *MERIP Reports* 89 (July–August 1980): 13–14; *Zarya Vostoka*, 12 May 1978, in *FBIS/SU*, 22 May 1978, p. J2.

110. Beattie, "Effects of the Saor Revolution."

111. *Izvestiya*, 1 June 1979, p. 5, in *FBIS/SU*, 12 June 1979, p. D3.

112. *Kabul Times*, 15 July 1979, in Afghan Council *Newsletter*, 4 September 1979.

113. *The Guardian*, 29 April 1979, in Afghan Council *Newsletter*, 4 September 1979; Moscow Radio, 27 July 1979, in *FBIS/SU*, 30 July 1979, p. D2; Tass from Kabul, 30 July and 5 August 1979, in *FBIS/SU*, 31 July and 7 August 1979, pp. D1 and D3–4; *New York Times*, 13 July 1979, p. 3.

114. Kabul Radio, 27 February 1980, in *FBIS/ME*, 3 March 1980, pp. S1–7.

115. *Novoye Vremya*, 11 April 1980, pp. 5–7, in *FBIS/SU*, 21 April 1980, pp. D6–9.

116. Ibid.; see also, *Kabul New Times*, 23 and 24 March 1980, p. 2, in *FBIS/SA*, 5 May 1980, pp. C10–14; *Pravda* (Bratislava), 31 December 1980, p. 6, in *FBIS/SA*, 7 January 1981, pp. C1–2; Kabul Radio, 27 February 1980, in *FBIS/ME*, 3 March 1980, p. S4.

117. *Pravda* (Moscow), 18 February 1980, in *FBIS/SU*, 21 February 1980, pp. D3–4.

118. Kabul Radio, 28 April 1980, in *FBIS/SA*, 29 April 1980, pp. C1–3.

119. *Pravda*, 17 October 1980, pp. 2–6, in *FBIS/SU*, 21 October 1980, pp. D4–11.

120. *Pakistani Progressive*, March–April 1980, reprinted in *MERIP Reports*, 89 (July–August 1980): 20–24. Ulyanovskiy added other factors: the absence "of an experienced and sufficiently large working class," "clan, tribal, local and religious prejudices," the taking of decisions "without careful preparations and without a thorough consideration of local conditions, traditions and religious customs," and others; see his "The Afghan Revolution," *USSR Report*, no. 1279, 20 July 1982, p. 11.

121. *Za Rubezhom*, 26 February 1981, p. 6, in *FBIS/SU*, 12 March 1981, pp. P8–10.

122. House of Commons, "Afghanistan," Appendix A.

123. Speech in Leningrad in *FBIS/SU*, 2 March 1979, p. R26.

124. *FBIS Trends*, 7 May 1980, p. 15.

125. Dastarac and Levant, "What Went Wrong," pp. 6–7.

126. Tass from Ulan Bator, 30 May 1979.

127. Tass, 5 December 1978, in *FBIS/SU*, 6 December 1978, pp. J10–13.

128. Foreign and Commonwealth Office [hereafter FCO], "Soviet Bloc Network of Friendship Treaties" (London, 1980).

129. *Current Digest of the Soviet Press*, 18, 3 (1966): 7–8.

130. Tass, 5 December 1978, in *FBIS/SU*, 6 December 1978, pp. J10–13.

131. Ibid.

132. Ibid.

133. *Kommunist*, 2 (1979), quoted in FCO, "Soviet Bloc Network."

134. *FBIS Trends*, 25 April 1979, pp. 1–3.

135. *FBIS Trends*, 13 December 1978, p. 6.

136. Moscow Radio, 5 December 1978, in *FBIS/SU*, 5 December 1978, p. J2.

137. Interviews with U.S. officials, who denied published reports that Dubs had frequent lengthy discussions with Amin in an effort to educate him on the dangers of getting too close to the Soviet Union. Dubs' reports to Washington, which the interviewed officials received, did not indicate he felt that he was making any progress toward convincing Afghan officials that they should resist Soviet influence.

138. State Department, "The Kidnapping and Death of Ambassador Adolph Dubs, Summary of Report of Investigation," Washington, D.C., made public 1980 [hereafter cited as "Kidnapping and Death"].

139. Ibid.

140. *The Guardian*, London, 29 April 1979, in Afghan Council *Newsletter*, 4 September 1979.

141. Amnesty International, "Violations of Human Rights," p. 7 and appendix C.

142. Kabul Radio, 8 June 1980, in *FBIS/SA*, 9 June 1980, pp. C2–3. Two years later a Soviet newspaper said that Kalakani's Chinese-supported terrorist organization had recently been smashed by Afghan government security units and Kalakani executed; see *Sovetskaya Rossiya*, 20 July 1982, p. 3, in *FBIS/SU*, 28 July 1982, p. D1. But another Soviet publication, in an article approved for publication on 22 July 1982, said the same organization had stepped up "subversive actions"; see *Za Rubezhom*, No. 30 for 1982, pp. 12–13, in *FBIS/SU*, 29 July 1982, pp. D1–3. *Sovetskaya Rossiya*'s retelling of Kalakani's demise two years later, and presenting it as a recent victory over the *mujahideen*, suggested a paucity of official successes to publicize.

143. Halliday, "Revolution in Afghanistan," p. 28.

144. State Department, "The Kidnapping and Death"; Tass, 17 February 1979, in *FBIS/SU*, 22 February 1979, p. J1.

145. *New York Times*, 23 February 1979, p. 3.

146. State Department press briefing record, 23 July 1979. At the time of the April coup, there were about 1,000 Americans in Afghanistan, including embassy personnel and dependents, about 45 families of aid personnel, and 95 Peace Corps volunteers; see State Department briefing memorandum, "Situation in Afghanistan," 30 April 1978.

147. CRS, "Afghanistan," p. 3.

148. U.S. State Department, "Country Reports on Human Rights Practices," Washington, D.C., 1981, p. 935.

149. Kabul Radio, 30 March 1980, in *FBIS/SA*, 3 April 1980, pp. C2–3. A month before this

version was given, a Soviet propaganda radio for the Third World, Radio Peace and Progress, said Dubs was killed by CIA agents "for the sole purpose of placing the blame . . . on the Taraki government and using this as an excuse to break off diplomatic relations with Afghanistan and cancel all agreements of economic aid to the country"; broadcast 23 February 1980.

150. Interviews with U.S. officials.

151. *New York Times*, 16 April 1979, p. 1. Some reports of these training camps said Chinese army instructors were involved, and this became a standard Soviet accusation. Ulyanovskiy, "The Afghan Revolution," in *USSR Report*, no. 1279, 20 July 1982, p. 12, says that "With the help of Beijing, in January 1979 an attempt was made to unite the scattered groups of Afghan pro-Maoists. Their congress which was held illegally in Herat defined the overthrow of the government of the [DRA] as a program task." This apparently referred to *Shu'la-ya-Jawed*, *Setem-i-Melli*, and other splinter groups. Another Soviet publication said in 1982 that "Numerous underground pro-Maoist groups planted and directed by Beijing have stepped up their subversive actions." One was identified as *Shu'la-ya-Jawed* and another was an "Organization for the Liberation of the People of Afghanistan" that seems to have been the same as, or linked with, *Setem-i-Melli*. See *Za Rubezhom*, no. 30 for 1982, pp. 12–13, in *FBIS/SU*, 29 July 1982, pp. D1–3.

152. *The Guardian*, undated, in Afghan Council *Newsletter*, January 1980; *The Economist*, 19 May 1979, p. 78. There were unconfirmed reports that Soviet pilots bombed and strafed the Afghan army's mutinous 17th Division in Herat, but whether they were flying Afghan planes in their role as advisers, or Soviet air force units were called in, was not clear from these reports: see *Los Angeles Times*, 7 January 1980, p. 17.

153. *New York Times*, 19 and 22 March 1979, pp. 14 and 5, and 13 June 1979, p. 11; *DRA Annual*, 1979, pp. 1,316–17.

154. *FBIS Trends*, 20 June 1979, p. 8.

155. *DRA Annual*, 1979, pp. 593–99 and 619.

156. *Kabul Times*, 16 May 1979, in Afghan Council *Newsletter*, 3 June 1979.

157. Interviews with Western intelligence specialists.

158. *Washington Post*, 28 March and 10 May 1979, pp. A16 and A33; *New York Times*, 4 May 1979, p. 7.

159. *The Economist*, 4 August 1979, p. 44; *Washington Post*, 9 October 1979, p. A1.

160. *Krasnaya Zvezda*, 25 April 1979, p. 3, in *FBIS/SU*, 1 May 1979, pp. D1–3.

161. Ulyanovskiy, "The Afghan Revolution," in *USSR Report*, No. 1279, 20 July 1982, pp. 13–14.

162. *Krasnaya Zvezda*, 25 April 1979, p. 3, in *FBIS/SU*, 1 May 1979, pp. D1–3.

163. *FBIS Trends*, 11 April 1979, p. 30; "The USSR Shows Concern Over Afghanistan," *Radio Liberty Research*, RL92/79, 20 March 1979.

164. *FBIS Trends*, 6 and 13 June 1979, pp. 8–10 and 7–8.

165. Moscow Radio, 11 June 1979, in *FBIS/SU*, 14 June 1979, p. D1.

166. *Pravda*, 31 December 1979, in *FBIS/SU*, 31 December 1979, pp. D7–10.

167. Information on Safronchuk from U.S. officials who monitored his work through diplomatic and intelligence reports.

168. *New York Times*, 2 August 1979, p. 10; *Washington Post*, 10 May 1979, p. A43.

169. *FBIS Trends*, 18 July and 1 August 1979, pp. 3–4 and 4.

170. *Far Eastern Economic Review*, 23 January 1981, pp. 28–29.

171. State Department briefing memorandum, "Soviet–Afghan Relations: Is Moscow's Patience Wearing Thin?," 24 May 1979.

172. Ibid.

173. *Kabul Times*, 5 May 1979, in Amnesty International, "Violations of Human Rights," p. 5.

174. Dastarac and Levant, "What Went Wrong."

175. Telegram no. 5470, U.S. Embassy, Kabul, date unclear (probably 31 July or 1 August 1979), as relayed by State Department telegram no. 199533 to U.S. Embassy, Canberra, on 1 August 1979.

176. *FBIS Trends*, 1 August 1979, p. 4; Tass from Kabul, 28 July 1979, in *FBIS/SU*, 30 July 1979, p. D1.

177. Telegram no. 5470, U.S. Embassy, Kabul (see note 175 on dating). Quotations are from the telegram, not direct words of the source. The non-Pushtun ministers named by the source as members of an anti-Amin alignment were Abdul Karim Misaq, finance, a Hazara; Abdul Hakim Sharaie, justice, an Uzbek; Dastagir Panjshiri, public works, a Tajik; and Mohammed Hassan Bareq Shafi'i, information and culture, also Tajik. The embassy noted that there were other non-Pushtun ministers who were not named, such as Abdul Qudus Ghorbandi, commerce, Tajik, and Mohammand Ismail Danesh, mines and industries, Kizilbash.

178. Telegram no. 6605, U.S. Embassy, Kabul, 2 September 1979.

179. Telegram no. 5470, U.S. Embassy, Kabul (see note 175 on dating).

180. Interviews with former diplomats in Kabul; telegram no. 7784, U.S. Embassy, Kabul, 30 October 1979.

181. Telegram no. 6959, U.S. Embassy, Kabul, 18 September 1979.

182. Telegram no. 6605, U.S. Embassy, Kabul, 2 September 1979.

183. Ibid.

184. *Washington Post*, 9 October 1979, p. A11; Dastarac and Levant, "What Went Wrong."

185. AFP from Peshawar, Pakistan, 4 February 1980, in *FBIS/ME*, 4 February 1980, pp. S11-12.

186. *The Economist*, 23 June 1979, p. 70.

187. Western intelligence officials who declined to be identified.

188. *New York Times*, 6 September 1979, p. 2; House of Commons, "Afghanistan."

189. *The Economist*, 11 August 1979, p. 53; *Washington Post*, 7 August 1979, p. A13.

190. Kabul Radio, 10 September 1979, in *FBIS/ME*, 12 September 1979, pp. S4-5.

191. *New York Times*, 20 September 1979, p. 10; *The Economist*, 25 August 1979.

192. Moscow Radio, 16 August 1979, in *FBIS/SU*, 20 August 1979, p. D2.

193. Moscow Radio, 17 August 1979, in *FBIS/SU*, 20 August 1979, p. D4.

194. *FBIS Trends*, 22 August 1979, pp. 7-9.

195. Telegram no. 6606, U.S. Embassy, Kabul, 2 September 1979.

Chapter 6. Amin's Hundred Days

1. Havana Television, 5 September 1979, in *FBIS/Latin America*, 11 September 1979, pp. AA3-10.

2. Tass from Moscow 10 September 1979, in *FBIS/SU*, 12 September 1979, p. D1.

3. Tass from Moscow, 11 September 1979, in *FBIS/SU*, 12 September 1979, p. D4.

4. Ibid.; Kabul Radio, 10 and 11 September 1979, in *FBIS/ME*, 11 and 12 September 1979, p. S2.

5. Feroz Ahmed in *MERIP Reports*, 89 (July-August 1980); 16; *The Economist*, 22 September 1979, p. 60.

6. Dastarac and Levant, "What Went Wrong."

7. Ibid.

8. Moscow Television, 26 January 1980, in *FBIS/SU*, 5 February 1980, p. A7.

9. Reported by diplomats who were given an account of Brezhnev's remarks by the visitor on condition that they not identify him.

10. Kabul Radio, 11 September 1979, in *FBIS/ME*, 12 September 1979, p. S3. On the cult of personality, see *Washington Post*, 11 June 1979, p. A21, and Kabul Radio, 4 September 1979, in *FBIS/ME*, 7 September 1979, p. S2.

11. Kabul Radio, 11 September 1979, in *FBIS/ME*, 12 September 1979, p. S3.

12. *The Economist*, 22 September 1979, p. 60.

13. Interviews with Asian officials who declined to be identified.

14. Kabul Radio, 14 September 1979, in *FBIS/ME*, 15 September 1979, p. S1.

15. Dastarac and Levant, "What Went Wrong"; *The Economist*, 22 September 1979, p. 60; interviews with diplomats then in Kabul; telegram no. 7784, U.S. Embassy, Kabul, 30 October 1979.

16. Dastarac and Levant, "What Went Wrong"; interviews with diplomats then in Kabul.

17. Telegram no. 6914, U.S. Embassy, Kabul, 16 September 1979.

18. Kabul Radio, 8 December 1979, in *FBIS/ME*, 11 December 1979, pp. S1-6.

19. Dastarac and Levant, "What Went Wrong"; interviews with diplomats then in Kabul. Taraki was initially reported to have been killed in the gunbattle, a report probably at least partially based on his disappearance from official mention.

20. Telegram no. 6936, U.S. Embassy, Kabul, 17 September 1979.

21. Telegram no. 6959, U.S. Embassy, Kabul, 18 September 1979.

22. Kabul Radio, 16 September 1979, in *FBIS/ME*, 17 September 1979, pp. S1-2.

23. Telegram no. 6914, U.S. Embassy, Kabul, 16 September 1979.

24. Kabul Radio, 16 September 1979, in *FBIS/ME*, 17 September 1979, pp. S1-2.

25. Tanjug from Kabul, 2 November 1979, in *FBIS/ME*, 6 November 1979, pp. S2-3; *Washington Post*, 9 October 1979, p. A11; telegram no. 7428, U.S. Embassy, Kabul, 11 October 1979.

26. Kabul Radio, 16 September 1979, in *FBIS/ME*, 17 September 1979, pp. S1-2.

27. Kabul Radio, 17 September 1979, in *FBIS/ME*, 18 September 1979, p. S6; Karachi Radio, 17 September 1979, in *FBIS/ME*, 18 September 1979, p. S6.

28. *New York Times*, 17 September 1979; telegrams nos. 6936, 7502, and 7784, U.S. Embassy, Kabul, 17 September, 15 and 30 October 1979.

29. Kabul Radio, 14 September 1979, in *FBIS/ME*, 19 September 1979, pp. S5-7.

30. Kabul Radio, 17 and 18 September 1979, in *FBIS/ME*, 18 and 25 September 1979, pp. S1-5 and S5-10.

31. Kabul Radio, 26 September 1979, in *FBIS/ME*, 27 September 1979, pp. S1-5.

32. *Kabul Times*, 10 October 1979, in Afghan Council *Newsletter*, 1 January 1980.

33. Tass from Kabul, 5, 14, and 18 January 1980, in *FBIS/SU*, 7, 15, and 21 January 1980, pp. D3, D4 and D8-9.

34. Kabul Radio, 8 June 1980, in *FBIS/SA*, 9 June 1980, pp. C2-3.

35. *FBIS Trends*, 19 September 1979, pp. 6-7.

36. Tass from Kabul, 16 and 17 September 1979, in *FBIS/SU*, 17 September 1979, p. D1; Moscow Radio, 17 September 1979, in *FBIS/SU*, 18 and 19 September 1979, pp. D1-2.

37. Kabul Radio, 17 September 1979, in *FBIS/ME*, 18 September 1979, p. S5.

38. *Pravda*, 18 September 1979, p. 1, in *FBIS/SU*, 19 September 1979, p. D1.

39. Moscow Radio, 21 September 1979, in *FBIS/SU*, 21 September 1979, pp. D1-2.

40. *Izvestiya*, 21 September 1979, in *FBIS/SU*, 25 September 1979, p. D2.

41. *Washington Star*, 19 September 1979, p. 2.

42. *Washington Post*, 2 January 1980, p. A2.

43. State Department press briefing record, 19 September 1979.

44. *FBIS Trends*, 3 October 1979, pp. 15-16.

45. Telegrams nos. 7444 and 7784, U.S. Embassy, Kabul, 11 and 30 October 1979; House of Commons, "Afghanistan," p. 42; *The Economist*, 3 November 1979, pp. 52-53. Safronchuk reportedly asked Wali how he knew Watanjar was at the Soviet embassy, and Wali replied that Watanjar had telephoned the Kabul military commander from there; see telegram no. 7444. Safronchuk later told diplomats in Kabul that Puzanov's role on 14 September had been an effort to preserve peace between warring factions of the PDPA; see telegram no. 7784. Nayar, *Report on Afghanistan*, p. 43, says that Amin did in fact accept a Soviet invitation to visit Moscow. On a brief visit "in early December," Nayar says, Amin was kissed on both cheeks by Brezhnev and treated as a comrade. Amin "began to imagine" that the Soviets "had adopted him," and "his suspicion that the Russians wanted to eliminate him receded into the background." This reported trip lacks confirmation, seems inconsistent with the available facts, and should be treated with extreme skepticism.

46. *The Economist*, 3 November 1979, pp. 52-53.

47. Kabul Radio, 19 November 1979, in *FBIS/ME*, 20 November 1979, p. S4.

48. Kabul Radio, 1 December 1979, in *FBIS/ME*, 3 December 1979, p. S1.

49. Interviews with Western specialists on Soviet affairs.

50. Kabul Radio, 6 November 1979, in *FBIS/ME*, 7 November 1979, pp. S1-3.

51. Telegrams nos. 7726 and 8117, U.S. Embassy, Kabul, 28 October and 21 November 1979.

52. Kabul Radio, 7 November 1979, in *FBIS/ME*, 9 November 1979, pp. S1-3.

53. *FBIS Trends*, 28 March 1979, p. 7.

54. Tass, 8 December 1980, in *FBIS/SU*, 8 December 1980, p. D8.

55. Kabul Radio, 7 November 1979, in *FBIS/ME*, 9 November 1979, p. S3.

56. Mirmukhsin, "Chadrali ayal" ["Woman in Chador"], *Sharq yulduzi* 10 (1979) described by James Critchlow, "Afghan Revolutionary Leaders as Viewed by Soviet Publication in Tashkent," *Radio Liberty Research*, RL 21/80, 10 January 1980.

57. Kabul Radio, 18 September 1979, in *FBIS/ME*, 25 September 1979, pp. S5-10.

58. *Strategic Mid-East & Africa*, 5 (7 November 1979): 6, as quoted by Mark Heller, "The Soviet Invasion of Afghanistan," *The Washington Quarterly*, 3 (Summer 1980): 39.

59. Kabul Radio, 23 September 1979, and subsequent days, in *FBIS/ME*, 24 September 1979, and subsequent, pp. S4 and other S-section pages.

60. *Kabul New Times* (the *Kabul Times* renamed by the Karmal regime), 3 January 1980, in Afghan Council *Newsletter*, 2 March 1980.

61. *Kabul Times*, 10 October 1979, in Afghan Council *Newsletter*, 1 January 1980.

62. *Kabul Times*, 18 November 1979, in Afghan Council *Newsletter*, 1 January 1980; Kabul Radio, 20 November 1979, in *FBIS/ME*, 21 November 1979, pp. S1-2.

63. *Turkmenskaya Iskra*, 9 December 1979, p. 4, in *FBIS/SU*, 20 December 1979, p. D1.

64. *FBIS Trends*, 3 October 1979, p. 15; *Asian/Pacific Population Program News*, Bangkok, undated.

65. *Kabul New Times*, 3 January 1980, in Afghan Council *Newsletter*, 2 March 1980.

66. *New York Times*, 9 October 1979, p. 8.

67. *New York Times*, 17 October 1979, p. 10; *The Economist*, 3 November 1979, pp. 52–53.

68. AFP from Islamabad, 13 December 1979, in *FBIS/ME*, 14 December 1979, p. S1.

69. *Amnesty International Report 1980* (London, 1980), p. 177; interviews with diplomats formerly in Kabul; Dupree, "Red Flag Over the Hindu Kush, Part 6: Repressions, or Security Through Terror," *AUFS/A*, 29, 9 (1980).

70. Telegram no. 7218, U.S. Embassy, Kabul, 27 September 1979.

71. Moscow Radio, 26 January 1980, in *FBIS/SU*, 28 January 1980, p. D2.

72. *Der Spiegel*, 31 March 1980, pp. 139–46, in *FBIS/SA*, 2 April 1980, pp. C1–9.

73. Kabul Radio, 9 January 1980, in *FBIS/ME*, 10 January 1980, pp. S3–4.

74. Kabul Radio, 18 June 1980, in *FBIS/SA*, 20 June 1980, C1–5; *Der Spiegel*, 31 March 1980, pp. 139–46, in *FBIS/SA*, 2 April 1980, pp. C1–9.

75. Kabul Radio, 21 December 1980, in *FBIS/SA*, 23 December 1980, pp. C2–3.

76. State Department, "Country Reports," p. 930.

77. *Amnesty International Report 1980*, p. 179.

78. Telegram no. 7876, U.S. Embassy, Kabul, 6 November 1979. This reports that, among other gestures, Amin had "a tame group of religious figures . . . declare him 'olelamar' . . . a secular leader who rules through the authority of Allah," whose commands "have the force of divine sanction." Taraki had been so designated shortly before his downfall.

79. Interview with senior Asian official who declined to be identified.

80. Kabul Radio, 17 September 1979, in *FBIS/ME*, 18 September 1979, pp. S1–5.

81. Kabul Radio, 8 and 15 November, 10 and 16 December 1979, in *FBIS/ME*, 14 and 20 November 12 and 16 December 1979, pp. S1–5.

82. Interview with senior Asian official who declined to be identified.

83. *Indian Express* (New Delhi), 13 February 1980, p. 6, in *FBIS/ME*, 21 February 1980, pp. S1–2.

84. Telegram no. 282436, Secretary of State, Washington, D.C., to U.S. Embassy, Islamabad, 29 October 1979. It said the State Department's "conclusion [was] that at the maximum we regard our current dialogue with the Afghans as a means of exploring the possibilities for a less contentious relationship, and we are not overly sanguine that even this limited objective can be sustained." See also exchange between the State Department and Chargé Blood in telegrams nos. 275088 from Washington and 7645 from Kabul, 22 and 23 October 1979. There is nothing in the telegrams made public during the first few years after the Communists came to power in Afghanistan to substantiate speculations that the United States tried, or even hoped, to lure Amin away from the Soviets and take him under U.S. influence; for an example of such speculations, see K. P. Misra, ed., *Afghanistan in Crisis* (New Delhi, 1981), p. 13.

85. "A Chronology of Soviet Afghan Relations: April 1978–January 1980," *Radio Liberty Research*, RL 17/80, 2 January 1980; the estimates of Soviet personnel in Afghanistan in the autumn of 1979 are those made by the U.S. government. Other estimates run significantly higher.

86. *The Economist*, 17 November 1979, pp. 68–69; AFP from Islamabad, 8 November 1979, in *FBIS/ME*, 9 November 1979, pp. S1–2.

87. International Institute for Strategic Studies, *Strategic Survey, 1979*, London, 1980, pp. 50–52.

88. Interviews with Western officials.

89. U.S. State Department, "Chronology of Recent Developments Related to Afghanistan," 1980.

90. Tass, 4 December 1979, in *FBIS/SU*, 11 December 1979, p. D3.

91. *Pravda*, 7 December 1979, p. 5, in *FBIS/SU*, 11 December 1979, p. D1.

92. *Pravda*, 7 December 1979, p. 1, in *FBIS/SU*, 11 December 1979, pp. D1–2.

93. *FBIS Trends*, 19 December 1979, pp. 3–4.

94. *Pravda*, 7 December 1979, p. 1, in *FBIS/SU*, 11 December 1979, p. D2.

95. *FBIS Trends*, 19 December 1979, pp. 3–4.

Chapter 7. The Correlation of Forces

1. *U.S. Department of State Bulletin*, 26 June 1972.

2. Tass, 7 October 1977, in *FBIS/SU*, Supplement 10, 14 October 1977, pp. 6–7.

3. *Pravda*, 21 February 1980, p. 2, in *FBIS/SU*, 26 February 1980, p. R10.

4. Moscow Radio, 24 February 1976, in *FBIS/SU*, Supplement 16, 25 February 1976, p. 15 (which translates Brezhnev's "correlation of forces" as "balance of forces").

5. *Pravda*, 14 February 1980, p. 2, in *FBIS/SU*, 19 February 1980, p. R3. For a general discussion of the correlation of forces concept as it applied in the early 1980s, see Vernon V. Aspaturian "Soviet Global Power and the Correlation of Forces," *Problems of Communism* 29 (May-June 1980): 1−18.

6. *Pravda*, 17 October 1980, p. 2, in *FBIS/SU*, 21 October 1980, p. D4.

7. International Institute for Strategic Studies, *The Military Balance 1980−1981*, (London, 1980), p. 13.

8. Permanent Select Committee on Intelligence, U.S. House of Representatives, "CIA Estimates of Soviet Defense Spending," Washington, D.C., 1980, pp. 6 and 28; Committee on Armed Services, U.S. Senate, "Soviet Defense Expenditures and Related Programs," Washington, D.C., 1980, p. 4.

9. Abraham Becker, "The Meaning and Measure of Soviet Military Expenditures," in Joint Economic Committee, U.S. Congress, *Soviet Economy in a Time of Change* (Washington, 1979), p. 359.

10. John M. Collins, *U.S.-Soviet Military Balance: Concepts and Capabilities, 1960−1980* (Washington, 1980), p. 84, note 20.

11. Permanent Select Committee on Intelligence, U.S. House of Representatives, "CIA Estimates of Soviet Defense Spending," Washington, D.C., 1980, pp. 6 and 28.

12. Ibid. See also Max Beloff, "The Military Factor in Soviet Foreign Policy," *Problems of Communism* 30 (January-February 1981): 70−73.

13. William F. Scott and Harriet Fast Scott, "Soviet Projection of Military Presence and Power, Vol. II, A Review and Assessment of Soviet Policy and Concepts on the Projections of Military Presence and Power" (McLean, Va., 1979), p. xiii; Andrew Marshall, "Sources of Soviet Power: The Military Potential in the 1980s," in *Adelphi Papers*, no. 152, "Prospects of Soviet Power in the 1980s, Part II" (London, 1979), pp. 12−13.

14. Ibid.

15. Collins, *U.S.-Soviet Military Balance*, pp. 34, 37−38, 274, 509−13, 527−30, and 532−33.

16. Ibid.

17. The 1943 withdrawal from Sinkiang was a special wartime case with political overtones.

18. Scott and Scott, "Soviet Projection of Military Presence."

19. G. A. Fedorov et al., *Marxism-Leninism on War and the Army* (Moscow, 1961, 1968, and 1977 editions), quoted by Scott and Scott, "Soviet Projection," pp. 9, 45−47.

20. N. N. Inozemtsev, *International Relations After the Second World War* (Moscow, 1965), quoted by Scott and Scott, "Soviet Projection," pp. 11−12.

21. Fedorov, *Marxism-Leninism on War*, in Scott and Scott, "Soviet Projection," pp. 45−47.

22. Ibid.

23. Grechko quoted by Scott and Scott, "Soviet Projection," p. 5, with the latter quote from "The Leading Role of the CPSU in Building the Army of a Developed Socialist Society," in *Problems of History of the CPSU* (Moscow, May 1974) (emphasis added by the current author).

24. V. M. Kulish, ed., *Military Force and International Relations* (Moscow, 1972; English edition, Arlington, 1973), p. 103 (emphasis added).

25. V. Servriannikov and M. Iasiukov, "Peaceful Coexistence and Defense of the Socialist Fatherland," in *Kommunist Voorushennykh Sil* (August 1972): 15−16, quoted by Avigdor Haselkorn, "The 'External Function' of Soviet Armed Forces," *Naval War College Review* 33 (January−February 1980): 35−45.

26. A. I. Sorokin, ed., *V. I. Lenin on the Defense of the Socialist Fatherland* (Moscow, 1977), quoted by Scott and Scott, "Soviet Projection," p. 76 (emphasis added by author).

27. Editorial in *Krasnaya Zvezda*, 15 March 1980, p. 1, in *FBIS/SU*, 21 March 1980, p. V1.

28. Mikhail S. Kapitsa, *KNR: Dva Desiatiletiia-dve Politiki* (Moscow, 1969), cited in Stephen S. Kaplan, *Diplomacy of Power: Soviet Armed Forces as a Political Instrument* (Washington, 1981), pp. 331−32. It is worth noting that, while no more than 2,000 Russians fought with the republican Loyalists in Spain, Stalin managed to be paid for his shipments of military equipment to the Loyalists, whereas other foreign involvement in the civil war seems to have been at the expense of the intervening power, especially Nazi Germany and Fascist Italy on the Falange side. This parallels the 1960s and 1970s Soviet practice of insuring payment for military aid whenever possible but providing little or no economic aid. See Hugh Thomas, *The Spanish Civil War* (London, 1965), pp. 795−97.

29. Scott and Scott, "Soviet Projection", pp. 70−71.

30. Ibid., p. vi.

31. The growing Soviet emphasis on its armed forces' role outside the socialist community was accompanied in the 1970s by a rewriting of treaties linking the Soviet Union to its East European allies.

The purpose was to extend the allies' responsibility to provide military support for the Soviet Union outside the Warsaw Pact area. The new concept included a joint defense of the entire socialist community—whatever that was defined to be at any time. This was resisted by some East European countries, especially Romania. Although Afghanistan was in a few Soviet references indicated to be a socialist country—see chapter 5—it was unclear whether East Europeans had any obligation to help protect it from the alleged outside attacks. Up to two years and more after the Soviet invasion, none of the Soviet Union's allies had been reliably reported to have sent military personnel there, although some did contribute military equipment, medical aid, and other help. On the basis of the known Soviet coercion of East European countries to provide aid for North Vietnam in the mid-1960s, this help can be presumed to have been a requirement of "proletarian internationalism" set by Moscow. On the treaty rewriting, see Avigdor Haselkorn, "The Expanding Soviet Collective Security Network," in *Strategic Review* (Summer 1978): 64.

32. Yepishev, *V. I Lenin on the Defense*, quoted by the Scotts, "Soviet Projection," pp. 74–75.

33. *Pravda*, 26 September 1968, p. 4, in *Current Digest of the Soviet Press*, 16 October 1978, Vol. XX, No. 39, pp. 10–12.

34. *Pravda*, 13 November 1968, pp. 1–2, in ibid., Vol. XX, No. 46, pp. 3–5.

35. And perhaps Cuba, too. A number of American specialists concluded after the 1979 excitement about a Soviet brigade in Cuba—discussed below—that its primary purpose probably was to serve as an emergency praetorian guard for the Communist regime in Havana, protecting it against any indigenous attempt to oust it. The brigade might be able to hold long enough for more Soviet soldiers to be flown in.

36. *Novoye Vremya*, 18 January 1980, pp. 8–10, in *FBIS/SU*, 23 January 1980, pp. BB1–5.

37. Bovin, "Apropos the Afghan Revolution." This 15 April 1980 article that "Non-interference is a good thing" was paraphrased in a letter signed by Borin and Yevgeniy Primakov to the Italian Communist Party newspaper *L'Unita*, which had criticized the Afghan intervention. The letter concluded that "There are exceptional situations, when non-interference becomes shameful and a betrayal. Such situations demand extraordinary solutions and the courage to adopt them." *L'Unita*, 25 April 1980, quoted in *Soviet World Outlook* 5, 6 (15 June 1980): 4.

38. *Pravda*, 14 February 1980, p. 2, in *FBIS/SU*, 19 February 1980, p. R4.

39. *Novoye Vremya*, no. 17, April 1980, quoted in *Soviet World Outlook* 5, 6 (15 June 1980): 4–5.

40. Kaplan, *Diplomacy of Power*, pp. 27–46, 689–93. The incidents listed by Kaplan do not include the Soviet and Communist allies' involvement in the June 1978 change of government in the People's Democratic Republic of [South] Yemen, which might be variously counted as fitting into all three categories of preserving fraternal Communist regimes, or else categorized as an expansion of Soviet authority, depending on how the regime before June 1978 is viewed.

41. *Izvestiya*, 6 February 1980, p. 5, in *FBIS/SU*, 8 February 1980, p. A4.

42. Kulish, *Military Force*, p. 105 of English edition.

43. *Izvestiya*, 6 February 1975, quoted by Dimitri K. Simes, "The Death of Détente?," *International Security*, 5 (Summer 1980): 10.

44. Henry A. Kissinger, *The White House Years* (Boston, 1979), p. 1,250.

45. Moscow Radio, 24 February 1976, in *FBIS/SU*, Supplement 16, 25 February 1976, pp. 27–28. The unidentified critics of Brezhnev were described as "leftist opportunists," a term of opprobrium since Lenin's time, in a later Soviet article that paraphrased his argument; see A. S. Milovidov and Ye. A. Zhdanov, "Sociophilosophical Problems of War and Peace," *Voprosy Filosofii*, 10 (1980): 32–51, in *FBIS/SU Annex*, 17 December 1980, p. 3.

46. Nathaniel Davis, "The Angola Decision of 1975: A Personal Memoir," *Foreign Affairs* 57 (Fall 1978): 109–24; Neil C. Livingstone and Manfred von Nordheim, "The United States Congress and the Angola Crisis," *Strategic Review* (Spring 1977): 34–44.

47. Colin Legum, "Angola and the Horn of Africa," in Kaplan, *Diplomacy of Power*, pp. 591–96; testimony of David D. Newsom, undersecretary of state for political affairs, before the U.S. House subcommittee on African affairs, 18 October 1979.

48. Scott and Scott, "Soviet Projection," p. ix. The Soviet attitude toward Third World clients was shown by Moscow's purchase of Angolan coffee, which is particularly prized by makers of instant coffee, at 15 percent below the world price of the 1976 crop and 30 percent below the 1977 crop price, then reselling it in world markets, thus diverting to the Soviet Union hard-currency earnings needed by Angola.

49. *New York Times*, 3 October 1977, p. 1 (a summary of the situation; see other dates for the running story).

50. Legum, "Angola and the Horn of Africa," pp. 610–37.

51. *Public Papers of the Presidents: Jimmy Carter, 1978* (Washington, 1979), p. 442.

52. FCO, "Ethiopia: Problems for the USSR" (London, 1980). Haile Selassie had thriftily accumulated considerable foreign exchange reserves; the Soviet Union quickly cleaned these out in return for military equipment. This left the Ethiopian government with major economic problems as a number of insurrections in Mengistu's empire of disparate ethnic and cultural groups disrupted the economy. As other countries found, Moscow was happy to sell weapons but refused to provide meaningful amounts of economic aid.

53. FCO, "PDRY (South Yemen); Soviet Client State in the Arab World" (London, 1980); Charles T. Creekman, Jr., "Sino-Soviet Competition in the Yemens," *Naval War College Review* 32 (June–July 1979): 80.

54. Ibid.

55. FCO, "PDRY"; J. B. Kelly, "East & West: The Road to Kabul: The Kremlin and the Gulf," *Encounter* 54 (April 1980): 84–90; *FBIS Trends*, 19 September 1979, p. 9.

56. Ibid.

57. *FBIS Trends*, 31 October 1979, p. 21.

58. House of Commons, "Afghanistan," p. 5.

59. FCO, "PDRY".

60. *Pravda*, 1 March 1979, p. 2, in *FBIS/SU*, 2 March 1979, p. R26.

61. Interviews with senior American officials directly involved in relations with the Soviet Union, who declined to be identified.

62. *New York Times*, 2 October 1979, p. 1.

63. *New York Times*, 3 October 1979, p. 1.

64. Interviews with American officials.

65. Ibid.; *FBIS Trends*, 15 November through 12 December 1979, pp. 1ff.

Chapter 8. The View from the Kremlin

1. State Department Press Briefing Record, 23 March 1979.

2. House of Commons, "Afghanistan," p. xxxiv.

3. *New York Times*, 3 August 1979, p. 1.

4. Interviews with senior U.S. officials who were personally involved with the warnings but declined to be identified by name.

5. *Washington Post*, 2 January 1981, p. A14.

6. U.S. House subcommittee on Europe and the Middle East, "East-West Relations in the Aftermath of Soviet Invasion of Afghanistan" (Washington, 1980), p. 117.

7. *Pravda*, 13 January 1980, p. 1, in *FBIS/SU*, 14 January 1980, pp. A1–6.

8. Moscow Television, 26 January 1980, in *FBIS/SU*, 5 February 1980, pp. A1–11.

9. House of Commons, "Afghanistan," pp. 37–38.

10. House subcommittee, "East-West Relations," pp. 30, 33–34, and 117–19.

11. *Washington Star*, 19 September 1979, p. A-2.

12. The six meetings were on 4, 8, 11, 15, 17, and 27 December 1979.

13. House subcommittee, "East-West Relations," pp. 111–13, 119.

14. House of Commons, "Afghanistan," p. xxxv.

15. *Washington Star*, 21 and 23 December 1979, p. A-1.

16. Tass from Kabul, 6 December 1980, in *FBIS/SU*, 8 December 1980, p. D12; Moscow Radio, 8 January 1980, in *FBIS/SU*, 9 January 1980, p. D11; *Pravda*, 14 and 19 January 1980, pp. 6 and 4, in *FBIS/SU*, 16 and 21 January 1980, pp. D10–12 and A1–5.

17. NHK Television, Tokyo, 14 January 1980, in *FBIS/ME*, 15 January 1980, p. S3.

18. Ulyanovskiy, "The Afghan Revolution," in *USSR Report*, no. 1279, 20 July 1982, p. 14.

19. Ibid., pp. 15 and 17.

20. *Fifty Years of the Soviet Union's Armed Might* (Moscow, 1968), pp. 219, 221, 229, 233.

21. *Pravda*, 31 December 1979, in *FBIS/SU*, 31 December 1979, pp. D7–10.

22. *Pravda*, 3 January 1980, in *FBIS/SU*, 4 January 1980, pp. D2–3.

23. *Pravda*, 13 January 1980, p. 1, in *FBIS/SU*, 14 January 1980, pp. A1–6.

24. Tass, 23 June 1980, in *FBIS/SU*, 24 June 1980, p. R4.

25. Ibid., p. R7.

26. *Pravda*, 21 February 1981, p. 2, in *FBIS/SU*, 23 February 1981, pp. V1–5; Moscow Television, 26 January and 1 June 1980, in *FBIS/SU*, 5 February and 2 June 1980, pp. A1–11 and CC10;

Moscow Radio, 2 January and 18 February 1980, in *FBIS/SU*, 3 January and 19 February 1980, pp. D8 and R6–13.

27. *Kommunist Tadzhikistana* (Dushanbe), 31 October 1980, p. 2, in *FBIS/SU*, 12 November 1980, pp. R3–5; FCO, "Soviet Attitude to Muslim Believers" (London, 1981).

28. *Turkmenskaya Iskra* (Ashkhabad), 13 November 1979, and 17 January 1981, pp. 2–5, in *FBIS/SU*, 27 November 1979, and 12 February 1981, pp. F2–5 and R16.

29. *Bakinskiy Rabochiy* (Baku) 19 December 1980, p. 3, in *FBIS/SU*, 7 January 1981, pp. R1–3.

30. Dupree, "Red Flag Over the Hindu Kush, Part V," p. 10.

31. "Early Retirement of Foreign Minister of the Kirgiz SSR," *Radio Liberty Research*, RL 152/80, 1980.

32. *Moskovskaya Pravda*, 6 February 1980, pp. 2–3, in *FBIS/SU*, 14 February 1980, p. R22.

33. *Pravda*, 13 January 1980, p. 1, in *FBIS/SU*, 14 January 1980, pp. A1–6.

34. Text of Chervonenko's speech to the International Diplomatic Academy, Paris, in French, obtained privately.

35. Kulish, *Military Force*, p. 98 in English edition.

36. *Pravda*, 13 January 1980, p. 1, in *FBIS/SU*, 14 January 1980, pp. A1–6.

37. House of Commons, "Afghanistan," p. 35, and also pp. 24–25, 81, 86.

38. Budget Committee, U.S. Senate, hearings record, 26 February 1980, pp. 5, 10, 37, also pp. 182–83.

39. Craig Whitney, "The View from the Kremlin," *New York Times Magazine* (20 April 1980): 32.

40. Robert C. Tucker, "Swollen State, Spent Society: Stalin's Legacy to Brezhnev's Russia," *Foreign Affairs* 60 (Winter 1981/82): 429.

41. Moscow Television, 26 January 1980, in *FBIS/SU*, 5 February 1980, pp. A1–11; *Pravda*, 6 January and 3 March 1980, pp. 4 and 6, in *FBIS/SU*, 8 January and 5 March 1980, pp. A4–8 and A1–6; Tass, 28 January 1980, in *FBIS/SU*, 29 January 1980, pp. A1–5; *Krasnaya Zvezda*, 26 February 1980, p. 1, in *FBIS/SU*, 7 March 1980, pp. CC1–2; Moscow Radio, 6 January, 25 February, 9 June, and 14 July 1980, in *FBIS/SU*, 7 January, 25 February, 10 June, and 15 July 1980, pp. C1–8, R5, and A1–4.

42. *FBIS Trends*, 14 and 21 June, 30 August, and 27 September 1978.

43. Moscow Television, 31 May 1980, in *FBIS/SU*, 9 June 1980, p. CC14.

44. *FBIS Trends*, 7 June 1978.

45. International Institute for Strategic Studies, "Strategic Survey 1979," p. 100.

46. Legum, "Angola and the Horn of Africa," pp. 620–22.

47. Interviews with Western officials and scholars.

48. *Washington Post*, 20 August 1980, p. A2.

49. A key Soviet affairs specialist of the Carter administration who was interviewed on the condition that he not be identified.

50. Tass, 27 November 1979, in *FBIS/SU*, 28 November 1979, pp. R1–3.

51. Moscow Radio, 28 November 1979, in *FBIS/SU*, 29 November 1979, pp. R1–13.

52. EFE news agency from Moscow, 10 January 1980, in *FBIS/SU*, 11 January 1980, pp. D9–11.

53. For a study of the 1968 decision, see Jiři Valenta, *Soviet Intervention in Czechoslovakia, 1968: Anatomy of a Decision* (Baltimore, 1979).

54. *Pravda*, 14 May 1957, quoted by Valenta, *Soviet Intervention*, p. 140 and notes 63 and 65, p. 186.

55. *Pravda*, 13 January 1980, p. 1, in *FBIS/SU*, 14 January 1980, pp. A1–6.

56. Moscow Radio, 22 March 1980, in *FBIS/SU*, 25 March 1980, pp. D1–2.

57. Paris Radio, 18 January 1980, in FBIS, *Daily Report, West Europe*, 21 January 1980, p. K1.

58. *Asahi Shimbun*, 8 March 1980, quoted in Jiri Valenta, "From Prague to Kabul: the Soviet Style of Invasion," *International Security*, 5, (Fall 1980): 127.

59. Moscow Radio, 23 February 1981, in *FBIS/SU Supplement*, 24 February 1981, p. 47 (emphasis added).

60. Recounted to the author by a senior U.S. diplomat stationed in Moscow at the time, on condition that he not be identified. A leading Soviet dissident, Nobel Peace Prize winner Andrei D. Sakharov, said that "The Soviet policy makers may have decided that it was now or never" to influence the situation in Afghanistan because of deteriorating conditions there and the U.S. distraction in Iran; see *New York Times*, 3 January 1980, p. A13.

61. An examination of the speeches that Soviet leaders made in February 1980 during their unopposed campaigns for Supreme Soviet seats yields faint suggestions, but no real analytical evidence, of differences over the Afghanistan action. For instance, Ponomarev and Gromyko were more out-

spokenly defensive about it, while Suslov touched on it only briefly without explaining or defending it, and some politburo members ignored it. See *FBIS/SU* reports for the period.

Chapter 9. Invasion

1. Charles R. Bawden, *The Modern History of Mongolia* (London, 1968), p. 323.

2. Ulam, *Expansion & Coexistence*, pp. 289–92; Hugh Seton-Watson *From Lenin to Khrushchev: The History of World Communism* (New York, 1960), pp. 301–2.

3. FCO, "The Baltic States: 40 Years Under Soviet Rule" (London, 1980).

4. Ferenc A. Vali, *Rift and Revolt in Hungary: Nationalism versus Communism* (Cambridge, 1961), pp. 276–77, 363–79, 445; FCO, "Afghanistan: Soviet Occupation" (London, 1980); Ulam, *Expansion & Coexistence*, pp. 596–600.

5. H. Gordon Skilling, *Czechoslovakia's Interrupted Revolution* (Princeton, 1976), pp. 713–19; Harry Schwartz, *Prague's 200 Days: The Struggle for Democracy in Czechoslovakia* (New York, 1969), pp. 214–17; FCO, "Afghanistan: Soviet Occupation"; Donald R. Shanor, *Soviet Europe* (New York, 1975), p. 75; Valenta, *Soviet Intervention*, pp. 146 and 187.

6. *New York Times*, 4 December 1978, p. 1, and subsequent January 1979 accounts of Cambodian developments.

7. Kabul Radio, 10 September 1979, in *FBIS/ME*, 12 September 1979, p. S2.

8. Delhi Radio, 4 November 1979, in *FBIS/ME*, 5 November 1979, pp. S1–2; JPS (Japanese Press Service), Tokyo, 16 December 1980, in *FBIS/SA Annex*, 17 December 1980, p. 2.

9. *Izvestiya*, 1 January 1980, p. 4, in *FBIS/SU*, 4 January 1980, pp. D7–10; Moscow Radio, 22 March 1980, in *FBIS/SU*, 25 March 1980, p. D1; Tass, 23 April 1980, in *FBIS/SU*, 24 April 1980, p. D1; AFP from Islamabad, 28 September 1980, in *FBIS/SU*, 1 October 1980, p. D6; Kabul Radio, 11 May 1981, in *FBIS/SA*, 12 May 1981, pp. C1–4.

10. See the same references in footnote 9, above. Karmal said on 10 January 1980 that Amin did not ask for Soviet troops; on 11 May 1981, he said Amin did; see Kabul Radio, 11 January 1980, and 11 May 1981, in *FBIS/ME*, 14 January 1980, p. S5, and *FBIS/SA*, 12 May 1981, p. C3. There were many other such conflicts.

11. Bovin, "Apropos the Afghan Revolution."

12. Kabul Radio, 11 January 1980, in *FBIS/ME*, 14 January 1980, p. S5.

13. Andreas Kohlschuetter, "Points of the Compass: The Day of the Kabul Rising (& After), in Afghanistan," *Encounter* 55 (August-September 1980): 68.

14. Western intelligence officials who declined to be identified.

15. *Mlada Fronta* (Prague) 1 September 1980, in *FBIS/SA*, 8 September 1980, p. C3. Karmal's claim that he walked across the Durand Line into Paktia province and then made his way to Kabul is heroic, in the best tradition of Nadir Khan and others, but seems very unlikely. His return to Afghanistan could only have been under Soviet auspices, and, if in fact he did return while Amin was still in power, Moscow would hardly have exposed him to the risks of rebellious Paktia. Smuggling him off a Soviet plane seems more probable.

16. Kabul Radio, 11 January 1980, in *FBIS/ME*, 14 January 1980, p. S3; *Current*, 16 February 1980, p. 10; *Der Spiegel*, 31 March 1980, pp. 139–46, in *FBIS/SA*, 2 April 1980, pp. C1–9.

17. Nayar, *Report on Afghanistan*, p. 13.

18. *Current*, 16 February 1980, p. 10.

19. *Patriot*, 7 February 1980, pp. 1 and 7, in *FBIS/ME*, 12 February 1980, pp. S1-3; Kabul Radio, 11 January 1980, in *FBIS/ME*, 14 January 1980, p. S3.

20. Ibid.

21. Kabul Radio, 21 January 1980, in *FBIS/ME*, 22 January 1980, pp. S1–5.

22. Bakhtar News Agency (Kabul), 17 February 1981, in *FBIS/SA*, 18 February 1981, pp. C9–15.

23. Tass from Kabul (quoting Kabul Radio), 28 December 1979, in *FBIS/SU*, 28 December 1979, p. D5.

24. Ibid.

25. *Novoye Vremya*, quoted by Tass, 23 April 1980, in *FBIS/SU*, 24 April 1980, p. D1.

26. Kabul Radio, 11 January 1980, in *FBIS/ME*, 14 January 1980, pp. S2–5.

27. *Der Spiegel*, 31 March 1980, pp. 139–46, in *FBIS/SA*, 2 April 1980, pp. C1–9.

28. Budapest Radio, 12 January 1980, in *FBIS/ME*, 14 January 1980, p. S10.

29. Interviews with Western intelligence officials who declined to be identified.

30. *Washington Post*, 7 December 1979, p. A29.

31. Chronologies published in House of Commons, "Afghanistan," and by the U.S. State Department (distributed in mimeographed form).

32. *Der Spiegel*, 16 June 1980, pp. 112–14, in *FBIS/SU*, 20 June 1980, pp. R1–3.

33. Chronologies, House of Commons and State Department.

34. *Washington Star*, 13 December 1979, p. A-10.

35. Chronologies, House of Commons and State Department.

36. Moscow Radio, 18 December 1979, in *FBIS/SU*, 19 December 1979, pp. D1–2.

37. Moscow Radio, 22 December 1979, in *FBIS/SU*, 31 December 1979, pp. D11–12.

38. *Pravda*, 23 December 1979, p. 5, in *FBIS/SU*, 26 December 1979, p. D1.

39. Kabul Radio, 11 May 1981, in *FBIS/SA*, 12 May 1981, p. C4.

40. Biographical information from U.S. government files, provided by officials who declined to be identified.

41. "Soviet Media Coverage of Events in Afghanistan in the Weeks Before the Coup," *Radio Liberty Research*, RL 62/80, 1980.

42. Kabul Radio, 30 November 1979, in *FBIS/ME*, 3 December 1979, pp. S1–2.

43. Kabul Radio, 2 December 1979, in *FBIS/ME*, 3 December 1979, pp. S1–2.

44. Kabul Radio, 13 December 1979, in *FBIS/ME*, 14 December 1979, pp. S1–2.

45. FCO, "Afghanistan: Soviet Occupation,"; *The Guardian*, 2 January 1980, in Afghan Council *Newsletter*, dated 1 January 1980, but issued later (this account gives the date of the shootout as 19 December instead of 17); *New York Times*, 2 January 1980, p. 1.

46. Kabul Radio, 20 December 1979, in *FBIS/ME*, 21 December 1979, pp. S1–2; FCO, "Afghanistan: Soviet Occupation."

47. BBC (London), 1 January 1980, in *FBIS/ME*, 2 January 1980, p. S11.

48. Moscow Radio, 16 January 1980, in *FBIS/SU*, 17 January 1980, p. D8.

49. Nayar, *Report on Afghanistan*, p. 5.

50. Kabul Radio, 20 December 1979, in *FBIS/ME*, 21 December 1979, pp. S1–2.

51. Interview with a senior Asian official who declined to be identified.

52. House subcommittee on Europe and the Middle East, "East-West Relations," p. 37.

53. State Department chronology.

54. Ibid.; House of Commons, "Afghanistan," pp. 3 and 44.

55. *Washington Post*, 27 December 1979, p. A12.

56. BBC (London), 1 January 1980, in *FBIS/ME*, 2 January 1980, pp. S11–12.

57. Kabul Radio, 24 and 27 December 1979, in *FBIS/ME*, 27 and 28 December 1979, p. S1.

58. James E. Taylor, "Afghanistan: Eyewitness Story of the Soviet Invasion," *Department of State Newsletter* (March 1980): 4–5.

59. FCO, "Afghanistan: Chronology of Events Since April 1978," 1980.

60. Telegram no. 333161 from State Department to many embassies overseas, 28 December 1979.

61. Ibid.

62. Tass, 27 December 1979, in *FBIS/SU*, 28 December 1979, pp. D1–2.

63. AFP from Tehran, 27 December 1979, in *FBIS/ME*, 28 December 1979, pp. S2–4.

64. Ibid.

65. Taylor, "Afghanistan: Eyewitness"; interviews with Westerners who were in Kabul at the time.

66. Tass, 27 December 1979, in *FBIS/SU*, 28 December 1979, pp. D1–2.

67. Kabul Radio, 27 December 1979 (dated in Greenwich time), in *FBIS/ME*, 28 December 1979, p. S1. Karmal's Parchami comrade Nur Ahmad Nur was added to the presidium in early January.

68. Kabul Radio, 27 December 1979, in *FBIS/ME*, 28 December 1979, p. S2.

69. Ibid.

70. A military attaché interviewed in Washington, December 1980, who declined to be identified. Nayar, *Report on Afghanistan*, p. 6, reports without attribution a story not known from other sources that Amin might have been poisoned by Soviet cooks on 27 December. "It is believed that he was dead before the shooting began," Nayar says.

71. Tass, 19 March 1980, in *FBIS/SU*, 21 March 1980, pp. D1–3; see also Tass, 23 April 1980, in *FBIS/SU*, 24 April 1980, pp. D1–3.

72. *Sotsialisticheskaya Industriya*, 6 February 1980, p. 3, in *FBIS/SU*, 8 February 1980, pp. D3–4.

73. *Der Spiegel*, 31 March 1980, pp. 139–46, in *FBIS/SA*, 2 April 1980, pp. C1–9 (emphasis added).

74. Interviews with diplomats formerly in Kabul.

75. *Pravda*, 3 January 1980, p. 6, in *FBIS/SU*, 9 January 1980, p. R7.

76. *FBIS Trends*, 19 March 1980, p. 14.

77. Interviews with diplomats then in Moscow.

78. Telegrams nos. 94 and 1395, U.S. Embassy, Moscow, 3 and 25 January 1980. U. S. Ambassador Thomas J. Watson reported in the 25 January telegram that "the story circulating in university circles is that Amin shot Paputin personally in his (Amin's) office and was in turn shot by the Soviets, who moved in to retaliate." A Western news agency reported that a posthumous award to Paputin was given to his wife, but no public record of this is known, and Western intelligence analysts treated this as nothing more than an unlikely rumor because it was inconsistent with the obituary treatment.

79. *FBIS Trends*, 19 March 1980, p. 14.

80. *Pravda*, 4 March 1981, p. 2, in *FBIS/SU Supplement*, 9 March 1981, p. 4.

81. Chronologies, House of Commons and State Department.

82. House subcommittee on Europe and the Middle East, "East-West Relations," p. 50.

83. "The Ethnic Composition of Soviet Forces in Afghanistan," *Radio Liberty Research*, RL 20/80, 1980; House of Commons, "Afghanistan," p. 80.

84. Benningsen, "Soviet Muslims," p. 41n.

85. Interviews with Western intelligence specialists.

86. Moscow Radio, 28 December 1979, in *FBIS/SU*, 28 December 1979,p. D3; Tass, 28 December 1979, in *FBIS/SU*, 31 December 1979, p. D5 (emphasis added).

87. AFP from New Delhi, 28 December 1979, in *FBIS/ME*, 28 December 1979, p. S6.

88. DPA (West German news agency) from Bonn, 28 December 1979, in *FBIS/SU*, 28 December 1979, p. D4.

89. FCO, "Afghanistan: Soviet Occupation," 1980, p. 4; *Nedelya*, Moscow, No. 1, 1980, p. 2, in *FBIS/SU*, 9 January 1980, pp. D9–11.

90. Tass from Kabul, 28 December 1979, in *FBIS/SU*, 28 December 1979, p. D5.

91. Tass from Moscow, 28 December 1979, in *FBIS/SU*, 28 December 1979, p. D5.

92. Moscow Radio, 1 January 1980, in *FBIS/SU*, 2 January 1980, p. D3.

93. *FBIS Trends*, 28 December 1979, pp. 3–4.

94. *Pravda*, December 31, 1979, in *FBIS/SU*, 31 December 1979, pp. D7–10.

95. FCO, "Afghanistan: Soviet Occupation," p. 3.

96. *Far Eastern Economic Review*, 25 January 1980, p. 9.

97. *Weekly Compilation of Presidential Documents* [hereafter *Presidential Documents*], 16, (14 January 1980): 25.

98. Tass from Kabul, 29 December 1979, in *FBIS/SU*, 31 December 1979, p. D1.

99. Ibid.

100. Kabul Radio, 1 January 1980, in *FBIS/ME*, 2 January 1980, pp. S1–5.

101. Tass from Kabul, 30 December 1979, in *FBIS/SU*, 31 December 1979, pp. D1–5.

102. Ibid.

103. Tass from Kabul, 29 December 1979, in *FBIS/SU*, 31 December 1979, p. D2.

104. Ibid.

105. Tass from Kabul, 30 December 1979, in *FBIS/SU*, 31 December 1979, p. D4.

106. Kabul Radio, 1 January 1980, in *FBIS/ME*, 2 January 1980, pp. S1–5.

107. Moscow Radio, 29 December 1979, in *FBIS/SU*, 31 December 1979, pp. D5–6.

108. Moscow Radio, 26 February 1980, in *FBIS/SU*, 27 February 1980, p. D1.

109. Interviews with officials receiving reports from Kabul.

110. For the new appointments announced 10 January 1980, see Kabul Radio on that date and on 12 January 1980, in *FBIS/ME*, 11 and 14 January 1980, pp. S1–3 and S6–7. The announcements did not specify which persons were Khalqis and which Parchamis; for this, names were compared with the PDPA secret history. The PDPA politburo members were Karmal, Sarwari, Ratebzad, Keshtmand, Ziray, Panjshiri, and Nur. Ziray and Panjshiri were the two Khalqis. Party secretaries were Ziray and Nur. Panjshiri had been reported wounded in the 14 September palace shooting that toppled Taraki; he was then flown to Moscow for medical treatment. On 26 December 1979, Kabul media reported his return, stirring rumors then that Moscow was considering replacing Amin with some of the Afghan leaders whom it had been harboring; see FCO, "Afghanistan: Soviet Occupation," p. 2.

111. Kabul Radio, 9 January 1980, in *FBIS/ME*, 10 January 1980, pp. S2–3; see also Kabul Radio, 5 January 1980, in *FBIS/ME*, 7 January 1980, pp. S2–3.

112. *L'Humanite*, 11 July 1980, p. 8, in *FBIS/SA*, 18 July 1980, pp. C1–3.

113. *Amnesty International Report 1980*, p. 180.

114. AFP from Kabul, 11 and 12 January 1980, in *FBIS/ME*, 14 January 1980, pp. S13–15.

115. *The Times of India*, 11 February 1981, p. 1, in *FBIS/SA*, 23 February 1981, pp. C1–2.

Chapter 10. Consequences

1. *Presidential Documents* 16 (14 January 1980): 41.

2. *Presidential Documents* 15 (31 December 1979): 2,287; *New York Times*, 29 December 1979, p. 5.

3. *Presidential Documents* 16 (14 January 1980): 25.

4. Ibid., p. 40 (emphasis added).

5. *Presidential Documents*, 16 (21 January 1980): 87.

6. *Presidential Documents* 16 (28 January 1980): 196 (emphasis added).

7. *Presidential Documents* 15 (31 December 1979): 2287.

8. *Presidential Documents* 16 (14 January 1980): 25.

9. Tass from Kabul, 4 January 1980, in *FBIS/SU*, 4 January 1980, pp. D1⁻2.

10. Tass from Kabul, 31 December 1979, in *FBIS/SU*, 2 January 1980, pp. D1⁻2.

11. *Kabul New Times*, 10 January 1980, p. 1, in *FBIS/ME*, 28 January 1980, pp. S6⁻7.

12. *Der Spiegel*, 31 March 1980, pp. 139⁻46, in *FBIS/SA*, 2 April 1980, p. C5.

13. *New York Times*, 30 December 1979, p. 1.

14. *New York Times*, 1 January 1980, p. 4.

15. Ibid.

16. Ibid.

17. *Presidential Documents* 16 (28 January 1980): 111.

18. *Presidential Documents* 16 (25 February 1980): 346⁻47.

19. *Pravda*, 8 January 1980, p. 5, in *FBIS/SU*, 10 January 1980, pp. A7⁻8.

20. *Presidential Documents* 16 (3 March 1980): 387.

21. CRS, "Afghanistan: Soviet Invasion," p. 27.

22. Moscow Radio, 2 January 1980, in *FBIS/SU*, 3 January 1980, p. A2.

23. Tass, 6 January 1980, in *FBIS/SU*, 7 January 1980, pp. A1⁻4; *FBIS Trends*, 16 January 1980, p. 2.

24. *Izvestiya*, 11 January 1980, p. 4, in *FBIS/SU*, 14 January 1980, pp. A22⁻23. See also *Pravda*, 10 January 1980, p. 4, in *FBIS/SU*, 14 January 1980, pp. A24⁻26.

25. Transcript, "Issues and Answers," ABC News, 30 December 1979.

26. See transcript in *New York Times*, 29 October 1980.

27. U.S. House subcommittee on Europe and the Middle East, "NATO After Afghanistan" (1980) p. 7.

28. *Presidential Documents* 16 (14 January 1980): 41.

29. *Presidential Documents* 16 (28 January 1980): 165.

30. Ibid., p. 185.

31. Ibid., p. 197.

32. *Washington Star*, 24 January 1980, p. 1; David D. Newsom "America EnGulfed," *Foreign Policy* 43 (Summer 1981): 17⁻32. Newsom, who was under secretary of state for political affairs at the time, says "the Carter doctrine" "grew out of last-minute pressures for a presidential speech. . . . As far as is known, neither the current [Reagan] administration nor the previous [Carter] one has ever conducted a detailed study of the implications of the policy or its alternatives." See also Defense Secretary Harold Brown's statement to the Senate budget committee, 27 February 1980, in committee hearing report, vol. 1 (1980), p. 93.

33. Vance quoted by Vernon V. Aspaturian, "Superpower Maneuvers—1: Moscow's Afghan Gamble," *The New Leader* 28 January 1980, p. 9.

34. Briefing by Muskie 5 June 1980, in State Department Current Policy Paper No. 194.

35. *Presidential Documents* 16 (14 January 1980): 41.

36. *New York Times*, 1 January 1980, p. 4.

37. *Presidential Documents* 16 (7 January 1980): 11; *New York Times*, 3 January 1980, p. 1.

38. *Presidential Documents* 16 (7 January 1980): 12.

39. Transcript, "Issues and Answers."

40. Interviews with U.S. officials who declined to be identified.

41. *Presidential Documents* 16 (14 January 1980): 25⁻27.

42. Ibid. Background on Carter's announced steps is drawn from U.S. House subcommittee on Europe and the Middle East, "An Assessment of the Afghanistan Sanctions: Implications for Trade

and Diplomacy in the 1980's (Washington, April 1981), pp. 1–2, 7–8, 24, 88, 93, 97; from CRS, "Afghanistan: Soviet Invasion," pp. 28–29; and from *Washington Post*, 5 January 1980, p. 1.

43. Ibid.

44. Ibid.

45. Ibid.

46. Ibid.

47. *Presidential Documents* 17 (27 April 1981): 466.

48. Statement by Richard N. Cooper, under secretary of state for economic affairs, to the Senate banking committee, 20 August 1980.

49. House subcommittee on Europe and the Middle East, "An Assessment," p. 88.

50. Ibid., p. 8. This study, written primarily by John P. Hardt of the Congressional Research Service, gives a detailed account of the sanctions. It notes that, in addition to steps announced 4 January, Carter a month later blocked what Secretary of Commerce Philip M. Klutznick called "this country's largest long-term cooperative project with the Soviet Union." This was a $20 billion deal made in 1973 for Occidental Petroleum Co. to sell the Soviet Union over twenty years from 1978 liquid phosphate concentrate used to make fertilizer and to buy in return anhydrous ammonia, potash and urea, which are also fertilizer ingredients. Reagan unblocked the deal at the same time he lifted the grain embargo. Carter also restricted U.S. landing rights for the Soviet government airline Aeroflot. See "Assessment," pp. 53–64 and 94, and *Presidential Documents* 17 (27 April 1981): 466. The Carter administration's own assessment of sanctions, and its extension of them just before it left office, is given in Secretary Klutznick's letter to House Speaker T. P. O'Neill Jr. and Senate President Walter F. Mondale on 31 December 1980.

51. *Presidential Documents* 16 (11 February 1980): 289.

52. *Pravda*, 6 January 1980, p. 4, in *FBIS/SU*, 8 January 1980, pp. A1–8.

53. Tass, 6 January 1980, in *FBIS/SU*, 7 January 1980, pp. A1–4.

54. Moscow Radio, 10 January 1980, in *FBIS/SU*, 11 January 1980, pp. A1–2.

55. *Pravda*, 13 January 1980, p. 1, in *FBIS/SU*, 14 January 1980, pp. A1–8.

56. Ibid.

57. *Presidential Documents* 16 (14 January 1980): 27.

58. *FBIS Trends*, 16 January 1980, pp. 26–28.

59. *Pravda*, 20 February 1980, p. 2, in *FBIS/SU*, 22 February 1980, p. R12.

60. FCO, "Soviet Foreign Trade: 1979–80" (London, 1981), p. 2.

61. *FBIS Trends*, 30 April 1980, pp. 8–9.

62. *Pravda*, 28 February 1981, pp. 2–4, in *FBIS/SU Supplement*, 3 March 1981, p. 30.

63. Interviews with U.S. officials who declined to be identified.

64. *Presidential Documents* 16 (14 January 1980): 27.

65. FCO, "Afghanistan: Response to Soviet Intervention" (London, 1980), pp. 1–2.

66. Transcript, "Issues and Answers."

67. CRS, "Afghanistan: Soviet Invasion," pp. 16–17.

68. *Washington Post*, 16 September 1981, p. A7.

69. Karachi Radio, 13 and 15 January 1980, in *FBIS/ME*, 14 and 16 January 1980, pp. S9 and S12.

70. House of Commons, "Afghanistan," p. 13.

71. *New York Times*, 12 December 1980, p. A11.

72. Neville Chamberlain, 27 September 1938, after the Munich agreement, quoted in Winston S. Churchill, *The Second World War: The Gathering Storm*, (Boston, 1948), p. 315.

73. House subcommittee on Europe and the Middle East, "NATO After Afghanistan," p. 1.

74. Richard Lowenthal, "The Shattered Balance: Estimating the Dangers of War & Peace," *Encounter* 55 (November 1980): 12–13; *FBIS Trends*, 5 March 1980, pp. 12–13.

75. CRS, "Afghanistan: Soviet Invasion," pp. 19–20.

76. *Frankfurter Allgemeine*, 21 January 1980, p. 3, in *JPRS*, No. 75113, 12 February 1980, pp. 1–2.

77. *Helsingin Sanomat*, Helsinki, 3 January 1980, p. 2, in *JPRS*, No. 75021, 29 January 1980, pp. 72–73. See also Pierre Hassner, "Moscow and the Western Alliance," *Problems of Communism* 30 (May–June 1981): 48–49.

78. Telegram no. 333359, State Department to more than sixty U.S. missions abroad, 28 December 1979, summarized the facts of the Soviet invasion as then understood in Washington and instructed the missions to "brief host governments soonest at highest available level" on them. "Since the Soviets are

likely to be sensitive to the fact that their intervention in Afghanistan may incur significant political costs in the non-aligned and Moslem world," the telegram said, "we want to encourage opposition in these areas to the Soviet role in Afghanistan."

79. Reuter from Islamabad, 29 January 1980, in *FBIS/ME*, 30 January 1980, pp. A3–5; CRS, "Afghanistan: Soviet Invasion," pp. 12–13.

80. Karachi Radio, 22 May 1980, in *FBIS/SA*, 23 May 1980, pp. A1–6.

81. *Washington Post*, 26 January 1981, p. A6.

82. FCO, "Muslim Conference in Tashkent" (London, 1980).

83. "Soviet Moslem Publication Plays Down Tashkent Conference," *Radio Liberty Research*, RL 241/81, 1981.

84. FCO, "Cuban Setbacks in the Non-Aligned Movement" (London, 1980).

85. AFP from New Delhi, 13 February 1981, in *FBIS/SA*, 17 February 1981, pp. A16–17.

86. *Washington Post*, 7 December 1980, p. 1; CRS, "Afghanistan: Soviet Invasion," pp. 17–18.

87. FCO, "Afghanistan: Response to Soviet Intervention."

88. *Beijing Review* (7 January 1980): 3.

89. *Beijing Review* (14 January 1980): 9–12.

90. *FBIS Trends*, 30 January 1980, pp. 13–16.

91. House of Commons, "Afghanistan," pp. 258–59; FCO, "Afghanistan: Chronology of Events" (London, 1981).

92. Ibid.

93. *Washington Post*, 19 November 1981, p. A24. U.N. members voting against the January resolution were Afghanistan, Angola, Bulgaria, Byelorussia (USSR), Cuba, Czechoslovakia, East Germany, Ethiopia, Grenada, Hungary, Laos, Mongolia, Mozambique, South Yemen, Poland, Soviet Union, Ukraine (USSR), and Vietnam. They were joined in November 1980 by Madagascar, Sao Tome and Principe, Seychelles, and Syria. Abstaining in January were Algeria, Benin, Burundi, Congo, Cyprus, Equatorial Guinea, Finland, Guinea, Guinea-Bissau, India, Madagascar, Mali, Nicaragua, North Yemen, Sao Tome and Principe, Syria, Uganda, and Zambia. Absent in January were Bhutan, Cape Verde, Central African Republic, Chad, Comoros, Dominica, Libya, Romania, Seychelles, Solomon Islands, and Sudan.

94. *FBIS Trends*, 4, 16, and 23 January, 30 April 1980, pp. 6–12; FCO, "Afghanistan" and "Afghanistan: Further Responses" (London, 1980).

95. "Cuba Continues to Take an Ambiguous Stand on Soviet Actions in Afghanistan," *Radio Liberty Research*, RL 56/80, 1980.

96. FCO, "Afghanistan," and "Afghanistan: Further Responses;" State Department, "Soviet Invasion of Afghanistan," Special Report no. 70, 1980.

97. Tass, quoting *Novoye Vremya*, 23 April 1980, in *FBIS/SU*, 24 April 1980, pp. D1–2.

98. *Die Welt*, 14 January 1980, p. 1, in *FBIS/SU*, 15 January 1980, pp. A4–6.

99. *Pravda*, 29 January 1980, in *FBIS/SU*, 29 January 1980, pp. A1–5.

100. *Izvestiya*, 16 January 1980, p. 5, in *FBIS/SU*, 17 January 1980, pp. A1–4.

101. Moscow Radio, 21 February 1980, in *FBIS/SU*, 22 February 1980, p. R7 (emphasis added).

102. *FBIS Trends*, 23 April 1980, Appendix.

103. *FBIS Trends*, 6 February 1980, pp. 1–4.

104. Tass, 26 April 1980, in *FBIS/SU*, 28 April 1980, pp. D5–8.

105. Moscow Radio, 22 February 1980, in *FBIS/SU*, 25 February 1980, p. R7.

106. *FBIS Trends*, 5 March 1980, pp. 1–4.

107. The CIA projections were controversial among Western analysts of Soviet oil production and prospects. They did, however, affect Carter administration thinking about Gulf security.

108. *Pravda*, 11 December 1980, p. 2, in *FBIS/SU*, 11 December 1980, p. D7.

109. Moscow Radio, 23 February 1981, in *FBIS/SU Supplement*, 24 February 1981, p. 20.

Chapter 11. Quagmire

1. State Department officials, from briefings given to the press as part of the Carter administration's policy of trying to keep the public informed on and aware of the Afghan situation. See also FCO, "Afghanistan: Chronology of Events Since April 1978."

2. International Institute for Strategic Studies, *The Military Balance, 1977–1978*, p. 55; FCO, "Afghanistan: Chronology."

3. Western intelligence officials who declined to be identified.

4. Ibid.

5. The Taraki government changed the number of provinces by reorganization.

6. FCO, "Afghanistan Report" (London, July and November, 1980, February 1981); State Department, "Afghanistan: A Year of Occupation," Special Report no. 79 (Washington, 1981). Bakhtar news agency said 20 October 1982 (*FBIS/SA*, 22 October 1982, p. C9) that 1,438 elementary and 230 upper schools had been destroyed "by the counterrevolution."

7. *Pravda*, 17 October 1980, p. 2, in *FBIS/SU*, 21 October 1980, pp. D4–11.

8. AFP from Kabul, 22 February 1980, in *FBIS/ME*, 25 February 1980, p. S15.

9. *Le Monde*, 29 February 1980, p. 6, in *FBIS/ME*, 3 March 1980, p. S14.

10. FCO, "Afghanistan Report," July 1980.

11. FCO, "Afghanistan: Chronology."

12. *Suddeutsche Zeitung* reported in June 1981 that the population of Kabul had swollen to 1,400,000 persons; see *World Press Review* (September 1981): 29–31.

13. FCO, "Afghanistan: Chronology"; FCO, "Afghanistan Report" (May 1980); AFP from New Delhi, 21 January 1981, in *FBIS/SA*, 22 January 1981, p. C6. For a description of the April 1980 demonstrations, see U.S. House of Representatives, Foreign Affairs Committee, subcommittee on human rights and international organizations, "Soviet Violation of Helsinki Final Act: Invasion of Afghanistan," 22 July 1981, pp. 6ff.

14. FCO, "Afghanistan: Chronology"; FCO, "Afghanistan Report" (May 1980). U.S. Defense Department reports cited much higher casualty figures in the Kabul demonstrations: 500 to 2,000 deaths in February, and 100 to 120 in late April and early May; see State Department, "Soviet Dilemmas in Afghanistan," Special Report no. 72, June 1980.

15. Interviews with diplomats formerly in Kabul.

16. Briefings given to the press by the Carter administration.

17. Ibid.

18. House of Commons, "Afghanistan," pp. 250–51; FCO, "Afghanistan: Chronology."

19. Statements by Stoessel, State Department news conference, 14 September 1981.

20. Statements by a State Department official who declined to be identified, same news conference.

21. Sterling Seagrave, *Yellow Rain: A Journey Through the Terror of Chemical Warfare* (New York, 1981), pp. 135–44, 254.

22. U.S. State Department, "Chemical Warfare in Southeast Asia and Afghanistan," Special Report no. 98 (Washington, D.C., 1982), p. 6

23. For typical denials of/using poison gas, see Bakhtar statement for Afghan government, 15 September 1981, in *FBIS/SA*, 16 September 1981, pp. AA3–4, and *Pravda*, 17 September 1981, p. 9, in *FBIS/SU*, 22 September 1981, pp. AA1–2.

24. Briefings by U.S. officials for Washington journalists.

25. Tass, 5 February 1980, in *FBIS/SU*, 6 February 1980, pp. D3–4.

26. *Pravda*, 10 February 1980, p. 4, in *FBIS/SU*, 12 February 1980, pp. A3–4.

27. *Le Soir*, Brussels, 22 May 1980, p. 3, in *FBIS/SA*, 29 May 1980, p. C2.

28. State Department, "Soviet Dilemmas." For the bridge opening, see *FBIS/SA*, 13 May 1982, p. C1.

29. Kabul Radio, 15 March 1980, in *FBIS/ME*, 17 March 1980, pp. S5–6.

30. Kabul Radio, 4 April 1980, in *FBIS/SA*, 7 April 1980, p. C1. The first precedent seems to have been an agreement in August 1921 for the Soviet troops that had established a Bolshevik regime in Ulan Bator to remain in Mongolia "pending the complete removal of the threat from the common enemy," who was unidentified; see Carr, *Bolshevik Revolution*, 3: 508. The Soviet Union had in 1980 similar agreements in force with Hungary, East Germany, and other allies.

31. FCO, "Soviet Network of Friendship Treaties" (London, 1980).

32. Kabul Radio, 22 June 1980, in *FBIS/SA* 23 June 1980, pp. C1–4; Tass from Kabul, 22 June 1980, in *FBIS/SU*, 23 June 1980, p. D1.

33. FCO, "Afghanistan Report" (November 1980); State Department, "Afghanistan: A Year of Occupation."

34. Kabul Radio, 24 October 1980, in *FBIS/SA*, 28 October 1980, pp. C1–4.

35. FCO, "Afghanistan Report" (February 1981); State Department, "Afghanistan: A Year of Occupation."

36. FCO, "The Sovietisation of Afghanistan" (London, 1980).

37. Kabul Radio, 7 September 1981, in *FBIS/SA*, 8 September 1981, pp. C1–2. This broadcast

said the Council of Ministers' resolution called up discharged soldiers *under* thirty-five years old, but Kabul Radio the next day, in *FBIS/SA*, 10 September 1981, p. C3, quoted the order as saying those "over the age of 35" were exempt. Kabul University classes were reported from mid-1980 onward to be thinly attended because so many male students had fled to avoid conscription.

38. "*Krasnaya Zvezda* Describes Reception of Soviet Troops in Afghanistan," *Radio Liberty Research*, RL 109/80, 1980.

39. *Turkmenskaya Iskra*, 23 February 1980, p. 3, in *FBIS/SU*, 5 March 1980, pp. V2–3; *Pravda Vostoka*, 21 February 1980, p. 3, in ibid., pp. V5–6.

40. *Pravda*, 21 February 1981, p. 2, in *FBIS/SU*, 21 February 1981, pp. V1–5.

41. *Pravda*, 5 February 1980, p. 3, in *FBIS/SU*, 6 February 1980, pp. R10–14.

42. Tass, 26 April 1980, in *FBIS/SU*, 28 April 1980, pp. D5–8.

43. Moscow Television, 19 October 1980, in *FBIS/SU*, 20 October 1980, pp. D3–4.

44. Interviews with Western officials who cited diplomatic reports.

45. *FBIS Trends*, 27 February 1980, pp. 5–6.

46. Interview with an American official of Russian ancestry, who declined to be identified, quoting a relative living in Moscow whose Soviet government work gave him access to such information.

47. *Le Monde*, 3 December 1980, p. 6, in *FBIS/SA*, 12 December 1980, pp. C4–5. Such leaflets might have been written by Chinese government psychological warfare experts and passed by them to guerrillas.

48. See, for example, *Krasnaya Zvezda*, 25 and 30 September and 10 and 18 October 1981, pp. 1 and 3, in *FBIS/SU*, 30 September, 7, 15, and 23 October 1981, pp. D1–6.

49. A winner of the Soviet Union's highest combat award, Hero of the Soviet Union (which is also used as a political award), was publicized as a delegate to the Communist Party's twenty-sixth congress in late February and early March 1981. He was Major Vasiliy Vasilyevich Shcherbakov, the commander of a helicopter squadron in Afghanistan up to the autumn of 1980. His heroism meant that a helicopter crew's "combat comrades were saved" under circumstances not made public. Curiously, his action was publicized afresh in October 1981 as if it had just occurred, suggesting a paucity of good examples for Soviet internal propaganda. See *Krasnaya Zvezda*, 14 March 1981, described in "*Krasnaya Zvezda's* 'Afghan Notebook'," *Radio Liberty Research*, RL 133/81, 26 March 1981, and *Krasnaya Zvezda*, 10 October 1981, in *FBIS/SU*, 15 October 1981, p. D1.

50. *Komsomolskaya Pravda*, 22 September 1981, p. 3, in *FBIS/SU*, 7 October 1981, p. D1.

51. *Komsomolskaya Pravda*, 7 August 1981, p. 2, in *FBIS/SU*, 13 August 1981, pp. D5–9.

52. *Voennye Znaniya*, No. 3, 1981, pp. 4–5, described in "*Voennye Znaniya* Reports on Conditions Experienced by Soviet Troops in Afghanistan," *Radio Liberty Research*, RL 176/81, 23 April 1981.

53. *The Sun*, 9 April 1981, p. A6.

54. *Izvestiya*, 25 July 1981, p. 5, in *FBIS/SU*, 5 August 1981, pp. D4–6; *Pravda*, 28 September 1981, p. 4, in *FBIS/SU*, 1 October 1981, p. D2.

55. *Izvestiya*, 21 August 1981, p. 5, in *FBIS/SU*, 27 August 1981, p. D2.

56. Associated Press from Islamabad, 22 October 1982; *Renmin Ribao*, Beijing, 24 September 1982, p. 7, in *FBIS Daily Report, China*, 12 October 1982, p. C1.

57. Interviews with Western specialists on Afghanistan.

58. FCO, "Afghanistan Report" (June 1980).

59. *New York Times*, 9 October 1980, p. A20.

60. State Department, "Afghanistan: A Year of Occupation;" FCO, "Afghanistan Report" (November 1980); *The Economist*, 23 August 1980, pp. 33-34; Kabul Radio, 17 January 1981, in *FBIS/SA*, 21 January 1981, pp. C1–2; Tass, 20 February 1981, in *FBIS/SU*, 23 February 1981, pp. P7–8.

61. Eliza Van Hollen, State Department, "Afghanistan: 2 Years of Occupation," Special Report no. 91, December 1981, p. 2.

62. Mashhad Radio, 27 October 1981, in *FBIS/SA*, 28 October 1981, pp. I1–2.

63. Kabul Radio, 18 March 1980, in *FBIS/ME*, 19 March 1980, pp. S1–3.

64. Kabul Radio, 18 June and 10 August 1981, in *FBIS/SA*, 18 June and 20 August 1981, pp. C1–2.

65. *Sovietskaya Rossiya*, 10 July 1980, p. 1, in *FBIS/SU*, 15 July 1980, pp. D1–2.

66. FCO, "Afghanistan: Opposition Groups" (London, 1980); *The Economist*, 2 February 1980, pp. 52–53; Kohlschuetter, "The Day of the Kabul Uprising," pp. 75–77; *Le Monde*, 8–10 March 1980, pp. 4–5, in *FBIS/ME*, 13 March 1980, pp. S6–11.

67. *Die Welt*, 16 February 1981, p. 1, in *FBIS/SA*, 19 February 1981, p. C3.

68. FCO, "Afghanistan: Opposition Groups"; *The Economist*, 2 February 1980, pp. 52–53.

69. See sources in note 66.

70. FCO "Afghanistan Report," May 1980.

71. *Far Eastern Economic Review*, 23 January 1981, pp. 25−29; Nayar, *Report on Afghanistan*, p. 136; State Department, "Afghanistan: A Year of Occupation." Some more conservative resistance groups joined in early 1982 in an Islamic Union of Afghan *mujahideen* that was in close touch with Saudi Arabia and some other oil-wealthy countries; see *Al-Madinah*, Jiddah, 11 July 1982, p. 11, in *FBIS/SA*, 14 July 1982, p. C3. Nayar, *Report on Afghanistan*, pp. 136−37, says that the KGB "fanned differences among insurgent groups," using as one channel for bribes the Mangal tribe. A member of the tribe, Habib Mangal, was named in November 1980 as the Afghan ambassador in Moscow, after a curiously long time into the Karmal regime without an ambassador there.

72. FCO, "Afghanistan: Opposition Groups."

73. *Washington Post*, 27 November 1980, p. E10.

74. *Le Monde*, 9 January 1980, p. 3, in *FBIS/ME*, 10 January 1980, pp. S6−7. *Hezb-i-Islami*, which wanted an Afghanistan ruled by religious leaders, said in early 1981 that 500,000 Afghans had died and 3 million gone into exile as a result of the Communist forces whose unleashing it blamed on Zahir Shah, and it talked of kidnapping him from Rome and putting him on trial in an eventually liberated Kabul for having ruined the country; see *Corriere della Sera*, 4 March 1981, p. 3 in *FBIS/SA Annex*, 10, March 1981, pp. 2−3.

75. Letter to the author, 10 October 1982, from a former Afghan government minister working in Pakistan with Pazhwak on unification efforts.

76. *Al-Bayan*, 17 May 1980, p. 13, in *FBIS/SA*, 20 May 1980, pp. C5−6; AFP from Peshawar, 19 January 1980, in *FBIS/ME*, 21 January 1980, pp. S9−10.

77. Ibid.

78. Karachi Radio, 6 and 13 January 1980, in *FBIS/ME*, 7 and 14 January 1980, pp. S17 and S9.

79. Karachi Radio, 26 and 28 September 1980, and 12 September 1981, in *FBIS/SA*, 30 September 1980, p. C1, and 16 September 1981, p. F1. Kabul initially denied such incidents and countered with accusations of Pakistani border provocations; see Kabul Radio, 29 September 1980, in *FBIS/SA*, 30 September 1980, p. C1. Pakistan allowed clandestine *mujahideen* radio stations to operate from Peshawar and Quetta in Pushtun, Dari, and Uzbek, and Soviet media charged that Pakistani officials even helped with programming; see Naby, "Ethnic Factors," and *Novoye Vremya*, 8 February 1980, pp. 10−11, in *FBIS/SU*, 21 February 1980, pp. D7−8.

80. *Washington Post*, 2 February 1979, p. A23; *New York Times*, 16 April 1979, p. 1.

81. Tass from Kabul, 19 January 1980, in *FBIS/SU*, 21 January 1980, p. D10; *Literaturnaya Gazeta*, 23 January 1980, p. 9, in *FBIS/SU*, 31 January 1980, pp. D3−4 (which charged that Chinese "'advisers' systematically participate with their 'protégés' in raids on our soil"); *L'Humanite*, 11 July 1980, p. 8, in *FBIS/SA*, 18 July 1980, pp. C1−3; *FBIS Trends*, 6 June 1979; Tass from New York, 18 November 1980, in *FBIS/SU*, 19 November 1980, p. CC6; Kabul Radio, 20 March 1980, in *FBIS/ME*, 24 March 1980, pp. S1−5; *Patriot*, 7 February 1980, pp. 1 and 7, in *FBIS/ME*, 12 February 1980, pp. S1−4; Tass, 20 February 1981, in *FBIS/SU*, 23 February 1981, pp. P7−8.

82. *Der Spiegel*, 31 March 1980, pp. 139−46, in *FBIS/SA*, 2 April 1980, pp. C1−9.

83. *Pravda*, 11 and 19 January 1980, pp. 5 and 4, in *FBIS/SU*, 15 and 21 January 1980, pp. D3 and A1−5.

84. Kabul Radio, 12 January 1980, in *FBIS/ME*, 14 January 1980, pp. S8−10.

85. *FBIS Trends*, 4 September 1980, pp. 11−12.

86. *Iran Times*, 8 January 1980, quoting *Tehran Times*, in *Afghan Council Newsletter*, 2 March 1980.

87. *Izvestiya*, 17 January 1981, p. 4, in *FBIS/SU*, 22 January 1981, pp. D4−5.

88. *Pravda*, 25 June 1980, p. 5, in *FBIS/SU*, 27 June 1980, pp. D1−2.

89. *Izvestiya*, 25 October 1981, p. 5, in *FBIS/SU*, 30 October 1981, p. D1 (reprinting an article from the Nicosia newspaper *Dhimokratia*).

90. *Le Monde*, 18−19 May 1980, p. 3, in *FBIS/SA*, 6 June 1980, pp. C6−8.

91. *Washington Post*, 23 and 24 September 1981, pp. A23 and A24.

92. *The Sunday Telegraph*, 8 February 1981, p. 2, in *FBIS/SA*, 10 February 1981, p. C3; Halliday, "The Limits of Russian Imperialism"; *Far Eastern Economic Review*, 23 January 1981, p. 28; *Washington Post*, 14 February 1980, p. 1. See also Bakhtar news agency, 13 March 1980, in "White Book of the Democratic Republic of Afghanistan" (Kabul, 1980), pp. 102−9.

93. Carl Bernstein, "Arms for Afghanistan," *New Republic*, 18 July 1981, pp. 8−10.

94. *Pravda*, 8 January 1980, p. 4, in *FBIS/SU*, 10 January 1980, pp. D7−8.

95. Soviet embassy, Washington, material mailed to journalists 23 January 1981.

96. Moscow Radio, 10 July 1981, in *FBIS/SU*, 14 July 1981, p. A3.

97. Bernstein, "Arms for Afghanistan"; *FBIS Trends*, 19 March 1980; *Boston Globe*, 5 January 1980.

98. Ibid.; Halliday, "The Limits of Russian Imperialism"; transcript of "Today," NBC Television, 9 January 1980; *Washington Post*, 15 February 1980, p. 1; *New York Times*, 16 February 1980, p. 1; *Columbia Journalism Review*, New York, March/April 1981, pp. 5–7.

99. *Beijing Review*, No. 12, 24 March 1980, pp. 8–9; see also *Beijing Review*, No. 11, 17 March 1980, p. 3.

100. Halliday, "The Limits of Russian Imperialism"; interviews with Western officials who declined to be identified.

101. *New York Times*, 10 March 1981, p. 1.

102. *Pravda*, 11 March 1981, p. 3, in *FBIS/SU*, 16 March 1981, pp. A3–4.

103. Kabul Radio, 20 March 1980, in *FBIS/ME*, 24 March 1980, pp. S1–5; Kabul Radio, 21 and 22 November 1980, in *FBIS/SA*, 25 November 1980, pp. C4–5; *The Economist*, 14 March 1981, pp. 38–39. The Pakistani opposition organization led by Murtaza Bhutto, son of the former prime minister who was executed by Zia's government for murder, operated from Kabul, which necessarily had to involve Soviet support.

104. *Pravda*, 13 January 1980, p. 1, in *FBIS/SU*, 14 January 1980, pp. A1–6.

105. Moscow Radio, 22 February 1980, in *FBIS/SU*, 25 February 1980, p. R6; "Brezhnev Introduces New Element in USSR's Position on Afghanistan," *Radio Liberty Research*, RL 85/80, 1980.

106. *FBIS Trends*, 27 February and 5 March 1980, pp. 1–5.

107. Kabul Radio, 14 May 1980, in *FBIS/SA*, 15 May 1980, pp. C1–3.

108. *FBIS Trends*, 29 May 1980, pp. 1–5.

109. See, for example, *FBIS Trends*, 18 June and 2 July 1980, pp. 1–5; Kabul Radio, 24 August 1981, in *FBIS/SA*, 25 August 1981, pp. C1–3; Bakhtar, 28 September 1981, in *FBIS/SA*, 29 September 1981, pp. C1–2; Tass, 10 July 1981, from Moscow, and 13 July 1981, from Kabul, in *FBIS/SU*, 13 and 14 July 1981, p. D1; *New York Times*, 7 August 1981, p. 1. Cuba tried in March and April 1980 to work out some solution that would have South Asian nations accept Karmal's government. This repeated the Cuban effort to head off the Ethiopian-Somali clash in 1977 so as to enable its patron, the Soviet Union, to avoid a choice between those two countries. But Cuba was no more successful in this new diplomatic service to Moscow, which never commented publicly on it; see FCO, "Afghanistan and the 'Brezhnev Doctrine'" (London, 1980).

110. *The Daily Telegraph*, 22 January 1980, p. 4; AFP from Kabul, 14 February 1980, in *FBIS/ME*, 14 February 1980, p. S4; AFP from Islamabad, 11 June 1980, in *FBIS/SA*, 13 June 1980, pp. C3.

111. AFP from New Delhi, 17 June 1980, in *FBIS/SA*, 18 June 1980, pp. C1–2.

112. *Der Spiegel*, 30 June 1980, pp. 113–18, in *FBIS/SA*, 1 July 1980, p. C6.

113. *Pravda*, 27 April 1980, p. 1, in *FBIS/SU*, 30 April 1980, pp. D1–2.

114. Diplomatic reports, cited by U.S. officials who declined to be identified.

115. Moscow Radio, 16 October 1980, in *FBIS/SU*, 17 October 1980, pp. D3–4.

116. Tass, 19 October 1980, in *FBIS/SU*, 20 October 1980, p. D5 (emphasis added). This characterization of the talks is from Tass in Russian. In its English language service, Tass substituted "comradely *sincerity*" for the correct translation of the word "*otkrovennost*" ("frankness") in the Russian original and the equivalent in Dari (Kabul Radio, 19 October 1980, in *FBIS/SU*, 22 October 1980, p. D3). This substitution presumably was intended to deceive foreigners, who depended mainly upon the English version, about the underlying problems in Soviet-Afghan relations. There was another possible problem, too. An unusually large number of Soviet leaders turned out for the statement's signing. Under the normal rules of Kremlinology, and following the logic of protesting too much, this raised questions of whether there had been dissension within the leadership over the policies that had created trouble in Afghanistan, and a show of unity was therefore needed to reassure other Soviet officials; see "Babrak Karmal's Moscow Visit," *Radio Liberty Research*, RL 389/80, 1980.

117. Kabul Radio, 19 October 1980, in *FBIS/SU*, 22 October 1980, p. D3; *Pravda*, 17 and 18 October 1980, p. 2, in *FBIS/SU*, 21 and 22 October 1980, pp. D4–11 and D1.

118. *Pravda*, 17 October 1980, p. 2, in *FBIS/SU*, 21 October 1980, pp. D4–11.

119. Kabul Radio, 14 November 1980, in *FBIS/SA*, 17 November 1980, pp. C1–7.

120. *Pravda*, 5 February 1980, p. 3, in *FBIS/SU*, 6 February 1980, pp. R10–14.

121. *FBIS Trends*, 6 February 1980, p. 2.

122. *The Economist*, 14 June 1980, p. 43; AFP from Islamabad, 10 June 1980, in *FBIS/SA*, 10

June 1980, p. C1; FCO, "The Sovietisation of Afghanistan"; FCO, "Afghanistan Report" (June and August 1980); Nayar, *Report on Afghanistan*, p. 185 (which estimates the number of Soviet advisers at the end of 1980 to have been between 6,000 and 8,000).

123. AFP from Asadabad, 30 October 1980, in *FBIS/SA*, 31 October 1980, pp. C2–3.

124. *The Daily Telegraph*, 19 July 1980, p. 5; State Department, "Soviet Military and Civilian Control in Afghanistan," unpublished paper distributed to journalists, 1980.

125. CIA, "Communist Aid Activities in Non-Communist Less Developed Countries, 1979 and 1954–79," p. 23; Moscow Radio, 3 February 1981, in *FBIS/SU*, 5 February 1981, pp. D2–3. At the end of 1979 there were also 2,430 Afghan students in East Europe. This total of about 6,500 in the Soviet bloc in 1979 compared with just 950 in 1976; see CIA, "Communist Aid to the Less Developed Countries of the Free World, 1976" (Washington, 1977), p. 10. Presumably large new groups of Afghan students also went to East Europe in 1980.

126. Tass, 4 November 1980, in *FBIS/SA*, 5 November 1980, p. C1.

127. Kabul Radio, 14 November 1980, in *FBIS/SA*, 17 November 1980, pp. C1–7.

128. Ibid.

129. Kabul Radio, 29 April 1980, in *FBIS/SA*, 30 April 1980, p. C1.

130. Kabul Radio, 12 July 1980, in *FBIS/SA*, 14 July 1980, pp. C6–7.

131. PAP (Polish press agency) from Kabul, 23 February 1981, in *FBIS/SA*, 25 February 1981, p. C3.

132. *Novoye Vremya*, 11 April 1980, pp. 5–7, in *FBIS/SU*, 21 April 1980, pp. D6–9.

133. Press Trust of India (news agency) from Kabul, 10 and 14 April 1980, in *FBIS/SA*, 10 and 14 April 1980, pp. C1 and C9 (both as quoted by AFP).

134. FCO, "Afghanistan Report" (July 1980); FCO, "Afghanistan: Chronology."

135. Ibid.

136. Kabul Radio, 8 and 14 June 1980, in *FBIS/SA*, 9 and 16 June 1980, pp. C1–3.

137. Ibid. For attacks on Amin's nepotism, see Telegram No. 6605, U.S. Embassy, Kabul, 2 September 1979.

138. State Department, "Country Reports on Human Rights Practices," pp. 929–30; FCO, "Afghanistan Report" (September 1980).

139. Kabul Radio, 20 July 1980, in *FBIS/SA*, 21 July 1980, pp. C1–5.

140. *FBIS Trends*, 23 July 1980, pp. 3–4.

141. Montsame News Agency (of Mongolia), 15 August 1980, in *FBIS/SA*, 25 August 1980, p. C5.

142. Kabul Radio, 12 and 13 June 1981, in *FBIS/SA*, 15 June 1981, pp. C1–5; Bakhtar, 12 and 14 June 1981, in *FBIS/SA*, 15 June 1981, pp. C2–3.

143. Ibid. The cabinet, but not the council, had had non-party members from the beginning, but a 11 January 1980 decision to include them in the council apparently was not carried out, because Barialay said 13 June 1981 that they had just gained membership; see Kabul Radio, 11 January 1980 and 13 June 1981, in *FBIS/ME*, 14 January 1980, p. S1, and *FBIS/SA*, 15 June 1981, p. C9. Keshtmand was inexplicably absent from Kabul from mid-October to mid-December 1981, reportedly in Moscow, and his name was not mentioned by Afghan media. This suggested political trouble for him; however, there was in 1981 and 1982 a Soviet program of giving senior Afghan officials special training in the Soviet Union better to qualify them for their duties, and it is possible that Keshtmand was involved in one of these. See Eliza Van Hollen, State Department, "Afghanistan: 2 Years of Occupation," (Washington, D.C., 1981) p. 4.

144. State Department, "Afghanistan: A Year of Occupation."

145. Interviews with State Department officials.

146. Kabul Radio, 17 August 1981, in *FBIS/SA*, 18 August 1981, pp. C1–3.

147. Karmal in *World Marxist Review*, quoted by Tass from Prague, 21 May 1981, in *FBIS/SU*, 22 May 1981, p. D2.

148. Budapest Radio, 11 December 1980, in *FBIS/SA*, 12 December 1980, pp. C1–2.

149. DRA, "White Book," p. 4.

150. Chaffetz, "Afghanistan, Russia's Vietnam?" p. 6.

151. *Voprosy Filosofii*, Moscow, No 8 for 1980, pp. 60–71, in *FBIS/SU Annex*, 6 October 1980, pp. 1–12.

152. Kabul Radio, 25 January 1980, in *FBIS/ME*, 28 January 1980, pp. S1–2; Kabul Radio, 18 June 1980, in *FBIS/SA*, 20 June 1980, pp. C1–6.

153. Kohlschuetter, "The Day of the Kabul Rising," pp. 70–71.

154. Kabul Radio, 17 April 1980, in *FBIS/SA*, 22 April 1980, pp. C1–6.

155. Kabul Radio, 19 April 1980, in *FBIS/SA*, 23 April 1980, p. C2.

156. *Pravda*, 18 February 1980, p. 6, in *FBIS/SU*, 21 February 1980, pp. D3−4.

157. *Der Spiegel*, 31 March 1980, pp. 139−46, in *FBIS/SA*, 2 April 1980, pp. C1−9.

158. Kabul Radio, 17 April 1980, in *FBIS/SA*, 22 April 1980, pp. C1−9. In his first speech after coming to power, Karmal said that "our immediate task in the present conditions is not the introduction of socialism"; see Tass from Kabul, 30 December 1979, in *FBIS/SU*, 31 December 1979, p. D3. This was, however, qualified in such a way as to make the eventual goal of a Soviet-style socialism clear; ibid. A year later, Karmal said that "our present revolution is not a socialist one"; see *Times of India*, 11 February 1981, p. 1, in *FBIS/SA*, 23 February 1981, p. C1.

159. AFP from Islamabad, 10 July 1980, in *FBIS/SA*, 10 July 1980, pp. C3−4. In his speech to the Moslem conference, Karmal denied that Islam had been suppressed in the Soviet Union, and he invited delegates to go there at government expense "to see for yourselves that Islam exists there and has even achieved progress"; 88 persons, most Shi'ites, went and visited the government-controlled Islamic institutions in Soviet Central Asia; see "White Book," p. 66, and *FBIS Trends*, 16 July 1980, pp. 3−5.

160. *FBIS Trends*, 16 July 1980, pp. 3−5.

161. Radio Kabul, 19 September 1981, in *FBIS/SA*, 22 September 1981, p. C2. The Council of *Ulema* said, after the government had called soldiers and non-commissioned officers back to active duty, that "military service is obligatory and incumbent on all Moslem and patriotic people . . . on the basis of the following injunction of God: 'Prepare as much as you are able the means of confrontation against the enemies of the homeland'." Those who avoided this duty, the statement said, "are subject to the anger and wrath of God"; see ibid.

162. *Washington Post*, 15 September 1980, p. A12.

163. Interviews with Afghan exiles who declined to be identified.

164. Tass from Kabul, 29 December 1979, in *FBIS/SU*, 31 December 1979, pp. D1−5.

165. Tass from Kabul, 11 January 1980, in *FBIS/SU*, 14 January 1980, pp. D2−3; Kabul Radio, 11 January 1980, in *FBIS/ME*, 14 January 1980, p. S1. The three non-PDPA ministers headed the relatively nonsensitive ministries of commerce, agriculture and land reforms, and health.

166. In March 1980, Kabul Radio said 53 out of 122 persons appointed to government posts since 27 December were not PDPA members, and in announcing 37 further appointments in April it said 8 were not; see Kabul Radio, 13 March 1980, in *FBIS/ME*, 17 March 1980, pp. S10−11, and 10 April 1980, in *FBIS/SA*, 11 April 1980, p. C4; see also Moscow Radio, 6 January 1981, in *FBIS/SU*, 7 January 1981, p. D1.

167. State Department, "Afghanistan: A Year of Occupation."

168. *Rabotnichesko Delo*, 26 January 1980, pp. 1 and 6, in *FBIS/ME*, 30 January 1980, pp. S1−3.

169. Hugh Seton-Watson, *The East European Revolution* (3rd ed., New York, 1956), pp. 94, 169−71.

170. Jacques Guillermaz, *The Chinese Communist Party in Power, 1949−1976* (Boulder, 1976), pp. 14−15.

171. *Pravda*, 17 October 1980, p. 2, in *FBIS/SU*, 21 October 1980, pp. D3−11.

172. Kabul Radio, 8 September 1980, in *FBIS/SA*, 10 September 1980, p. C2; see also reports on meetings of women and of agricultural cooperatives, on Kabul Radio, 27 November and 12 December 1980, in *FBIS/SA*, 1 and 16 December 1980, pp. C1−6.

173. FCO, "The Sovietisation of Afghanistan."

174. Tass from Kabul, 7 March 1981, in *FBIS/SU*, 9 March 1981, p. D1.

175. *Pravda*, 27 September 1980, p. 5, in *FBIS/SU*, 28 September 1980, pp. D3−11; Tass from Kabul, 26 September 1980, in *FBIS/SU*, 29 September 1980, p. D1; Kabul Radio, 25 September 1980, in *FBIS/SA*, 26 September 1980, pp. C4−5.

176. *Pravda*, 28 September 1980, p. 5, in *FBIS/SU*, 2 October 1980, p. D3.

177. *Mlada Fronta*, 18 February 1981, p. 3, in *FBIS/SA*, 6 March 1981, p. C2.

178. FCO, "The Sovietisation of Afghanistan."

179. Ibid.; Kabul Radio, 27 November 1980, in *FBIS/SA*, 1 December 1980, p. C1.

180. *Pravda*, 31 January 1981, p. 4, in *FBIS/SU*, 5 February 1981, pp. D3−6.

181. Kabul Radio, 27 December 1980, in *FBIS/SA*, 30 December 1980, pp. C1−5.

182. Ibid.

183. Ibid.

184. Tass from Kabul, 29 December 1980, in *FBIS/SU*, 30 December 1980, pp. D2−3.

185. *The Times of India*, 11 February 1981, p. 1, in *FBIS/SA*, 23 February 1981, pp. C1−2.

186. Kabul Radio, 27 December 1980, in *FBIS/SA*, 30 December 1980, p. C1; *FBIS Trends*, 31 December 1980, p. 8.

187. FCO, "Afghanistan Report" (June 1981).

188. Bakhtar, 14 June 1981, in *FBIS/SA*, 15 June 1981, p. C1.

189. Bakhtar, 16 June 1981, in *FBIS/SA*, 19 June 1981, p. C1; Karmal's text is in ibid., pp. C4-15; see also FCO, "Afghanistan Report" (June 1981).

190. Kabul Radio, 15 June 1981, in *FBIS/SA*, 19 June 1981, pp. C23-24.

191. Bakhtar, 15 June 1981, in *FBIS/SA*, 19 June 1981, pp. C16-19.

192. Ibid., p. C17.

193. Ibid., p. C18. The constitution listed "the collective founding members" as the PDPA, the trade unions organization, the Union of Agricultural Cooperatives, the Democratic Organization of Youth, the Democratic Organization of Women, the Union of Poets and Writers, the Union of Journalists, the Union of Artists, the Peace, Solidarity and Friendship Organization, the Economic Consultative Council, the Council of Scholars and Clergies, and the High Jirgah of Tribal Representatives. Ziray later said (Kabul Radio, 31 October 1981, in *FBIS/SA*, 3 November 1981, pp. C2-4) that provincial branches of the NFF included, in addition to these groups, "guilds, merchants, owners of small industries," and other individuals. The constitution's statement on Soviet ties is similar to Article 89(e) of the Mongolian national constitution of 1960; see Robert A. Rupen, *Mongols of the Twentieth Century, Part I* (Bloomington, 1964), p. 425.

194. Diplomatic reports from Kabul, cited by U.S. officials.

195. Moscow Television, 27 December 1980, in *FBIS/SU*, 5 January 1981, pp. CC6-7.

196. Xinhua news agency from Beijing, 12 June 1981, in *FBIS/SU*, 19 June 1981, p. C1.

197. *The Economist*, 30 August 1980, p. 34.

198. Nayar, *Report on Afghanistan*, p. 180; *Washington Star*, 27 December 1980, p. A7.

199. FCO, "The Sovietisation of Afghanistan."

200. Interviews with Afghan exiles who declined to be identified.

201. *Komsomolskaya Pravda*, 16 October 1980, in *FBIS/SU*, 22 October 1980, pp. D6-7.

202. Kabul Radio, 25 August 1981, in *FBIS/SA*, 26 August 1981, pp. C1-3.

203. Kabul Radio, 27 August 1981, in *FBIS/SA*, 27 August 1981, pp. C1-3.

204. Ibid.

205. *Vneshnyaya Torgovlya SSSR*, for 1978 and 1980, quoted by Theodore Shabad, "The Soviet Union and Afghanistan: Some Economic Aspects," paper presented to the American Association for the Advancement of Slavic Studies, September 1981.

206. Interviews with Afghan exiles.

207. MTI (Hungarian news agency) from Kabul, 20 February 1981, in *FBIS/SA*, 23 February 1981, p. C3. The pattern had been set by 1980 agreements for Soviet aid to Afghanistan; see Kabul Radio, 8 March 1980, in *FBIS/ME*, 10 March 1980, pp. S5-6, and 26 December 1980, in *FBIS/SA*, 30 December 1980, pp. C7-8.

208. Diplomatic reports from Kabul, cited by U.S. officials.

209. Kabul Radio, 14 November 1980, in *FBIS/SA*, 17 November 1980, p. C5.

210. Kabul Radio, 26 June 1980, in *FBIS/SA*, 27 June 1980, pp. C1-7.

211. FCO, "Afghanistan Report" (February 1981).

212. MTI from Kabul, 23 January 1980, in *FBIS/ME*, 24 January 1980, pp. S6-7.

213. *Komsomolskaya Pravda*, 16 October 1980, in *FBIS/SU*, 22 October 1980, pp. D6-7.

214. Kabul Radio, 10 August and 5 September 1981, in *FBIS/SA*, 20 August and 10 September 1981, pp. C1-3. The basic decision to revive "just and democratic land reform" was taken by the PDPA politburo on 20 June 1981, but implementation began almost two months later.

Chapter 12. Soviet Afghanistan

1. *Pravda*, 17 October 1980, p. 2, in *FBIS/SU*, 21 October 1980, pp. D2-3.

2. Klein, "Basmachi," pp. 42-59; Pipes, *Formation of the Soviet Union*, pp. 259-60.

3. *Bol'shaya Sovetskaya Entsiklopediya* (1st ed. 1927), quoted by Klein, "Basmachi," p. 42.

4. *News Tibet* 15 (January-March 1980): 2.

5. Walther Heissig, *The Religions of Mongolia* (London, 1980): 26.

6. Bawden, *Modern History of Mongolia*, pp. 303-27; see also Henry S. Bradsher, "The Sovietization of Mongolia," *Foreign Affairs* 50 (April 1972): 547-48.

Bibliography

Documents

Afghanistan Task Force, Foreign Affairs and National Defense Division, The Library of Congress, Congressional Research Service. "Afghanistan: Soviet Invasion and U.S. Response," Issue Brief Number IB80006, as updated 13 June 1980 and 22 December 1980. Washington, 1980.

Agency for International Development. "Congressional Presentation, FY '81." Washington, 1980.

―――. "U.S. Overseas Loans and Grants." Washington, 1979.

Amnesty International. "Violations of Human Rights and Fundamental Freedoms in the Democratic Republic of Afghanistan." London, May 1979.

Becker, Abraham. "The Meaning and Measure of Soviet Military Expenditures," in Joint Economic Committee, U.S. Congress, *Soviet Economy in a Time of Change*. Washington, 1979.

British Broadcasting Corporation. *Summary of World Broadcasts, Far East*. London, 1973.

Central Intelligence Agency. "Changing Patterns in Soviet-LDC Trade, 1976–77." Washington, 1978.

―――. "Communist Aid Activities in Non-Communist Less Developed Countries, 1979 and 1954–79." Washington, 1980.

―――. "Communist Aid to the Less Developed Countries of the Free World, 1976" Washington, 1977.

―――. "Iran's International Position (NIE [National Intelligence Estimate] 34–61)." Washington, 1961.

Cooper, Richard N. Transcript of statement to U.S. Senate Banking Committee. Washington, 20 August 1980.

Cooper, William H. The Library of Congress, Congressional Research Service, "Soviet Policy Towards the Third World," Issue Brief Number IB79102, as updated 10 January 1980. Washington, 1980.

The Declassified Documents Quarterly Catalog. Washington, 1981.

The Declassified Documents Retrospective Collection. Washington, 1976.

The Declassified Documents 1977, 1978, 1979, 1980 Collections. Washington, 1977, 1978, 1979, 1980.

Department of State. "Afghanistan: A Year of Occupation," Special Report No. 79. Washington, 1981.

―――. "Assessment of Soviet Use of Chemical Warfare in Afghanistan." Paper distributed to journalists. Washington, 1980.

―――. *Bulletin*. Washington.

―――. "Chronology of Recent Developments Related to Afghanistan." Washington, 1980.

―――. "Country Reports on Human Rights Practices." Washington, 1981.

―――. *Foreign Relations of the United States, 1948, Vol. V, The Near East, South Asia, and Africa, Part 1*. Published 1975; *1949, Vol. VI*. published 1977; *1950, Vol. V*. published 1978. Washington.

―――. *Foreign Relations of the United States, 1951, Vol. VI, Asia and the Pacific, Part 2*. Published 1977. Washington.

————. *Foreign Relations of the United States, Diplomatic Papers, 1934, Vol. 2, Europe, Near East and Africa*. Washington, 1951.

————. "The Kidnapping and Death of Ambassador Adolph Dubs, Summary of Report of Investigation." Washington, made public in 1980.

————. *Papers Relating to the Foreign Relations of the United States, 1921, Vol. 1*. Published 1936; *1926, Vol. 1*. published 1941; *1931, Vol. 1*. published 1946. Washington.

————. Press Briefing Record. Washington.

————. "Soviet Invasion of Afghanistan," Special Report No. 72. Washington, 1980.

————. "Soviet Military and Civilian Control in Afghanistan." Paper made available to journalists. Washington, 1980.

Embassy of the United States. "Helping People." Kabul, 1976.

Embassy of the Soviet Union. Material mailed to American journalists on 23 January 1981. Washington.

"Expansion of Soviet Influence in Afghanistan and U.S. Countermeasures." Undated U.S. government study done in late 1950s, in *Declassified Documents 1980 Collection*. Washington, 1980.

Foreign Broadcast Information Service. *Daily Report, China*. Washington.

————. *Daily Report, Latin America*. Washington.

————. *Daily Report, Middle East and North Africa* (covering Afghanistan and the Indian subcontinent up to 1 April 1980). Washington.

————. *Daily Report, South Asia* (covering Afghanistan and the Indian subcontinent from 1 April 1980). Washington.

————. *Daily Report, Soviet Union*. Washington.

————. *Daily Report, West Europe*. Washington.

————. *Trends in Communist Media*. Washington.

Foreign and Commonwealth Office. "Afghanistan." London, 1980.

————. "Afghanistan and the 'Brezhnev Doctrine'." London, 1980.

————. "Afghanistan: Chronology of Events Since April 1978." London, 1980.

————. "Afghanistan: Further Responses." London, 1980.

————. "Afghanistan: Opposition Groups." London, 1980.

————. "Afghanistan Report." London, issued periodically.

————. "Afghanistan: Response to Soviet Intervention." London, 1980.

————. "Afghanistan: Soviet Occupation." London, 1980.

————. "Cuban Setbacks in the Non-Aligned Movement." London, 1980.

————. "Ethiopia: Problems for the USSR." London, 1980.

————. "Muslim Conference in Tashkent." London, 1980.

————. "PDRY (South Yemen): Soviet Client State in the Arab World." London, 1980.

————. "Soviet Attitude to Muslim Believers." London, 1981.

————. "Soviet Bloc Network of Friendship Treaties." London, 1980.

————. "Soviet Foreign Trade: 1979–80." London, 1981.

————. "The Sovietisation of Afghanistan." London, 1980.

————. "The Baltic States: 40 Years Under Soviet Rule." London, 1980.

The Geographer, Bureau of Intelligence and Research, Department of State. *International Boundary Study* series: No. 6, Afghanistan-Iran. Published 1961; No. 26, Afghanistan-USSR. 1963; No. 64, China-USSR. 1966; No. 85, China-Pakistan. 1968; No. 89, Afghanistan-China. 1969. Washington.

House of Commons. "Afghanistan: The Soviet Invasion and Its Consequences for British Policy." London, 1980.

International Cooperation Administration. "Soviet Bloc Economic Activities in the Near East and Asia, as of November 25, 1955." Washington, 1955, in *The Declassified Documents Retrospective Collection*, Washington, 1976.

Labour Press Service. Release LPS/09A/80/E. New Delhi, 1980.

Lay, James S., Jr. "Note by the Executive Secretary to the National Security Council on U.S. Policy Toward South Asia." 7 December 1956, in *Declassified Documents Quarterly Catalog* 5 (January–March 1979), Washington.

Muskie, Edmund S. press briefing, 5 June 1980, in Department of State Current Policy Paper No. 194. Washington, 1980.

Newsom, David D. Transcript of statement before U.S. Congress, House of Representatives, Committee on Foreign Affairs, Subcommittee on African Affairs. 18 October 1979, Washington.

Polk, W. R. Department of State, "Elements of U.S. Policy Toward Afghanistan." Washington, 1962, in *Declassified Documents 1978 Collection*, Washington, 1978.

Security Assistance Agency, Department of Defense. "Fiscal Year Series, 1979." Washington, 1979.

Taylor, James E. "Afghanistan: Eyewitness Story of the Soviet Invasion." *Department of State Newsletter*, March 1980, Washington, pp. 4-5.

U.S. Congress, House of Representatives, Committee on Foreign Affairs, Subcommittee on Europe and the Middle East. "An Assessment of the Afghanistan Sanctions: Implications for Trade and Diplomacy in the 1980's." Washington, April 1981.

————. "East-West Relations in the Aftermath of Soviet Invasion of Afghanistan." Washington, 1980.

————. "NATO After Afghanistan." Washington, 1980.

U.S. Congress, House of Representatives, Committee on Foreign Affairs, Subcommittee on Human Rights and International Organizations. "Soviet Violation of Helsinki Final Act: Invasion of Afghanistan." Hearing transcript, 22 July 1981. Washington, 1981.

U.S. Congress, House of Representatives, Permanent Select Committee on Intelligence. "CIA Estimates of Soviet Defense Spending." Washington, 1980.

U.S. Congress, Senate, Committee on Armed Services. "Soviet Defense Expenditures and Related Programs." Washington, 1980.

U.S. Congress, Senate, Committee on the Budget. "First Concurrent Resolution on the Budget—Fiscal Year 1981, National Defense." Hearing transcript, 26 February 1980. Washington, 1980.

Van Hollen, Eliza. "Soviet Dilemmas in Afghanistan," Department of State Special Report No. 72. Washington, 1980.

Vneshnyaya Torgovlya SSSR. Moscow, annual series.

Weekly Compilation of Presidential Documents. Washington.

Broadcast and News Agency Sources

Agence France Presse, French news agency

Bakhtar, Afghan news agency

British Broadcasting Corporation, London

Budapest Radio, Hungary

Delhi Radio, India

Havana Radio, Cuba

"Issues and Answers," ABC News, transcript of broadcast, 30 December 1979, from Washington, D.C.

Japan Press Service, Tokyo
Kabul Radio, Afghanistan
Karachi Radio, Pakistan
Mashhad Radio, Iran
Montsame, Mongolian news agency
Moscow Radio, USSR
Moscow Television, USSR
MTI, Hungarian news agency
NHK Television, Tokyo, Japan
PAP, Polish news agency
Press Trust of India, Indian news agency
Radio Peace and Progress, Moscow and Tashkent, USSR
Tanjug, Yugoslav news agency
Tass, Soviet news agency
Tehran Radio, Iran
"Today," NBC Television, transcript of broadcast, 9 January 1980, from Washington, D.C.
Xinhua, Chinese news agency

Periodicals and Newspapers

Adelphi Papers, London
Al-Bayan, Dubai
Al-Madinah, Jiddah, Saudi Arabia
American Universities Field Staff Reports, New York and Hanover, N. H.
Asia, New York
Asian/Pacific Population Program News, Bangkok, Thailand
Asian Survey, Berkeley, Calif.
Asiaweek, Hong Kong
Batinskiy Rabochiy, Baku, USSR
Beijing Review, Beijing, China
Boston Globe
Broadway, New York
Business Week, New York
Central Asian Review, London
China Quarterly, London
Columbia Journalism Review, New York
Corriere della Sera, Milan, Italy
Current, Bombay, India
Current Digest of the Soviet Press, New York
Daily Telegraph, London
Demography, Washington, D.C.
Der Spiegel, Hamburg, Germany
Dhimokratia, Nicosia, Cyprus
Die Welt, Bonn, Germany
Die Zeit, Hamburg, Germany
The Economist, London
The Economist Intelligence Unit, "Quarterly Economic Review: Pakistan, Bangladesh, Afghanistan," London

Encounter, London
Far Eastern Economic Review, Hong Kong
Foreign Affairs, New York
Foreign Policy, Washington, D.C.
Frankfurter Allgemeine, Frankfurt, Germany
Geographical Review, New York
The Guardian, London
Helsingin Sanomat, Helsinki, Finland
Hong Kong Standard
Indian Express, Bombay and New Delhi editions
International Affairs, London
International Affairs, Moscow
International Journal of Middle East Studies, Cambridge, England
International Security, Cambridge, Mass.
International Studies, New Delhi
Iran Times, Tehran
Izvestiya, Moscow (most citations are to the international edition, which is dated the day
    after the main Moscow afternoon publication)
Journal of Social and Political Studies, Washington, D.C.
Kabul New Times (renamed this in 1980)
Kabul Times (before 1980)
Kharavyi, Nicosia, Cyprus
Kommunist, Moscow
Kommunist Tadzhikistana, Dushanbe, USSR
Kommunist Voorushennykh Sil, Moscow
Komsomolskaya Pravda, Moscow
Krasnaya Zvezda, Moscow
Le Monde, Paris
Le Monde Diplomatique, Paris
Le Soir, Brussels
L'Humanite, Paris
Literaturnaya Gazeta, Moscow
Los Angeles Times
L'Unita, Rome
The Fletcher Forum, Medford, Mass.
MERIP Reports, Washington, D.C.
The Middle East Journal, Washington, D.C.
Mlada Fronta, Prague, Czechoslovakia
Moscow News Weekly
Moskovskaya Pravda, Moscow
Naval War College Review, Newport, R.I.
Nedelya, Moscow
The New Leader, New York
New Left Review, London
The New Republic, Washington, D.C.
New Statesman, London
The New York Review
The New York Times

Newsletter, Afghanistan Council, The Asia Society, New York
News Tibet, New York
Novoye Vremya, Moscow
Orbis, Philadelphia, Pa.
Party Life, New Delhi
Patriot, New Delhi
Political Affairs, Theoretical Journal of the Communist Party, USA, New York
Pravda, Bratislava, Czechoslovakia
Pravda, Moscow
Problems of Communism, Washington, D.C.
Problems of History of the Soviet Communist Party, Moscow
Rabotnichesko Delo, Sofia, Bulgaria
Radio Liberty Research reports, Munich, Germany
Ramparts, San Francisco, Calif.
Scientific American, New York
The Socialist, Sydney, Australia
Sotsialisticheskaya Industriya, Moscow
Soviet World Outlook, Washington, D.C.
Sovietskaya Rossiya, Moscow
Strategic Review, Washington, D.C.
Suddeutsche Zeitung, Munich, Germany
The Sun, Baltimore, Maryland
The Sunday Telegraph, London
Survey, London
Survival, London
Tariqust Al-Shaab, Baghdad, Iraq
The Times of India, Bombay
Turkmenskaya Iskra, Ashkhabad, USSR
United Nations *Treaty Series*, New York
Voprosy Filosofii, Moscow
The Washington Post
The Washington Quarterly
The Washington Review of Strategic and International Studies
The Washington Star (in 1973, *The Washington Star-News*)
World Marxist Review, Prague, Czechoslovakia
World Press Review, New York
The World Today, London
Za Rubezhom, Moscow
Zarya Vostoka, Tbilisi, USSR

Books

Adamec, Ludwig W. *Afghanistan's Foreign Affairs to the Mid-Twentieth Century: Relations with the USSR, Germany and Britain*. Tucson, 1974.
Afghan Information Bureau. *Pakhtunistan: The Khyber Pass as the Focus of the New State of Pakhtunistan: an important political development in Central Asia*. London, [1952?].
Agabekov, Grigorii S. *OGPU: The Russian Secret Terror*. New York, 1931.
Aitchison, C. U. *A Collection of Treaties, Engagements and Sanads Relating to India and*

Neighbouring Countries, Vol. XIII, Containing the Treaties &c. Relating to Persia and Afghanistan. Calcutta, 1933.

Akhramovich, Roman T. *Outline History of Afghanistan After the Second World War.* Moscow, 1966.

Amnesty International. *Amnesty International Report 1980.* London, 1980.

Ayub Khan, Mohammad. *Friends Not Masters: A Political Autobiography.* London, 1967.

Barnds, William J. *India, Pakistan, and the Great Powers.* New York, 1972.

Baryalai, A. M., ed. *Democratic Republic of Afghanistan Annual, Saur 7, 1358.* Kabul, 1979.

Bawden, C. R. *The Modern History of Mongolia.* London, 1968.

Becker, Seymour. *Russia's Protectorates in Central Asia: Bukhara and Khiva, 1865–1924.* Cambridge, Mass., 1968.

Bennigsen, Alexandre A., and S. Enders Wimbush, *Muslim National Communism in the Soviet Union: A Revolutionary Strategy for the Colonial World.* Chicago, 1979.

Berliner, Joseph S. *Soviet Economic Aid: the New Aid and Trade Policy in Underdeveloped Countries.* New York, 1958.

Bulganin, N. A., and N. S. Khrushchev. *Speeches During Sojourn in India, Burma and Afghanistan, November–December 1955.* New Delhi, 1956.

Bureau of Intelligence and Research, Department of State. *World Strength of Communist Party Organizations, 24th annual report, 1972 edition.* Washington, 1972.

Callard, Keith. *Pakistan: A Political Study.* London, 1957.

Caroe, Olaf. *The Pathans: 550 B.C.–A.D. 1957,* London, 1958.

———. *Soviet Empire: The Turks of Central Asia and Stalinism.* London, 1953.

Carr, Edward H. *A History of Soviet Russia: The Bolshevik Revolution, 1917–1923.* Vol. 3. London: Pelican ed., 1966.

———. *A History of Soviet Russia: The Interregnum, 1923–1924.* Baltimore: Penguin ed., 1969.

———. *A History of Soviet Russia: Socialism in One Country, 1924–1926,* Vol. 3. London: Pelican ed., 1972.

Churchill, Winston S. *The Second World War: The Gathering Storm.* Boston, 1948.

Collins, John M. *U.S.-Soviet Military Balance: Concepts and Capabilities, 1960–1980.* Washington, 1980.

Daoud, Mohammed. *The Republic of Afghanistan: Statements, Messages, and Press Interviews of the National Leader and the Founder of the Republic, No. 1.* Kabul, 1973.

Dupree, Louis. *Afghanistan.* Princeton, 1980.

Elphinstone, Mountstuart. *Account of the Kingdom of Caubul.* London, 1815.

Fedorov, G.A., et al., *Marxism-Leninism on War and the Army.* Moscow, 1961, 1968, 1977.

Fifty Years of the Soviet Union's Armed Might. Moscow, 1968.

Fischer, Louis. *The Soviets in World Affairs.* London, 1930.

Franck, Peter G. *Afghanistan Between East and West.* Washington, 1960.

Fraser-Tytler, W. Kerr. *Afghanistan: A Study of Political Developments in Central and Southern Asia.* 2d ed. London, 1953.

Friters, Gerard M. *Outer Mongolia and Its International Position.* Baltimore, 1949.

Grassmuck, George, and Ludwig W. Adamec. *Afghanistan: Some New Approaches,* Ann Arbor, 1969.

Gregorian, Vartan. *The Emergence of Modern Afghanistan: Politics of Reform and Modernization, 1880–1946.* Stanford, 1969.

Goldman, Marshall I. *Soviet Foreign Aid.* New York, 1967.

Guillermaz, Jacques. *The Chinese Communist Party in Power, 1949–1976*, Boulder, 1976.

Habberton, William. *Anglo-Russian Relations Concerning Afghanistan, 1837–1907*. Urbana, 1937.

Harrison, Selig S. *In Afghanistan's Shadow: Baluch Nationalism and Soviet Temptations.* New York, 1981.

Heissig, Walther. *The Religions of Mongolia*. London, 1980.

Hurewitz, J. C. *Diplomacy in the Near and Middle East, A Documentary Record, 1914–1956*. Princeton, 1956.

———. *Middle East Politics: The Military Dimension*. New York, 1969.

Hussain, Syed Shabbir, with Abdul Hamid Alvi, and Absar Hussain Rizvi, *Afghanistan Under Soviet Occupation*. Islamabad, 1980.

Information Department, Ministry of Foreign Affairs. *Undeclared War: Armed Intervention and Other Forms of Interference in the Internal Affairs of the Democratic Republic of Afghanistan*. Kabul, 1980.

———. *White Book of the Democratic Republic of Afghanistan: Documents and Materials about Interference in the Internal Affairs of the Democratic Republic of Afghanistan and about the DRA Government's Initiatives in Peaceful Settlement of the Situation around Afghanistan*. Kabul, n.d. [1980?].

Inozemtsev, N. N. *International Relations After the Second World War*. Moscow, 1965.

International Institute for Strategic Studies. *The Military Balance, 1977–78*. London, 1977.

———. *The Military Balance, 1980–81*. London, 1980.

———. *Strategic Survey, 1979*. London, 1980.

Kapitsa, Mikhail S. *KNR: Dva Desiatiletiia-dve Politiki*. Moscow, 1969.

Kaplan, Stephen S. *Diplomacy of Power: Soviet Armed Forces as a Political Instrument*. Washington, 1981.

Kavalsky, Basil G. "Afghanistan, the Journey to Economic Development." Study for the World Bank, unpublished. Washington, 1977.

Khrushchev, Nikita S. *Khrushchev Remembers*. Boston, 1971.

Kissinger, Henry A. *The White House Years*. Boston, 1979.

Klein, David. "The *Basmachi*—A Case Study in Soviet Policy Toward National Minorities." State Department study, unpublished. Washington, 1952.

Kolarz, Walter. *Russia and Her Colonies*. London, 1952.

Kulish, V. M., ed. *Military Force and International Relations*. Moscow, 1972. English edition. Arlington, 1973.

Lenczowski, George. *Russia and the West in Iran, 1918–1948: A Study in Big-Power Rivalry*. Ithaca, 1949.

Majumdar, R. C., H. C. Raychaudhuri, and Kalikinkar Datta, *An Advanced History of India*. 2nd ed. London, 1960.

Masani, M. R. *The Communist Party of India: A Short History*. London, 1954.

Murphy, George G. S. *Soviet Mongolia: A Study of the Oldest Political Satellite*. Berkeley, 1966.

Nachukdorji, Sh. *Life of Sukebatur*. Ulan Bator, 1943; translated in Owen Lattimore. *Nationalism and Revolution in Mongolia*. Leiden, 1955.

Nayar, Kuldip. *Report on Afghanistan*. New Delhi, 1981.

Newell, Nancy Peabody, and Richard S. Newell, *The Struggle for Afghanistan*. Ithaca, 1981.

Newell, Richard S. *The Politics of Afghanistan*. Ithaca, 1972.

Nollau, Gunther, and Hans Jurgen Wiehe, *Russia's South Flank: Soviet Operations in Iran, Turkey and Afghanistan*. New York, 1963.

Nove, Alec. *An Economic History of the U.S.S.R..* London, 1969.

Novosti Press Agency. *The Truth About Afghanistan: Documents, Facts, Eyewitness Reports.* Moscow, 1980.

Overstreet, Gene D., and Marshall Windmiller, *Communism in India.* Bombay, 1960.

Pahlavi, Mohammed Reza. *Answer to History.* New York, 1980.

Pennell, Theodore L. *Among the Wild Tribes of the Afghan Frontier.* London, 1927.

Pipes, Richard. *The Formation of the Soviet Union: Communism and Nationalism, 1917–1923.* Rev. ed. Cambridge, Mass., 1964.

Prescott, J. R. V. *Map of Mainland Asia by Treaty.* Melbourne, 1975.

Public Papers of the Presidents: Jimmy Carter, 1978. Washington, 1980.

Ra'anan, Uri. *The USSR Arms the Third World: Case Studies in Soviet Foreign Policy.* Cambridge, Mass., 1969.

Reid, Warren R., ed. *Public Papers of the Presidents of the United States: Harry S. Truman, 1949.* Washington, 1964.

Riasanovsky, Nicholas V. *A History of Russia.* New York, 1963.

Rubinstein, Alvin Z. *The Foreign Policy of the Soviet Union.* New York, 1960.

Rupen, Robert A. *Mongols of the Twentieth Century, Part I.* Bloomington, 1964.

Saikal, Amin. *The Rise and Fall of the Shah.* Princeton, 1980.

Schwartz, Harry. *Prague's 200 Days: The Struggle for Democracy in Czechoslovakia.* New York, 1969.

Scott, William F., and Harriet Fast Scott, *Soviet Projection of Military Presence and Power, Vol. II, A Review and Assessment of Soviet Policy and Concepts on the Projections of Military Presence and Power.* McLean, 1979.

Seagrave, Sterling. *Yellow Rain: A Journey Through the Terror of Chemical Warfare.* New York, 1981.

Seton-Watson, Hugh. *The East European Revolution.* 3rd ed. New York, 1956.

———. *From Lenin to Khrushchev: The History of World Communism.* New York, 1960.

Shah, Ikbal Ali. *Afghanistan of the Afghans.* London, 1928.

Shanor, Donald R. *Soviet Europe.* New York, 1975.

Shirendev, B., and others, eds. *The History of the Mongolian People's Republic.* Ulan Bator, 1969. Translated by William A. Brown and Urgunge Onon, Cambridge, Mass., 1976.

Skilling, H. Gordon. *Czechoslovakia's Interrupted Revolution.* Princeton, 1976.

Smith, Harvey H., and others. *Area Handbook for Afghanistan.* 4th ed. Washington, 1973.

Sontag, R. J., and J. S. Beddie, eds. *Nazi-Soviet Relations, 1939–1941: Documents from the Archives of the German Foreign Office.* Washington, 1948.

Sorokin, A. I., ed., *V. I. Lenin on the Defense of the Socialist Fatherland.* Mosow, 1977.

Sykes, Percy Molesworth. *A History of Afghanistan.* London, 1940.

Tang, Peter S. H. *Russian and Soviet Policy in Manchuria and Outer Mongolia, 1911–1931.* Durham, 1959.

Thomas, Hugh. *The Spanish Civil War.* London; Penguin ed. 1965.

Ulam, Adam B. *Expansion & Coexistence: The History of Soviet Foreign Policy, 1917–1967.* New York, 1968.

Valenta, Jiri. *Soviet Intervention in Czechoslovakia, 1968: Anatomy of a Decision.* Baltimore, 1979.

Vali, Ferenc A. *Rift and Revolt in Hungary: Nationalism versus Communism.* Cambridge, Mass., 1961.

Vambery, Arminius. *Western Culture in Eastern Lands.* New York, 1906.

Wheeler, Geoffrey. *The Modern History of Soviet Central Asia.* London, 1964.

Wilber, Donald N., ed. *Country Survey Series: Afghanistan.* New Haven, 1956.

Articles

Abidi, A. H. H. "Irano-Afghan Dispute over the Helmand Waters." *International Studies* (New Delhi) (1977): 357–78.

Adamec, Ludwig W. "Germany, Third Power in Afghanistan's Foreign Relations." In George Grassmuck and Ludwig W. Adamec, eds., *Afghanistan: Some New Approaches.* Ann Arbor, 1969.

Ahmed, Feroz. Interview. *MERIP Reports* 89 (1980): 13–20.

Amin, Hafizullah. "Afghan Youth Movement." In Nassimi, Mohammed Yassin, ed. *Yearbook of the Associated Students of Afghanistan in the United States.* No place of publication given, 1964.

Aslanov, M. G. et al., "Peoples of Afghanistan." In Kisliakov, N. A., and A. I. Pershits, eds. *Narody Peredenei Asii* (Moscow, 1957). Translated by Mark and Greta Slobin, in George Grassmuck and Ludwig W. Adamec, eds., *Afghanistan: Some New Approaches.* Ann Arbor, 1969.

Aspaturian, Vernon V. "Soviet Global Power and the Correlation of Forces." *Problems of Communism*, 29 (1980): 1–18.

———. "Superpower Maneuvers—1: Moscow's Afghan Gamble." *The New Leader.* 28 January 1980, p. 9.

Barfield, Thomas. "Afghans Fight Old Battles in a New War." *Asia* 2 (March/April 1980): 12–15, 46–47.

"The *Basmachis*: The Central Asian Resistance Movement, 1918–1924." *Central Asian Review* 7 (1959): 236–50.

Beattie, H. "Effects of the Saor Revolution in the Nahrin Area of Northern Afghanistan." Paper presented to the American Anthropological Assn., Washington, D.C., December 1980.

Beloff, Max. "The Military Factor in Soviet Foreign Policy." *Problems of Communism*, 30 (1981): 70–73.

Bennigsen, Alexandre. "Soviet Muslims and the World of Islam." *Problems of Communism*, 29 (1980): 38–51.

Bernstein, Carl. "Arms for Afghanistan." *New Republic*, 18 July 1981, pp. 8–10.

Bovin, Alexander. "Apropos the Afghan Revolution." *Moscow News Weekly*, No. 16 (1980), p. 7.

Bradsher, Henry S. ("a correspondent"). "Afghanistan: Change in Kabul." *The Economist*, 8 June 1963, p. 1006.

———. "Kabul Remains Shaky After July Coup." *Washington Star-News*, 24 November 1973, p. B-back.

——— "The Sovietization of Mongolia." *Foreign Affairs* 50 (1972): 546–53.

Chaffetz, David. "Afghanistan in Turmoil." *International Affairs* (London)(January 1980): 15–36.

———. "Afghanistan, Russia's Vietnam?" Afghanistan Council Special Paper No. 4, The Asia Society, New York, Summer 1979.

"Conversation with the Readers: With Regard to the Khalq Party of Afghanistan." *Tariqust Al-Shaab* (Baghdad), nos. 740 (22 February 1976), and 841 (23 June 1976).

Creekman, Charles T., Jr. "Sino-Soviet Competition in the Yemens." *Naval War College Review* 32 (July-August 1979): 73–82.

Dastarac, Alexandre, and M. Levant, "What Went Wrong in Afghanistan." *Le Monde Diplomatique* (February 1980): 6–7. In *Near East/North Africa Report,* No. 2093, Joint Publications Research Service, 21 March 1980.

Davis, Nathaniel. "The Angola Decision of 1975: A Personal Memoir." *Foreign Affairs* 57 (1978): 109–24.

Demohenko, P., and L. Moronov, "The Revolution's Difficult Steps." *Pravda*, 14 January 1980, p. 6.

Dupree, Louis. "Afghanistan Under the Khalq." *Problems of Communism* 28 (1979): 34–50.

――――. "Afghanistan's Big Gamble: Part II, the Economic and Strategic Aspects of Soviet Aid," *American Universities Field Staff Reports, South Asia* 4, 4 (1960).

――――. "Asia Society Occasional Paper." New York, Spring 1976.

――――. "The Mountains Go to Mohammad Zahir: Observations on Afghanistan's Reactions to Visits from Nixon, Bulganin-Khrushchev, Eisenhower and Khrushchev." *American Universities Field Staff Reports, South Asia* 4, 6 (1960).

――――. "Afghanistan's Slow March to Democracy; Reflections on Kabul's Municipal Balloting." *American Universities Field Staff Reports, South Asia* 7, 1 (1963).

――――. "The Decade of Daoud Ends: Implications of Afghanistan's Change of Government." *American Universities Field Staff Reports, South Asia* 7, 7 (1963).

――――. "An Informal Talk with King Mohammad Zahir of Afghanistan." *Afghanistan Universities Field Staff Reports, South Asia* 7, 9 (1963).

――――. "Constitutional Development and Cultural Change, Part VIII: The Future of Constitutional Law in Afghanistan and Pakistan," *American Universities Field Staff Reports, South Asia*, New York 9, 10 (1965).

――――. "Afghanistan: 1966; Comments on a Comparatively Calm State of Affairs with Reference to the Turbulence of Late 1965." *American Universities Field Staff Reports, South Asia* 10, 4 (1966).

――――. "The Chinese Touch Base and Strike Out: Observations on China's Relations with Pakistan and Afghanistan," *American Universities Field Staff Reports, South Asia* 10, 11 (1966).

――――. "Afghanistan: 1968, Part III: Problems of a Free Press," *American Universities Field Staff Reports, South Asia* 12, 6 (1968).

――――. "A Note on Afghanistan: 1974," *American Universities Field Staff Reports, South Asia* 18, 8 (1974).

――――. "Afghanistan 1977: Does Trade Plus Aid Guarantee Development?," *American Universities Field Staff Reports, Asia* 21, 3 (1977).

――――. "The Democratic Republic of Afghanistan, 1979," *American Universities Field Staff Reports, Asia* 3 (1979).

――――. "Red Flag over Hindu Kush, Part 1: Leftist Movements in Afghanistan," *American Universities Field Staff Reports, Asia* 44 (1979).

――――. "Red Flag over Hindu Kush, Part 2: The Accidental Coup, or Taraki in Blunderland," *American Universities Field Staff Reports, Asia* 45 (1979).

――――. "Red Flag Over the Hindu Kush, Part III: Rhetoric and Reforms, or Promises! Promises!," *American Universities Field Staff Reports, Asia* 23 (1980).

――――. "Red Flag Over the Hindu Kush, Part V: Repressions, or Security Through Terror Purges, I-IV," *American Universities Field Staff Reports, Asia* 28 (1980).

Dupree, Nancy Hatch. "Revolutionary Rhetoric and Afghan Women." Paper presented to the American Anthropological Assn., Washington, D.C., December 1980.

The Editors. "How the CIA Turns Foreign Students into Traitors." *Ramparts* (April 1967): 3–4.

Eliot, Theodore L., Jr. "Afghanistan After the 1978 Revolution." *Strategic Review* 7 (1979): 57–62.

———. "The 1978 Afghan Revolution: Some Internal Aspects." *The Fletcher Forum* 3 (1979): 82–87.

Field, Neil C. "The Amu Darya: A Study in Resource Geography." *Geographical Review* (October 1954): 528–42.

Fine, Daniel I. "An Underlying Impetus for Soviet Invasion." *Business Week*, 29 September 1980, p. 62.

Fromkin, David. "The Great Game in Asia." *Foreign Affairs*, 58 (1980): 936–51.

Garver, John W. "The Sino-Soviet Territorial Dispute in the Pamir Mountains Region." *The China Quarterly* 85 (1981): 107–18.

Grechko, A. A. "The Leading Role of the CPSU in Building the Army of a Developed Socialist Society." *Problems of History of the Soviet Communist Party* (May 1974).

Halliday, Fred. "Afghanistan: The Limits of Russian Imperialism." *New Statesman*, 5 December 1980, pp. 10–12.

———. "Afghanistan—A Revolution Consumes Itself." *The Nation*, 17 November 1979, pp. 492–95.

———. "Revolution in Afghanistan." *New Left Review*, No. 112 (1978), pp. 3–44.

Harrison, Selig S. "Dateline Afghanistan: Exit Through Finland?" *Foreign Policy* 41 (1980–81): 163–87.

———. "The Shah, Not Kremlin, Touched Off Afghan Coup." *The Washington Post*, 13 May 1979, pp. C1 and C5.

Haselkorn, Avigdor. "The Expanding Soviet Collective Security Network." *Strategic Review* 6 (Summer 1978): 62–73.

———. "The 'External Function' of Soviet Armed Forces." *Naval War College Review* 33 (1980): 35–45.

Hassner, Pierre. "Moscow and the Western Alliance." *Problems of Communism* 30 (1981): 37–54.

Hauner, Milan. "Afghanistan Between the Great Powers, 1938–1945." Paper presented to the Middle East Studies Assn., Washington, D.C., November 1980.

Heller, Mark. "The Soviet Invasion of Afghanistan." *The Washington Quarterly* (Summer 1980): 36–59.

"Interview with an Afghan Marxist." *Pakistani Progressive* (March–April 1980). In *MERIP Reports*, 89 (1980): 20–24.

Kakar, Hasan. "The Fall of the Afghan Monarchy in 1973." *International Journal of Middle East Studies* 9 (1978): 195–214.

Kanet, Roger E. "Soviet Attitudes Toward Developing Nations Since Stalin." In Roger E. Kanet, *The Soviet Union and the Developing Nations.* Baltimore, 1974, pp. 27–50.

Kazemzadeh, Firuz. "Afghanistan: The Imperial Dream." *The New York Review*, 21 February 1980, pp. 10–14.

———. "Russia and the Middle East." In Ivo J. Lederer, ed. *Russian Foreign Policy: Essays in Historical Perspective.* New Haven, 1962, pp. 489–530.

Kelly, John B. "East & West: The Road to Kabul: The Kremlin and the Gulf." *Encounter* 54 (1980): 84–90.

Khalilzad, Zalmay. "Afghanistan and the Crisis in American Foreign Policy." *Survival* 22 (1980): 151–60.

Kohlschuetter, Andreas. "Points of the Compass: The Day of the Kabul Rising (& After), in Afghanistan." *Encounter* 55 (August/September 1980): 68–79.

Krishnan, N. K. "Prospects of Democratic Advance in Afghanistan." *Party Life*, 22 May 1976.

Lapchinskiy, A. N. "The Organization and Use of Airborne Landing Parties." In A. B. Kadishev, ed. *Problems of Tactics in Soviet Military Works, 1917–1940. Moscow, 1970.*

Legum, Colin. "Angola and the Horn of Africa." In Stephen S. Kaplan, Diplomacy of Power: Soviet Armed Forces as a Political Instrument. Washington, 1981, pp. 570–637.

Livingston, Neil C. and Manfred von Nordheim. "The United States Congress and the Angola Crisis." *Strategic Review* 5 (Spring 1977): 34–44.

Lowenthal, Richard. "Soviet 'Counterimperialism'." *Problems of Communism* 25 (1976): 52–63.

———. "The Shattered Balance: Estimating the Dangers of War & Peace." *Encounter* 55 (1980): 12–13.

Marshall, Andrew. "Sources of Soviet Power: The Military Potential in the 1980s." In *Adelphi Papers*, No. 152, "Prospects of Soviet Power in the 1980s, Part II." London, 1979.

Milovidov, A. S., and Ye. A. Zhdanov, "Sociophilosophical Problems of War and Peace." *Voprosy Filosofii*, No. 10, 1980.

Mironov, L., and G. Polyakov, "Afghanistan: the Beginning of a New Life." *International Affairs* (Moscow)(March 1979): 46–54.

Molnar, Peter, and Paul Tapponnier, "The Collision Between India and Eurasia." *Scientific American*, April 1977, pp. 30–41.

Montgomery, David O. "The Uzbeks in Two States: Soviet and Afghan Policies Toward an Ethnic Minority." In William O. McCagg, Jr., and Brian D. Silver, eds. *Soviet Asian Ethnic Frontiers.* New York, 1979.

Mukerjee, Dilip. "Afghanistan Under Daud: Relations with Neighboring States." *Asian Survey* 15 (1975): 301–12.

Naby, Eden. "The Ethnic Factor in Soviet-Afghan Relations." *Asian Survey* 20 (1980): 237–56.

———. "The Iranian Frontier Nationalities: The Kurds, the Assyrians, the Baluchis, and the Turkmens." In William O. McCagg, Jr., and Brian D. Silver, eds. *Soviet Asian Ethnic Frontiers.* New York, 1979, pp. 83–114.

Negaran, Hannah (pseudonym). "The Afghan Coup of April 1978: Revolution and International Security." *Orbis* 23 (1979): 93–113.

Neumann, Robert G. "Afghanistan." *The Washington Review of Strategic and International Studies* (July 1978): 115–18.

———. "Afghanistan Under the Red Flag." in Z. Michael Szaz, ed. *The Impact of the Iranian Events Upon Persian Gulf & United States Security.* Washington, 1979.

Newell, Richard S. "The Government of Mustafa Shafiq: Prelude to Disaster." Paper presented to the Middle East Studies Assn., Washington, D.C., November 1980.

———. "Soviet Intervention in Afghanistan." *The World Today* (July 1980): 250–58.

Newsom, David D. "America EnGulfed." *Foreign Policy*, No. 43 (1981): 17–32.

Noorani, A. G. "Soviet Ambitions in South Asia." *International Security* 4 (1979–80): 31–59.

Peterzell, Jay. "Chronicle: The New Afghanistanism." *Columbia Journalism Review* (March/April 1981): 5–7.

Philips, James. "Afghanistan: Islam versus Marxism." *Journal of Social and Political Studies* 4 (1979): 305–20.

Poullada, Leon B. "Afghanistan and the United States: The Crucial Years." *The Middle East Journal* 35 (1981): 178–90.

———. "The Pushtun Role in the Afghan Political System." Occasional Paper No. 1, The Afghanistan Council of The Asia Society, New York, 1970.

Primakov, Yevgeniy M. "Islam and Progress in the Social Progress of Foreign Countries in the East." *Voprosy Filosofii* No. 8 (1980): pp. 60–71.

Radio Liberty Research. "The USSR Shows Concern Over Afghanistan." RL92/79, 1979.

———. "A Chronology of Soviet-Afghan Relations: April 1978–January 1980." RL17/80, 1980.

———. "The Ethnic Composition of Soviet Forces in Afghanistan." RL20/80, 1980.

———. "Afghan Revolutionary Leaders as Viewed by Soviet Publication in Tashkent." RL21/80, 1980.

———. "Cuba Continues to Take an Ambiguous Stand on Soviet Actions in Afghanistan." RL56/80, 1980.

———. "Soviet Media Coverage of Events in Afghanistan in the Weeks Before the Coup." RL62/80, 1980.

———. "Brezhnev Introduces New Element in USSR's Position on Afghanistan." RL85/80, 1980.

———. "*Krasnaya Zvezda* Describes Reception of Soviet Troops in Afghanistan." RL109/80, 1980.

———. "The National Composition of the Population of the USSR According to the Census of 1979." RL123/80, 1980.

———. "Early Retirement of Foreign Minister of the Kirgiz SSR." RL152/80, 1980.

———. "Babrak Karmal's Moscow Visit." RL389/80, 1980.

———. "*Voennye Znaniya* Reports on Conditions Experienced by Soviet Troops in Afghanistan." RL176/81, 1981.

———. "*Krasnaya Zvezda's* 'Afghan Notebook'." RL133/81, 1981.

———. "Soviet Moslem Publication Plays Down Tashkent Conference." RL241/81, 1981.

———. "The Soviet Military Air Transport Force." RL385/81, 1981.

Reardon, Patrick J. "Modernization and Reform: The Contemporary Endeavor." In George Grassmuck and Ludwig W. Adamec, eds., *Afghanistan: Some New Approaches*. Ann Arbor, 1969, pp. 149–203.

Schwartz, Morton. "The USSR and Leftist Regimes in Less-Developed Countries." *Survey* 19 (1973): 209–44.

Servriannikov, V., and M. Iasiukov, "Peaceful Coexistence and Defense of the Socialist Fatherland." *Kommunist Voorushennykh Sil*, August 1972.

Shabad, Theodore. "The Soviet Union and Afghanistan: Some Economic Aspects." Paper presented to the American Assn. for the Advancement of Slavic Studies, Monterey, Calif., September 1981.

Sikoyev, Ruslan. "Afghanistan: Revolution in the Interests of the Working People." *Political Affairs, Theoretical Journal of the Communist Party, USA* 58 (1979): 10–16.

Simes, Dimitri K. "The Death of Detente?" *International Security* 5 (1980): 3–25.

Spitler, James F., and Nancy B. Frank, "Afghanistan, A Demographic Uncertainty." International Research Document No. 6, U.S. Department of Commerce, Bureau of the Census, Washington, September 1978.

Stepanov, V. "Islamabad Falsifiers." *Izvestiya*, 29 August 1980, p. 5.

Trussell, James, and Eleanor Brown, "A Close Look at the Demography of Afghanistan." *Demography* 16 (1979): 137–56.

Tucker, Robert C. "Swollen State, Spent Society: Stalin's Legacy to Brezhnev's Russia." *Foreign Affairs* 60 (Winter 1981/82): 414–35.

Ulyanovskiy, Rostislav A., "The Afghan Revolution at the Current Stage," *Problems of History of the Soviet Communist Party* 4 (1982): 84–95.

———. "The Third World—Problems of Socialist Orientation." *International Affairs* (Moscow) 9 (1971): 26–35.

Valenta, Jiri. "From Prague to Kabul: the Soviet Style of Invasion." *International Security* 5 (1980): 114–41.

Valkenier, Elizabeth Kridl. "Soviet Economic Relations with the Developing Nations." In Roger E. Kanet, ed. *The Soviet Union and Developing Nations*. Baltimore, 1974.

———. "The USSR, the Third World, and the Global Economy." *Problems of Communism*, 28 (1979): 17–33.

Whitney, Craig. "The View from the Kremlin." *The New York Times Magazine*, 20 April 1980: 30–33.

Yakobson, Sergius. "Russia and Africa." In Ivo J. Lederer, ed. *Russian Foreign Policy: Essays in Historical Perspective*. New Haven, 1962, pp. 453–87.

Index

Henry S. Bradsher worked in Afghanistan as an Associated Press correspondent in the early 1960s, visited the country again in the 1970s for *The Washington Star*, and has written about it for *The Economist* and other publications. Long a specialist in Soviet affairs, he was AP bureau chief in Moscow from 1964 to 1968. As *The Star*'s Hong Kong correspondent from 1969 to 1975, he won one of the most important prizes in American journalism, the George Polk Memorial Award, for his analysis of Chinese affairs. In 1968–69 he was a Nieman fellow at Harvard University, and in 1980–81 he was a guest scholar at the Kennan Institute for Advanced Russian Studies of the Smithsonian Institution's Wilson Center, where he wrote this book. He has written for *Foreign Affairs* and other journals.